MEDITERRANEAN
Diet Cookbook
— FOR BEGINNERS —

1000 Affordable and Delicious Recipes for Healthy Living (21 Days Meal Plan Included)

Catharine White

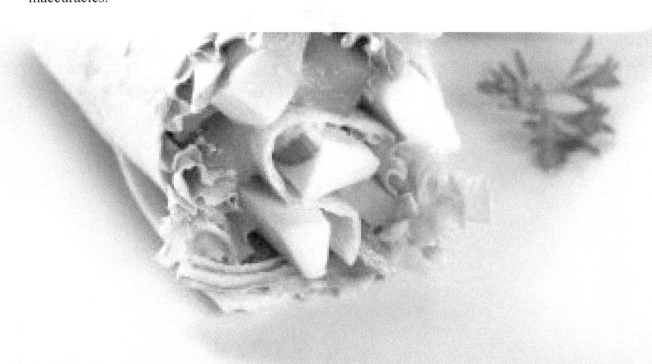

CONTENT

INTRODUCTION

I have never been able to understand why the Mediterranean diet isn't more popular. I've heard of and tried all of the popular fad diets, but there hasn't been any success. In fact, they often made me feel worse physically, and the only thing many of them were designed to address was weightloss.

There is so much more to one's health than just a number on a scale. How about pain and aches? How about organ function? How about my mental health as well my physical health? Popular diets didn't focus on these things at all, and they were incredibly unsatisfying.

With these struggles in the back of my head, I did my research and found the Mediterranean diet.

This isn't like many of the other popular diets out there. Rather than being based on a specific aspect of nutritional science, the Mediterranean diet is a cultural practice.

The Mediterranean Sea is bordered by four European countries. Greece, Spain, France, and Italy all have access to a healthy supply of fish thanks to this geography. In addition to this, their climate allows for them to consume some of the same foods, but in a much different fashion.

This diet has been studied for years because of the incredible health benefits (Gunnars & Link, 2021). That was one of the first reasons I had been drawn to it. It doesn't just focus on your weight, like many other diets do.

The health benefits include brain health as well. I have always tried to use my brain to its maximum capacity. When other diets created a brain fog, I was left feeling extremely frustrated at the fact that I couldn't get more work done.

The Mediterranean diet also focuses heavily on fresh food sources.

One of my favorite parts of healthy eating has always been the fresh food. It tastes better and I do notice a difference in my body when I cook with these ingredients. It can take up some extra time during the week, but to save myself that trouble, I've set aside time to prepare meals on the weekends and that makes a difference (and I'm less tempted to go out for food, because what I need is already there).

Through many ways, the Mediterranean diet connects me to a culture of health and helps me feel great.

Once the basics are understood, it is very easy to follow!

Chapter 1 Understanding and Managing Chronic Inflammation

What is the Mediterranean Diet?

The Mediterranean diet is more of a cultural eating pattern than a full blown diet. It's origins come from Europe, particularly in the areas surrounding the Mediterranean Sea. It came to the attention of scientists because unlike the rest of the world, who tended to rely on similar foods (though in different quantities), this area wasn't facing epidemics of obesity, heart disease, diabetes, etc. This was jaw dropping to the era of people who were just discovering the role diet plays in overall health (Gunnars & Link, 2021). The answer was found to be in the way they eat their food.

Unlike nearly every popular diet, the Mediterranean diet isn't centered around what you can't eat. Rather it focuses on how much of something you should eat, and the type of something you should eat. Due to the geography of the area, fish is a huge part of their diet. The climate of this area is also perfect for plant growth. Thanks to this, it's easier for those in this area to get a hold of fresh food than it is for them to get a hold of anything processed.

With the fresh fruits and vegetables being in easy reach, it makes up a major portion of the diet.

What isn't so easy to get a hold of in this area is red meat. Because of that, it is severely limited. White meats are included much more in this diet, but not as often as fish.

Finally, if you are an alcohol lover, you will like this! The Mediterranean diet does include wine. Vineyards are not hard to come by in the Mediterranean region.

Health Benefits of the Mediterranean Diet

One health benefit is that people in this area just seem to live longer. Their average age of death is higher because they don't have to worry about a lot of these common killers, which will often make up the top ten deaths in places like the United States.

One of these killers is heart disease. While it makes up a significant portion of deaths in the U.S., the Mediterranean diet aids the region due to it's low-fat content. There is evidence to suggest that it doesn't lead to nearly as much plaque build up in the arteries (Gunnars & Link, 2021).

It can have a great impact on your brain as well. Diseases such as Alzheimer's are much less common in those who follow this diet. It has also shown to help with overall brain function, with those who have been on it reporting that they can think and focus better (Gunnars & Link, 2021).

It protects us against diabetes. Much of the issues with diabetes come from highly processed foods and red meat that are not common in this area. The Mediterranean diet helps with inflammation and body function, and it can have positive effects on those who already have diabetes, and help others who are at risk avoid getting it altogether (Gunnars & Link, 2021).

Finally, there are certain cancers that are linked to diet. Liver cancer, for example, can stem from fatty liver which is a result of obesity. The Mediterranean diet protects against this.

The Mediterranean Food Pyramid

Most culture-based diets do have a food pyramid that their diet is based on. This can be in common use around the country, or created by researchers as something that others scientists and

curious individuals can reference.

The Mediterranean pyramid, in particular, has five slots. Four of these slots are dedicated to the food that should be consumed, and one is dedicated to the lifestyle. The outside of the food pyramid talks about two important liquids. Water is essential to the Mediterranean diet, and wine can be consumed in moderation.

Part of the Mediterranean diet involves its lifestyle. Physical activity and enjoying meals with others are a part of the diet. These things do actually affect how you eat and how food is metabolized in your body. Exercising engages your metabolism and changes how the food is going to be processed. Another aspect to consider is that eating with others has been proven to slow you down. You receive your fullness cue on time instead of when you have already eaten too much.

Foods to Eat

First of all, fruit is very important! Fruit contains vital vitamins and minerals, and in this way of eating, you don't have to limit your consumption of them! Apples, oranges and other citruses, berries, peaches, mangoes, grapes, and more are all ready and waiting for you to make them a part of your diet. A little tip if you are craving something sweet is to have cut up fruit with you. Oftentimes, this will do the trick!

Vegetables, as you might imagine, are next on the list. Like fruit, vegetables also contain items that are vital to your health. Carrots, broccoli, spinach, lettuce, onions, and more are all now a major part of the diet. It's worth noting that the traditional Mediterranean diet also includes potatoes, but there will be a difference in the level of processing between their potatoes and ours. At the end of the day, if you want to enjoy a starchy treat, it's best to be able to name all of the ingredients it contains.

Whole grains are your next item in this section. This will mean a lot of substitution. Many breaded and carb items are filled with refined grains which are stripped of their minerals and tend to harm us more than they help us. Whole wheat bread, pasta, rice, and other breaded items are all fantastic options for some of your favorite carb rich dishes.

Olive oil is a huge part of the Mediterranean diet. Because this diet is low on processed items, dressings and cooking sprays are often out of the picture. However, olives grow naturally in this area, so it's understandable that they are such a big part of the diet. You can cook with it, add it to baked goods, make dips out of it, and use it in dressing. If you're bored of the same olive oil, specialty stores often carry a wide variety of flavors!

Up next are beans. Beans can be very filling and they are a great source of protein. With the Mediterranean diet, you won't be consuming as much meat, so these will become important!

We can't forget about nuts and seeds. A lot of vitamins and minerals will come from them, and some nuts even have protein! Finally, there are herbs and spices. They add flavor to your food and they are full of rich vitamins and minerals for your body.

Foods to Eat in Moderation

Anything listed above is something that should be a part of your diet every day. They take up a main portion of every meal. This next list, however, doesn't need to be included as often.

The most important ones on this list are fish, shellfish, and other seafood. You should be aiming to eat this at least two times a week. As discussed above, fish is a huge part of the Mediterranean diet. It provides a good source of healthy fat and protein. You should aim for fresh fish if you can!

Up next is poultry, which includes white meats such as chicken and turkey. These aren't nearly as hard on your heart as red meat tends to be. They still provide a great source of protein. You should be aiming for this anywhere from daily to weekly.

Up next are eggs. Like poultry items, eggs provide a great source of protein, but they aren't as important to the diet as items in the first category. You should also be aiming for a daily to weekly intake of this.

Next are the dairy products. This includes milk, cheese, and yogurt. Because these items have to go through some processing in order to be created, they aren't as involved in the diet, but they do contain some much needed nutrients (like Vitamin D). They can also be a healthy source of fat in some cases. Try to aim for less processed options if possible and consume them anywhere from a daily to a weekly basis.

Finally, there is wine. Wine is a wonderful part of the Mediterranean diet, and is also something that should be consumed in moderation. That means something different to everyone. Whether you chose to have a single glass with a meal, or you chose to have a couple of drinks on the weekend with friends is up to you!

Foods That Won't Be the Main Part of the Diet

The cool thing about the Mediterranean diet is that it doesn't really eliminate foods, instead it relies on amounts and limits.

The main thing for this will be processed foods. This is incredibly hard in countries like America, where everything does seem to have a lot of processing to it, but that processing is hurting us! In countries in the Mediterranean region, it's actually harder to get a hold of processed foods than it is to get a hold of regular food types. This may link to why their health seems to be a lot better as a population.

Steer away from processed options as much as your budget will allow. White breaded items can be swapped for whole grains (which is something to consume daily) at almost no cost. Aim for fresh fruits and vegetables if you can, but if you have budget concerns, or if you know they will go bad, start reading labels very carefully. These can provide clues as to what's been processed more.

Running along the line of processed foods are candy. These should only be consumed once a week at most. They are often highly processed and even when they aren't, they still contain things that aren't very good for us. If you like sweet things, make fruit a go-to in your diet. Dates are also a fantastic way to satisfy your sweet tooth. If you are still really craving that sugar, aim for dark chocolate. It still has many great minerals for you and it hasn't been nearly as processed.

Finally, there is red meat. Red meat has been linked to a variety of issues, including raised cholesterol, heart disease, obesity, blood pressure, diabetes, etc. No one is certain on why it seems to be causing us so much trouble, but everyone can agree that it is problematic and that cutting it down in our diet would help us. The Mediterranean region has never had the same access to red meat that we do and as a result, they are in better internal shape. You should be eating this, at most, weekly.

Extra Virgin Olive Oil: The Core of the Mediterranean Diet

You may have heard before that substituting canola and vegetable oil with olive oil was a better choice. This is more than true!

Olive oil is a huge part of the Mediterranean diet. It can be cooked with, made into dips and dressings, and more. Olive oil is rich in the healthy fats you need, and finding the right kind means that you have an unprocessed oil to cook with.

When thinking of olive oil, you may just be thinking of the plain brand that ends up in every store, but there is more to it than that. If you know where to look, you can find specialty stores that sell olive oil in a variety of flavors with different processes to make them. Each one can add something amazing to your cooking!

If it is within your budget, I absolutely recommend trying out one of these speciality stores for your olive oil needs. They will have little to no processing, and their taste is impeccable.

If this isn't an option for you, then read the labels at your local grocery store carefully. Refined olive oil will be the most processed. Then there is virgin olive oil. Finally, anything labeled extra virgin olive oil will have the least amount of process, and it is associated with the most health benefits.

For extra virgin olive oil, you don't need to refrigerate it. With the other two, this is your best option. Do not store your olive oil next to the stove, as the heat can harm the potency of the oil and shorten its life. Keep it in a dark place and at room temperature. If you don't use it within a year, it may start to break down on you.

Chapter 2: Eight Steps to Getting Started

1.Eat LOTS of Vegetables

Vegetables are a major part of the Mediterranean diet. Technically, it's supposed to be a major part of all diets, but that isn't necessarily what happens. In many countries, fresh vegetables are often exalted, but they are expensive. When people think that frozen or canned items aren't good for them, they tend to leave without any vegetables. Whether it's fresh, frozen, or canned though, vegetables still have amazing benefits.

2.Change the Way You Think About Meat

We are taught that protein is vital to our diet. It is stressed to us from a young age, and it often leaves us to believe that we should consume it in every meal. This isn't true.

Meat isn't the only protein source out there. Beans, nuts, wholegrains, and even dairy all contain what we need. Furthermore, we don't need meat with every meal. Having a protein source in our diet once a day will satisfy our body's needs most of the time.

Meat, in particular, can be dangerous if over consumed. Heart disease and it's cousins, high cholesterol, high blood pressure, obesity, and diabetes, are all associated with over consumption of meat.

3.Enjoy Some Dairy Products

People tend to over or under do it when it comes to dairy.

If you eat too little, you aren't getting enough of the vitamins and minerals that contribute to bone growth. If you are eating too much then you run the same risk that you do when you eat too much meat.

The Mediterranean diet says to consume dairy on a daily to weekly basis. You don't need it every day, but you should be having it more than once a week.

4.Eat Seafood Twice a Week

If your diet doesn't usually contain seafood, then this is a great place to start. Eating seafood twice a week can provide protein the same way meat can, and it provides you with healthy fats. Fresh fish is going to be your best bet if you can get a hold of it!

5.Cook a Vegetarian Meal One Night a Week

How much do you consume when it comes to vegetables? With the Mediterranean diet, you should be consuming them with just about every meal. Cooking in a vegetarian manner allows you to do just that, and opens your mind to more possibilities. If you want to ensure your meal is filling, add beans or whole grains…or both!

6.Use Good Fats

Olive oil! We are absolutely talking about olive oil here. Canola and other oils are extremely refined and can really hurt you in the long run. Olive oil, on the other hand, involves minimal processing and it is associated with great health benefits.

7.Switch to Whole Grains

Even though other diets have tried to eliminate them, carbohydrates are important to your diet…it's the kind of carb that will matter. White grains are extremely processed and have had all of the vital vitamins and minerals removed from them. Whole grain options let you get your carbs in while also containing what your body needs!

8.Use Fresh Fruit to Satisfy Your Sweet Tooth

Fresh fruit is incredibly sweet and full of nutrients. If you are like me and you get a sweet tooth, have something on hand from your local farmer's market! These won't contain processed additives that will do more harm than good, and they will make you feel better at the end of the day.

Living the Mediterranean Way

The Mediterranean region also has certain lifestyle aspects that will make a huge difference in how this diet works for you.

The Mediterranean region is, as a whole, more active. Their outdoor spaces are open and inviting (how could you not want to walk on the Mediterranean beach), and they have shorter commute times that usually render a car unnecessary. These mild things make a difference, and with these changes, they naturally make time for exercise too.

These changes can affect your metabolism and make a huge difference in how your body might handle things! You can try to go out for morning walks, or find some workout videos if you have an area at home. Going to a gym regularly can also be of great benefit.

The Mediterranean region is also in the habit of being social when it comes to food. Eating with the family, and having big gatherings that surround food as a culture are major. They also take time with lunch, even on the working day. Eating with people encourages you to slow down and taste what you are eating. You won't be trying to get it all down as quickly as possible.

Finally, they are wary of processed and outsourced food items. They can get everything they need rather easily, so why would they need anything processed. Processed and outsourced items can cost more in this region.

Small changes like these make a world of difference. The data proves it!

21 Days Mediterranean Diet Meal Plan

DAYS	BREAKFAST	LUNCH	DINNER	SNACK/DESSERT
1	Gluten-Free Granola Cereal	Cucumber Basil Sandwiches	Cornish Hens with Honey-Lime Glaze	S'mores
2	Spinach and Mushroom Mini Quiche	Powerhouse Arugula Salad	Honey-Balsamic Salmon	Olive Oil Ice Cream
3	Smoky Sausage Patties	Creamy Spring Vegetable Linguine	Nigerian Peanut-Crusted Flank Steak	Cinnamon-Apple Chips
4	Cauliflower Avocado Toast	Lebanese Rice and Broken Noodles with Cabbage	Beef and Mushroom Stroganoff	Parmesan French Fries
5	Homemade Pumpkin Parfait	French Lentils with Swiss Chard	Braised Striped Bass with Zucchini and Tomatoes	Grilled Pineapple and Melon
6	Baked Egg and Mushroom Cups	Classic Margherita Pizza	Citrus–Marinated Scallops	Garlic Edamame
7	Spinach and Feta Egg Bake	Lemon Farro Bowl with Avocado	Flounder with Tomatoes and Basil	Marinated Feta and Artichokes
8	Poached Eggs on Whole Grain Avocado Toast	Warm Fennel, Cherry Tomato, and Spinach Salad	Whole-Roasted Spanish Chicken	Crispy Apple Phyllo Tart
9	Power Peach Smoothie Bowl	Asparagus and Mushroom Farrotto	Mediterranean-Style Cod	Goat Cheese–Mackerel Pâté
10	Garlic Scrambled Eggs with Basil	Rigatoni with Lamb Meatballs	Pilaf with Eggplant and Raisins	Fig-Pecan Energy Bites
11	Crostini with Smoked Trout	Cauliflower Steaks with Olive Citrus Sauce	Spicy Trout over Sautéed Mediterranean Salad	Strawberry-Pomegranate Molasses Sauce
12	Garlicky Beans and Greens with Polenta	Marinated Greek Salad with Oregano and Goat Cheese	Herb-Crusted Lamb Chops	S'mores
13	Mediterranean Breakfast Pita Sandwiches	Moroccan Lamb Wrap with Harissa	Bocadillo with Herbed Tuna and Piquillo Peppers	Smoky Baba Ghanoush
14	Fig and Ricotta Toast with Walnuts and Honey	Spicy Lentil Patties	Mussels with Tomatoes and Herbs	Warm Olives with Rosemary and Garlic
15	Egg in a "Pepper Hole" with Avocado	Melon Caprese Salad	Kofta with Vegetables in Tomato Sauce	Cherry Tomato Bruschetta
16	Quickie Honey Nut Granola	Whole-Wheat Spaghetti à la Puttanesca	Cornish Hens with Honey-Lime Glaze	Fresh Figs with Chocolate Sauce
17	Gluten-Free Granola Cereal	Pilaf with Eggplant and Raisins	Braised Striped Bass with Zucchini and Tomatoes	Italian Crepe with Herbs and Onion
18	Spinach and Mushroom Mini Quiche	Turkey Burgers with Feta and Dill	Greek-Style Pea Casserole	Grilled Stone Fruit
19	Smoky Sausage Patties	Insalata Caprese	Pork Tenderloin with Chermoula Sauce	Spiced Maple Nuts
20	Cauliflower Avocado Toast	Puglia-Style Pasta with Broccoli Sauce	Mediterranean-Style Cod	Sweet Potato Hummus
21	Spinach and Feta Egg Bake	Mexican Pizza	Pesto Chicken and Potatoes	Cretan Cheese Pancakes

Chapter 3 Beans and Grains

Freehold Pilaf with Dates and Pistachios

Prep time: 15 minutes | Cook time: 6 minutes | Serves 4 to 6

2 tablespoons extra-virgin olive oil, plus extra for drizzling
1 shallot, minced
1½ teaspoons grated fresh ginger
½ teaspoon table salt
¼ teaspoon ground coriander
¼ teaspoon ground cumin
¼ teaspoon pepper
1¾ cups water
1½ cups cracked freekeh, rinsed
3 ounces (85 g) pitted dates, chopped (½ cup)
¼ cup shelled pistachios, toasted and coarsely chopped
1½ tablespoons lemon juice
¼ cup chopped fresh mint

1. Using highest sauté function, heat oil in Instant Pot until shimmering. Add shallot, ginger, salt, coriander, cumin, and pepper and cook until shallot is softened, about 2 minutes. Stir in water and freekeh. 2. Lock lid in place and close pressure release valve. Select high pressure cook function and cook for 4 minutes. Turn off Instant Pot and quick-release pressure. Carefully remove lid, allowing steam to escape away from you. 3. Add dates, pistachios, and lemon juice and gently fluff freekeh with fork to combine. Season with salt and pepper to taste. Transfer to serving dish, sprinkle with mint, and drizzle with extra oil. Serve.

Per Serving
Calories: 280 | fat: 8g | protein: 8g | carbs: 46g | fiber: 9g | sodium: 200mg

French Lentils with Swiss Chard

Prep time: 15 minutes | Cook time: 17 minutes | Serves 6

2 tablespoons extra-virgin olive oil, plus extra for drizzling
12 ounces (340 g) Swiss chard, stems chopped fine, leaves sliced into ½-inch-wide strips
1 onion, chopped fine
½ teaspoon table salt
2 garlic cloves, minced
1 teaspoon minced fresh thyme or ¼ teaspoon dried
2½ cups water
1 cup French green lentils, picked over and rinsed
3 tablespoons whole-grain mustard
½ teaspoon grated lemon zest plus 1 teaspoon juice
3 tablespoons sliced almonds, toasted
2 tablespoons chopped fresh parsley

1. Using highest sauté function, heat oil in Instant Pot until shimmering. Add chard stems, onion, and salt and cook until vegetables are softened, about 5 minutes. Stir in garlic and thyme and cook until fragrant, about 30 seconds. Stir in water and lentils. 2. Lock lid in place and close pressure release valve. Select high pressure cook function and cook for 11 minutes. Turn off Instant Pot and let pressure release naturally for 15 minutes. Quick-release any remaining pressure, then carefully remove lid, allowing steam to escape away from you. 3. Stir chard leaves into lentils, 1 handful at a time, and let cook in residual heat until wilted, about 5 minutes. Stir in mustard and lemon zest and juice. Season with salt and pepper to taste. Transfer to serving dish, drizzle with extra oil, and sprinkle with almonds and parsley. Serve.

Per Serving
Calories: 190 | fat: 8g | protein: 9g | carbs: 23g | fiber: 6g | sodium: 470mg

Wild Mushroom Farrotto

Prep time: 15 minutes | Cook time: 20 minutes | Serves 4 to 6

1½ cups whole farro
3 tablespoons extra-virgin olive oil, divided, plus extra for drizzling
12 ounces (340 g) cremini or white mushrooms, trimmed and sliced thin
½ onion, chopped fine
½ teaspoon table salt
¼ teaspoon pepper
1 garlic clove, minced
¼ ounce dried porcini
mushrooms, rinsed and chopped fine
2 teaspoons minced fresh thyme or ½ teaspoon dried
¼ cup dry white wine
2½ cups chicken or vegetable broth, plus extra as needed
2 ounces (57 g) Parmesan cheese, grated (1 cup), plus extra for serving
2 teaspoons lemon juice
½ cup chopped fresh parsley

1. Pulse farro in blender until about half of grains are broken into smaller pieces, about 6 pulses. 2. Using highest sauté function, heat 2 tablespoons oil in Instant Pot until shimmering. Add cremini mushrooms, onion, salt, and pepper, partially cover, and cook until mushrooms are softened and have released their liquid, about 5 minutes. Stir in farro, garlic, porcini mushrooms, and thyme and cook until fragrant, about 1 minute. Stir in wine and cook until nearly evaporated, about 30 seconds. Stir in broth. 3. Lock lid in place and close pressure release valve. Select high pressure cook function and cook for 12 minutes. Turn off Instant Pot and quick-release pressure. Carefully remove lid, allowing steam to escape away from you. 4. If necessary adjust consistency with extra hot broth, or continue to cook farrotto, using highest sauté function, stirring frequently, until proper consistency is achieved. (Farrotto should be slightly thickened, and spoon dragged along bottom of multicooker should leave trail that quickly fills in.) Add Parmesan and remaining 1 tablespoon oil and stir vigorously until farrotto becomes creamy. Stir in lemon juice and season with salt and pepper to taste. Sprinkle individual portions with parsley and extra Parmesan, and drizzle with extra oil before serving.

Per Serving
Calories: 280 | fat: 10g | protein: 13g | carbs: 35g | fiber: 4g | sodium: 630mg

Bulgur with Chickpeas, Spinach, and Za'atar

Prep time: 15 minutes | Cook time: 7 minutes | Serves 4 to 6

3 tablespoons extra-virgin olive oil, divided
1 onion, chopped fine
½ teaspoon table salt
3 garlic cloves, minced
2 tablespoons za'atar, divided
1 cup medium-grind bulgur, rinsed

1 (15-ounce / 425-g) can chickpeas, rinsed
1½ cups water
5 ounces (142 g) baby spinach, chopped
1 tablespoon lemon juice, plus lemon wedges for serving

1. Using highest sauté function, heat 2 tablespoons oil in Instant Pot until shimmering. Add onion and salt and cook until onion is softened, about 5 minutes. Stir in garlic and 1 tablespoon za'atar and cook until fragrant, about 30 seconds. Stir in bulgur, chickpeas, and water. 2. Lock lid in place and close pressure release valve. Select high pressure cook function and cook for 1 minute. Turn off Instant Pot and quick-release pressure. Carefully remove lid, allowing steam to escape away from you. 3. Gently fluff bulgur with fork. Lay clean dish towel over pot, replace lid, and let sit for 5 minutes. Add spinach, lemon juice, remaining 1 tablespoon za'atar, and remaining 1 tablespoon oil and gently toss to combine. Season with salt and pepper to taste. Serve with lemon wedges.

Per Serving
Calories: 200 | fat: 8g | protein: 6g | carbs: 28g | fiber: 6g | sodium: 320mg

Barley Salad with Lemon-Tahini Dressing

Prep time: 15 minutes | Cook time: 10 minutes | Serves 4 to 6

1½ cups pearl barley
5 tablespoons extra-virgin olive oil, divided
1½ teaspoons table salt, for cooking barley
¼ cup tahini
1 teaspoon grated lemon zest plus ¼ cup juice (2 lemons)
1 tablespoon sumac, divided
1 garlic clove, minced
¾ teaspoon table salt

1 English cucumber, cut into ½-inch pieces
1 carrot, peeled and shredded
1 red bell pepper, stemmed, seeded, and chopped
4 scallions, sliced thin
2 tablespoons finely chopped jarred hot cherry peppers
¼ cup coarsely chopped fresh mint

1. Combine 6 cups water, barley, 1 tablespoon oil, and 1½ teaspoons salt in Instant Pot. Lock lid in place and close pressure release valve. Select high pressure cook function and cook for 8 minutes. Turn off Instant Pot and let pressure release naturally for 15 minutes. Quick-release any remaining pressure, then carefully remove lid, allowing steam to escape away from you. Drain barley, spread onto rimmed baking sheet, and let cool completely, about 15 minutes. 2. Meanwhile, whisk remaining ¼ cup oil, tahini, 2 tablespoons water, lemon zest and juice, 1 teaspoon sumac, garlic, and ¾ teaspoon salt in large bowl until combined; let sit for 15 minutes. 3. Measure out and reserve ½ cup dressing for serving. Add barley, cucumber,

carrot, bell pepper, scallions, and cherry peppers to bowl with dressing and gently toss to combine. Season with salt and pepper to taste. Transfer salad to serving dish and sprinkle with mint and remaining 2 teaspoons sumac. Serve, passing reserved dressing separately.

Per Serving
Calories: 370 | fat: 18g | protein: 8g | carbs: 47g | fiber: 10g | sodium: 510mg

Brown Rice Pilaf with Golden Raisins

Prep time: 5 minutes |Cook time: 15 minutes| Serves: 6

1 tablespoon extra-virgin olive oil
1 cup chopped onion (about ½ medium onion)
½ cup shredded carrot (about 1 medium carrot)
1 teaspoon ground cumin
½ teaspoon ground cinnamon

2 cups instant brown rice
1¾ cups 100% orange juice
¼ cup water
1 cup golden raisins
½ cup shelled pistachios
Chopped fresh chives (optional)

1. In a medium saucepan over medium-high heat, heat the oil. Add the onion and cook for 5 minutes, stirring frequently. Add the carrot, cumin, and cinnamon, and cook for 1 minute, stirring frequently. Stir in the rice, orange juice, and water. Bring to a boil, cover, then lower the heat to medium-low. Simmer for 7 minutes, or until the rice is cooked through and the liquid is absorbed. 2. Stir in the raisins, pistachios, and chives (if using) and serve.

Per Serving
Calories: 337 | fat: 8.5g | protein: 7.4g | carbs: 71.3g | fiber: 5g | sodium: 154mg

Fava and Garbanzo Bean Fūl

Prep time: 10 minutes | Cook time: 10 minutes | Serves 6

1 (16-ounce / 454-g) can garbanzo beans, rinsed and drained
1 (15-ounce / 425-g) can fava beans, rinsed and drained
3 cups water

½ cup lemon juice
3 cloves garlic, peeled and minced
1 teaspoon salt
3 tablespoons extra-virgin olive oil

1. In a 3-quart pot over medium heat, cook the garbanzo beans, fava beans, and water for 10 minutes. 2. Reserving 1 cup of the liquid from the cooked beans, drain the beans and put them in a bowl. 3. Mix the reserved liquid, lemon juice, minced garlic, and salt together and add to the beans in the bowl. Using a potato masher, mash up about half the beans in the bowl. 4. After mashing half the beans, give the mixture one more stir to make sure the beans are evenly mixed. 5. Drizzle the olive oil over the top. 6. Serve warm or cold with pita bread.

Per Serving
Calories: 199 | fat: 9g | protein: 10g | carbs: 25g | fiber: 9g | sodium: 395mg

No-Stir Polenta with Arugula, Figs, and Blue Cheese

Prep time: 15 minutes | Cook time: 40 minutes | Serves 4

1 cup coarse-ground cornmeal	2 ounces (57 g) baby arugula
½ cup oil-packed sun-dried tomatoes, chopped	4 figs, cut into ½-inch-thick wedges
1 teaspoon minced fresh thyme or ¼ teaspoon dried	1 tablespoon balsamic vinegar
½ teaspoon table salt	2 ounces (57 g) blue cheese, crumbled (½ cup)
¼ teaspoon pepper	2 tablespoons pine nuts, toasted
3 tablespoons extra-virgin olive oil, divided	

1. Arrange trivet included with Instant Pot in base of insert and add 1 cup water. Fold sheet of aluminum foil into 16 by 6-inch sling, then rest 1½-quart round soufflé dish in center of sling. Whisk 4 cups water, cornmeal, tomatoes, thyme, salt, and pepper together in bowl, then transfer mixture to soufflé dish. Using sling, lower soufflé dish into pot and onto trivet; allow narrow edges of sling to rest along sides of insert. 2. Lock lid in place and close pressure release valve. Select high pressure cook function and cook for 40 minutes. Turn off Instant Pot and quick-release pressure. Carefully remove lid, allowing steam to escape away from you. 3. Using sling, transfer soufflé dish to wire rack. Whisk 1 tablespoon oil into polenta, smoothing out any lumps. Let sit until thickened slightly, about 10 minutes. Season with salt and pepper to taste. 4. Toss arugula and figs with vinegar and remaining 2 tablespoons oil in bowl, and season with salt and pepper to taste. Divide polenta among individual serving plates and top with arugula mixture, blue cheese, and pine nuts. Serve.

Per Serving

Calories: 360 | fat: 21g | protein: 7g | carbs: 38g | fiber: 8g | sodium: 510mg

Garlic-Asparagus Israeli Couscous

Prep time: 5 minutes |Cook time: 25 minutes| Serves: 6

1 cup garlic-and-herb goat cheese (about 4 ounces / 113 g)	½ teaspoon)
1½ pounds (680 g) asparagus spears, ends trimmed and stalks chopped into 1-inch pieces (about 2¾ to 3 cups chopped)	¼ teaspoon freshly ground black pepper
	1¾ cups water
	1 (8-ounce / 227-g) box uncooked whole-wheat or regular Israeli couscous (about 1⅓ cups)
1 tablespoon extra-virgin olive oil	
1 garlic clove, minced (about	¼ teaspoon kosher or sea salt

1. Preheat the oven to 425°F (220°C). Put the goat cheese on the counter to bring to room temperature. 2. In a large bowl, mix together the asparagus, oil, garlic, and pepper. Spread the asparagus on a large, rimmed baking sheet and roast for 10 minutes, stirring a few times. Remove the pan from the oven, and spoon the asparagus into a large serving bowl. 3. While the asparagus is roasting, in a medium saucepan, bring the water to a boil. Add the couscous and salt. Reduce the heat to medium-low, cover, and cook for 12 minutes, or until the water is absorbed. 4. Pour the hot couscous into the bowl with the asparagus. Add the goat cheese, mix thoroughly until completely melted, and serve.

Per Serving

Calories: 98 | fat: 1.3g | protein: 10.2g | carbs: 13.5g | fiber: 3.67g | sodium: 262mg

Lemon Farro Bowl with Avocado

Prep time: 5 minutes |Cook time: 25 minutes| Serves: 6

1 tablespoon plus 2 teaspoons extra-virgin olive oil, divided	2 cups low-sodium or no-salt-added vegetable broth
1 cup chopped onion (about ½ medium onion)	1 cup uncooked pearled or 10-minute farro
2 garlic cloves, minced (about 1 teaspoon)	2 avocados, peeled, pitted, and sliced
1 carrot, shredded (about 1 cup)	1 small lemon
	¼ teaspoon kosher or sea salt

1. In a medium saucepan over medium-high heat, heat 1 tablespoon of oil. Add the onion and cook for 5 minutes, stirring occasionally. Add the garlic and carrot and cook for 1 minute, stirring frequently. Add the broth and farro, and bring to a boil over high heat. Lower the heat to medium-low, cover, and simmer for about 20 minutes or until the farro is plump and slightly chewy (al dente). 2. Pour the farro into a serving bowl, and add the avocado slices. Using a Microplane or citrus zester, zest the peel of the lemon directly into the bowl of farro. Halve the lemon, and squeeze the juice out of both halves using a citrus juicer or your hands. Drizzle the remaining 2 teaspoons of oil over the bowl, and sprinkle with salt. Gently mix all the ingredients and serve.

Per Serving

Calories: 212 | fat: 11.2g | protein: 3.4g | carbs: 28.7g | fiber: 7g | sodium: 147mg

Lemon Orzo with Fresh Herbs

Prep time: 10 minutes | Cook time: 10 minutes | Serves 4

2 cups orzo	½ cup extra-virgin olive oil
½ cup fresh parsley, finely chopped	⅓ cup lemon juice
½ cup fresh basil, finely chopped	1 teaspoon salt
	½ teaspoon freshly ground black pepper
2 tablespoons lemon zest	

1. Bring a large pot of water to a boil. Add the orzo and cook for 7 minutes. Drain and rinse with cold water. Let the orzo sit in a strainer to completely drain and cool. 2. Once the orzo has cooled, put it in a large bowl and add the parsley, basil, and lemon zest. 3. In a small bowl, whisk together the olive oil, lemon juice, salt, and pepper. Add the dressing to the pasta and toss everything together. Serve at room temperature or chilled.

Per Serving

Calories: 568 | fat: 29g | protein: 11g | carbs: 65g | fiber: 4g | sodium: 586mg

Greek Chickpeas with Coriander and Sage

Prep time: 20 minutes | Cook time: 22 minutes | Serves 6 to 8

1½ tablespoons table salt, for brining
1 pound (454 g) dried chickpeas, picked over and rinsed
2 tablespoons extra-virgin olive oil, plus extra for drizzling
2 onions, halved and sliced thin
¼ teaspoon table salt

1 tablespoon coriander seeds, cracked
¼–½ teaspoon red pepper flakes
2½ cups chicken broth
¼ cup fresh sage leaves
2 bay leaves
1½ teaspoons grated lemon zest plus 2 teaspoons juice
2 tablespoons minced fresh parsley

1. Dissolve 1½ tablespoons salt in 2 quarts cold water in large container. Add chickpeas and soak at room temperature for at least 8 hours or up to 24 hours. Drain and rinse well. 2. Using highest sauté function, heat oil in Instant Pot until shimmering. Add onions and ¼ teaspoon salt and cook until onions are softened and well browned, 10 to 12 minutes. Stir in coriander and pepper flakes and cook until fragrant, about 30 seconds. Stir in broth, scraping up any browned bits, then stir in chickpeas, sage, and bay leaves. 3. Lock lid in place and close pressure release valve. Select low pressure cook function and cook for 10 minutes. Turn off Instant Pot and let pressure release naturally for 15 minutes. Quick-release any remaining pressure, then carefully remove lid, allowing steam to escape away from you. 4. Discard bay leaves. Stir lemon zest and juice into chickpeas and season with salt and pepper to taste. Sprinkle with parsley. Serve, drizzling individual portions with extra oil.

Per Serving
Calories: 190 | fat: 6g | protein: 11g | carbs: 40g | fiber: 1g | sodium: 360mg

Mediterranean Lentils and Rice

Prep time: 5 minutes |Cook time: 25 minutes| Serves: 4

2¼ cups low-sodium or no-salt-added vegetable broth
½ cup uncooked brown or green lentils
½ cup uncooked instant brown rice
½ cup diced carrots (about 1 carrot)
½ cup diced celery (about 1 stalk)
1 (2¼-ounce / 64-g) can sliced olives, drained (about ½ cup)
¼ cup diced red onion (about

⅛ onion)
¼ cup chopped fresh curly-leaf parsley
1½ tablespoons extra-virgin olive oil
1 tablespoon freshly squeezed lemon juice (from about ½ small lemon)
1 garlic clove, minced (about ½ teaspoon)
¼ teaspoon kosher or sea salt
¼ teaspoon freshly ground black pepper

1. In a medium saucepan over high heat, bring the broth and lentils to a boil, cover, and lower the heat to medium-low. Cook for 8 minutes. 2. Raise the heat to medium, and stir in the rice. Cover the pot and cook the mixture for 15 minutes, or until the liquid is absorbed. Remove the pot from the heat and let it sit, covered, for 1 minute, then stir. 3. While the lentils and rice are cooking, mix together the carrots, celery, olives, onion, and parsley in a large serving bowl. 4. In a small bowl, whisk together the oil, lemon juice, garlic, salt, and pepper. Set aside. 5. When the lentils and rice are cooked, add them to the serving bowl. Pour the dressing on top, and mix everything together. Serve warm or cold, or store in a sealed container in the refrigerator for up to 7 days.

Per Serving
Calories: 183 | fat: 6g | protein: 4.9g | carbs: 29.5g | fiber: 3.3g | sodium: 552mg

Lebanese Rice and Broken Noodles with Cabbage

Prep time: 5 minutes |Cook time: 25 minutes| Serves: 6

1 tablespoon extra-virgin olive oil
1 cup (about 3 ounces / 85 g) uncooked vermicelli or thin spaghetti, broken into 1- to 1½-inch pieces
3 cups shredded cabbage (about half a 14-ounce package of coleslaw mix or half a small head of cabbage)
3 cups low-sodium or no-salt-

added vegetable broth
½ cup water
1 cup instant brown rice
2 garlic cloves
¼ teaspoon kosher or sea salt
⅛ to ¼ teaspoon crushed red pepper
½ cup loosely packed, coarsely chopped cilantro
Fresh lemon slices, for serving (optional)

1. In a large saucepan over medium-high heat, heat the oil. Add the pasta and cook for 3 minutes to toast, stirring often. Add the cabbage and cook for 4 minutes, stirring often. Add the broth, water, rice, garlic, salt, and crushed red pepper, and bring to a boil over high heat. Stir, cover, and reduce the heat to medium-low. Simmer for 10 minutes. 2. Remove the pan from the heat, but do not lift the lid. Let sit for 5 minutes. Fish out the garlic cloves, mash them with a fork, then stir the garlic back into the rice. Stir in the cilantro. Serve with the lemon slices (if using).

Per Serving
Calories: 150 | fat: 3.6g | protein: 3g | carbs: 27g | fiber: 2.8g | sodium: 664mg

Spanish Rice

Prep time: 10 minutes | Cook time: 20 minutes | Serves 4

2 tablespoons extra-virgin olive oil
1 medium onion, finely chopped
1 large tomato, finely diced

2 tablespoons tomato paste
1 teaspoon smoked paprika
1 teaspoon salt
1½ cups basmati rice
3 cups water

1. In a medium pot over medium heat, cook the olive oil, onion, and tomato for 3 minutes. 2. Stir in the tomato paste, paprika, salt, and rice. Cook for 1 minute. 3. Add the water, cover the pot, and turn the heat to low. Cook for 12 minutes. 4. Gently toss the rice, cover, and cook for another 3 minutes.

Per Serving
Calories: 328 | fat: 7g | protein: 6g | carbs: 60g | fiber: 2g | sodium: 651mg

Moroccan White Beans with Lamb

Prep time: 25 minutes | Cook time: 22 minutes | Serves 6 to 8

1½ tablespoons table salt, for brining
1 pound (454 g) dried great Northern beans, picked over and rinsed
1 (12-ounce / 340-g) lamb shoulder chop (blade or round bone), ¾ to 1 inch thick, trimmed and halved
½ teaspoon table salt
2 tablespoons extra-virgin olive oil, plus extra for serving
1 onion, chopped
1 red bell pepper, stemmed, seeded, and chopped
2 tablespoons tomato paste
3 garlic cloves, minced
2 teaspoons paprika
2 teaspoons ground cumin
1½ teaspoons ground ginger
¼ teaspoon cayenne pepper
½ cup dry white wine
2 cups chicken broth
2 tablespoons minced fresh parsley

1. Dissolve 1½ tablespoons salt in 2 quarts cold water in large container. Add beans and soak at room temperature for at least 8 hours or up to 24 hours. Drain and rinse well. 2. Pat lamb dry with paper towels and sprinkle with ½ teaspoon salt. Using highest sauté function, heat oil in Instant Pot for 5 minutes (or until just smoking). Brown lamb, about 5 minutes per side; transfer to plate. 3. Add onion and bell pepper to fat left in pot and cook, using highest sauté function, until softened, about 5 minutes. Stir in tomato paste, garlic, paprika, cumin, ginger, and cayenne and cook until fragrant, about 30 seconds. Stir in wine, scraping up any browned bits, then stir in broth and beans. 4. Nestle lamb into beans and add any accumulated juices. Lock lid in place and close pressure release valve. Select high pressure cook function and cook for 1 minute. Turn off Instant Pot and let pressure release naturally for 15 minutes. Quick-release any remaining pressure, then carefully remove lid, allowing steam to escape away from you. 5. Transfer lamb to cutting board, let cool slightly, then shred into bite-size pieces using 2 forks; discard excess fat and bones. Stir lamb and parsley into beans, and season with salt and pepper to taste. Drizzle individual portions with extra oil before serving.

Per Serving
Calories: 350 | fat: 12g | protein: 20g | carbs: 40g | fiber: 15g | sodium: 410mg

White Bean Cassoulet

Prep time: 30 minutes | Cook time: 45 minutes | Serves 8

1 tablespoon olive oil
1 medium onion, peeled and diced
2 cups dried cannellini beans, soaked overnight and drained
1 medium parsnip, peeled and diced
2 medium carrots, peeled and diced
2 stalks celery, diced
1 medium zucchini, trimmed
and chopped
½ teaspoon fennel seed
¼ teaspoon ground nutmeg
½ teaspoon garlic powder
1 teaspoon sea salt
½ teaspoon ground black pepper
2 cups vegetable broth
1 (14½-ounce / 411-g) can diced tomatoes, including juice
2 sprigs rosemary

1. Press the Sauté button on the Instant Pot® and heat oil. Add onion and cook until translucent, about 5 minutes. Add beans and toss. 2. Add a layer of parsnip, then a layer of carrots, and next a layer of celery. Finally, add a layer of zucchini. Sprinkle in fennel seed, nutmeg, garlic powder, salt, and pepper. Press the Cancel button. 3. Gently pour in broth and canned tomatoes. Top with rosemary. 4. Close lid, set steam release to Sealing, press the Bean button, and cook for the default time of 30 minutes. When the timer beeps, let pressure release naturally for 10 minutes. Quick-release any remaining pressure until the float valve drops and open lid. Press the Cancel button. 5. Press the Sauté button, then press the Adjust button to change the temperature to Less, and simmer bean mixture uncovered for 10 minutes to thicken. Transfer to a serving bowl and carefully toss. Remove and discard rosemary and serve.

Per Serving
Calories: 128 | fat: 2g | protein: 6g | carbs: 21g | fiber: 5g | sodium: 387mg

Confetti Couscous

Prep time: 5 minutes | Cook time: 20 minutes | Serves 4 to 6

3 tablespoons extra-virgin olive oil
1 large onion, chopped
2 carrots, chopped
1 cup fresh peas
½ cup golden raisins
1 teaspoon salt
2 cups vegetable broth
2 cups couscous

1. In a medium pot over medium heat, gently toss the olive oil, onions, carrots, peas, and raisins together and let cook for 5 minutes. 2. Add the salt and broth, and stir to combine. Bring to a boil, and let ingredients boil for 5 minutes. 3. Add the couscous. Stir, turn the heat to low, cover, and let cook for 10 minutes. Fluff with a fork and serve.

Per Serving
Calories: 511 | fat: 12g | protein: 14g | carbs: 92g | fiber: 7g | sodium: 504mg

Herbed Green Lentil Rice Balls

Prep time: 5 minutes | Cook time: 11 minutes | Serves 6

½ cup cooked green lentils
2 garlic cloves, minced
¼ white onion, minced
¼ cup parsley leaves
5 basil leaves
1 cup cooked brown rice
1 tablespoon lemon juice
1 tablespoon olive oil
½ teaspoon salt

1. Preheat the air fryer to 380ºF (193ºC). 2. In a food processor, pulse the cooked lentils with the garlic, onion, parsley, and basil until mostly smooth. (You will want some bits of lentils in the mixture.) 3. Pour the lentil mixture into a large bowl, and stir in brown rice, lemon juice, olive oil, and salt. Stir until well combined. 4. Form the rice mixture into 1-inch balls. Place the rice balls in a single layer in the air fryer basket, making sure that they don't touch each other. 5. Fry for 6 minutes. Turn the rice balls and then fry for an additional 4 to 5 minutes, or until browned on all sides.

Per Serving
Calories: 87 | fat: 3g | protein: 2.6g | carbs: 13g | fiber: 2g | sodium: 212mg

Lentils and Bulgur with Caramelized Onions

Prep time: 10 minutes | Cook time: 50 minutes | Serves 6

½ cup extra-virgin olive oil
4 large onions, chopped
2 teaspoons salt, divided
6 cups water
2 cups brown lentils, picked

over and rinsed
1 teaspoon freshly ground black pepper
1 cup bulgur wheat

1. In a medium pot over medium heat, cook the olive oil and onions for 7 to 10 minutes until the edges are browned. 2. Turn the heat to high, add the water, cumin, and salt, and bring this mixture to a boil, boiling for about 3 minutes. 3. Add the lentils and turn the heat to medium-low. Cover the pot and cook for 20 minutes, stirring occasionally. 4. Stir in the rice and cover; cook for an additional 20 minutes. 5. Fluff the rice with a fork and serve 1.In a large pot over medium heat, cook and stir the olive oil, onions, and 1 teaspoon of salt for 12 to 15 minutes, until the onions are a medium brown/golden color. 2. Put half of the cooked onions in a bowl. 3. Add the water, remaining 1 teaspoon of salt, and lentils to the remaining onions. Stir. Cover and cook for 30 minutes. 4. Stir in the black pepper and bulgur, cover, and cook for 5 minutes. Fluff with a fork, cover, and let stand for another 5 minutes. 5. Spoon the lentils and bulgur onto a serving plate and top with the reserved onions. Serve warm.

Per Serving
Calories: 479 | fat: 20g | protein: 20g | carbs: 60g | fiber: 24g | sodium: 789mg

Mediterranean Creamed Green Peas

Prep time: 5 minutes | Cook time: 25 minutes | Serves 4

1 cup cauliflower florets, fresh or frozen
½ white onion, roughly chopped
2 tablespoons olive oil
½ cup unsweetened almond milk
3 cups green peas, fresh or frozen

3 garlic cloves, minced
2 tablespoons fresh thyme leaves, chopped
1 teaspoon fresh rosemary leaves, chopped
½ teaspoon salt
½ teaspoon black pepper
Shredded Parmesan cheese, for garnish
Fresh parsley, for garnish

1. Preheat the air fryer to 380°F (193°C). 2. In a large bowl, combine the cauliflower florets and onion with the olive oil and toss well to coat. 3. Put the cauliflower-and-onion mixture into the air fryer basket in an even layer and bake for 15 minutes. 4. Transfer the cauliflower and onion to a food processor. Add the almond milk and pulse until smooth. 5. In a medium saucepan, combine the cauliflower purée, peas, garlic, thyme, rosemary, salt, and pepper and mix well. Cook over medium heat for an additional 10 minutes, stirring regularly. 6. Serve with a sprinkle of Parmesan cheese and chopped fresh parsley.

Per Serving
Calories: 313 | fat: 16.4g | protein: 14.7g | carbs: 28.8g | fiber: 8.3g | sodium: 898mg

Red Lentil and Goat Cheese Stuffed Tomatoes

Prep time: 10 minutes | Cook time: 15 minutes | Serves 4

4 tomatoes
½ cup cooked red lentils
1 garlic clove, minced
1 tablespoon minced red onion
4 basil leaves, minced

¼ teaspoon salt
¼ teaspoon black pepper
4 ounces (113 g) goat cheese
2 tablespoons shredded Parmesan cheese

1. Preheat the air fryer to 380°F (193°C). 2. Slice the top off of each tomato. 3. Using a knife and spoon, cut and scoop out half of the flesh inside of the tomato. Place it into a medium bowl. 4. To the bowl with the tomato, add the cooked lentils, garlic, onion, basil, salt, pepper, and goat cheese. Stir until well combined. 5. Spoon the filling into the scooped-out cavity of each of the tomatoes, then top each one with ½ tablespoon of shredded Parmesan cheese. 6. Place the tomatoes in a single layer in the air fryer basket and bake for 15 minutes.

Per Serving
Calories: 249 | fat: 11.6g | protein: 16.3g | carbs: 21.5g | fiber: 4.2g | sodium: 318mg

Sweet Potato Black Bean Burgers

Prep time: 10 minutes | Cook time: 10 minutes | Serves 4

1 (15-ounce / 425-g) can black beans, drained and rinsed
1 cup mashed sweet potato
½ teaspoon dried oregano
¼ teaspoon dried thyme
¼ teaspoon dried marjoram
1 garlic clove, minced
¼ teaspoon salt
¼ teaspoon black pepper
1 tablespoon lemon juice
1 cup cooked brown rice

¼ to ½ cup whole wheat bread crumbs
1 tablespoon olive oil
For serving:
Whole wheat buns or whole wheat pitas
Plain Greek yogurt
Avocado
Lettuce
Tomato
Red onion

1. Preheat the air fryer to 380°F (193°C). 2. In a large bowl, use the back of a fork to mash the black beans until there are no large pieces left. 3. Add the mashed sweet potato, oregano, thyme, marjoram, garlic, salt, pepper, and lemon juice, and mix until well combined. 4. Stir in the cooked rice. 5. Add in ¼ cup of the whole wheat bread crumbs and stir. Check to see if the mixture is dry enough to form patties. If it seems too wet and loose, add an additional ¼ cup bread crumbs and stir. 6. Form the dough into 4 patties. Place them into the air fryer basket in a single layer, making sure that they don't touch each other. 7. Brush half of the olive oil onto the patties and bake for 5 minutes. 8. Flip the patties over, brush the other side with the remaining oil, and bake for an additional 4 to 5 minutes. 9. Serve on toasted whole wheat buns or whole wheat pitas with a spoonful of yogurt and avocado, lettuce, tomato, and red onion as desired.

Per Serving
Calories: 112 | fat: 4.3g | protein: 2.8g | carbs: 17g | fiber: 3g | sodium: 161mg

Orzo-Veggie Pilaf

Prep time: 20 minutes | Cook time: 10 minutes | Serves 6

2 cups orzo
1 pint (2 cups) cherry tomatoes, cut in half
1 cup Kalamata olives
½ cup fresh basil, finely chopped
½ cup extra-virgin olive oil
⅓ cup balsamic vinegar
1 teaspoon salt
½ teaspoon freshly ground black pepper

1. Bring a large pot of water to a boil. Add the orzo and cook for 7 minutes. Drain and rinse the orzo with cold water in a strainer. 2. Once the orzo has cooled, put it in a large bowl. Add the tomatoes, olives, and basil. 3. In a small bowl, whisk together the olive oil, vinegar, salt, and pepper. Add this dressing to the pasta and toss everything together. Serve at room temperature or chilled.

Per Serving
Calories: 476 | fat: 28g | protein: 8g | carbs: 48g | fiber: 3g | sodium: 851mg

Venetian-Style Pasta E Fagioli

Prep time: 15 minutes | Cook time: 50 minutes | Serves 2

1 cup uncooked borlotti (cranberry) beans or pinto beans
3 tablespoons extra virgin olive oil, divided
1 small carrot, finely chopped
½ medium onion (white or red), finely chopped
1 celery stalk, finely chopped
1 bay leaf
1 tablespoon tomato paste
2 cups cold water
1 rosemary sprig plus ½ teaspoon chopped fresh
rosemary needles
¼ teaspoon fine sea salt
¼ teaspoon freshly ground black pepper plus more to taste
1½ ounces (43 g) uncooked egg fettuccine or other egg noodles
1 garlic clove, peeled and finely sliced
¼ teaspoon red pepper flakes
2 teaspoons grated Parmesan cheese
Pinch of coarse sea salt, for serving

1. Place the beans in a large bowl and cover with cold water by 3 inches (7.5cm) to allow for expansion. Soak for 12 hours or overnight, then drain and rinse. 2. Add 2 tablespoons of the olive oil to a medium pot over medium heat. When the oil begins to shimmer, add the carrot, onions, celery, and bay leaf. Sauté for 3 minutes, then add the tomato paste and continue sautéing and stirring for 2 more minutes. 3. Add the beans, cold water, and rosemary sprig. Cover, bring to a boil, then reduce the heat to low and simmer for 30–40 minutes or until the beans are soft, but not falling apart. Remove the rosemary sprig and bay leaf. Use a slotted spoon to remove about 1 cup of the beans. Set aside. 4. Using an immersion blender, blend the remaining beans in the pot, then add the whole beans back to the pot along with the sea salt and ¼ teaspoon of the black pepper. Increase the heat to medium. When the mixture begins to bubble, add the pasta and cook until done, about 3 minutes. 5. While the pasta is cooking, heat 1 teaspoon of the olive oil in a small pan over medium heat. Add the garlic, red pepper flakes, and chopped rosemary needles. Sauté for 2 minutes, then transfer the mixture to the beans and stir. 6. When the pasta is done cooking, remove from the heat and set aside to cool for 5 minutes before dividing between 2 plates. Drizzle 1 teaspoon of the olive oil and sprinkle 1 teaspoon of the grated Parmesan over each serving. Season with freshly ground pepper to taste and a pinch of coarse sea salt. This dish is best served promptly, but can be stored in the refrigerator for up to 2 days.

Per Serving
Calories: 409 | fat: 22g | protein: 12g | carbs: 42g | fiber: 11g | sodium: 763mg

Baked Farro Risotto with Sage

Prep time: 5 minutes | Cook time: 35 minutes | Serves 6

Olive oil cooking spray
1½ cups uncooked farro
2½ cups chicken broth
1 cup tomato sauce
1 yellow onion, diced
3 garlic cloves, minced
1 tablespoon fresh sage, chopped
½ teaspoon salt
2 tablespoons olive oil
1 cup Parmesan cheese, grated, divided

1. Preheat the air fryer to 380ºF (193ºC). Lightly coat the inside of a 5-cup capacity casserole dish with olive oil cooking spray. (The shape of the casserole dish will depend upon the size of the air fryer, but it needs to be able to hold at least 5 cups.) 2. In a large bowl, combine the farro, broth, tomato sauce, onion, garlic, sage, salt, olive oil, and ½ cup of the Parmesan. 3. Pour the farro mixture into the prepared casserole dish and cover with aluminum foil. 4. Bake for 20 minutes, then uncover and stir. Sprinkle the remaining ½ cup Parmesan over the top and bake for 15 minutes more. 5. Stir well before serving.

Per Serving
Calories: 227 | fat: 11.3g | protein: 7.3g | carbs: 27g | fiber: 3.4g | sodium: 889mg

Slow Cooker Vegetarian Chili

Prep time: 20 minutes | Cook time: 4 to 6 hours | Serves 4

1 (28-ounce / 794-g) can chopped whole tomatoes, with the juice
1 medium green bell pepper, chopped
1 (15-ounce / 425-g) can red beans, drained and rinsed
1 (15-ounce / 425-g) can black beans, drained and rinsed
1 yellow onion, chopped
1 tablespoon olive oil
1 tablespoon onion powder
1 teaspoon garlic powder
1 teaspoon cayenne pepper
1 teaspoon paprika
½ teaspoon sea salt
½ teaspoon black pepper
1 large hass avocado, pitted, peeled, and chopped, for garnish

1. Combine the tomatoes, bell pepper, red beans, black beans, and onion in the slow cooker. Sprinkle with the onion powder, garlic powder, cayenne pepper, paprika, ½ teaspoon salt, and ½ teaspoon black pepper. 2. Cover and cook on high for 4 to 6 hours or on low for 8 hours, or until thick. 3. Season with salt and black pepper if needed. Served hot, garnished with some of the avocado.

Per Serving
Calories: 446 | fat: 15.4g | protein: 20.9g | carbs: 61g | fiber: 21.5g | sodium: 599mg

Moroccan Vegetables and Chickpeas

Prep time: 25 minutes | Cook time: 6 hours | Serves 6

1 large carrot, cut into ¼-inch rounds
2 large baking potatoes, peeled and cubed
1 large bell pepper, any color, chopped
6 ounces (170 g) green beans, trimmed and cut into bite-size pieces
1 large yellow onion, chopped
2 garlic cloves, minced
1 teaspoon peeled, grated fresh ginger
1 (15-ounce / 425-g) can diced tomatoes, with the juice
3 cups canned chickpeas, rinsed and drained
1¾ cups vegetable stock
1 tablespoon ground coriander
1 teaspoon ground cumin
¼ teaspoon ground red pepper
Sea salt
Black pepper
8 ounces (227 g) fresh baby spinach
¼ cup diced dried apricots
¼ cup diced dried figs
1 cup plain greek yogurt

1. Put the carrot, potatoes, bell pepper, green beans, onion, garlic, and ginger in the slow cooker. Stir in the diced tomatoes, chickpeas, and vegetable stock. Sprinkle with coriander, cumin, red pepper, salt, and black pepper. 2. Cover and cook on high for 6 hours or until the vegetables are tender. 3. Add the spinach, apricots, figs, and Greek yogurt, and cook and stir until the spinach wilts, about 4 minutes. Serve hot.

Per Serving

Calories: 307 | fat: 5g | protein: 13g | carbs: 57g | fiber: 12g | sodium: 513mg

Spicy Lentil Patties

Prep time: 15 minutes | Cook time: 10 minutes | Serves 4

1 cup cooked brown lentils
¼ cup fresh parsley leaves
½ cup shredded carrots
¼ red onion, minced
¼ red bell pepper, minced
1 jalapeño, seeded and minced
2 garlic cloves, minced
1 egg
2 tablespoons lemon juice
2 tablespoons olive oil, divided
½ teaspoon onion powder
½ teaspoon smoked paprika
½ teaspoon dried oregano
¼ teaspoon salt
¼ teaspoon black pepper
½ cup whole wheat bread crumbs
For serving:
Whole wheat buns or whole wheat pitas
Plain Greek yogurt
Tomato
Lettuce
Red Onion

1. Preheat the air fryer to 380ºF (193ºC). 2. In a food processor, pulse the lentils and parsley mostly smooth. (You will want some bits of lentils in the mixture.) 3. Pour the lentils into a large bowl, and combine with the carrots, onion, bell pepper, jalapeño, garlic, egg, lemon juice, and 1 tablespoon olive oil. 4. Add the onion powder, paprika, oregano, salt, pepper, and bread crumbs. Stir everything together until the seasonings and bread crumbs are well distributed. 5. Form the dough into 4 patties. Place them into the air fryer basket in a single layer, making sure that they don't touch each other. Brush the remaining 1 tablespoon of olive oil over the patties. 6. Bake for 5 minutes. Flip the patties over and bake for an additional 5 minutes. 7.

Serve on toasted whole wheat buns or whole wheat pitas with a spoonful of yogurt and lettuce, tomato, and red onion as desired.

Per Serving

Calories: 225 | fat: 10.3g | protein: 9.3g | carbs: 25g | fiber: 5.7g | sodium: 285mg

Creamy Yellow Lentil Soup

Prep time: 15 minutes | Cook time: 20 minutes | Serves 6

2 tablespoons olive oil
1 medium yellow onion, peeled and chopped
1 medium carrot, peeled and chopped
2 cloves garlic, peeled and minced
1 teaspoon ground cumin
½ teaspoon ground black pepper
¼ teaspoon salt
2 cups dried yellow lentils, rinsed and drained
6 cups water

1. Press the Sauté button on the Instant Pot® and heat oil. Add onion and carrot and cook until just tender, about 3 minutes. Add garlic, cumin, pepper, and salt and cook until fragrant, about 30 seconds. Press the Cancel button. 2. Add lentils and water, close lid, set steam release to Sealing, press the Manual button, and set time to 15 minutes. When the timer beeps, let pressure release naturally, about 15 minutes. 3. Open lid and purée with an immersion blender or in batches in a blender. Serve warm.

Per Serving

Calories: 248 | fat: 5g | protein: 15g | carbs: 35g | fiber: 8g | sodium: 118mg

Savory Gigantes Plaki (Baked Giant White Beans)

Prep time: 5 minutes | Cook time: 30 minutes | Serves 4

Olive oil cooking spray
1 (15-ounce / 425-g) can cooked butter beans, drained and rinsed
1 cup diced fresh tomatoes
½ tablespoon tomato paste
2 garlic cloves, minced
½ yellow onion, diced
½ teaspoon salt
¼ cup olive oil
¼ cup fresh parsley, chopped

1. Preheat the air fryer to 380ºF (193ºC). Lightly coat the inside of a 5-cup capacity casserole dish with olive oil cooking spray. (The shape of the casserole dish will depend upon the size of the air fryer, but it needs to be able to hold at least 5 cups.) 2. In a large bowl, combine the butter beans, tomatoes, tomato paste, garlic, onion, salt, and olive oil, mixing until all ingredients are combined. 3. Pour the mixture into the prepared casserole dish and top with the chopped parsley. 4. Bake in the air fryer for 15 minutes. Stir well, then return to the air fryer and bake for 15 minutes more.

Per Serving

Calories: 199 | fat: 18.6g | protein: 2g | carbs: 8g | fiber: 3g | sodium: 300mg

Spanakorizo (Greek Spinach and Rice)

Prep time: 5 minutes | Cook time: 27 minutes | Serves 2

3½ tablespoons extra virgin olive oil, divided
1 pound (454 g) fresh spinach, rinsed and torn into large pieces
2 tablespoons fresh lemon juice plus juice of ½ lemon, for serving
1 medium red onion, chopped
1 teaspoon dried mint
2 tablespoons chopped fresh dill
⅓ cup uncooked medium-grain rice
⅔ cup hot water
½ teaspoon fine sea salt
¼ teaspoon freshly ground black pepper

1. Add 1½ teaspoons of olive oil to a deep pan over medium heat. When the oils starts to shimmer, add the spinach and 2 tablespoons lemon juice. Using tongs, toss the spinach until it's wilted and develops a bright green color, about 2–3 minutes, then transfer to a colander and set aside to drain. 2. In a separate large pot placed over medium heat, combine the onions with 2 tablespoons of the olive oil. Sauté until the onions are soft, about 3 minutes. 3. Add the cooked spinach, mint, dill, and rice to the pot and then stir to coat the spinach and rice in the olive oil. Continue sautéing for 1 minute, then add the hot water, sea salt, and black pepper. Stir, then increase the heat slightly and bring the mixture to a boil. 4. Once the mixture comes to a boil, reduce the heat to low and simmer for 20 minutes or until the rice is soft, adding more warm water as needed if the rice becomes too dry. 5. Serve warm or at room temperature with a squeeze of lemon juice and 1½ teaspoons of the olive oil drizzled over each serving. Store covered in the refrigerator for up to 3 days.

Per Serving

Calories: 421 | fat: 26g | protein: 11g | carbs: 42g | fiber: 9g | sodium: 768mg

Brown Rice with Apricots, Cherries, and Toasted Pecans

Prep time: 10 minutes | Cook time: 55 minutes | Serves 2

2 tablespoons olive oil
2 green onions, sliced
½ cup brown rice
1 cup chicken stock
4–5 dried apricots, chopped
2 tablespoons dried cherries
2 tablespoons pecans, toasted and chopped
Sea salt and freshly ground pepper, to taste

1. Heat the olive oil in a medium saucepan, and add the green onions. 2. Sauté for 1–2 minutes, and add the rice. Stir to coat in oil, then add the stock. 3. Bring to a boil, reduce heat, and cover. Simmer for 50 minutes. 4. Remove the lid, add the apricots, cherries, and pecans, and cover for 10 more minutes. 5. Fluff with a fork to mix the fruit into the rice, season with sea salt and freshly ground pepper, and serve.

Per Serving

Calories: 429 | fat: 21g | protein: 8g | carbs: 54g | fiber: 4g | sodium: 43mg

Buckwheat Bake with Root Vegetables

Prep time: 15 minutes | Cook time: 30 minutes | Serves 6

Olive oil cooking spray
2 large potatoes, cubed
2 carrots, sliced
1 small rutabaga, cubed
2 celery stalks, chopped
½ teaspoon smoked paprika
¼ cup plus 1 tablespoon olive
oil, divided
2 rosemary sprigs
1 cup buckwheat groats
2 cups vegetable broth
2 garlic cloves, minced
½ yellow onion, chopped
1 teaspoon salt

1. Preheat the air fryer to 380ºF (193ºC). Lightly coat the inside of a 5-cup capacity casserole dish with olive oil cooking spray. (The shape of the casserole dish will depend upon the size of the air fryer, but it needs to be able to hold at least 5 cups.) 2. In a large bowl, toss the potatoes, carrots, rutabaga, and celery with the paprika and ¼ cup olive oil. 3. Pour the vegetable mixture into the prepared casserole dish and top with the rosemary sprigs. Place the casserole dish into the air fryer and bake for 15 minutes. 4. While the vegetables are cooking, rinse and drain the buckwheat groats. 5. In a medium saucepan over medium-high heat, combine the groats, vegetable broth, garlic, onion, and salt with the remaining 1 tablespoon olive oil. Bring the mixture to a boil, then reduce the heat to low, cover, and cook for 10 to 12 minutes. 6. Remove the casserole dish from the air fryer. Remove the rosemary sprigs and discard. Pour the cooked buckwheat into the dish with the vegetables and stir to combine. Cover with aluminum foil and bake for an additional 15 minutes. 7. Stir before serving.

Per Serving

Calories: 229 | fat: 10.2g | protein: 4g | carbs: 32.2g | fiber: 4.6g | sodium: 720mg

Peppers

Prep time: 5 minutes | Cook time: 15 minutes | Serves 4

Olive oil cooking spray
2 (15-ounce / 425-g) cans white beans, or cannellini beans, drained and rinsed
1 red bell pepper, diced
½ red onion, diced
3 garlic cloves, minced
1 tablespoon olive oil
¼ to ½ teaspoon salt
½ teaspoon black pepper
1 rosemary sprig
1 bay leaf

1. Preheat the air fryer to 360ºF (182ºC). Lightly coat the inside of a 5-cup capacity casserole dish with olive oil cooking spray. (The shape of the casserole dish will depend upon the size of the air fryer, but it needs to be able to hold at least 5 cups.) 2. In a large bowl, combine the beans, bell pepper, onion, garlic, olive oil, salt, and pepper. 3. Pour the bean mixture into the prepared casserole dish, place the rosemary and bay leaf on top, and then place the casserole dish into the air fryer. 4. Roast for 15 minutes. 5. Remove the rosemary and bay leaves, then stir well before serving.

Per Serving

Calories: 77 | fat: 4.2g | protein: 2.2g | carbs: 9.6g | fiber: 3.3g | sodium: 150mg

Apple Couscous with Curry

Prep time: 10 minutes | Cook time: 10 minutes | Serves 4

2 teaspoons olive oil
2 leeks, white parts only, sliced
1 Granny Smith apple, diced
2 cups cooked whole-wheat

couscous
2 tablespoons curry powder
½ cup chopped pecans

1. Heat the olive oil in a large skillet on medium heat and add leeks. Cook until soft and tender, about 5 minutes. 2. Add diced apple and cook until soft. 3. Add couscous and curry powder, then stir to combine. Remove from heat, mix in nuts, and serve.

Per Serving

Calories: 255 | fat: 12g | protein: 5g | carbs: 34g | fiber: 6g | sodium: 15mg

Sweet Potato and Chickpea Moroccan Stew

Prep time: 10 minutes | Cook time: 40 minutes | Serves 4

6 tablespoons extra virgin olive oil
2 medium red or white onions, finely chopped
6 garlic cloves, minced
3 medium carrots (about 8 ounces /227 g), peeled and cubed
1 teaspoon ground cumin
1 teaspoon ground coriander
½ teaspoon smoked paprika
½ teaspoon ground turmeric
1 cinnamon stick
½ pound (227 g) butternut squash, peeled and cut into

½-inch cubes
2 medium sweet potatoes, peeled and cut into ½-inch cubes
4 ounces (113 g) prunes, pitted
4 tomatoes (any variety), chopped, or 20 ounces (567g) canned chopped tomatoes
14 ounces (397 g) vegetable broth
14 ounces (397 g) canned chickpeas
½ cup chopped fresh parsley, for serving

1. Place a deep pan over medium heat and add the olive oil. When the oil is shimmering, add the onions and sauté for 5 minutes, then add the garlic and carrots, and sauté for 1 more minute. 2. Add the cumin, coriander, paprika, turmeric, and cinnamon stick. Continue cooking, stirring continuously, for 1 minute, then add the squash, sweet potatoes, prunes, tomatoes, and vegetable broth. Stir, cover, then reduce the heat to low and simmer for 20 minutes, stirring occasionally and checking the water levels, until the vegetables are cooked through. (If the stew appears to be drying out, add small amounts of hot water until the stew is thick.) 3. Add the chickpeas to the pan, stir, and continue simmering for 10 more minutes, adding more water if necessary. Remove the pan from the heat, discard the cinnamon stick, and set the stew aside to cool for 10 minutes. 4. When ready to serve, sprinkle the chopped parsley over the top of the stew. Store covered in the refrigerator for up to 4 days.

Per Serving

Calories: 471 | fat: 23g | protein: 9g | carbs: 63g | fiber: 12g | sodium: 651mg

Earthy Lentil and Rice Pilaf

Prep time: 5 minutes | Cook time: 50 minutes | Serves 6

¼ cup extra-virgin olive oil
1 large onion, chopped
6 cups water
1 teaspoon ground cumin

1 teaspoon salt
2 cups brown lentils, picked over and rinsed
1 cup basmati rice

1. In a medium pot over medium heat, cook the olive oil and onions for 7 to 10 minutes until the edges are browned. 2. Turn the heat to high, add the water, cumin, and salt, and bring this mixture to a boil, boiling for about 3 minutes. 3. Add the lentils and turn the heat to medium-low. Cover the pot and cook for 20 minutes, stirring occasionally. 4. Stir in the rice and cover; cook for an additional 20 minutes. 5. Fluff the rice with a fork and serve warm.

Per Serving

Calories: 397 | fat: 11g | protein: 18g | carbs: 60g | fiber: 18g | sodium: 396mg

Pilaf with Eggplant and Raisins

Prep time: 10 minutes | Cook time: 30 minutes | Serves 4

4 eggplant (preferably thinner, about 6 ounces / 170 g each) cut into ¼-inch thick slices (if the slices are too large, cut them in half)
1½ teaspoons fine sea salt, divided
½ cup extra virgin olive oil
1 medium onion (any variety), diced
4 garlic cloves, thinly sliced
¼ cup white wine

1 cup uncooked medium-grain rice
1 (15-ounce / 425-g) can crushed tomatoes
3 cups hot water
4 tablespoons black raisins
4 teaspoons finely chopped fresh parsley
4 teaspoons finely chopped fresh mint
¼ teaspoon freshly ground black pepper to serve

1. Place the eggplant in a colander and sprinkle with ½ teaspoon of the sea salt. Set aside to rest for 10 minutes, then rinse well and squeeze to remove any remaining water. 2. Add the olive oil to a medium pot placed over medium heat. When the oil begins to shimmer, add the eggplant and sauté for 7 minutes or until soft, moving the eggplant continuously, then add the onions and continue sautéing and stirring for 2 more minutes. 3. Add the garlic and sauté for 1 additional minute, then add the white wine and deglaze the pan. After about 1 minute, add the rice and stir until the rice is coated with the oil. 4. Add the crushed tomatoes, hot water, and remaining sea salt. Stir and bring to a boil, then reduce the heat to low and simmer for 20 minutes. Add more hot water, ¼ cup at a time, if the water level gets too low. 5. Add the raisins, stir, then cover the pot and remove from the heat. Set aside to cool for 15 minutes. 6. To serve, sprinkle 1 teaspoon of the mint and 1 teaspoon of the parsley over each serving, then season each serving with black pepper. Store covered in the refrigerator for up to 3 days.

Per Serving

Calories: 612 | fat: 29g | protein: 11g | carbs: 84g | fiber: 21g | sodium: 859mg

Baked Mushroom-Barley Pilaf

Prep time: 5 minutes | Cook time: 37 minutes | Serves 4

Olive oil cooking spray
2 tablespoons olive oil
8 ounces (227 g) button mushrooms, diced
½ yellow onion, diced
2 garlic cloves, minced
1 cup pearl barley

2 cups vegetable broth
1 tablespoon fresh thyme, chopped
½ teaspoon salt
¼ teaspoon smoked paprika
Fresh parsley, for garnish

1. Preheat the air fryer to 380ºF (193ºC). Lightly coat the inside of a 5-cup capacity casserole dish with olive oil cooking spray. (The shape of the casserole dish will depend upon the size of the air fryer, but it needs to be able to hold at least 5 cups.) 2. In a large skillet, heat the olive oil over medium heat. Add the mushrooms and onion and cook, stirring occasionally, for 5 minutes, or until the mushrooms begin to brown. 3. Add the garlic and cook for an additional 2 minutes. Transfer the vegetables to a large bowl. 4. Add the barley, broth, thyme, salt, and paprika. 5. Pour the barley-and-vegetable mixture into the prepared casserole dish, and place the dish into the air fryer. Bake for 15 minutes. 6. Stir the barley mixture. Reduce the heat to 360ºF (182ºC), then return the barley to the air fryer and bake for 15 minutes more. 7. Remove from the air fryer and let sit for 5 minutes before fluffing with a fork and topping with fresh parsley.

Per Serving
Calories: 428 | fat: 9.2g | protein: 10.7g | carbs: 84.7g | fiber: 9.2g | sodium: 775mg

Tomato Rice

Prep time: 10 minutes | Cook time: 25 minutes | Serves 3

2 tablespoons extra virgin olive oil
1 medium onion (any variety), chopped
1 garlic clove, finely chopped
1 cup uncooked medium-grain rice
1 tablespoon tomato paste
1 pound (454 g) canned

crushed tomatoes, or 1 pound (454 g) fresh tomatoes (puréed in a food processor)
¾ teaspoon fine sea salt
1 teaspoon granulated sugar
2 cups hot water
2 tablespoons chopped fresh mint or basil

1. Heat the olive oil in a wide, deep pan over medium heat. When the oil begins to shimmer, add the onion and sauté for 3–4 minutes or until soft, then add the garlic and sauté for an additional 30 seconds. 2. Add the rice and stir until the rice is coated with the oil, then add the tomato paste and stir rapidly. Add the tomatoes, sea salt, and sugar, and then stir again. 3. Add the hot water, stir, then reduce the heat to low and simmer, covered, for 20 minutes or until the rice is soft. (If the rice appears to need more cooking time, add a small amount of hot water to the pan and continue cooking.) Remove the pan from the heat. 4. Add the chopped mint or basil, and let the rice sit for 10 minutes before serving. Store covered in the refrigerator for up to 4 days.

Per Serving
Calories: 359 | fat: 11g | protein: 7g | carbs: 60g | fiber: 6g | sodium: 607mg

Lentil Pâté

Prep time: 10 minutes | Cook time: 34 minutes | Serves 12

2 tablespoons olive oil, divided
1 cup diced yellow onion
3 cloves garlic, peeled and minced
1 teaspoon red wine vinegar
2 cups dried green lentils,

rinsed and drained
4 cups water
1 teaspoon salt
¼ teaspoon ground black pepper

1. Press the Sauté button on the Instant Pot® and heat 1 tablespoon oil. Add onion and cook until translucent, about 3 minutes. Add garlic and vinegar, and cook for 30 seconds. Add lentils, water, remaining 1 tablespoon oil, and salt to pot and stir to combine. Press the Cancel button. 2. Close lid, set steam release to Sealing, press the Bean button, and allow to cook for default time of 30 minutes. When the timer beeps, let pressure release naturally for 10 minutes. Quick-release any remaining pressure until the float valve drops, then open lid. 3. Transfer lentil mixture to a food processor or blender, and blend until smooth. Season with pepper and serve warm.

Per Serving
Calories: 138 | fat: 3g | protein: 8g | carbs: 20g | fiber: 10g | sodium: 196mg

Greek-Style Pea Casserole

Prep time: 5 minutes | Cook time: 45 minutes | Serves 3

⅓ cup extra virgin olive oil
1 medium onion (any variety), diced
1 medium carrot, peeled and sliced
1 medium white potato, peeled and cut into bite-sized pieces
1 pound (454 g) peas (fresh or frozen)
3 tablespoons chopped fresh

dill
2 medium tomatoes, grated, or 12 ounces (340 g) canned crushed tomatoes
½ teaspoon fine sea salt
¼ teaspoon freshly ground black pepper
½ cup hot water
Salt to taste

1. Add the olive oil to a medium pot over medium heat. When the oil starts to shimmer, add the onions and sauté for 2 minutes. Add the carrots and potatoes, and sauté for 3 more minutes. 2. Add the peas and dill. Stir until the peas are coated in the olive oil. 3. Add the tomatoes, sea salt, black pepper, and hot water. Mix well. Bring to the mixture to a boil, then cover, reduce the heat to low, and simmer for 40 minutes or until the peas and carrots are soft and the casserole has thickened. (Check the water levels intermittently, adding more hot water if the mixture appears to be getting too dry.) 4. Remove the casserole from the heat, uncover, and set aside for 20 minutes. Add salt to taste before serving. Store covered in the refrigerator for up to 3 days.

Per Serving
Calories: 439 | fat: 26g | protein: 12g | carbs: 45g | fiber: 13g | sodium: 429mg

Fasolakia (Greek Green Beans)

Prep time: 5 minutes | Cook time: 45 minutes | Serves 2

⅓ cup olive oil (any variety)	3 medium tomatoes, grated, or 1 (15-ounce / 425-g) can crushed tomatoes
1 medium onion (red or white), chopped	¼ cup chopped fresh parsley
1 medium russet or white potato, sliced into ¼-inch thick slices	1 teaspoon granulated sugar
	½ teaspoon salt
1 pound (454 g) green beans (fresh or frozen)	¼ teaspoon freshly ground black pepper

1. Add the olive oil a medium pot over medium-low heat. When the oil begins to shimmer, add the onions and sauté until soft, about 5 minutes. 2. Add the potatoes to the pot, and sauté for an additional 2–3 minutes. 3. Add the green beans and stir until the beans are thoroughly coated with the olive oil. Add the tomatoes, parsley, sugar, salt, and black pepper. Stir to combine. 4. Add just enough hot water to the pot to cover half the beans. Cover and simmer for 40 minutes or until there is no water left in the pot and the beans are soft. (Do not allow the beans to boil.) 5. Allow the beans to cool until they're warm or until they reach room temperature, but do not serve hot. Store in refrigerator for up to 3 days.

Per Serving
Calories: 536 | fat: 37g | protein: 9g | carbs: 50g | fiber: 11g | sodium: 617mg

Chickpeas with Spinach and Sun-Dried Tomatoes

Prep time: 10 minutes | Cook time: 2 hours 30 minutes | Serves 3

½ pound (227 g) uncooked chickpeas	(packed in oil), drained, rinsed, and chopped
4 tablespoons extra virgin olive oil, divided	1 tablespoon chopped fresh mint
2 spring onions (white parts only), sliced	1 tablespoon chopped fresh dill
1 small onion (any variety), diced	6 tablespoons fresh lemon juice, divided
1 pound (454 g) fresh spinach, washed and chopped	¼ teaspoon freshly ground black pepper
½ cup white wine	¾ teaspoon fine sea salt
½ cup sun-dried tomatoes	

1. Place the chickpeas in a large bowl and cover with cold water by 3 inches (7.5cm) to allow for expansion. Soak overnight or for 12 hours. 2. When ready to cook, drain and rinse the chickpeas. Place them in a large pot and cover with cold water. Place the pot over high heat and bring to a boil (using a slotted spoon to remove any foam), then reduce the heat to low and simmer until the chickpeas are tender but not falling apart, about 1 to 1½ hours, checking the chickpeas every 30 minutes to ensure they aren't overcooking. Use the slotted spoon to transfer the chickpeas a medium bowl and then reserve the cooking water. Set aside. 3. In a deep pan, heat 3 tablespoons of the olive oil over medium heat. When the oil begins to shimmer, add the spring onions and diced onions, and sauté for 5 minutes or until soft, then add the spinach. Toss and continue cooking for 5–7 minutes or until the spinach has wilted. Add the wine and continue cooking for 2 minutes or until the liquid has evaporated. 4. Add the cooked chickpeas, sun-dried tomatoes, mint, dill, 3 tablespoons of the lemon juice, black pepper, and 1½ cups of the chickpea cooking water. Bring the mixture to a boil and then reduce the heat to low and simmer for 30–45 minutes or until the liquid has been absorbed and the chickpeas have thickened, adding more water as needed if the chickpeas appear to be too dry. About 5 minutes before removing the chickpeas from the heat, add the remaining 1 tablespoon of olive oil, a tablespoon of the lemon juice, and the sea salt. Mix well, then remove the pan from the heat, keeping it covered, and set aside to rest for 5 minutes. 5. Divide the mixture between three bowls and top each serving with 1 tablespoon of the lemon juice. Store covered in the refrigerator for up to 3 days.

Per Serving
Calories: 599 | fat: 24g | protein: 24g | carbs: 81g | fiber: 17g | sodium: 764mg

Roasted White Beans with Lentil and Zucchini Boats

Prep time: 15 minutes | Cook time: 50 minutes | Serves 4

1 cup dried green lentils, rinsed and drained	1 cup marinara sauce
¼ teaspoon salt	¼ teaspoon crushed red pepper flakes
2 cups water	4 medium zucchini, trimmed and cut lengthwise
1 tablespoon olive oil	
½ medium red onion, peeled and diced	½ cup shredded part-skim mozzarella cheese
1 clove garlic, peeled and minced	¼ cup chopped fresh flat-leaf parsley

1. Add lentils, salt, and water to the Instant Pot®. Close lid, set steam release to Sealing, press the Manual button, and set time to 12 minutes. When the timer beeps, quick-release the pressure until the float valve drops. Press the Cancel button. Open lid and drain off any excess liquid. Transfer lentils to a medium bowl. Set aside. 2. Press the Sauté button and heat oil. Add onion and cook until tender, about 3 minutes. Add garlic and cook until fragrant, about 30 seconds. Add marinara sauce and crushed red pepper flakes and stir to combine. Press the Cancel button. Stir in lentils. 3. Preheat oven to 350ºF (180ºC) and spray a 9" × 13" baking dish with nonstick cooking spray. 4. Using a teaspoon, hollow out each zucchini half. Lay zucchini in prepared baking dish. Divide lentil mixture among prepared zucchini. Top with cheese. Bake for 30–35 minutes, or until zucchini are tender and cheese is melted and browned. Top with parsley and serve hot.

Per Serving
Calories: 326 | fat: 10g | protein: 22g | carbs: 39g | fiber: 16g | sodium: 568mg

Moroccan-Style Rice and Chickpea Bake

Prep time: 10 minutes | Cook time: 45 minutes | Serves 6

Olive oil cooking spray
1 cup long-grain brown rice
2¼ cups chicken stock
1 (15½-ounce / 439-g) can chickpeas, drained and rinsed
½ cup diced carrot
½ cup green peas
1 teaspoon ground cumin
½ teaspoon ground turmeric
½ teaspoon ground ginger
½ teaspoon onion powder
½ teaspoon salt
¼ teaspoon ground cinnamon
¼ teaspoon garlic powder
¼ teaspoon black pepper
Fresh parsley, for garnish

1. Preheat the air fryer to 380°F (193°C). Lightly coat the inside of a 5-cup capacity casserole dish with olive oil cooking spray. (The shape of the casserole dish will depend upon the size of the air fryer, but it needs to be able to hold at least 5 cups.) 2. In the casserole dish, combine the rice, stock, chickpeas, carrot, peas, cumin, turmeric, ginger, onion powder, salt, cinnamon, garlic powder, and black pepper. Stir well to combine. 3. Cover loosely with aluminum foil. 4. Place the covered casserole dish into the air fryer and bake for 20 minutes. Remove from the air fryer and stir well. 5. Place the casserole back into the air fryer, uncovered, and bake for 25 minutes more. 6. Fluff with a spoon and sprinkle with fresh chopped parsley before serving.

Per Serving
Calories: 223 | fat: 3.3g | protein: 8.6g | carbs: 40.1g | fiber: 5g | sodium: 462mg

Greek Baked Beans

Prep time: 5 minutes | Cook time: 30 minutes | Serves 4

Olive oil cooking spray
1 (15-ounce / 425-g) can cannellini beans, drained and rinsed
1 (15-ounce / 425-g) can great northern beans, drained and rinsed
½ yellow onion, diced
1 (8-ounce / 227-g) can tomato sauce
1½ tablespoons raw honey
¼ cup olive oil
2 garlic cloves, minced
2 tablespoons chopped fresh dill
½ teaspoon salt
½ teaspoon black pepper
1 bay leaf
1 tablespoon balsamic vinegar
2 ounces (57 g) feta cheese, crumbled, for serving

1. Preheat the air fryer to 360°F (182°C). Lightly coat the inside of a 5-cup capacity casserole dish with olive oil cooking spray. (The shape of the casserole dish will depend upon the size of the air fryer, but it needs to be able to hold at least 5 cups.) 2. In a large bowl, combine all ingredients except the feta cheese and stir until well combined. 3. Pour the bean mixture into the prepared casserole dish. 4. Bake in the air fryer for 30 minutes. 5. Remove from the air fryer and remove and discard the bay leaf. Sprinkle crumbled feta over the top before serving.

Per Serving
Calories: 336 | fat: 19g | protein: 11g | carbs: 34g | fiber: 9.4g | sodium: 497mg

Gigantes (Greek Roasted Butter Beans)

Prep time: 10 minutes | Cook time: 1 hour 45 minutes | Serves 4

1 pound (454 g) uncooked gigantes or butter beans
2 bay leaves
¾ cup extra virgin olive oil, divided
2 medium red onions, chopped
4 garlic cloves, thinly sliced
1½ cups canned crushed tomatoes
2 tablespoons tomato paste mixed with 2 tablespoons water
1 teaspoon paprika
1 teaspoon dried oregano
3 tablespoons chopped fresh parsley
2 tablespoons chopped fresh dill
1 teaspoon fine sea salt, divided
¼ teaspoon freshly ground black pepper
Pinch of kosher salt

1. Place the beans in a large bowl and cover with cold water. Soak for 10 hours or overnight, then drain and rinse. 2. When ready to cook, add the beans to a large pot and fill the pot with enough fresh water to cover the beans. Add the bay leaves and place the pot over high heat. Bring the beans to a boil, cover, and reduce the heat to low. Simmer for about 40 minutes to 1 hour or until the beans are soft but not mushy. 3. While the beans are cooking, begin preparing the sauce by adding ¼ cup olive oil to a medium pan placed over medium heat. When the oil begins to shimmer, add the onions and sauté for 5 minutes or until the onions are soft. Add the garlic and sauté for 1 more minute. 4. Add the crushed tomatoes, tomato paste mixture, paprika, oregano, parsley, dill, ½ teaspoon of the sea salt, black pepper, and another ¼ cup of the olive oil, then stir to combine. Let the sauce simmer for about 10 minutes or until it thickens. 5. Preheat the oven to 350° (180°C). When the beans are done cooking, remove them from the heat. Reserve 2 cups of the cooking water, drain the remaining water from the pot, and remove the bay leaves. 6. Add the sauce to the beans, then add the remaining ½ teaspoon of sea salt, and mix gently. Pour the mixture into a baking dish and spread it evenly. Add the reserved cooking water to one corner of the dish and tilt the dish to spread the water across the beans. Drizzle the remaining ¼ cup of olive oil over the beans. Transfer the beans to the oven and bake for 45 minutes or until the sauce is thick and the beans are tender. 7. Remove the beans from the oven and set aside to cool for 15 minutes. Sprinkle a pinch of kosher salt over the top before serving warm or at room temperature. Store covered in the refrigerator for up to 3 days.

Per Serving
Calories: 564 | fat: 42g | protein: 2g | carbs: 13g | fiber: 3g | sodium: 596mg

Greek Chickpeas and Rice with Tahini and Lemon

Prep time: 10 minutes | Cook time: 1 hour 45 minutes | Serves 2

¾ cup uncooked chickpeas
1 tablespoon tahini
3 tablespoons fresh lemon juice plus juice of 1 lemon for serving
4 tablespoons water
2 tablespoons extra virgin olive oil
1 medium onion (any variety), chopped
1 garlic clove, minced

¾ cup uncooked medium-grain rice
¾ teaspoon fine sea salt
½ teaspoon freshly ground black pepper
1 bay leaf
2½ cups reserved cooking water
4 teaspoons chopped fresh parsley

1. Place the chickpeas in a large bowl and cover with cold water by 3 inches to allow for expansion. Soak overnight or for 12 hours. 2. In a small bowl, combine the tahini with the lemon juice and 4 tablespoons of water. Whisk with a fork. Set aside. 3. When ready to cook, drain and rinse the chickpeas. Fill a large pot with cold water, place it over high heat, and add the chickpeas. Bring to a boil (removing any foam with a slotted spoon), then reduce the heat to medium-low and simmer until the chickpeas are tender but not falling apart, about 60–90 minutes. (Some chickpeas will cook faster, so begin checking after 30 minutes.) Reserve 2½ cups of the cooking water and then drain the chickpeas. Set aside. 4. Add the olive oil to a medium pot placed over medium heat. When the oil begins to shimmer, add the onions and sauté for 4–5 minutes or until the onions are soft. Add the garlic and sauté for more 1 minute, then add the rice and stir until the rice is coated in the oil. 5. Add the tahini-lemon juice mixture to the pot, followed by the sea salt, black pepper, bay leaf, and 1½ cups of the cooking water (if using canned chickpeas, use 1½ cups tap water instead). Reduce the heat to medium-low and simmer for about 10 minutes, then add the chickpeas and continue simmering until the rice is cooked and the water has been absorbed, about 10 minutes, then remove the pot from the heat. (Add more hot water in small amounts if the mixture appears to be too dry.) Remove the pot from the heat. 6. Discard the bay leaf and transfer the mixture to two bowls. Squeeze half a lemon over each serving, then sprinkle 2 teaspoons of the parsley over each serving. Store covered in the refrigerator for up to 3 days.

Per Serving
Calories: 842 | fat: 25g | protein: 25g | carbs: 134g | fiber: 27g | sodium: 863mg

Garbanzo and Pita No-Bake Casserole

Prep time: 10 minutes | Cook time: 10 minutes | Serves 4

4 cups Greek yogurt
3 cloves garlic, minced
1 teaspoon salt
2 (16-ounce / 454-g) cans arbanzo beans, rinsed and drained

2 cups water
4 cups pita chips
5 tablespoons unsalted butter

1. In a large bowl, whisk together the yogurt, garlic, and salt. Set aside. 2. Put the garbanzo beans and water in a medium pot. Bring to a boil; let beans boil for about 5 minutes. 3. Pour the garbanzo beans and the liquid into a large casserole dish. 4. Top the beans with pita chips. Pour the yogurt sauce over the pita chip layer. 5. In a small saucepan, melt and brown the butter, about 3 minutes. Pour the brown butter over the yogurt sauce.

Per Serving
Calories: 772 | fat: 36g | protein: 39g | carbs: 73g | fiber: 13g | sodium: 1,003mg

Chapter 4 Beef, Pork, and Lamb

Herbed Lamb Steaks

Prep time: 30 minutes | Cook time: 15 minutes | Serves 4

½ medium onion	1 teaspoon cayenne pepper
2 tablespoons minced garlic	1 teaspoon salt
2 teaspoons ground ginger	4 (6-ounce / 170-g) boneless
1 teaspoon ground cinnamon	lamb sirloin steaks
1 teaspoon onion powder	Oil, for spraying

1. In a blender, combine the onion, garlic, ginger, cinnamon, onion powder, cayenne pepper, and salt and pulse until the onion is minced. 2. Place the lamb steaks in a large bowl or zip-top plastic bag and sprinkle the onion mixture over the top. Turn the steaks until they are evenly coated. Cover with plastic wrap or seal the bag and refrigerate for 30 minutes. 3. Preheat the air fryer to 330ºF (166ºC). Line the air fryer basket with parchment and spray lightly with oil. 4. Place the lamb steaks in a single layer in the prepared basket, making sure they don't overlap. You may need to work in batches, depending on the size of your air fryer. 5. Cook for 8 minutes, flip, and cook for another 7 minutes, or until the internal temperature reaches 155ºF (68ºC).

Per Serving
Calories: 255 | fat: 10g | protein: 35g | carbs: 5g | fiber: 1g | sodium: 720mg

Nigerian Peanut-Crusted Flank Steak

Prep time: 30 minutes | Cook time: 8 minutes | Serves 4

Suya Spice Mix:	1 teaspoon kosher salt
¼ cup dry-roasted peanuts	½ teaspoon cayenne pepper
1 teaspoon cumin seeds	Steak:
1 teaspoon garlic powder	1 pound (454 g) flank steak
1 teaspoon smoked paprika	2 tablespoons vegetable oil
½ teaspoon ground ginger	

1. For the spice mix: In a clean coffee grinder or spice mill, combine the peanuts and cumin seeds. Process until you get a coarse powder. (Do not overprocess or you will wind up with peanut butter! Alternatively, you can grind the cumin with ⅓ cup ready-made peanut powder, such as PB2, instead of the peanuts.) 2. Pour the peanut mixture into a small bowl, add the garlic powder, paprika, ginger, salt, and cayenne, and stir to combine. This recipe makes about ½ cup suya spice mix. Store leftovers in an airtight container in a cool, dry place for up to 1 month. 3. For the steak: Cut the flank steak into ½-inch-thick slices, cutting against the grain and at a slight angle. Place the beef strips in a resealable plastic bag and add the oil and 2½ to 3 tablespoons of the spice mixture. Seal the bag and massage to coat all of the meat with the oil and spice mixture. Marinate at room temperature for 30 minutes or in the refrigerator for up to 24 hours. 4. Place the beef strips in the air fryer basket. Set the air fryer to 400ºF (204ºC) for 8 minutes, turning the strips halfway through the cooking time. 5. Transfer the meat to a serving platter. Sprinkle with additional spice mix, if desired.

Per Serving
Calories: 275 | fat: 17g | protein: 27g | carbs: 3g | fiber: 1g | sodium: 644mg

Beef Sliders with Pepper Slaw

Prep time: 10 minutes |Cook time: 10 minutes| Serves: 4

Nonstick cooking spray	divided
1 (8-ounce / 227-g) package	¼ teaspoon freshly ground
white button mushrooms	black pepper
2 tablespoons extra-virgin	1 tablespoon balsamic vinegar
olive oil, divided	2 bell peppers of different
1 pound (454 g) ground beef	colors, sliced into strips
(93% lean)	2 tablespoons torn fresh basil
2 garlic cloves, minced (about	or flat-leaf (Italian) parsley
1 teaspoon)	Mini or slider whole-grain
½ teaspoon kosher or sea salt,	rolls, for serving (optional)

1. Set one oven rack about 4 inches below the broiler element. Preheat the oven broiler to high. 2. Line a large, rimmed baking sheet with aluminum foil. Place a wire cooling rack on the aluminum foil, and spray the rack with nonstick cooking spray. Set aside. 3. Put half the mushrooms in the bowl of a food processor and pulse about 15 times, until the mushrooms are finely chopped but not puréed, similar to the texture of ground meat. Repeat with the remaining mushrooms. 4. In a large skillet over medium-high heat, heat 1 tablespoon of oil. Add the mushrooms and cook for 2 to 3 minutes, stirring occasionally, until the mushrooms have cooked down and some of their liquid has evaporated. Remove from the heat. 5. In a large bowl, combine the ground beef with the cooked mushrooms, garlic, ¼ teaspoon of salt, and pepper. Mix gently using your hands. Form the meat into 8 small (½-inch-thick) patties, and place on the prepared rack, making two lines of 4 patties down the center of the pan. 6. Place the pan in the oven so the broiler heating element is directly over as many burgers as possible. Broil for 4 minutes. Flip the burgers and rearrange them so any burgers not getting brown are nearer to the heat source. Broil for 3 to 4 more minutes, or until the internal temperature of the meat is 160ºF (71ºC) on a meat thermometer. Watch carefully to prevent burning. 7. While the burgers are cooking, in a large bowl, whisk together the remaining 1 tablespoon of oil, vinegar, and remaining ¼ teaspoon of salt. Add the peppers and basil, and stir gently to coat with the dressing. Serve the sliders with the pepper slaw as a topping or on the side. If desired, serve with the rolls, burger style.

Per Serving
Calories: 252 | fat: 13g | protein: 27g | carbs: 9g | fiber: 2g | sodium: 373mg

Herb-Crusted Lamb Chops

Prep time: 10 minutes | Cook time: 5 minutes | Serves 2

1 large egg
2 cloves garlic, minced
¼ cup pork dust
¼ cup powdered Parmesan cheese
1 tablespoon chopped fresh oregano leaves
1 tablespoon chopped fresh rosemary leaves
1 teaspoon chopped fresh thyme leaves
½ teaspoon ground black pepper
4 (1-inch-thick) lamb chops
For Garnish/Serving (Optional):
Sprigs of fresh oregano
Sprigs of fresh rosemary
Sprigs of fresh thyme
Lavender flowers
Lemon slices

1. Spray the air fryer basket with avocado oil. Preheat the air fryer to 400°F (204°C). 2. Beat the egg in a shallow bowl, add the garlic, and stir well to combine. In another shallow bowl, mix together the pork dust, Parmesan, herbs, and pepper. 3. One at a time, dip the lamb chops into the egg mixture, shake off the excess egg, and then dredge them in the Parmesan mixture. Use your hands to coat the chops well in the Parmesan mixture and form a nice crust on all sides; if necessary, dip the chops again in both the egg and the Parmesan mixture. 4. Place the lamb chops in the air fryer basket, leaving space between them, and air fry for 5 minutes, or until the internal temperature reaches 145°F (63°C) for medium doneness. Allow to rest for 10 minutes before serving. 5. Garnish with sprigs of oregano, rosemary, and thyme, and lavender flowers, if desired. Serve with lemon slices, if desired. 6. Best served fresh. Store leftovers in an airtight container in the fridge for up to 4 days. Serve chilled over a salad, or reheat in a 350°F (177°C) air fryer for 3 minutes, or until heated through.

Per Serving
Calories: 510 | fat: 42g | protein: 30g | carbs: 3g | fiber: 1g | sodium: 380mg

Asian Glazed Meatballs

Prep time: 15 minutes | Cook time: 10 minutes per batch | Serves 4 to 6

1 large shallot, finely chopped
2 cloves garlic, minced
1 tablespoon grated fresh ginger
2 teaspoons fresh thyme, finely chopped
1½ cups brown mushrooms, very finely chopped (a food processor works well here)
2 tablespoons soy sauce
Freshly ground black pepper, to taste
1 pound (454 g) ground beef
½ pound (227 g) ground pork
3 egg yolks
1 cup Thai sweet chili sauce (spring roll sauce)
¼ cup toasted sesame seeds
2 scallions, sliced

1. Combine the shallot, garlic, ginger, thyme, mushrooms, soy sauce, freshly ground black pepper, ground beef and pork, and egg yolks in a bowl and mix the ingredients together. Gently shape the mixture into 24 balls, about the size of a golf ball. 2. Preheat the air fryer to 380°F (193°C). 3. Working in batches, air fry the meatballs for 8 minutes, turning the meatballs over halfway through the cooking time. Drizzle some of the Thai sweet chili sauce on top of each meatball and return the basket to the air fryer, air frying for another 2 minutes. Reserve the remaining Thai sweet chili sauce for serving. 4. As soon as the meatballs are done, sprinkle with toasted sesame seeds and transfer them to a serving platter. Scatter the scallions around and serve warm.

Per Serving
Calories: 274 | fat: 11g | protein: 29g | carbs: 14g | fiber: 4g | sodium: 802mg

Indian Mint and Chile Kebabs

Prep time: 30 minutes | Cook time: 15 minutes | Serves 4

1 pound (454 g) ground lamb
½ cup finely minced onion
¼ cup chopped fresh mint
¼ cup chopped fresh cilantro
1 tablespoon minced garlic
½ teaspoon ground turmeric
½ teaspoon cayenne pepper
¼ teaspoon ground cardamom
¼ teaspoon ground cinnamon
1 teaspoon kosher salt

1. In the bowl of a stand mixer fitted with the paddle attachment, combine the lamb, onion, mint, cilantro, garlic, turmeric, cayenne, cardamom, cinnamon, and salt. Mix on low speed until you have a sticky mess of spiced meat. If you have time, let the mixture stand at room temperature for 30 minutes (or cover and refrigerate for up to a day or two, until you're ready to make the kebabs). 2. Divide the meat into eight equal portions. Form each into a long sausage shape. Place the kebabs in a single layer in the air fryer basket. Set the air fryer to 350°F (177°C) for 10 minutes. Increase the air fryer temperature to 400°F (204°C) and cook for 3 to 4 minutes more to brown the kebabs. Use a meat thermometer to ensure the kebabs have reached an internal temperature of 160°F / 71°C (medium).

Per Serving
Calories: 231 | fat: 14g | protein: 23g | carbs: 3g | fiber: 1g | sodium: 648mg

Blackened Cajun Pork Roast

Prep time: 20 minutes | Cook time: 33 minutes | Serves 4

2 pounds (907 g) bone-in pork loin roast
2 tablespoons oil
¼ cup Cajun seasoning
½ cup diced onion
½ cup diced celery
½ cup diced green bell pepper
1 tablespoon minced garlic

1. Cut 5 slits across the pork roast. Spritz it with oil, coating it completely. Evenly sprinkle the Cajun seasoning over the pork roast. 2. In a medium bowl, stir together the onion, celery, green bell pepper, and garlic until combined. Set aside. 3. Preheat the air fryer to 360°F (182°C). Line the air fryer basket with parchment paper. 4. Place the pork roast on the parchment and spritz with oil. 5. Cook for 5 minutes. Flip the roast and cook for 5 minutes more. Continue to flip and cook in 5-minute increments for a total cook time of 20 minutes. 6. Increase the air fryer temperature to 390°F (199°C). 7. Cook the roast for 8 minutes more and flip. Add the vegetable mixture to the basket and cook for a final 5 minutes. Let the roast sit for 5 minutes before serving.

Per Serving
Calories: 400 | fat: 16g | protein: 52g | carbs: 8g | fiber: 2g | sodium: 738mg

Pork and Beef Egg Rolls

Prep time: 30 minutes | Cook time: 7 to 8 minutes per batch | Makes 8 egg rolls

¼ pound (113 g) very lean ground beef
¼ pound (113 g) lean ground pork
1 tablespoon soy sauce
1 teaspoon olive oil
½ cup grated carrots
2 green onions, chopped
2 cups grated Napa cabbage
¼ cup chopped water chestnuts
¼ teaspoon salt
¼ teaspoon garlic powder
¼ teaspoon black pepper
1 egg
1 tablespoon water
8 egg roll wraps
Oil for misting or cooking spray

1. In a large skillet, brown beef and pork with soy sauce. Remove cooked meat from skillet, drain, and set aside. 2. Pour off any excess grease from skillet. Add olive oil, carrots, and onions. Sauté until barely tender, about 1 minute. 3. Stir in cabbage, cover, and cook for 1 minute or just until cabbage slightly wilts. Remove from heat. 4. In a large bowl, combine the cooked meats and vegetables, water chestnuts, salt, garlic powder, and pepper. Stir well. If needed, add more salt to taste. 5. Beat together egg and water in a small bowl. 6. Fill egg roll wrappers, using about ¼ cup of filling for each wrap. Roll up and brush all over with egg wash to seal. Spray very lightly with olive oil or cooking spray. 7. Place 4 egg rolls in air fryer basket and air fry at 390°F (199°C) for 4 minutes. Turn over and cook 3 to 4 more minutes, until golden brown and crispy. 8. Repeat to cook remaining egg rolls.

Per Serving
Calories: 176 | fat: 5g | protein: 11g | carbs: 22g | fiber: 2g | sodium: 339mg

Greek Stuffed Tenderloin

Prep time: 10 minutes | Cook time: 10 minutes | Serves 4

1½ pounds (680 g) venison or beef tenderloin, pounded to ¼ inch thick
3 teaspoons fine sea salt
1 teaspoon ground black pepper
2 ounces (57 g) creamy goat cheese
½ cup crumbled feta cheese (about 2 ounces / 57 g)
¼ cup finely chopped onions
2 cloves garlic, minced
For Garnish/Serving (Optional):
Prepared yellow mustard
Halved cherry tomatoes
Extra-virgin olive oil
Sprigs of fresh rosemary
Lavender flowers

1. Spray the air fryer basket with avocado oil. Preheat the air fryer to 400°F (204°C). 2. Season the tenderloin on all sides with the salt and pepper. 3. In a medium-sized mixing bowl, combine the goat cheese, feta, onions, and garlic. Place the mixture in the center of the tenderloin. Starting at the end closest to you, tightly roll the tenderloin like a jelly roll. Tie the rolled tenderloin tightly with kitchen twine. 4. Place the meat in the air fryer basket and air fry for 5 minutes. Flip the meat over and cook for another 5 minutes, or until the internal temperature reaches 135°F (57°C) for medium-rare. 5. To serve, smear a line of prepared yellow mustard on a platter, then place the meat next to it and add halved cherry tomatoes on the side, if desired. Drizzle with olive oil and garnish with rosemary sprigs and lavender flowers, if desired. 6. Best served fresh. Store leftovers in an airtight container in the fridge for 3 days. Reheat in a preheated 350°F (177°C) air fryer for 4 minutes, or until heated through.

Per Serving
Calories: 345 | fat: 17g | protein: 43g | carbs: 2g | fiber: 0g | sodium: 676mg

Garlic-Marinated Flank Steak

Prep time: 30 minutes | Cook time: 8 to 10 minutes | Serves 6

½ cup avocado oil
¼ cup coconut aminos
1 shallot, minced
1 tablespoon minced garlic
2 tablespoons chopped fresh oregano, or 2 teaspoons dried
1½ teaspoons sea salt
1 teaspoon freshly ground black pepper
¼ teaspoon red pepper flakes
2 pounds (907 g) flank steak

1. In a blender, combine the avocado oil, coconut aminos, shallot, garlic, oregano, salt, black pepper, and red pepper flakes. Process until smooth. 2. Place the steak in a zip-top plastic bag or shallow dish with the marinade. Seal the bag or cover the dish and marinate in the refrigerator for at least 2 hours or overnight. 3. Remove the steak from the bag and discard the marinade. 4. Set the air fryer to 400°F (204°C). Place the steak in the air fryer basket (if needed, cut into sections and work in batches). Air fry for 4 to 6 minutes, flip the steak, and cook for another 4 minutes or until the internal temperature reaches 120°F (49°C) in the thickest part for medium-rare (or as desired).

Per Serving
Calories: 373 | fat: 26g | protein: 33g | carbs: 1g | fiber: 0g | sodium: 672mg

Smoky Pork Tenderloin

Prep time: 5 minutes | Cook time: 19 to 22 minutes | Serves 6

1½ pounds (680 g) pork tenderloin
1 tablespoon avocado oil
1 teaspoon chili powder
1 teaspoon smoked paprika
1 teaspoon garlic powder
1 teaspoon sea salt
1 teaspoon freshly ground black pepper

1. Pierce the tenderloin all over with a fork and rub the oil all over the meat. 2. In a small dish, stir together the chili powder, smoked paprika, garlic powder, salt, and pepper. 3. Rub the spice mixture all over the tenderloin. 4. Set the air fryer to 400°F (204°C). Place the pork in the air fryer basket and air fry for 10 minutes. Flip the tenderloin and cook for 9 to 12 minutes more, until an instant-read thermometer reads at least 145°F (63°C). 5. Allow the tenderloin to rest for 5 minutes, then slice and serve.

Per Serving
Calories: 149 | fat: 5g | protein: 24g | carbs: 1g | fiber: 0g | sodium: 461mg

Pork Tenderloin with Chermoula Sauce

Prep time: 15 minutes | Cook time: 20 minutes | Serves 2

½ cup fresh parsley
½ cup fresh cilantro
6 small garlic cloves
3 tablespoons olive oil, divided
3 tablespoons freshly squeezed lemon juice
1 teaspoon smoked paprika
2 teaspoons cumin
½ teaspoon salt, divided
Pinch freshly ground black pepper
1 (8-ounce / 227-g) pork tenderloin

1. Preheat the oven to 425°F (220°C) and set the rack to the middle position. 2. In the bowl of a food processor, combine the parsley, cilantro, garlic, 2 tablespoons of olive oil, the lemon juice, paprika, cumin, and ¼ teaspoon of salt. Pulse 15 to 20 times, or until the mixture is fairly smooth. Scrape the sides down as needed to incorporate all of the ingredients. Transfer the sauce to a small bowl and set aside. 3. Season the pork tenderloin on all sides with the remaining ¼ teaspoon of salt and a generous pinch of pepper. 4. Heat the remaining 1 tablespoon of olive oil in a sauté pan. Add the pork and sear for 3 minutes, turning often, until it's golden on all sides. 5. Transfer the pork to an oven-safe baking dish and roast for 15 minutes, or until the internal temperature registers 145°F (63°C).
Per Serving
Calories: 168 | fat: 13g | protein: 11g | carbs: 3g | fiber: 1g | sodium: 333mg

Beef Bourguignon with Egg Noodles

Prep time: 15 minutes | Cook time: 8 hours | Serves 8

2 pounds (907 g) lean beef stew meat
6 tablespoons all-purpose flour
2 large carrots, cut into 1-inch slices
16 ounces (454 g) pearl onions, peeled fresh or frozen, thawed
8 ounces (227 g) mushrooms, stems removed
2 garlic cloves, minced
¾ cup beef stock
½ cup dry red wine
¼ cup tomato paste
1½ teaspoons sea salt
½ teaspoon dried rosemary
¼ teaspoon dried thyme
½ teaspoon black pepper
8 ounces (227 g) uncooked egg noodles
¼ cup chopped fresh thyme leaves

1. Place the beef in a medium bowl, sprinkle with the flour, and toss well to coat. 2. Place the beef mixture, carrots, onions, mushrooms, and garlic in the slow cooker. 3. Combine the stock, wine, tomato paste, salt, rosemary, thyme, and black pepper in a small bowl. Stir into the beef mixture. 4. Cover and cook on low for 8 hours. 5. Cook the noodles according to package directions, omitting any salt. 6. Serve the beef mixture over the noodles, sprinkled with the thyme.
Per Serving
Calories: 397 | fat: 6g | protein: 34g | carbs: 53g | fiber: 6g | sodium: 592mg

Lamb and Vegetable Bake

Prep time: 20 minutes | Cook time: 1 hour 20 minutes | Serves 8

¼ cup olive oil
1 pound (454 g) boneless, lean lamb, cut into ½-inch pieces
2 large red potatoes, scrubbed and diced
1 large onion, coarsely chopped
2 cloves garlic, minced
1 (28-ounce / 794-g) can diced tomatoes with liquid (no salt added)
2 medium zucchini, cut into
½-inch slices
1 red bell pepper, seeded and cut into 1-inch cubes
2 tablespoons flat-leaf parsley, chopped
1 teaspoon dried thyme
1 tablespoon paprika
½ teaspoon ground cinnamon
½ cup red wine
Sea salt and freshly ground pepper, to taste

1. Preheat the oven to 325°F (165°C). 2. Heat the olive oil in a large stew pot or cast-iron skillet over medium-high heat. 3. Add the lamb and brown the meat, stirring frequently. Transfer the lamb to an ovenproof baking dish. 4. Cook the potatoes, onion, and garlic in the skillet until tender, then transfer them to the baking dish. 5. Pour the tomatoes, zucchini, and pepper into the pan along with the herbs and spices, and simmer for 10 minutes. 6. Cover the lamb, onions, and potatoes with the tomato and pepper sauce and wine. 7. Cover with aluminum foil and bake for 1 hour. Uncover during the last 15 minutes of baking. 8. Season to taste, and serve with a green salad.
Per Serving
Calories: 264 | fat: 12g | protein: 15g | carbs: 24g | fiber: 5g | sodium: 75mg

Baked Lamb Kofta Meatballs

Prep time: 15 minutes | Cook time: 30 minutes | Serves 2

¼ cup walnuts
½ small onion
1 garlic clove
1 roasted piquillo pepper
2 tablespoons fresh parsley
2 tablespoons fresh mint
¼ teaspoon salt
¼ teaspoon cumin
¼ teaspoon allspice
Pinch cayenne pepper
8 ounces (227 g) lean ground lamb

1. Preheat the oven to 350°F (180°C) and set the rack to the middle position. Line a baking sheet with foil. 2. In the bowl of a food processor, combine the walnuts, onion, garlic, roasted pepper, parsley, mint, salt, cumin, allspice, and cayenne pepper. Pulse about 10 times to combine everything. 3. Transfer the spice mixture to the bowl and add the lamb. With your hands or a spatula, mix the spices into the lamb. 4. Roll into 1½-inch balls (about the size of golf balls). 5. Place the meatballs on the foil-lined baking sheet and bake for 30 minutes, or until cooked to an internal temperature of 160°F (71°C).
Per Serving
Calories: 408 | fat: 23g | protein: 22g | carbs: 7g | fiber: 3g | sodium: 429mg

Parmesan-Crusted Pork Chops

Prep time: 5 minutes | Cook time: 12 minutes | Serves 4

1 large egg
½ cup grated Parmesan cheese
4 (4-ounce / 113-g) boneless
pork chops
½ teaspoon salt
¼ teaspoon ground black
pepper

1. Whisk egg in a medium bowl and place Parmesan in a separate medium bowl. 2. Sprinkle pork chops on both sides with salt and pepper. Dip each pork chop into egg, then press both sides into Parmesan. 3. Place pork chops into ungreased air fryer basket. Adjust the temperature to 400ºF (204ºC) and air fry for 12 minutes, turning chops halfway through cooking. Pork chops will be golden and have an internal temperature of at least 145ºF (63ºC) when done. Serve warm.

Per Serving
Calories: 218 | fat: 9g | protein: 32g | carbs: 1g | fiber: 0g | sodium: 372mg

Quinoa Pilaf–Stuffed Pork

Prep time: 15 minutes | Cook time: 45 minutes | Serves 6

1 (1½-pound / 680-g) pork
tenderloin
2 tablespoons olive oil, divided
1 clove garlic, peeled and
minced
½ medium tomato, diced
¼ cup chopped fresh flat-leaf
parsley
1 tablespoon lemon juice
½ cup quinoa, rinsed and
drained
2 cups water, divided
¼ cup crumbled goat cheese
¼ teaspoon salt

1. Butterfly pork tenderloin. Open tenderloin and top with a sheet of plastic wrap. Pound pork out to ½" thick. Wrap and refrigerate until ready to use. 2. Press the Sauté button on the Instant Pot® and heat 1 tablespoon oil. Add garlic and cook 30 seconds, then add tomato, parsley, and lemon juice. Cook an additional minute. Transfer mixture to a small bowl. Press the Cancel button. 3. Add quinoa and 1 cup water to the pot. Close lid, set steam release to Sealing, press the Multigrain button, and set time to 20 minutes. When the timer beeps, let pressure release naturally, about 20 minutes, then open lid. Press the Cancel button. Fluff quinoa with a fork. Transfer quinoa to bowl with tomato mixture and mix well. 4. Spread quinoa mixture over pork. Top with goat cheese. Season with salt. Roll pork over filling. Tie pork every 2" with butcher's twine to secure. 5. Press Sauté on the Instant Pot® and heat remaining 1 tablespoon oil. Brown pork on all sides, about 2 minutes per side. Press the Cancel button. Remove pork and clean out pot. Return to machine, add remaining 1 cup water, place rack in pot, and place pork on rack. 6. Close lid, set steam release to Sealing, Press the Manual button, and set time to 20 minutes. When the timer beeps, quick-release the pressure until the float valve drops. Open lid and transfer pork to cutting board. Let rest for 10 minutes, then remove twine and cut into 1" slices. Serve hot.

Per Serving
Calories: 207 | fat: 9g | protein: 25g | carbs: 11g | fiber: 1g | sodium: 525mg

Ground Pork and Eggplant Casserole

Prep time: 20 minutes | Cook time: 18 minutes | Serves 8

2 pounds (907 g) lean ground
pork
1 large yellow onion, peeled
and diced
1 stalk celery, diced
1 medium green bell pepper,
seeded and diced
2 medium eggplants, cut into
½" pieces
4 cloves garlic, peeled and
minced
⅛ teaspoon dried thyme
1 tablespoon freeze-dried
parsley
3 tablespoons tomato paste
½ teaspoon hot sauce
2 teaspoons Worcestershire
sauce
1 teaspoon salt
½ teaspoon ground black
pepper
1 large egg, beaten
½ cup low-sodium chicken
broth

1. Press the Sauté button on the Instant Pot® and add pork, onion, celery, and bell pepper to the pot. Cook until pork is no longer pink, breaking it apart as it cooks, about 8 minutes. 2. Drain and discard any fat rendered from pork. Add eggplant, garlic, thyme, parsley, tomato paste, hot sauce, Worcestershire sauce, salt, pepper, and egg. Stir well, then press the Cancel button. 3. Pour in chicken broth. Close lid, set steam release to Sealing, press the Manual button, and set time to 10 minutes. When the timer beeps, let pressure release naturally, about 25 minutes. Open lid and serve hot.

Per Serving
Calories: 292 | fat: 18g | protein: 22g | carbs: 10g | fiber: 4g | sodium: 392mg

Mediterranean Chimichurri Skirt Steak

Prep time: 10 minutes | Cook time: 15 minutes | Serves 4

¾ cup fresh mint
¾ cup fresh parsley
⅔ cup extra-virgin olive oil
⅓ cup lemon juice
Zest of 1 lemon
2 tablespoons dried oregano
4 garlic cloves, peeled
½ teaspoon red pepper flakes
½ teaspoon kosher salt
1 to 1½ pounds (454 to 680 g)
skirt steak, cut in half if longer
than grill pan

1. In a food processor or blender, add the mint, parsley, olive oil, lemon juice, lemon zest, oregano, garlic, red pepper flakes, and salt. Process until the mixture reaches your desired consistency—anywhere from a slightly chunky to smooth purée. Remove a half cup of the chimichurri mixture and set aside. 2. Pour the remaining chimichurri mixture into a medium bowl or zip-top bag and add the steak. Mix together well and marinate for at least 30 minutes, and up to 8 hours in the refrigerator. 3. In a grill pan over medium-high heat, add the steak and cook 4 minutes on each side (for medium rare). Cook an additional 1 to 2 minutes per side for medium. 4. Place the steak on a cutting board, tent with foil to keep it warm, and let it rest for 10 minutes. Thinly slice the steak crosswise against the grain and serve with the reserved sauce.

Per Serving
Calories: 460 | fat: 38g | protein: 28g | carbs: 5g | fiber: 2g | sodium: 241mg

Greek-Inspired Beef Kebabs

Prep time: 15 minutes | Cook time: 15 minutes | Serves 2

6 ounces (170 g) beef sirloin tip, trimmed of fat and cut into 2-inch pieces
3 cups of any mixture of vegetables: mushrooms, zucchini, summer squash, onions, cherry tomatoes, red peppers
½ cup olive oil

¼ cup freshly squeezed lemon juice
2 tablespoons balsamic vinegar
2 teaspoons dried oregano
1 teaspoon garlic powder
1 teaspoon minced fresh rosemary
1 teaspoon salt

1. Place the meat in a large shallow container or in a plastic freezer bag. 2. Cut the vegetables into similar-size pieces and place them in a second shallow container or freezer bag. 3. For the marinade, combine the olive oil, lemon juice, balsamic vinegar, oregano, garlic powder, rosemary, and salt in a measuring cup. Whisk well to combine. Pour half of the marinade over the meat, and the other half over the vegetables. 4. Place the meat and vegetables in the refrigerator to marinate for 4 hours. 5. When you are ready to cook, preheat the grill to medium-high and grease the grill grate. 6. Thread the meat onto skewers and the vegetables onto separate skewers. 7. Grill the meat for 3 minutes on each side. They should only take 10 to 12 minutes to cook, but it will depend on how thick the meat is. 8. Grill the vegetables for about 3 minutes on each side or until they have grill marks and are softened.

Per Serving

Calories: 285 | fat: 18g | protein: 21g | carbs: 9g | fiber: 4g | sodium: 123mg

Pork and Cabbage Egg Roll in a Bowl

Prep time: 10 minutes | Cook time: 10 minutes | Serves 6

1 tablespoon light olive oil
1 pound (454 g) ground pork
1 medium yellow onion, peeled and chopped
1 clove garlic, peeled and minced
2 teaspoons minced fresh ginger

¼ cup low-sodium chicken broth
2 tablespoons soy sauce
2 (10-ounce / 283-g) bags shredded coleslaw mix
1 teaspoon sesame oil
1 teaspoon garlic chili sauce

1. Press the Sauté button on the Instant Pot® and heat olive oil. Add pork and sauté until cooked through, about 8 minutes. Add onion, garlic, and ginger, and cook until fragrant, about 2 minutes. Stir in chicken broth and soy sauce. Press the Cancel button. 2 Spread coleslaw mix over pork, but do not mix. Close lid, set steam release to Sealing, press the Manual button, and set time to 0 minutes. 3 When the timer beeps, quick-release the pressure until the float valve drops and open lid. Stir in sesame oil and garlic chili sauce. Serve hot.

Per Serving

Calories: 283 | fat: 24g | protein: 12g | carbs: 5g | fiber: 2g | sodium: 507mg

Herb-Marinated Grilled Lamb Loin Chops

Prep time: 5 minutes | Cook time: 10 to 12 minutes | Serves 4 to 6

3 tablespoons olive oil
Zest and juice of 1 lemon
2 tablespoons pomegranate molasses
1 cup finely chopped fresh mint
½ cup finely chopped fresh

cilantro or parsley
2 scallions (green onions), finely chopped
6 lamb loin chops
Freshly ground black pepper, to taste

1. In a small bowl, whisk together the olive oil, lemon zest, lemon juice, pomegranate molasses, mint, parsley, and scallions until well combined. Put the lamb in a large zip-top plastic bag. Add the marinade, seal the bag, and massage the marinade onto all sides of the chops. Refrigerate for at least 1 hour or up to overnight. 2. When ready to cook, heat a grill to medium. 3. Remove the chops from the marinade; discard the marinade. Season with pepper, if desired. Grill the chops for 10 to 12 minutes, turning once, for medium. Let rest for 10 minutes before serving.

Per Serving 1 cup:

Calories: 182 | fat: 11g | protein: 10g | carbs: 10g | fiber: 0g | sodium: 46mg

Beef Stew with Red Wine

Prep time: 15 minutes | Cook time: 46 minutes | Serves 8

1 pound (454 g) beef stew meat, cut into 1" pieces
2 tablespoons all-purpose flour
¼ teaspoon salt
¼ teaspoon ground black pepper
2 tablespoons olive oil, divided
1 pound (454 g) whole crimini mushrooms
2 cloves garlic, peeled and

minced
4 sprigs thyme
2 bay leaves
8 ounces (227 g) baby carrots
8 ounces (227 g) frozen pearl onions, thawed
1 cup red wine
½ cup beef broth
¼ cup chopped fresh parsley

1. In a medium bowl, toss beef with flour, salt, and pepper until thoroughly coated. Set aside. 2. Press the Sauté button on the Instant Pot® and heat 1 tablespoon oil. Add half of the beef pieces in a single layer, leaving space between each piece to prevent steaming, and brown well on all sides, about 3 minutes per side. Transfer beef to a medium bowl and repeat with remaining 1 tablespoon oil and beef. Press the Cancel button. 3. Add mushrooms, garlic, thyme, bay leaves, carrots, onions, wine, and broth to the Instant Pot®. Stir well. Close lid, set steam release to Sealing, press the Stew button, and set time to 40 minutes. When the timer beeps, quick-release the pressure until the float valve drops, open lid, and stir well. Remove and discard thyme and bay leaves. Sprinkle with parsley and serve hot.

Per Serving

Calories: 206 | fat: 13g | protein: 12g | carbs: 6g | fiber: 1g | sodium: 186mg

Pork Loin in Dried Fig Sauce

Prep time: 10 minutes | Cook time: 55 minutes | Serves 6

3 teaspoon fresh rosemary
1 tablespoon fresh thyme
Sea salt and freshly ground pepper, to taste
1 (3-pound / 1.4-kg) pork loin
½ cup olive oil
3 carrots, peeled and sliced
1 onion, diced
1 garlic clove, minced
1 cup dried figs, cut into small pieces
1 cup white wine
Juice of 1 lemon

1. Preheat the oven to 300°F (150°C). 2. Mix the rosemary, thyme, sea salt, and freshly ground pepper together to make a dry rub. Press the rub into the pork loin. 3. Heat the olive oil in a skillet. 4. Add the pork loin, carrots, onion, and garlic, and cook for 15 minutes, or until the pork is browned. 5. Transfer all to a shallow roasting pan. 6. Add the figs, white wine, and lemon juice. 7. Cover with aluminum foil and bake for 40–50 minutes, or until the meat is tender and internal temperature is about 145°F (63°C). 8. Transfer the meat to a serving dish, and cover with aluminum foil. Wait 15 minutes before slicing. 9. In the meantime, pour the vegetables, figs, and liquids into a blender. Process until smooth and strain through a sieve or strainer. 10. Transfer to a gravy dish, or pour directly over the sliced meat.

Per Serving

Calories: 546 | fat: 28g | protein: 52g | carbs: 22g | fiber: 4g | sodium: 139mg

Kofta with Vegetables in Tomato Sauce

Prep time: 15 minutes | Cook time: 6 to 8 hours | Serves 4

1 pound (454 g) raw ground beef
1 small white or yellow onion, finely diced
2 garlic cloves, minced
1 tablespoon dried parsley
2 teaspoons ground coriander
1 teaspoon ground cumin
½ teaspoon sea salt
½ teaspoon freshly ground black pepper
¼ teaspoon ground nutmeg
¼ teaspoon dried mint
¼ teaspoon paprika
1 (28-ounce / 794-g) can no-salt-added diced tomatoes
2 or 3 zucchini, cut into 1½-inch-thick rounds
4 ounces (113 g) mushrooms
1 large red onion, chopped
1 green bell pepper, seeded and chopped

1. In large bowl, mix together the ground beef, white or yellow onion, garlic, parsley, coriander, cumin, salt, pepper, nutmeg, mint, and paprika until well combined and all of the spices and onion are well blended into the meat. Form the meat mixture into 10 to 12 oval patties. Set aside. 2. In a slow cooker, combine the tomatoes, zucchini, mushrooms, red onion, and bell pepper. Stir to mix well. 3. Place the kofta patties on top of the tomato mixture. 4. Cover the cooker and cook for 6 to 8 hours on Low heat.

Per Serving

Calories: 263 | fat: 9g | protein: 27g | carbs: 23g | fiber: 7g | sodium: 480mg

One-Pot Pork Loin Dinner

Prep time: 35 minutes | Cook time: 28 minutes | Serves 6

1 tablespoon olive oil
1 small onion, peeled and diced
1 pound (454 g) boneless pork loin, cut into 1" pieces
½ teaspoon salt
¼ teaspoon ground black pepper
½ cup white wine
1 cup low-sodium chicken broth
1 large rutabaga, peeled and diced
1 large turnip, peeled and
diced
4 small Yukon Gold or red potatoes, quartered
4 medium carrots, peeled and diced
1 stalk celery, finely diced
½ cup sliced leeks, white part only
½ teaspoon mild curry powder
¼ teaspoon dried thyme
2 teaspoons dried parsley
3 tablespoons lemon juice
2 large Granny Smith apples, peeled, cored, and diced

1. Press the Sauté button on the Instant Pot® and heat oil. Add onion and cook until tender, about 3 minutes. Add pork and season with salt and pepper. Cook until pork begins to brown, about 5 minutes. Add wine, broth, rutabaga, and turnip and stir well. Add potatoes, carrots, celery, leeks, curry powder, thyme, parsley, and lemon juice to the pot. Stir to combine. Press the Cancel button. 2. Close lid, set steam release to Sealing, press the Manual button, and set time to 15 minutes. When the timer beeps, let pressure release naturally, about 25 minutes. Press the Cancel button. 3. Open lid and add diced apples. Press the Sauté button and simmer for 5 minutes or until apples are tender. Serve immediately in large bowls.

Per Serving

Calories: 271 | fat: 4g | protein: 14g | carbs: 30g | fiber: 5g | sodium: 316mg

Flank Steak and Blue Cheese Wraps

Prep time: 20 minutes | Cook time: 0 minutes | Serves 6

1 cup leftover flank steak, cut into 1-inch slices
¼ cup red onion, thinly sliced
¼ cup cherry tomatoes, chopped
¼ cup low-salt olives, pitted and chopped
¼ cup roasted red bell peppers, drained and coarsely chopped
¼ cup blue cheese crumbles
6 whole-wheat or spinach wraps
Sea salt and freshly ground pepper, to taste

1. Combine the flank steak, onion, tomatoes, olives, bell pepper, and blue cheese in a small bowl. 2. Spread ½ cup of this mixture on each wrap, and roll halfway. Fold the end in, and finish rolling like a burrito. 3. Cut on a diagonal if you'd like, season to taste, and serve.

Per Serving

Calories: 158 | fat: 8g | protein: 20g | carbs: 2g | fiber: 1g | sodium: 150mg

Garlic Balsamic London Broil

Prep time: 30 minutes | Cook time: 8 to 10 minutes | Serves 8

2 pounds (907 g) London broil
3 large garlic cloves, minced
3 tablespoons balsamic vinegar
3 tablespoons whole-grain mustard

2 tablespoons olive oil
Sea salt and ground black pepper, to taste
½ teaspoon dried hot red pepper flakes

1. Score both sides of the cleaned London broil. 2. Thoroughly combine the remaining ingredients; massage this mixture into the meat to coat it on all sides. Let it marinate for at least 3 hours. 3. Set the air fryer to 400°F (204°C); Then cook the London broil for 15 minutes. Flip it over and cook another 10 to 12 minutes. Bon appétit!

Per Serving

Calories: 240 | fat: 15g | protein: 23g | carbs: 2g | fiber: 0g | sodium: 141mg

One-Pan Greek Pork and Vegetables

Prep time: 10 minutes | Cook time: 40 minutes | Serves 3

1 pound (454 g) pork shoulder, cut into 1-inch cubes
¾ teaspoon fine sea salt, divided
½ teaspoon freshly ground black pepper, divided, plus more for serving
4 tablespoons extra virgin olive oil, divided

1 medium red onion, sliced
1 medium green bell pepper, seeded and sliced
1 medium carrot, peeled and julienned
¼ cup dry red wine
15 cherry tomatoes, halved
2 tablespoons hot water
½ teaspoon dried oregano

1. Scatter the cubed pork onto a cutting board and sprinkle with ¼ teaspoon of sea salt and ¼ teaspoon of black pepper. Flip the pieces over and sprinkle an additional ¼ teaspoon of sea salt and the remaining ¼ teaspoon of black pepper. 2. In a large pan wide enough to hold all the pork in a single layer, heat 3 tablespoons of olive oil over high heat. Once the oil is hot, add the pork pieces and brown for 2 minutes, then flip the pork pieces and brown for 2 more minutes. (Do not stir.) 3. Add the onions and sauté for 2 minutes and then add the bell peppers and carrots and sauté for 2 more minutes, ensuring all vegetables are coated with the oil. Reduce the heat to medium, cover the pan loosely, and cook for 5 minutes, stirring occasionally. 4. Add the wine and continue cooking for about 4 minutes, using a wooden spatula to scrape any browned bits from the bottom of the pan. Add about 20 cherry tomato halves and stir gently, then drizzle with the remaining 1 tablespoon of olive oil and add the hot water. Reduce the heat to low and simmer for 15–20 minutes or until all the liquids are absorbed. Remove the pan from the heat. 5. Sprinkle the oregano over the top. Top with the remaining cherry tomato halves and season to taste with the remaining ¼ teaspoon of sea salt and additional black pepper before serving. Store covered in the refrigerator for up to 3 days.

Per Serving

Calories: 407 | fat: 27g | protein: 30g | carbs: 8g | fiber: 2g | sodium: 700mg

Spaghetti Zoodles and Meatballs

Prep time: 30 minutes | Cook time: 11 to 13 minutes | Serves 6

1 pound (454 g) ground beef
1½ teaspoons sea salt, plus more for seasoning
1 large egg, beaten
1 teaspoon gelatin
¾ cup Parmesan cheese
2 teaspoons minced garlic
1 teaspoon Italian seasoning

Freshly ground black pepper, to taste
Avocado oil spray
Keto-friendly marinara sauce, for serving
6 ounces (170 g) zucchini noodles, made using a spiralizer or store-bought

1. Place the ground beef in a large bowl, and season with the salt. 2. Place the egg in a separate bowl and sprinkle with the gelatin. Allow to sit for 5 minutes. 3. Stir the gelatin mixture, then pour it over the ground beef. Add the Parmesan, garlic, and Italian seasoning. Season with salt and pepper. 4. Form the mixture into 1½-inch meatballs and place them on a plate; cover with plastic wrap and refrigerate for at least 1 hour or overnight. 5. Spray the meatballs with oil. Set the air fryer to 400°F (204°C) and arrange the meatballs in a single layer in the air fryer basket. Air fry for 4 minutes. Flip the meatballs and spray them with more oil. Air fry for 4 minutes more, until an instant-read thermometer reads 160°F (71°C). Transfer the meatballs to a plate and allow them to rest. 6. While the meatballs are resting, heat the marinara in a saucepan on the stove over medium heat. 7. Place the zucchini noodles in the air fryer, and cook at 400°F (204°C) for 3 to 5 minutes. 8. To serve, place the zucchini noodles in serving bowls. Top with meatballs and warm marinara.

Per Serving

Calories: 176 | fat: 8g | protein: 23g | carbs: 2g | fiber: 0g | sodium: 689mg

Moroccan Lamb Roast

Prep time: 15 minutes | Cook time: 6 to 8 hours | Serves 6

¼ cup low-sodium beef broth or low-sodium chicken broth
1 teaspoon dried ginger
1 teaspoon dried cumin
1 teaspoon ground turmeric
1 teaspoon paprika
1 teaspoon garlic powder
1 teaspoon red pepper flakes
½ teaspoon ground cinnamon
½ teaspoon ground coriander
½ teaspoon ground nutmeg

½ teaspoon ground cloves
½ teaspoon sea salt
½ teaspoon freshly ground black pepper
1 (3-pound / 1.4-kg) lamb roast
4 ounces (113 g) carrots, chopped
¼ cup sliced onion
¼ cup chopped fresh mint

1. Pour the broth into a slow cooker. 2. In a small bowl, stir together the ginger, cumin, turmeric, paprika, garlic powder, red pepper flakes, cinnamon, coriander, nutmeg, cloves, salt, and black pepper. Rub the spice mix firmly all over the lamb roast. Put the lamb in the slow cooker and add the carrots and onion. 3. Top everything with the mint. 4. Cover the cooker and cook for 6 to 8 hours on Low heat.

Per Serving

Calories: 601 | fat: 39g | protein: 56g | carbs: 4g | fiber: 1g | sodium: 398mg

Parmesan Herb Filet Mignon

Prep time: 20 minutes | Cook time: 13 minutes | Serves 4

1 pound (454 g) filet mignon
Sea salt and ground black pepper, to taste
½ teaspoon cayenne pepper
1 teaspoon dried basil
1 teaspoon dried rosemary
1 teaspoon dried thyme
1 tablespoon sesame oil
1 small-sized egg, well-whisked
½ cup Parmesan cheese, grated

1. Season the filet mignon with salt, black pepper, cayenne pepper, basil, rosemary, and thyme. Brush with sesame oil. 2. Put the egg in a shallow plate. Now, place the Parmesan cheese in another plate. 3. Coat the filet mignon with the egg; then lay it into the Parmesan cheese. Set the air fryer to 360°F (182°C). 4. Cook for 10 to 13 minutes or until golden. Serve with mixed salad leaves and enjoy!

Per Serving

Calories: 252 | fat: 13g | protein: 32g | carbs: 1g | fiber: 0g | sodium: 96mg

Pork Tenderloin with Vegetable Ragu

Prep time: 25 minutes | Cook time: 18 minutes | Serves 6

2 tablespoons light olive oil, divided
1 (1½-pound / 680-g) pork tenderloin
¼ teaspoon salt
¼ teaspoon ground black pepper
1 medium zucchini, trimmed and sliced
1 medium yellow squash, sliced
1 medium onion, peeled and chopped
1 medium carrot, peeled and grated
1 (14½-ounce / 411-g) can diced tomatoes, drained
2 cloves garlic, peeled and minced
¼ teaspoon crushed red pepper flakes
1 tablespoon chopped fresh basil
1 tablespoon chopped fresh oregano
1 sprig fresh thyme
½ cup red wine

1. Press the Sauté button on the Instant Pot® and heat 1 tablespoon oil. Season pork with salt and black pepper. Brown pork lightly on all sides, about 2 minutes per side. Transfer pork to a plate and set aside. 2. Add remaining 1 tablespoon oil to the pot. Add zucchini and squash, and cook until tender, about 5 minutes. Add onion and carrot, and cook until just softened, about 5 minutes. Add tomatoes, garlic, crushed red pepper flakes, basil, oregano, thyme, and red wine to pot, and stir well. Press the Cancel button. 3. Top vegetable mixture with browned pork. Close lid, set steam release to Sealing, press the Manual button, and set time to 3 minutes. When the timer beeps, quick-release the pressure until the float valve drops and open lid. Transfer pork to a cutting board and cut into 1" slices. Pour sauce on a serving platter and arrange pork slices on top. Serve immediately.

Per Serving

Calories: 190 | fat: 7g | protein: 23g | carbs: 9g | fiber: 2g | sodium: 606mg

Spaghetti with Meaty Mushroom Sauce

Prep time: 15 minutes | Cook time: 23 minutes | Serves 6

1 tablespoon olive oil
1 medium onion, peeled and diced
1 pound (454 g) sliced crimini mushrooms
½ pound (227 g) 90% lean ground beef
1 (14½-ounce / 411-g) can fire-roasted tomatoes, drained
1 clove garlic, peeled and minced
½ teaspoon ground fennel
2 sprigs thyme
2 sprigs oregano
1 pound (454 g) spaghetti, broken in half
1 (25-ounce / 709-g) jar marinara sauce
2 cups low-sodium chicken broth
1 cup grated Parmesan cheese

1. Press the Sauté button on the Instant Pot® and heat oil. Add onion and mushrooms, and cook until vegetables are tender, about 10 minutes. Add beef and cook, crumbling well, until no longer pink, about 5 minutes. Add tomatoes, garlic, fennel, thyme, and oregano. Stir well, then press the Cancel button. 2. Add spaghetti, sauce, and broth, and stir well. Close lid, set steam release to Sealing, press the Manual button, and set time to 8 minutes. 3. When the timer beeps, quick-release the pressure until the float valve drops, open lid, and stir well. Top with cheese and serve hot.

Per Serving

Calories: 188 | fat: 7g | protein: 23g | carbs: 8g | fiber: 2g | sodium: 595mg

Beef and Wild Mushroom Stew

Prep time: 15 minutes | Cook time: 1 hour 15 minutes | Serves 8

2 pounds (907 g) fresh porcini or morel mushrooms
⅓ cup olive oil
2 pounds (907 g) lean, boneless beef, cut into 2-inch cubes
2 medium onions, finely chopped
1 clove garlic, minced
1 cup dry white wine
1 teaspoon thyme, minced
Sea salt and freshly ground pepper, to taste

1. Wash the mushrooms carefully by soaking them in cold water and swirling them around. 2. Trim away any soft parts of the mushrooms. 3. Heat the olive oil in a heavy stew pot over medium-high heat. Brown the meat evenly on all sides, and set aside on a plate. 4. Add the onions, garlic, and mushrooms to the olive oil, and cook for 5–8 minutes, or until the onions are tender, stirring frequently. 5. Add the remaining ingredients and return the browned meat to the pot. Cover and bring to a boil, then reduce heat to low and simmer. Simmer for 1 hour, or until the meat is tender and flavorful. 6. Season with sea salt and freshly ground pepper to taste.

Per Serving

Calories: 343 | fat: 22g | protein: 26g | carbs: 9g | fiber: 2g | sodium: 93mg

Mediterranean Pork with Olives

Prep time: 10 minutes | Cook time: 6 to 8 hours | Serves 4

1 small onion, sliced
4 thick-cut, bone-in pork chops
1 cup low-sodium chicken broth
Juice of 1 lemon
2 garlic cloves, minced
1 teaspoon sea salt

1 teaspoon dried oregano
1 teaspoon dried parsley
½ teaspoon freshly ground black pepper
2 cups whole green olives, pitted
1 pint cherry tomatoes

1. Put the onion in a slow cooker and arrange the pork chops on top. 2. In a small bowl, whisk together the chicken broth, lemon juice, garlic, salt, oregano, parsley, and pepper. Pour the sauce over the pork chops. Top with the olives and tomatoes. 3. Cover the cooker and cook for 6 to 8 hours on Low heat.

Per Serving

Calories: 339 | fat: 14g | protein: 42g | carbs: 6g | fiber: 4g | sodium: 708mg

Mediterranean Beef Steaks

Prep time: 20 minutes | Cook time: 20 minutes | Serves 4

2 tablespoons coconut aminos
3 heaping tablespoons fresh chives
2 tablespoons olive oil
3 tablespoons dry white wine
4 small-sized beef steaks
2 teaspoons smoked cayenne

pepper
½ teaspoon dried basil
½ teaspoon dried rosemary
1 teaspoon freshly ground black pepper
1 teaspoon sea salt, or more to taste

1. Firstly, coat the steaks with the cayenne pepper, black pepper, salt, basil, and rosemary. 2. Drizzle the steaks with olive oil, white wine, and coconut aminos. 3. Finally, roast in the air fryer for 20 minutes at 340°F (171°C). Serve garnished with fresh chives. Bon appétit!

Per Serving

Calories: 320 | fat: 17g | protein: 37g | carbs: 5g | fiber: 1g | sodium: 401mg

Balsamic Beef and Vegetable Stew

Prep time: 30 minutes | Cook time: 54 minutes | Serves 8

1 pound (454 g) beef stew meat, cut into 1" pieces
2 tablespoons all-purpose flour
¼ teaspoon salt
¼ teaspoon ground black pepper
2 tablespoons olive oil, divided
2 medium carrots, peeled and sliced
2 stalks celery, sliced
1 medium onion, peeled and chopped
8 ounces (227 g) whole crimini

mushrooms, quartered
3 cloves garlic, peeled and minced
4 sprigs thyme
2 tablespoons chopped fresh oregano
2 bay leaves
¼ cup balsamic vinegar
1½ cups beef broth
1 (14½-ounce / 411-g) can diced tomatoes, drained
1 medium russet potato, cut into 1" pieces

1 (6-ounce / 170-g) can large black olives, drained and

quartered
¼ cup chopped fresh parsley

1. In a medium bowl, add beef, flour, salt, and pepper. Toss meat with seasoned flour until thoroughly coated. Set aside. 2. Press the Sauté button on the Instant Pot® and heat 1 tablespoon oil. Place half of the beef pieces in a single layer, leaving space between each piece to prevent steaming, and brown well on all sides, about 3 minutes per side. Transfer beef to a medium bowl and repeat with remaining 1 tablespoon oil and beef. 3. Add carrots, celery, and onion to the pot. Cook until tender, about 8 minutes. Add mushrooms, garlic, thyme, oregano, and bay leaves. Stir well. 4. Slowly add balsamic vinegar and beef broth, scraping bottom of pot well to release any brown bits. Add tomatoes, potato, and browned beef along with any juices. Press the Cancel button. 5. Close lid, set steam release to Sealing, press the Stew button, and set time to 40 minutes. When the timer beeps, quick-release the pressure until the float valve drops, open lid, and stir well. Remove and discard thyme and bay leaves. Stir in olives and parsley. Serve immediately.

Per Serving

Calories: 332| fat: 17g | protein: 16g | carbs: 15g | fiber: 5g | sodium: 404mg

Cheesy Low-Carb Lasagna

Prep time: 10 minutes | Cook time: 10 minutes | Serves 4

Meat Layer:
Extra-virgin olive oil
1 pound (454 g) 85% lean ground beef
1 cup prepared marinara sauce
¼ cup diced celery
¼ cup diced red onion
½ teaspoon minced garlic
Kosher salt and black pepper, to taste
Cheese Layer:

8 ounces (227 g) ricotta cheese
1 cup shredded Mozzarella cheese
½ cup grated Parmesan cheese
2 large eggs
1 teaspoon dried Italian seasoning, crushed
½ teaspoon each minced garlic, garlic powder, and black pepper

1. For the meat layer: Grease a cake pan with 1 teaspoon olive oil. 2. In a large bowl, combine the ground beef, marinara, celery, onion, garlic, salt, and pepper. Place the seasoned meat in the pan. 3. Place the pan in the air fryer basket. Set the air fryer to 375°F (191°C) for 10 minutes. 4. Meanwhile, for the cheese layer: In a medium bowl, combine the ricotta, half the Mozzarella, the Parmesan, lightly beaten eggs, Italian seasoning, minced garlic, garlic powder, and pepper. Stir until well blended. 5. At the end of the cooking time, spread the cheese mixture over the meat mixture. Sprinkle with the remaining ½ cup Mozzarella. Set the air fryer to 375°F (191°C) for 10 minutes, or until the cheese is browned and bubbling. 6. At the end of the cooking time, use a meat thermometer to ensure the meat has reached an internal temperature of 160°F (71°C). 7. Drain the fat and liquid from the pan. Let stand for 5 minutes before serving.

Per Serving

Calories: 555 | fat: 36g | protein: 45g | carbs: 10g | fiber: 2g | sodium: 248mg

Beef Meatballs in Garlic Cream Sauce

Prep time: 15 minutes | Cook time: 6 to 8 hours | Serves 4

For the Sauce:
1 cup low-sodium vegetable broth or low-sodium chicken broth
1 tablespoon extra-virgin olive oil
2 garlic cloves, minced
1 tablespoon dried onion flakes
1 teaspoon dried rosemary
2 tablespoons freshly squeezed lemon juice
Pinch sea salt
Pinch freshly ground black pepper

For the Meatballs:
1 pound (454 g) raw ground beef
1 large egg
2 tablespoons bread crumbs
1 teaspoon ground cumin
1 teaspoon salt
½ teaspoon freshly ground black pepper
To Finish:
2 cups plain Greek yogurt
2 tablespoons chopped fresh parsley

Make the Sauce: In a medium bowl, whisk together the vegetable broth, olive oil, garlic, onion flakes, rosemary, lemon juice, salt, and pepper until combined. Make the Meatballs: In a large bowl, mix together the ground beef, egg, bread crumbs, cumin, salt, and pepper until combined. Shape the meat mixture into 10 to 12 (2½-inch) meatballs. 1. Pour the sauce into the slow cooker. 2. Add the meatballs to the slow cooker. 3. Cover the cooker and cook for 6 to 8 hours on Low heat. 4. Stir in the yogurt. Replace the cover on the cooker and cook for 15 to 30 minutes on Low heat, or until the sauce has thickened. 5. Garnish with fresh parsley for serving.
Per Serving
Calories: 345 | fat: 20g | protein: 29g | carbs: 13g | fiber: 1g | sodium: 842mg

Herbed Lamb Meatballs

Prep time: 10 minutes | Cook time: 6 to 8 hours | Serves 4

1 (28-ounce / 794-g) can no-salt-added diced tomatoes
2 garlic cloves, minced, divided
1 pound (454 g) raw ground lamb
1 small onion, finely diced, or
1 tablespoon dried onion flakes
1 large egg

2 tablespoons bread crumbs
1 teaspoon dried basil
1 teaspoon dried oregano
1 teaspoon dried rosemary
1 teaspoon dried thyme
1 teaspoon sea salt
½ teaspoon freshly ground black pepper

1. In a slow cooker, combine the tomatoes and 1 clove of garlic. Stir to mix well. 2. In a large bowl, mix together the ground lamb, onion, egg, bread crumbs, basil, oregano, rosemary, thyme, salt, pepper, and the remaining 1 garlic clove until all of the ingredients are well-blended. Shape the meat mixture into 10 to 12 (2½-inch) meatballs. Put the meatballs in the slow cooker. 3. Cover the cooker and cook for 6 to 8 hours on Low heat.
Per Serving
Calories: 406 | fat: 28g | protein: 23g | carbs: 16g | fiber: 5g | sodium: 815mg

Balsamic Pork Chops with Figs and Pears

Prep time: 15 minutes | Cook time: 13 minutes | Serves 2

2 (8-ounce / 227-g) bone-in pork chops
½ teaspoon salt
1 teaspoon ground black pepper
¼ cup balsamic vinegar
¼ cup low-sodium chicken broth

1 tablespoon dried mint
2 tablespoons olive oil
1 medium sweet onion, peeled and sliced
3 medium pears, peeled, cored, and chopped
5 dried figs, stems removed and halved

1. Pat pork chops dry with a paper towel and season both sides with salt and pepper. Set aside. 2. In a small bowl, whisk together vinegar, broth, and mint. Set aside. 3. Press the Sauté button on the Instant Pot® and heat oil. Brown pork chops for 5 minutes per side. Remove chops and set aside. 4. Add vinegar mixture and scrape any brown bits from sides and bottom of pot. Layer onion slices in the pot, then scatter pears and figs over slices. Place pork chops on top. Press the Cancel button. 5. Close lid, set steam release to Sealing, press the Steam button, and set time to 3 minutes. When the timer beeps, let pressure release naturally for 10 minutes. Quick-release any remaining pressure until the float valve drops and then open lid. 6. Using a slotted spoon, transfer pork, onion, figs, and pears to a serving platter. Serve warm.
Per Serving
Calories: 672 | fat: 32g | protein: 27g | carbs: 68g | fiber: 13g | sodium: 773mg

Pork and Cannellini Bean Stew

Prep time: 15 minutes | Cook time: 1 hour | Serves 6

1 cup dried cannellini beans
¼ cup olive oil
1 medium onion, diced
2 pounds (907 g) pork roast, cut into 1-inch chunks
3 cups water
1 (8-ounce / 227-g) can tomato

paste
¼ cup flat-leaf parsley, chopped
½ teaspoon dried thyme
Sea salt and freshly ground pepper, to taste

1. Rinse and sort the beans. 2. Cover beans with water, and allow to soak overnight. Heat the olive oil in a large stew pot. 3. Add the onion, stirring occasionally, until golden brown. 4. Add the pork chunks and cook 5–8 minutes, stirring frequently, until the pork is browned. Drain and rinse the beans, and add to the pot. 5. Add the water, and bring to a boil. Reduce heat and simmer for 45 minutes, until beans are tender. 6. Add the tomato paste, parsley, and thyme, and simmer an additional 15 minutes, or until the sauce thickens slightly. Season to taste.
Per Serving
Calories: 373 | fat: 16g | protein: 39g | carbs: 19g | fiber: 4g | sodium: 107mg

Herb-Roasted Beef Tips with Onions

Prep time: 5 minutes | Cook time: 10 minutes | Serves 4

1 pound (454 g) rib eye steak, cubed
2 garlic cloves, minced
2 tablespoons olive oil
1 tablespoon fresh oregano

1 teaspoon salt
½ teaspoon black pepper
1 yellow onion, thinly sliced

1. Preheat the air fryer to 380ºF (193ºC). 2. In a medium bowl, combine the steak, garlic, olive oil, oregano, salt, pepper, and onion. Mix until all of the beef and onion are well coated. 3. Put the seasoned steak mixture into the air fryer basket. Roast for 5 minutes. Stir and roast for 5 minutes more. 4. Let rest for 5 minutes before serving with some favorite sides.

Per Serving

Calories: 380 | fat: 28g | protein: 28g | carbs: 3g | fiber: 0g | sodium: 646mg

Zesty Grilled Flank Steak

Prep time: 10 minutes | Cook time: 18 minutes | Serves 6

¼ cup olive oil
3 tablespoons red wine vinegar
1 teaspoon dried rosemary
1 teaspoon dried marjoram
1 teaspoon dried oregano

1 teaspoon paprika
2 cloves garlic, minced
1 teaspoon freshly ground pepper
2 pounds (907 g) flank steak

1. Combine the olive oil, vinegar, herbs, and seasonings in a small bowl. Place the flank steak in a shallow dish, and rub the marinade into the meat. Cover and refrigerate for up to 24 hours. 2. Heat a charcoal or gas grill to medium heat (375ºF / 190ºC). 3. Grill the steak for 18–21 minutes, turning once halfway through the cooking time. 4. An internal meat thermometer should read 140ºF (60ºC) when the meat is done. 5. Transfer the meat to a cutting board, and cover with aluminum foil. Let steak rest for at least 10 minutes. Slice against the grain very thinly and serve.

Per Serving

Calories: 292 | fat: 17g | protein: 33g | carbs: 1g | fiber: 0g | sodium: 81mg

Beef and Mushroom Stroganoff

Prep time: 15 minutes | Cook time: 31 minutes | Serves 6

2 tablespoons olive oil
1 medium onion, peeled and chopped
2 cloves garlic, peeled and minced
1 pound (454 g) beef stew meat, cut into 1" pieces
3 tablespoons all-purpose flour
¼ teaspoon salt

¼ teaspoon ground black pepper
2 cups beef broth
1 pound (454 g) sliced button mushrooms
1 pound (454 g) wide egg noodles
½ cup low-fat plain Greek yogurt

1. Press the Sauté button on the Instant Pot® and heat oil. Add onion and cook until soft, about 5 minutes. Add garlic and cook until fragrant, about 30 seconds. 2. Combine beef, flour, salt, and pepper in a medium bowl and toss to coat beef completely. Add beef to the pot and cook, stirring often, until browned, about 10 minutes. Stir in beef broth and scrape any brown bits from bottom of pot. Stir in mushrooms and press the Cancel button. 3. Close lid, set steam release to Sealing, press the Manual button, and set time to 10 minutes. When the timer beeps, quick-release the pressure until the float valve drops, open lid, and stir well. Press the Cancel button. 4. Add noodles and stir, making sure noodles are submerged in liquid. Close lid, set steam release to Sealing, press the Manual button, and set time to 5 minutes. 5. When the timer beeps, quick-release the pressure until the float valve drops. Open lid and stir well. Press the Cancel button and cool for 5 minutes, then stir in yogurt. Serve hot.

Per Serving

Calories: 446 | fat: 13g | protein: 19g | carbs: 63g | fiber: 4g | sodium: 721mg

Chapter 5 Breakfasts

Lemon–Olive Oil Breakfast Cakes with Berry Syrup

Prep time: 5 minutes | Cook time: 10 minutes | Serves 4

For the Pancakes:
1 cup almond flour
1 teaspoon baking powder
¼ teaspoon salt
6 tablespoon extra-virgin olive oil, divided
2 large eggs
Zest and juice of 1 lemon
½ teaspoon almond or vanilla extract
For the Berry Sauce:
1 cup frozen mixed berries
1 tablespoon water or lemon juice, plus more if needed
½ teaspoon vanilla extract

Make the Pancakes: 1. In a large bowl, combine the almond flour, baking powder, and salt and whisk to break up any clumps. 2. Add the 4 tablespoons olive oil, eggs, lemon zest and juice, and almond extract and whisk to combine well. 3. In a large skillet, heat 1 tablespoon of olive oil and spoon about 2 tablespoons of batter for each of 4 pancakes. Cook until bubbles begin to form, 4 to 5 minutes, and flip. Cook another 2 to 3 minutes on second side. Repeat with remaining 1 tablespoon olive oil and batter. Make the Berry Sauce: 1. In a small saucepan, heat the frozen berries, water, and vanilla extract over medium-high for 3 to 4 minutes, until bubbly, adding more water if mixture is too thick. Using the back of a spoon or fork, mash the berries and whisk until smooth.
Per Serving
Calories: 381 | fat: 35g | protein: 8g | carbs: 12g | fiber: 4g | sodium: 183mg

Mexican Breakfast Pepper Rings

Prep time: 5 minutes | Cook time: 10 minutes | Serves 4

Olive oil
1 large red, yellow, or orange bell pepper, cut into four ¾-inch rings
4 eggs
Salt and freshly ground black pepper, to taste
2 teaspoons salsa

1. Preheat the air fryer to 350°F (177°C). Lightly spray a baking pan with olive oil. 2. Place 2 bell pepper rings on the pan. Crack one egg into each bell pepper ring. Season with salt and black pepper. 3. Spoon ½ teaspoon of salsa on top of each egg. 4. Place the pan in the air fryer basket. Air fry until the yolk is slightly runny, 5 to 6 minutes or until the yolk is fully cooked, 8 to 10 minutes. 5. Repeat with the remaining 2 pepper rings. Serve hot.
Per Serving
Calories: 76 | fat: 4g | protein: 6g | carbs: 3g | fiber: 1g | sodium: 83mg

Butternut Squash and Ricotta Frittata

Prep time: 10 minutes | Cook time: 33 minutes | Serves 2 to 3

1 cup cubed (½-inch) butternut squash (5½ ounces / 156 g)
2 tablespoons olive oil
Kosher salt and freshly ground black pepper, to taste
4 fresh sage leaves, thinly sliced
6 large eggs, lightly beaten
½ cup ricotta cheese
Cayenne pepper

1. In a bowl, toss the squash with the olive oil and season with salt and black pepper until evenly coated. Sprinkle the sage on the bottom of a cake pan and place the squash on top. Place the pan in the air fryer and bake at 400°F (204°C) for 10 minutes. Stir to incorporate the sage, then cook until the squash is tender and lightly caramelized at the edges, about 3 minutes more. 2. Pour the eggs over the squash, dollop the ricotta all over, and sprinkle with cayenne. Bake at 300°F (149°C) until the eggs are set and the frittata is golden brown on top, about 20 minutes. Remove the pan from the air fryer and cut the frittata into wedges to serve.
Per Serving
Calories: 289 | fat: 22g | protein: 18g | carbs: 5g | fiber: 1g | sodium: 184mg

Gluten-Free Granola Cereal

Prep time: 7 minutes | Cook time: 30 minutes | Makes 3½ cups

Oil, for spraying
1½ cups gluten-free rolled oats
½ cup chopped walnuts
½ cup chopped almonds
½ cup pumpkin seeds
¼ cup maple syrup or honey
1 tablespoon toasted sesame oil or vegetable oil
1 teaspoon ground cinnamon
½ teaspoon salt
½ cup dried cranberries

1. Preheat the air fryer to 250°F (121°C). Line the air fryer basket with parchment and spray lightly with oil. (Do not skip the step of lining the basket; the parchment will keep the granola from falling through the holes.) 2. In a large bowl, mix together the oats, walnuts, almonds, pumpkin seeds, maple syrup, sesame oil, cinnamon, and salt. 3. Spread the mixture in an even layer in the prepared basket. 4. Cook for 30 minutes, stirring every 10 minutes. 5. Transfer the granola to a bowl, add the dried cranberries, and toss to combine. 6. Let cool to room temperature before storing in an airtight container.
Per Serving
Calories: 322 | fat: 17g | protein: 11g | carbs: 35g | fiber: 6g | sodium: 170mg

Spinach and Mushroom Mini Quiche

Prep time: 10 minutes | Cook time: 15 minutes | Serves 4

1 teaspoon olive oil, plus more for spraying
1 cup coarsely chopped mushrooms
1 cup fresh baby spinach, shredded
4 eggs, beaten
½ cup shredded Cheddar cheese
½ cup shredded Mozzarella cheese
¼ teaspoon salt
¼ teaspoon black pepper

1. Spray 4 silicone baking cups with olive oil and set aside. 2. In a medium sauté pan over medium heat, warm 1 teaspoon of olive oil. Add the mushrooms and sauté until soft, 3 to 4 minutes. 3. Add the spinach and cook until wilted, 1 to 2 minutes. Set aside. 4. In a medium bowl, whisk together the eggs, Cheddar cheese, Mozzarella cheese, salt, and pepper. 5. Gently fold the mushrooms and spinach into the egg mixture. 6. Pour ¼ of the mixture into each silicone baking cup. 7. Place the baking cups into the air fryer basket and air fry at 350°F (177°C) for 5 minutes. Stir the mixture in each ramekin slightly and air fry until the egg has set, an additional 3 to 5 minutes.

Per Serving
Calories: 156 | fat: 10g | protein: 14g | carbs: 2g | fiber: 1g | sodium: 411mg

Cauliflower Avocado Toast

Prep time: 15 minutes | Cook time: 8 minutes | Serves 2

1 (12-ounce / 340-g) steamer bag cauliflower
1 large egg
½ cup shredded Mozzarella cheese
1 ripe medium avocado
½ teaspoon garlic powder
¼ teaspoon ground black pepper

1. Cook cauliflower according to package instructions. Remove from bag and place into cheesecloth or clean towel to remove excess moisture. 2. Place cauliflower into a large bowl and mix in egg and Mozzarella. Cut a piece of parchment to fit your air fryer basket. Separate the cauliflower mixture into two, and place it on the parchment in two mounds. Press out the cauliflower mounds into a ¼-inch-thick rectangle. Place the parchment into the air fryer basket. 3. Adjust the temperature to 400°F (204°C) and set the timer for 8 minutes. 4. Flip the cauliflower halfway through the cooking time. 5. When the timer beeps, remove the parchment and allow the cauliflower to cool 5 minutes. 6. Cut open the avocado and remove the pit. Scoop out the inside, place it in a medium bowl, and mash it with garlic powder and pepper. Spread onto the cauliflower. Serve immediately.

Per Serving
Calories: 321 | fat: 22g | protein: 16g | carbs: 19g | fiber: 10g | sodium: 99mg

South of the Coast Sweet Potato Toast

Prep time: 5 minutes | Cook time: 15 minutes | Serves 4

2 plum tomatoes, halved
6 tablespoons extra-virgin olive oil, divided
Salt
Freshly ground black pepper
2 large sweet potatoes, sliced lengthwise
1 cup fresh spinach
8 medium asparagus, trimmed
4 large cooked eggs or egg substitute (poached, scrambled, or fried)
1 cup arugula
4 tablespoons pesto
4 tablespoons shredded Asiago cheese

1. Preheat the oven to 450°F (235°C). 2. On a baking sheet, brush the plum tomato halves with 2 tablespoons of olive oil and season with salt and pepper. Roast the tomatoes in the oven for approximately 15 minutes, then remove from the oven and allow to rest. 3. Put the sweet potato slices on a separate baking sheet and brush about 2 tablespoons of oil on each side and season with salt and pepper. Bake the sweet potato slices for about 15 minutes, flipping once after 5 to 7 minutes, until just tender. Remove from the oven and set aside. 4. In a sauté pan or skillet, heat the remaining 2 tablespoons of olive oil over medium heat and sauté the fresh spinach until just wilted. Remove from the pan and rest on a paper-towel-lined dish. In the same pan, add the asparagus and sauté, turning throughout. Transfer to a paper towel-lined dish. 5. Place the slices of grilled sweet potato on serving plates and divide the spinach and asparagus evenly among the slices. Place a prepared egg on top of the spinach and asparagus. Top this with ¼ cup of arugula. 6. Finish by drizzling with 1 tablespoon of pesto and sprinkle with 1 tablespoon of cheese. Serve with 1 roasted plum tomato.

Per Serving
Calories: 441 | fat: 35g | protein: 13g | carbs: 23g | fiber: 4g | sodium: 481mg

Buffalo Egg Cups

Prep time: 10 minutes | Cook time: 15 minutes | Serves 2

4 large eggs
2 ounces (57 g) full-fat cream cheese
2 tablespoons buffalo sauce
½ cup shredded sharp Cheddar cheese

1. Crack eggs into two ramekins. 2. In a small microwave-safe bowl, mix cream cheese, buffalo sauce, and Cheddar. Microwave for 20 seconds and then stir. Place a spoonful into each ramekin on top of the eggs. 3. Place ramekins into the air fryer basket. 4. Adjust the temperature to 320°F (160°C) and bake for 15 minutes. 5. Serve warm.

Per Serving
Calories: 354 | fat: 29g | protein: 21g | carbs: 3g | fiber: 0g | sodium: 343mg

Mediterranean Fruit Bulgur Breakfast Bowl

Prep time: 5 minutes |Cook time: 15 minutes| Serves: 6

1½ cups uncooked bulgur
2 cups 2% milk
1 cup water
½ teaspoon ground cinnamon
2 cups frozen (or fresh, pitted) dark sweet cherries

8 dried (or fresh) figs, chopped
½ cup chopped almonds
¼ cup loosely packed fresh mint, chopped
Warm 2% milk, for serving (optional)

1. In a medium saucepan, combine the bulgur, milk, water, and cinnamon. Stir once, then bring just to a boil. Cover, reduce the heat to medium-low, and simmer for 10 minutes or until the liquid is absorbed. 2. Turn off the heat, but keep the pan on the stove, and stir in the frozen cherries (no need to thaw), figs, and almonds. Stir well, cover for 1 minute, and let the hot bulgur thaw the cherries and partially hydrate the figs. Stir in the mint. 3. Scoop into serving bowls. Serve with warm milk, if desired. You can also serve it chilled.

Per Serving

Calories: 273 | fat: 7g | protein: 10g | carbs: 48g | fiber: 8g | sodium: 46mg

Smoky Sausage Patties

Prep time: 30 minutes | Cook time: 9 minutes | Serves 8

1 pound (454 g) ground pork
1 tablespoon coconut aminos
2 teaspoons liquid smoke
1 teaspoon dried sage
1 teaspoon sea salt

½ teaspoon fennel seeds
½ teaspoon dried thyme
½ teaspoon freshly ground black pepper
¼ teaspoon cayenne pepper

1. In a large bowl, combine the pork, coconut aminos, liquid smoke, sage, salt, fennel seeds, thyme, black pepper, and cayenne pepper. Work the meat with your hands until the seasonings are fully incorporated. 2. Shape the mixture into 8 equal-size patties. Using your thumb, make a dent in the center of each patty. Place the patties on a plate and cover with plastic wrap. Refrigerate the patties for at least 30 minutes. 3. Working in batches if necessary, place the patties in a single layer in the air fryer, being careful not to overcrowd them. 4. Set the air fryer to 400ºF (204ºC) and air fry for 5 minutes. Flip and cook for about 4 minutes more.

Per Serving

Calories: 70 | fat: 2g | protein: 12g | carbs: 0g | fiber: 0g | sodium: 329mg

Broccoli-Mushroom Frittata

Prep time: 10 minutes | Cook time: 20 minutes | Serves 2

1 tablespoon olive oil
1½ cups broccoli florets, finely chopped
½ cup sliced brown mushrooms
¼ cup finely chopped onion

½ teaspoon salt
¼ teaspoon freshly ground black pepper
6 eggs
¼ cup Parmesan cheese

1. In a nonstick cake pan, combine the olive oil, broccoli, mushrooms, onion, salt, and pepper. Stir until the vegetables are thoroughly coated with oil. Place the cake pan in the air fryer basket and set the air fryer to 400ºF (204ºC). Air fry for 5 minutes until the vegetables soften. 2. Meanwhile, in a medium bowl, whisk the eggs and Parmesan until thoroughly combined. Pour the egg mixture into the pan and shake gently to distribute the vegetables. Air fry for another 15 minutes until the eggs are set. 3. Remove from the air fryer and let sit for 5 minutes to cool slightly. Use a silicone spatula to gently lift the frittata onto a plate before serving.

Per Serving

Calories: 329 | fat: 23g | protein: 24g | carbs: 6g | fiber: 0g | sodium: 793mg

Mashed Chickpea, Feta, and Avocado Toast

Prep time: 10 minutes |Cook time: 0 minutes| Serves: 4

1 (15-ounce / 425-g) can chickpeas, drained and rinsed
1 avocado, pitted
½ cup diced feta cheese (about 2 ounces / 57 g)
2 teaspoons freshly squeezed

lemon juice or 1 tablespoon orange juice
½ teaspoon freshly ground black pepper
4 pieces multigrain toast
2 teaspoons honey

1. Put the chickpeas in a large bowl. Scoop the avocado flesh into the bowl. 2. With a potato masher or large fork, mash the ingredients together until the mix has a spreadable consistency. It doesn't need to be totally smooth. 3. Add the feta, lemon juice, and pepper, and mix well. 4. Evenly divide the mash onto the four pieces of toast and spread with a knife. Drizzle with honey and serve.

Per Serving

Calories: 301 | fat: 14g | protein: 12g | carbs: 35g | fiber: 11g | sodium: 450mg

Homemade Pumpkin Parfait

Prep time: 5 minutes | Cook time: 0 minutes | Serves 4

1 (15-ounce / 425-g) can pure pumpkin purée
4 teaspoons honey, additional to taste
1 teaspoon pumpkin pie spice

¼ teaspoon ground cinnamon
2 cups plain, unsweetened, full-fat Greek yogurt
1 cup honey granola

1. In a large bowl, mix the pumpkin purée, honey, pumpkin pie spice, and cinnamon. Cover and refrigerate for at least 2 hours. 2. To make the parfaits, in each cup, pour ¼ cup pumpkin mix, ¼ cup yogurt and ¼ cup granola. Repeat Greek yogurt and pumpkin layers and top with honey granola.

Per Serving

Calories: 264 | fat: 9g | protein: 15g | carbs: 35g | fiber: 6g | sodium: 90mg

Greek Egg and Tomato Scramble

Prep time: 10 minutes | Cook time: 25 minutes | Serves 4

¼ cup extra-virgin olive oil, divided
1½ cups chopped fresh tomatoes
¼ cup finely minced red onion
2 garlic cloves, minced
½ teaspoon dried oregano or 1 to 2 teaspoons chopped fresh oregano
½ teaspoon dried thyme or 1
to 2 teaspoons chopped fresh thyme
8 large eggs
½ teaspoon salt
¼ teaspoon freshly ground black pepper
¾ cup crumbled feta cheese
¼ cup chopped fresh mint leaves

1. In large skillet, heat the olive oil over medium heat. Add the chopped tomatoes and red onion and sauté until tomatoes are cooked through and soft, 10 to 12 minutes. 2. Add the garlic, oregano, and thyme and sauté another 2 to 4 minutes, until fragrant and liquid has reduced. 3. In a medium bowl, whisk together the eggs, salt, and pepper until well combined. 4. Add the eggs to the skillet, reduce the heat to low, and scramble until set and creamy, using a spatula to move them constantly, 3 to 4 minutes. Remove the skillet from the heat, stir in the feta and mint, and serve warm.

Per Serving

Calories: 355 | fat: 29g | protein: 17g | carbs: 6g | fiber: 1g | sodium: 695mg

Quickie Honey Nut Granola

Prep time: 10 minutes |Cook time: 20 minutes| Serves: 6

2½ cups regular rolled oats
⅓ cup coarsely chopped almonds
⅛ teaspoon kosher or sea salt
½ teaspoon ground cinnamon
½ cup chopped dried apricots
2 tablespoons ground flaxseed
¼ cup honey
¼ cup extra-virgin olive oil
2 teaspoons vanilla extract

1. Preheat the oven to 325°F (165°C). Line a large, rimmed baking sheet with parchment paper. 2. In a large skillet, combine the oats, almonds, salt, and cinnamon. Turn the heat to medium-high and cook, stirring often, to toast, about 6 minutes. 3. While the oat mixture is toasting, in a microwave-safe bowl, combine the apricots, flaxseed, honey, and oil. Microwave on high for about 1 minute, or until very hot and just beginning to bubble. (Or heat these ingredients in a small saucepan over medium heat for about 3 minutes.) 4. Stir the vanilla into the honey mixture, then pour it over the oat mixture in the skillet. Stir well. 5. Spread out the granola on the prepared baking sheet. Bake for 15 minutes, until lightly browned. Remove from the oven and cool completely. 6. Break the granola into small pieces, and store in an airtight container in the refrigerator for up to 2 weeks (if it lasts that long!).

Per Serving

Calories: 449 | fat: 17g | protein: 13g | carbs: 64g | fiber: 9g | sodium: 56mg

Red Pepper and Feta Frittata

Prep time: 10 minutes | Cook time: 20 minutes | Serves 4

Olive oil cooking spray
8 large eggs
1 medium red bell pepper, diced
½ teaspoon salt
½ teaspoon black pepper
1 garlic clove, minced
½ cup feta, divided

1. Preheat the air fryer to 360°F (182°C). Lightly coat the inside of a 6-inch round cake pan with olive oil cooking spray. 2. In a large bowl, beat the eggs for 1 to 2 minutes, or until well combined. 3. Add the bell pepper, salt, black pepper, and garlic to the eggs, and mix together until the bell pepper is distributed throughout. 4. Fold in ¼ cup of the feta cheese. 5. Pour the egg mixture into the prepared cake pan, and sprinkle the remaining ¼ cup of feta over the top. 6. Place into the air fryer and bake for 18 to 20 minutes, or until the eggs are set in the center. 7. Remove from the air fryer and allow to cool for 5 minutes before serving.

Per Serving

Calories: 204 | fat: 14g | protein: 16g | carbs: 4g | fiber: 1g | sodium: 606mg

Marinara Eggs with Parsley

Prep time: 5 minutes |Cook time: 15 minutes| Serves: 6

1 tablespoon extra-virgin olive oil
1 cup chopped onion (about ½ medium onion)
2 garlic cloves, minced (about 1 teaspoon)
2 (14½-ounce / 411-g) cans Italian diced tomatoes,
undrained, no salt added
6 large eggs
½ cup chopped fresh flat-leaf (Italian) parsley
Crusty Italian bread and grated Parmesan or Romano cheese, for serving (optional)

1. In a large skillet over medium-high heat, heat the oil. Add the onion and cook for 5 minutes, stirring occasionally. Add the garlic and cook for 1 minute. 2. Pour the tomatoes with their juices over the onion mixture and cook until bubbling, 2 to 3 minutes. While waiting for the tomato mixture to bubble, crack one egg into a small custard cup or coffee mug. 3. When the tomato mixture bubbles, lower the heat to medium. Then use a large spoon to make six indentations in the tomato mixture. Gently pour the first cracked egg into one indentation and repeat, cracking the remaining eggs, one at a time, into the custard cup and pouring one into each indentation. Cover the skillet and cook for 6 to 7 minutes, or until the eggs are done to your liking (about 6 minutes for soft-cooked, 7 minutes for harder cooked). 4. Top with the parsley, and serve with the bread and grated cheese, if desired.

Per Serving

Calories: 127 | fat: 7g | protein: 8g | carbs: 8g | fiber: 2g | sodium: 82mg

Strawberry Basil Honey Ricotta Toast

Prep time: 10 minutes | Cook time: 0 minutes | Serves 2

4 slices of whole-grain bread
½ cup ricotta cheese (whole milk or low-fat)
1 tablespoon honey
Sea salt
1 cup fresh strawberries, sliced
4 large fresh basil leaves, sliced into thin shreds

1. Toast the bread. 2. In a small bowl, combine the ricotta, honey, and a pinch or two of sea salt. Taste and add additional honey or salt if desired. 3. Spread the mixture evenly over each slice of bread (about 2 tablespoons per slice). 4. Top each piece with sliced strawberries and a few pieces of shredded basil.

Per Serving
Calories: 275 | fat: 8g | protein: 15g | carbs: 41g | fiber: 5g | sodium: 323mg

Quick Low-Carb Avocado Toasts

Prep time: 10 minutes | Cook time: 10 minutes | Makes 4 toasts

Quick Bread Base:
¼ cup flax meal
2 tablespoons coconut flour
2 teaspoons psyllium powder
⅛ teaspoon baking soda
Optional: ½ teaspoon dried herbs, ¼ teaspoon paprika or ground turmeric
Salt and black pepper, to taste
¼ teaspoon apple cider vinegar
1 teaspoon extra-virgin olive oil or ghee, plus more for greasing
1 large egg
2 tablespoons water
Avocado Topping:
1 large ripe avocado
¼ small red onion or 1 spring onion, minced
1 tablespoon extra-virgin olive oil
1 tablespoon fresh lemon juice
Salt, black pepper, and/or chile flakes, to taste
2 teaspoons chopped fresh herbs, such as parsley or chives
Optional: 2 ounces (57 g) smoked salmon and/or poached egg

1. Make the Bread Base: Combine all the dry ingredients in a bowl. Add the wet ingredients. Combine and set aside for 5 minutes. Divide the mixture between two wide ramekins lightly greased with the olive oil and microwave on high for about 2 minutes, checking every 30 to 60 seconds to avoid overcooking. (If the bread ends up too dry, you can "rehydrate" it: Pour 1 tablespoon [15 ml] of water evenly over it, then return it to the microwave for 30 seconds.) Let it cool slightly, then cut widthwise. Place on a dry nonstick pan and toast for 1 to 2 minutes per side. Set aside. 2. Make the Topping: In a bowl, mash the avocado with the onion, oil, lemon juice, salt, pepper, and chile flakes. To serve, spread the avocado mixture on top of the sliced bread and add fresh herbs. Optionally, top with smoked salmon. Store the bread separately from the topping at room temperature in a sealed container for 1 day, in the fridge for up to 5 days, or freeze for up to 3 months. Refrigerate the topping in a sealed jar for up to 3 days.

Per Serving
Calories: 112 | fat: 10g | protein: 3g | carbs: 4g | fiber: 3g | sodium: 71mg

Mushroom-and-Tomato Stuffed Hash Browns

Prep time: 10 minutes | Cook time: 20 minutes | Serves 4

Olive oil cooking spray
1 tablespoon plus 2 teaspoons olive oil, divided
4 ounces (113 g) baby bella mushrooms, diced
1 scallion, white parts and green parts, diced
1 garlic clove, minced
2 cups shredded potatoes
½ teaspoon salt
¼ teaspoon black pepper
1 Roma tomato, diced
½ cup shredded mozzarella

1. Preheat the air fryer to 380°F (193°C). Lightly coat the inside of a 6-inch cake pan with olive oil cooking spray. 2. In a small skillet, heat 2 teaspoons olive oil over medium heat. Add the mushrooms, scallion, and garlic, and cook for 4 to 5 minutes, or until they have softened and are beginning to show some color. Remove from heat. 3. Meanwhile, in a large bowl, combine the potatoes, salt, pepper, and the remaining tablespoon olive oil. Toss until all potatoes are well coated. 4. Pour half of the potatoes into the bottom of the cake pan. Top with the mushroom mixture, tomato, and mozzarella. Spread the remaining potatoes over the top. 5. Bake in the air fryer for 12 to 15 minutes, or until the top is golden brown. 6. Remove from the air fryer and allow to cool for 5 minutes before slicing and serving.

Per Serving
Calories: 165 | fat: 9g | protein: 6g | carbs: 16g | fiber: 3g | sodium: 403mg

Whole Wheat Banana-Walnut Bread

Prep time: 10 minutes | Cook time: 23 minutes | Serves 6

Olive oil cooking spray
2 ripe medium bananas
1 large egg
¼ cup nonfat plain Greek yogurt
¼ cup olive oil
½ teaspoon vanilla extract
2 tablespoons raw honey
1 cup whole wheat flour
¼ teaspoon salt
¼ teaspoon baking soda
½ teaspoon ground cinnamon
¼ cup chopped walnuts

1. Preheat the air fryer to 360°F (182°C). Lightly coat the inside of a 8-by-4-inch loaf pan with olive oil cooking spray. (Or use two 5 ½-by-3-inch loaf pans.) 2. In a large bowl, mash the bananas with a fork. Add the egg, yogurt, olive oil, vanilla, and honey. Mix until well combined and mostly smooth. 3. Sift the whole wheat flour, salt, baking soda, and cinnamon into the wet mixture, then stir until just combined. Do not overmix. 4. Gently fold in the walnuts. 5. Pour into the prepared loaf pan and spread to distribute evenly. 6. Place the loaf pan in the air fryer basket and bake for 20 to 23 minutes, or until golden brown on top and a toothpick inserted into the center comes out clean. 7. Allow to cool for 5 minutes before serving.

Per Serving
Calories: 255 | fat: 14g | protein: 6g | carbs: 30g | fiber: 4g | sodium: 154mg

Portobello Eggs Benedict

Prep time: 10 minutes | Cook time: 10 to 14 minutes | Serves 2

1 tablespoon olive oil
2 cloves garlic, minced
¼ teaspoon dried thyme
2 portobello mushrooms, stems removed and gills scraped out
2 Roma tomatoes, halved lengthwise
Salt and freshly ground black

pepper, to taste
2 large eggs
2 tablespoons grated Pecorino Romano cheese
1 tablespoon chopped fresh parsley, for garnish
1 teaspoon truffle oil (optional)

1. Preheat the air fryer to 400°F (204°C). 2. In a small bowl, combine the olive oil, garlic, and thyme. Brush the mixture over the mushrooms and tomatoes until thoroughly coated. Season to taste with salt and freshly ground black pepper. 3. Arrange the vegetables, cut side up, in the air fryer basket. Crack an egg into the center of each mushroom and sprinkle with cheese. Air fry for 10 to 14 minutes until the vegetables are tender and the whites are firm. When cool enough to handle, coarsely chop the tomatoes and place on top of the eggs. Scatter parsley on top and drizzle with truffle oil, if desired, just before serving.

Per Serving

Calories: 189 | fat: 13g | protein: 11g | carbs: 7g | fiber: 2g | sodium: 87mg

Honey-Apricot Granola with Greek Yogurt

Prep time: 10 minutes | Cook time: 30 minutes | Serves 6

1 cup rolled oats
¼ cup dried apricots, diced
¼ cup almond slivers
¼ cup walnuts, chopped
¼ cup pumpkin seeds
¼ cup hemp hearts
¼ to ⅓ cup raw honey, plus more for drizzling

1 tablespoon olive oil
1 teaspoon ground cinnamon
¼ teaspoon ground nutmeg
¼ teaspoon salt
2 tablespoons sugar-free dark chocolate chips (optional)
3 cups nonfat plain Greek yogurt

1. Preheat the air fryer to 260°F (127°C). Line the air fryer basket with parchment paper. 2. In a large bowl, combine the oats, apricots, almonds, walnuts, pumpkin seeds, hemp hearts, honey, olive oil, cinnamon, nutmeg, and salt, mixing so that the honey, oil, and spices are well distributed. 3. Pour the mixture onto the parchment paper and spread it into an even layer. 4. Bake for 10 minutes, then shake or stir and spread back out into an even layer. Continue baking for 10 minutes more, then repeat the process of shaking or stirring the mixture. Bake for an additional 10 minutes before removing from the air fryer. 5. Allow the granola to cool completely before stirring in the chocolate chips (if using) and pouring into an airtight container for storage. 6. For each serving, top ½ cup Greek yogurt with ⅓ cup granola and a drizzle of honey, if needed.

Per Serving

Calories: 342 | fat: 16g | protein: 20g | carbs: 31g | fiber: 4g | sodium: 146mg

Whole Wheat Blueberry Muffins

Prep time: 10 minutes | Cook time: 15 minutes | Serves 6

Olive oil cooking spray
½ cup unsweetened applesauce
¼ cup raw honey
½ cup nonfat plain Greek yogurt
1 teaspoon vanilla extract
1 large egg

1½ cups plus 1 tablespoon whole wheat flour, divided
½ teaspoon baking soda
½ teaspoon baking powder
½ teaspoon salt
½ cup blueberries, fresh or frozen

1. Preheat the air fryer to 360°F (182°C). Lightly coat the inside of six silicone muffin cups or a six-cup muffin tin with olive oil cooking spray. 2. In a large bowl, combine the applesauce, honey, yogurt, vanilla, and egg and mix until smooth. 3. Sift in 1½ cups of the flour, the baking soda, baking powder, and salt into the wet mixture, then stir until just combined. 4. In a small bowl, toss the blueberries with the remaining 1 tablespoon flour, then fold the mixture into the muffin batter. 5. Divide the mixture evenly among the prepared muffin cups and place into the basket of the air fryer. Bake for 12 to 15 minutes, or until golden brown on top and a toothpick inserted into the middle of one of the muffins comes out clean. 6. Allow to cool for 5 minutes before serving.

Per Serving

Calories: 186 | fat: 2g | protein: 7g | carbs: 38g | fiber: 4g | sodium: 318mg

Spinach and Swiss Frittata with Mushrooms

Prep time: 10 minutes | Cook time: 20 minutes | Serves 4

Olive oil cooking spray
8 large eggs
½ teaspoon salt
½ teaspoon black pepper
1 garlic clove, minced
2 cups fresh baby spinach
4 ounces (113 g) baby bella

mushrooms, sliced
1 shallot, diced
½ cup shredded Swiss cheese, divided
Hot sauce, for serving (optional)

1. Preheat the air fryer to 360°F (182°C). Lightly coat the inside of a 6-inch round cake pan with olive oil cooking spray. 2. In a large bowl, beat the eggs, salt, pepper, and garlic for 1 to 2 minutes, or until well combined. 3. Fold in the spinach, mushrooms, shallot, and ¼ cup of the Swiss cheese. 4. Pour the egg mixture into the prepared cake pan, and sprinkle the remaining ¼ cup of Swiss over the top. 5. Place into the air fryer and bake for 18 to 20 minutes, or until the eggs are set in the center. 6. Remove from the air fryer and allow to cool for 5 minutes. Drizzle with hot sauce (if using) before serving.

Per Serving

Calories: 207 | fat: 13g | protein: 18g | carbs: 4g | fiber: 1g | sodium: 456mg

Mediterranean Breakfast Pita Sandwiches

Prep time: 5 minutes | Cook time: 7 minutes | Serves 2

2 eggs
1 small avocado, peeled, halved, and pitted
¼ teaspoon fresh lemon juice
Pinch of salt
¼ teaspoon freshly ground black pepper
1 (8-inch) whole-wheat pocket pita bread, halved
12 (¼-inch) thick cucumber slices
6 oil-packed sun-dried tomatoes, rinsed, patted dry, and cut in half
2 tablespoons crumbled feta
½ teaspoon extra virgin olive oil

1. Fill a small saucepan with water and place it over medium heat. When the water is boiling, use a slotted spoon to carefully lower the eggs into the water. Gently boil for 7 minutes, then remove the pan from the heat and transfer the eggs to a bowl of cold water. Set aside. 2. In a small bowl, mash the avocado with a fork and then add the lemon juice and salt. Mash to combine. 3. Peel and slice the eggs, then sprinkle the black pepper over the egg slices. 4. Spread half of the avocado mixture over one side of the pita half. Top the pita half with 1 sliced egg, 6 cucumber slices, and 6 sun-dried tomato pieces. 5. Sprinkle 1 tablespoon crumbled feta over the top and drizzle ¼ teaspoon olive oil over the feta. Repeat with the other pita half. Serve promptly.

Per Serving
Calories: 427 | fat: 28g | protein: 14g | carbs: 36g | fiber: 12g | sodium: 398mg

Spiced Potatoes with Chickpeas

Prep time: 10 minutes | Cook time: 10 minutes | Serves 4

¼ cup olive oil
3 medium potatoes, peeled and shredded
2 cups finely chopped baby spinach
1 medium onion, finely diced
1 tablespoon minced fresh ginger
1 teaspoon ground cumin
1 teaspoon ground coriander
½ teaspoon ground turmeric
½ teaspoon salt
1 (15-ounce / 425-g) can chickpeas, drained and rinsed
1 medium zucchini, diced
¼ cup chopped cilantro
1 cup plain yogurt

1. Heat the olive oil in a large skillet over medium heat. Add the potatoes, spinach, onions, ginger, cumin, coriander, turmeric, and salt and stir to mix well. Spread the mixture out into an even layer and let cook, without stirring, for about 5 minutes until the potatoes are crisp and browned on the bottom. 2. Add the chickpeas and zucchini and mix to combine, breaking up the layer of potatoes. Spread the mixture out again into an even layer and continue to cook, without stirring, for another 5 minutes or so, until the potatoes are crisp on the bottom. 3. To serve, garnish with cilantro and yogurt.

Per Serving
Calories: 679 | fat: 20g | protein: 28g | carbs: 100g | fiber: 24g | sodium: 388mg

Savory Sweet Potato Hash

Prep time: 15 minutes | Cook time: 18 minutes | Serves 6

2 medium sweet potatoes, peeled and cut into 1-inch cubes
½ green bell pepper, diced
½ red onion, diced
4 ounces (113 g) baby bella mushrooms, diced
2 tablespoons olive oil
1 garlic clove, minced
½ teaspoon salt
½ teaspoon black pepper
½ tablespoon chopped fresh rosemary

1. Preheat the air fryer to 380ºF (193ºC). 2. In a large bowl, toss all ingredients together until the vegetables are well coated and seasonings distributed. 3. Pour the vegetables into the air fryer basket, making sure they are in a single even layer. (If using a smaller air fryer, you may need to do this in two batches.) 4. Roast for 9 minutes, then toss or flip the vegetables. Roast for 9 minutes more. 5. Transfer to a serving bowl or individual plates and enjoy.

Per Serving
Calories: 91 | fat: 5g | protein: 2g | carbs: 12g | fiber: 1g | sodium: 219mg

Greek Eggs and Potatoes

Prep time: 5 minutes | Cook time: 30 minutes | Serves 4

3 medium tomatoes, seeded and coarsely chopped
2 tablespoons fresh chopped basil
1 garlic clove, minced
2 tablespoons plus ½ cup olive oil, divided
Sea salt and freshly ground pepper, to taste
3 large russet potatoes
4 large eggs
1 teaspoon fresh oregano, chopped

1. Put tomatoes in a food processor and purée them, skins and all. 2. Add the basil, garlic, 2 tablespoons olive oil, sea salt, and freshly ground pepper, and pulse to combine. 3. Put the mixture in a large skillet over low heat and cook, covered, for 20–25 minutes, or until the sauce has thickened and is bubbly. 4. Meanwhile, dice the potatoes into small cubes. Put ½ cup olive oil in a nonstick skillet over medium-low heat. 5. Fry the potatoes for 5 minutes until crisp and browned on the outside, then cover and reduce heat to low. Steam potatoes until done. 6. Carefully crack the eggs into the tomato sauce. Cook over low heat until the eggs are set in the sauce, about 6 minutes. 7. Remove the potatoes from the pan and drain them on paper towels, then place them in a bowl. 8. Sprinkle with sea salt and freshly ground pepper to taste and top with the oregano. 9. Carefully remove the eggs with a slotted spoon and place them on a plate with the potatoes. Spoon sauce over the top and serve.

Per Serving
Calories: 548 | fat: 32g | protein: 13g | carbs: 54g | fiber: 5g | sodium: 90mg

Morning Buzz Iced Coffee

Prep time: 10 minutes | Cook time: 0 minutes | Serves 1

1 cup freshly brewed strong black coffee, cooled slightly
1 tablespoon extra-virgin olive oil
1 tablespoon half-and-half or
heavy cream (optional)
1 teaspoon MCT oil (optional)
⅛ teaspoon almond extract
⅛ teaspoon ground cinnamon

1. Pour the slightly cooled coffee into a blender or large glass (if using an immersion blender). 2. Add the olive oil, half-and-half (if using), MCT oil (if using), almond extract, and cinnamon. 3. Blend well until smooth and creamy. Drink warm and enjoy.
Per Serving
Calories: 124 | fat: 14g | protein: 0g | carbs: 0g | fiber: 0g | sodium: 5mg

Baked Egg and Mushroom Cups

Prep time: 5 minutes | Cook time: 15 minutes | Serves 6

Olive oil cooking spray
6 large eggs
1 garlic clove, minced
½ teaspoon salt
½ teaspoon black pepper
Pinch red pepper flakes
8 ounces (227 g) baby bella mushrooms, sliced
1 cup fresh baby spinach
2 scallions, white parts and green parts, diced

1. Preheat the air fryer to 320ºF (160ºC). Lightly coat the inside of six silicone muffin cups or a six-cup muffin tin with olive oil cooking spray. 2. In a large bowl, beat the eggs, garlic, salt, pepper, and red pepper flakes for 1 to 2 minutes, or until well combined. 3. Fold in the mushrooms, spinach, and scallions. 4. Divide the mixture evenly among the muffin cups. 5. Place into the air fryer and bake for 12 to 15 minutes, or until the eggs are set. 6. Remove and allow to cool for 5 minutes before serving.
Per Serving
Calories: 83 | fat: 5g | protein: 8g | carbs: 2g | fiber: 1g | sodium: 271mg

Hearty Berry Breakfast Oats

Prep time: 5 minutes | Cook time: 0 minutes | Serves 2

1½ cups whole-grain rolled or quick cooking oats (not instant)
¾ cup fresh blueberries,
raspberries, or blackberries, or a combination
2 teaspoons honey
2 tablespoons walnut pieces

1. Prepare the whole-grain oats according to the package directions and divide between 2 deep bowls. 2. In a small microwave-safe bowl, heat the berries and honey for 30 seconds. Top each bowl of oatmeal with the fruit mixture. Sprinkle the walnuts over the fruit and serve hot.
Per Serving
Calories: 556 | fat: 13g | protein: 22g | carbs: 92g | fiber: 14g | sodium: 3mg

Spinach, Sun-Dried Tomato, and Feta Egg Wraps

Prep time: 10 minutes | Cook time: 7 minutes | Serves 2

1 tablespoon olive oil
¼ cup minced onion
3 to 4 tablespoons minced sun-dried tomatoes in olive oil and herbs
3 large eggs, beaten
1½ cups packed baby spinach
1 ounce (28 g) crumbled feta cheese
Salt
2 (8-inch) whole-wheat tortillas

1. In a large skillet, heat the olive oil over medium-high heat. Add the onion and tomatoes and sauté for about 3 minutes. 2. Turn the heat down to medium. Add the beaten eggs and stir to scramble them. 3. Add the spinach and stir to combine. Sprinkle the feta cheese over the eggs. Add salt to taste. 4. Warm the tortillas in the microwave for about 20 seconds each. 5. Fill each tortilla with half of the egg mixture. Fold in half or roll them up and serve.
Per Serving
Calories: 435 | fat: 28g | protein: 17g | carbs: 31g | fiber: 6g | sodium: 552mg

Power Peach Smoothie Bowl

Prep time: 15 minutes | Cook time: 0 minutes | Serves 2

2 cups packed partially thawed frozen peaches
½ cup plain or vanilla Greek yogurt
½ ripe avocado
2 tablespoons flax meal
1 teaspoon vanilla extract
1 teaspoon orange extract
1 tablespoon honey (optional)

1. Combine all of the ingredients in a blender and blend until smooth. 2. Pour the mixture into two bowls, and, if desired, sprinkle with additional toppings.
Per Serving
Calories: 213 | fat: 13g | protein: 6g | carbs: 23g | fiber: 7g | sodium: 41mg

Greek Yogurt and Berries

Prep time: 5 minutes | Cook time: 30 minutes | Serves 4

4 cups plain full-fat Greek yogurt
1 cup granola
½ cup blackberries
2 bananas, sliced and frozen
1 teaspoon chia seeds, for
topping
1 teaspoon chopped fresh mint leaves, for topping
4 teaspoons honey, for topping (optional)

1. Evenly divide the yogurt among four bowls. Top with the granola, blackberries, bananas, chia seeds, mint, and honey (if desired), dividing evenly among the bowls. Serve.
Per Serving
Calories: 283 | fat: 9g | protein: 12g | carbs: 42g | fiber: 5g | sodium: 115mg

Garlic Scrambled Eggs with Basil

Prep time: 5 minutes | Cook time: 5 minutes | Serves 2

4 large eggs
2 tablespoons finely chopped fresh basil
2 tablespoons grated Gruyère cheese
1 tablespoon cream
1 tablespoon olive oil
2 cloves garlic, minced
Sea salt and freshly ground pepper, to taste

1. In a large bowl, beat together the eggs, basil, cheese, and cream with a whisk until just combined. 2. Heat the oil in a large, heavy nonstick skillet over medium-low heat. Add the garlic and cook until golden, about 1 minute. 3. Pour the egg mixture into the skillet over the garlic. Work the eggs continuously and cook until fluffy and soft. 4. Season with sea salt and freshly ground pepper to taste. Divide between 2 plates and serve immediately.

Per Serving
Calories: 267 | fat: 21g | protein: 16g | carbs: 3g | fiber: 0g | sodium: 394mg

Blueberry-Banana Bowl with Quinoa

Prep time: 5 minutes | Cook time: 20 minutes | Serves 4

1½ cups water
¾ cup uncooked quinoa, rinsed
2 tablespoons honey, divided
1 cup blueberries (preferably frozen)
2 bananas (preferably frozen), sliced
½ cup sliced almonds or crushed walnuts
½ cup dried cranberries
1 cup granola
1 cup milk or nondairy milk of your choice

1. Combine the water and quinoa in a medium saucepan. Bring to a boil over medium-high heat, cover, reduce the heat to low, and simmer for 15 to 20 minutes, until the water has been absorbed. Remove from the heat and fluff the quinoa with a fork. 2. Evenly divide the quinoa among four bowls, about ½ cup for each bowl. Evenly divide the honey among the bowls and mix it in well. Top evenly with the blueberries, bananas, almonds, cranberries, granola, and milk. Serve.

Per Serving
Calories: 469 | fat: 15g | protein: 12g | carbs: 77g | fiber: 9g | sodium: 31mg

Crostini with Smoked Trout

Prep time: 10 minutes | Cook time: 5 minutes | Serves 4

½ French baguette, cut into 1-inch-thick slices
1 tablespoon olive oil
¼ teaspoon onion powder
1 (4-ounce / 113-g) can
smoked trout
¼ cup crème fraîche
¼ teaspoon chopped fresh dill, for garnish

1. Drizzle the bread on both sides with the olive oil and sprinkle with the onion powder. 2. Place the bread in a single layer in a large skillet and toast over medium heat until lightly browned on both sides, 3 to 4 minutes total. 3. Transfer the toasted bread to a serving platter and place 1 or 2 pieces of the trout on each slice. Top with the crème fraîche, garnish with the dill, and serve immediately.

Per Serving
Calories: 206 | fat: 10g | protein: 13g | carbs: 15g | fiber: 1g | sodium: 350mg

Egg Salad with Red Pepper and Dill

Prep time: 5 minutes | Cook time: 10 minutes | Serves 6

6 large eggs
1 cup water
1 tablespoon olive oil
1 medium red bell pepper, seeded and chopped
¼ teaspoon salt
¼ teaspoon ground black pepper
½ cup low-fat plain Greek yogurt
2 tablespoons chopped fresh dill

1. Have ready a large bowl of ice water. Place rack or egg holder into bottom of the Instant Pot®. 2. Arrange eggs on rack or holder and add water to the Instant Pot®. Close lid, set steam release to Sealing, press the Manual button, and set time to 5 minutes. 3. When the timer beeps, let pressure release naturally for 5 minutes, then quick-release the remaining pressure until the float valve drops. Press the Cancel button and open lid. Carefully transfer eggs to the bowl of ice water. Let stand in ice water for 10 minutes, then peel, chop, and add eggs to a medium bowl. 4. Clean out pot, dry well, and return to machine. Press the Sauté button and heat oil. Add bell pepper, salt, and black pepper. Cook, stirring often, until bell pepper is tender, about 5 minutes. Transfer to bowl with eggs. 5. Add yogurt and dill to bowl, and fold to combine. Cover and chill for 1 hour before serving.

Per Serving
Calories: 111 | fat: 8g | protein: 8g | carbs: 3g | fiber: 0g | sodium: 178mg

Quinoa and Yogurt Breakfast Bowls

Prep time: 10 minutes | Cook time: 12 minutes | Serves 8

2 cups quinoa, rinsed and drained
4 cups water
1 teaspoon vanilla extract
¼ teaspoon salt
2 cups low-fat plain Greek yogurt
2 cups blueberries
1 cup toasted almonds
½ cup pure maple syrup

1. Place quinoa, water, vanilla, and salt in the Instant Pot®. Close lid and set steam release to Sealing. Press the Rice button and set time to 12 minutes. 2. When the timer beeps, let pressure release naturally, about 20 minutes. Open lid and fluff quinoa with a fork. 3. Stir in yogurt. Serve warm, topped with berries, almonds, and maple syrup.

Per Serving
Calories: 376 | fat: 13g | protein: 16g | carbs: 52g | fiber: 6g | sodium: 105mg

Harissa Shakshuka with Bell Peppers and Tomatoes

Prep time: 10 minutes | Cook time: 20 minutes | Serves 4

1½ tablespoons extra-virgin olive oil
2 tablespoons harissa
1 tablespoon tomato paste
½ onion, diced
1 bell pepper, seeded and diced
3 garlic cloves, minced
1 (28-ounce / 794-g) can no-salt-added diced tomatoes
½ teaspoon kosher salt
4 large eggs
2 to 3 tablespoons fresh basil, chopped or cut into ribbons

1. Preheat the oven to 375ºF (190ºC). 2. Heat the olive oil in a 12-inch cast-iron pan or ovenproof skillet over medium heat. Add the harissa, tomato paste, onion, and bell pepper; sauté for 3 to 4 minutes. Add the garlic and cook until fragrant, about 30 seconds. Add the diced tomatoes and salt and simmer for about 10 minutes. 3. Make 4 wells in the sauce and gently break 1 egg into each. Transfer to the oven and bake until the whites are cooked and the yolks are set, 10 to 12 minutes. 4. Allow to cool for 3 to 5 minutes, garnish with the basil, and carefully spoon onto plates.

Per Serving
Calories: 190 | fat: 10g | protein: 9g | carbs: 15g | fiber: 4g | sodium: 255mg

Red Pepper and Feta Egg Bites

Prep time: 5 minutes | Cook time: 8 minutes | Serves 6

1 tablespoon olive oil
½ cup crumbled feta cheese
¼ cup chopped roasted red peppers
6 large eggs, beaten
¼ teaspoon ground black pepper
1 cup water

1. Brush silicone muffin or poaching cups with oil. Divide feta and roasted red peppers among prepared cups. In a bowl with a pour spout, beat eggs with black pepper. 2. Place rack in the Instant Pot® and add water. Place cups on rack. Pour egg mixture into cups. Close lid, set steam release to Sealing, press the Manual button, and set time to 8 minutes. 3. When the timer beeps, quick-release the pressure until the float valve drops and open lid. Remove silicone cups carefully and slide eggs from cups onto plates. Serve warm.

Per Serving
Calories: 145 | fat: 11g | protein: 10g | carbs: 3g | fiber: 1g | sodium: 294mg

Quinoa Porridge with Apricots

Prep time: 10 minutes | Cook time: 12 minutes | Serves 4

1½ cups quinoa, rinsed and drained
1 cup chopped dried apricots
2½ cups water
1 cup almond milk
1 tablespoon rose water
½ teaspoon cardamom
¼ teaspoon salt

1. Place all ingredients in the Instant Pot®. Stir to combine. Close lid, set steam release to Sealing, press the Rice button, and set time to 12 minutes. When the timer beeps, let pressure release naturally, about 20 minutes. 2. Press the Cancel button, open lid, and fluff quinoa with a fork. Serve warm.

Per Serving
Calories: 197 | fat: 2g | protein: 3g | carbs: 44g | fiber: 4g | sodium: 293mg

Mediterranean Muesli and Breakfast Bowl

Prep time: 10 minutes | Cook time: 0 minutes | Serves 12

Muesli:
3 cups old-fashioned rolled oats
1 cup wheat or rye flakes
1 cup pistachios or almonds, coarsely chopped
½ cup oat bran
8 dried apricots, chopped
8 dates, chopped
8 dried figs, chopped

Breakfast Bowl:
½ cup Mediterranean Muesli (above)
1 cup low-fat plain Greek yogurt or milk
2 tablespoons pomegranate seeds (optional)
½ teaspoon black or white sesame seeds

1. To make the muesli: In a medium bowl, combine the oats, wheat or rye flakes, pistachios or almonds, oat bran, apricots, dates, and figs. Transfer to an airtight container and store for up to 1 month. 2. To make the breakfast bowl: In a bowl, combine the muesli with the yogurt or milk. Top with the pomegranate seeds, if using, and the sesame seeds.

Per Serving
Calories: 234 | fat: 6g | protein: 8g | carbs: 40g | fiber: 6g | sodium: 54mg

Garlicky Beans and Greens with Polenta

Prep time: 5 minutes | Cook time: 20 minutes | Serves 4

2 tablespoons olive oil, divided
1 (18-ounce / 510-g) roll precooked polenta, cut into ½"-thick slices
4 cloves garlic, minced
4 cups chopped greens, such as kale, mustard greens, collards,
or chard
2 tomatoes, seeded and diced
1 (15-ounce / 425-g) can small white beans, drained and rinsed
Kosher salt and ground black pepper, to taste

1. In a large skillet over medium heat, warm 1 tablespoon of the oil. Cook the polenta slices, flipping once, until golden and crispy, about 5 minutes per side. Remove the polenta and keep warm. 2. Add the remaining 1 tablespoon oil to the skillet. Cook the garlic until softened, 1 minute. Add the greens, tomatoes, and beans and cook until the greens are wilted and bright green and the beans are heated through, 10 minutes. Season to taste with the salt and pepper. To serve, top the polenta with the beans and greens.

Per Serving
Calories: 329 | fat: 8g | protein: 12g | carbs: 54g | fiber: 9g | sodium: 324mg

Flax, Date, and Walnut Steel-Cut Oats

Prep time: 5 minutes | Cook time: 5 minutes | Serves 4

1 tablespoon light olive oil
1 cup steel-cut oats
3 cups water
⅓ cup chopped pitted dates
¼ cup ground flax
¼ teaspoon salt
½ cup toasted chopped walnuts

1. Place oil, oats, water, dates, flax, and salt in the Instant Pot® and stir well. Close lid, set steam release to Sealing, press the Manual button, and set time to 5 minutes. 2. When the timer beeps, let pressure release naturally for 10 minutes, then quick-release the remaining pressure until the float valve drops. Press the Cancel button, open lid, and stir in walnuts. Serve hot.

Per Serving
Calories: 322 | fat: 18g | protein: 10g | carbs: 42g | fiber: 8g | sodium: 150mg

Breakfast Quinoa with Figs and Walnuts

Prep time: 10 minutes | Cook time: 12 minutes | Serves 4

1½ cups quinoa, rinsed and drained
2½ cups water
1 cup almond milk
2 tablespoons honey
1 teaspoon vanilla extract
½ teaspoon ground cinnamon
¼ teaspoon salt
½ cup low-fat plain Greek yogurt
8 fresh figs, quartered
1 cup chopped toasted walnuts

1. Place quinoa, water, almond milk, honey, vanilla, cinnamon, and salt in the Instant Pot®. Stir to combine. Close lid, set steam release to Sealing, press the Rice button, and set time to 12 minutes. When the timer beeps, let pressure release naturally, about 20 minutes. 2. Press the Cancel button, open lid, and fluff quinoa with a fork. Serve warm with yogurt, figs, and walnuts.

Per Serving
Calories: 413 | fat: 25g | protein: 10g | carbs: 52g | fiber: 7g | sodium: 275mg

Breakfast Farro with Dried Fruit and Nuts

Prep time: 10 minutes | Cook time: 20 minutes | Serves 8

16 ounces (454 g) farro, rinsed and drained
4½ cups water
¼ cup maple syrup
¼ teaspoon salt
1 cup dried mixed fruit
½ cup chopped toasted mixed nuts
2 cups almond milk

1. Place farro, water, maple syrup, and salt in the Instant Pot® and stir to combine. Close lid, set steam release to Sealing, press the Multigrain button, and set time to 20 minutes. When the timer beeps, let pressure release naturally, about 30 minutes. 2. Press the Cancel button, open lid, and add dried fruit. Close lid and let stand on the Keep Warm setting for 20 minutes. Serve warm with nuts and almond milk.

Per Serving
Calories: 347 | fat: 7g | protein: 9g | carbs: 65g | fiber: 9g | sodium: 145mg

Black Olive Toast with Herbed Hummus

Prep time: 5 minutes | Cook time: 5 minutes | Serves 2

¼ cup store-bought plain hummus
2 tablespoons finely chopped fresh flat-leaf parsley
1 tablespoon finely chopped fresh dill
1 tablespoon finely chopped fresh mint
1 teaspoon finely grated lemon peel
2 slices (½" thick) black olive bread
1 clove garlic, halved
1 tablespoon extra-virgin olive oil

1. In a small bowl, combine the hummus, herbs, and lemon peel. 2. Toast the bread. Immediately rub the warm bread with the garlic. 3. Spread half the hummus over each slice of bread and drizzle with the oil.

Per Serving
Calories: 197 | fat: 11g | protein: 6g | carbs: 20g | fiber: 4g | sodium: 177mg

Greek Yogurt Parfait with Granola

Prep time: 10 minutes | Cook time: 30 minutes | Serves 4

For the Granola:
¼ cup honey or maple syrup
2 tablespoons vegetable oil
2 teaspoons vanilla extract
½ teaspoon kosher salt
3 cups gluten-free rolled oats
1 cup mixed raw and unsalted nuts, chopped
¼ cup sunflower seeds
1 cup unsweetened dried cherries
For the Parfait:
2 cups plain Greek yogurt
1 cup fresh fruit, chopped (optional)

To Make the Granola: 1. Preheat the oven to 325ºF (163ºC). Line a baking sheet with parchment paper or foil. 2. Heat the honey, oil, vanilla, and salt in a small saucepan over medium heat. Simmer for 2 minutes and stir together well. 3. In a large bowl, combine the oats, nuts, and seeds. Pour the warm oil mixture over the top and toss well. Spread in a single layer on the prepared baking sheet. Bake for 30 minutes, stirring halfway through. 4. Remove from the oven and add in the dried cherries. Cool completely and store in an airtight container at room temperature for up to 3 months. To Make the Parfait: 5. For one serving: In a bowl or lowball drinking glass, spoon in ½ cup yogurt, ½ cup granola, and ¼ cup fruit (if desired). Layer in whatever pattern you like.

Per Serving
Calories: 370 | fat: 144g | protein: 19g | carbs: 44g | fiber: 6g | sodium: 100mg

Smoked Salmon Egg Scramble with Dill and Chives

Prep time: 5 minutes | Cook time: 5 minutes | Serves 2

4 large eggs
1 tablespoon milk
1 tablespoon fresh chives, minced
1 tablespoon fresh dill, minced
¼ teaspoon kosher salt
⅛ teaspoon freshly ground black pepper
2 teaspoons extra-virgin olive oil
2 ounces (57 g) smoked salmon, thinly sliced

1. In a large bowl, whisk together the eggs, milk, chives, dill, salt, and pepper. 2. Heat the olive oil in a medium skillet or sauté pan over medium heat. Add the egg mixture and cook for about 3 minutes, stirring occasionally. 3. Add the salmon and cook until the eggs are set but moist, about 1 minute.

Per Serving
Calories: 325 | fat: 26g | protein: 23g | carbs: 1g | fiber: 0g | sodium: 455mg

Polenta with Sautéed Chard and Fried Eggs

Prep time: 5 minutes | Cook time: 20 minutes | Serves 4

For the Polenta:
2½ cups water
½ teaspoon kosher salt
¾ cups whole-grain cornmeal
¼ teaspoon freshly ground black pepper
2 tablespoons grated Parmesan cheese
For the Chard:
1 tablespoon extra-virgin olive oil
1 bunch (about 6 ounces / 170 g) Swiss chard, leaves and stems chopped and separated
2 garlic cloves, sliced
¼ teaspoon kosher salt
⅛ teaspoon freshly ground black pepper
Lemon juice (optional)
For the Eggs:
1 tablespoon extra-virgin olive oil
4 large eggs

To Make the Polenta: 1. Bring the water and salt to a boil in a medium saucepan over high heat. Slowly add the cornmeal, whisking constantly. 2. Decrease the heat to low, cover, and cook for 10 to 15 minutes, stirring often to avoid lumps. Stir in the pepper and Parmesan, and divide among 4 bowls. To Make the Chard: 3. Heat the oil in a large skillet over medium heat. Add the chard stems, garlic, salt, and pepper; sauté for 2 minutes. Add the chard leaves and cook until wilted, about 3 to 5 minutes. 4. Add a spritz of lemon juice (if desired), toss together, and divide evenly on top of the polenta. To Make the Eggs: 5. Heat the oil in the same large skillet over medium-high heat. Crack each egg into the skillet, taking care not to crowd the skillet and leaving space between the eggs. Cook until the whites are set and golden around the edges, about 2 to 3 minutes. 6. Serve sunny-side up or flip the eggs over carefully and cook 1 minute longer for over easy. Place one egg on top of the polenta and chard in each bowl.

Per Serving
Calories: 310 | fat: 18g | protein: 17g | carbs: 21g | fiber: 1g | sodium: 500mg

Savory Cottage Cheese Breakfast Bowl

Prep time: 10 minutes | Cook time: 0 minutes | Serves 4

2 cups low-fat cottage cheese
2 tablespoons chopped mixed fresh herbs, such as basil, dill, flat-leaf parsley, and oregano
½ teaspoon ground black pepper
1 large tomato, chopped
1 small cucumber, peeled and chopped
¼ cup pitted kalamata olives, halved
1 tablespoon extra-virgin olive oil

1. In a medium bowl, combine the cottage cheese, herbs, and pepper. Add the tomato, cucumber, and olives and gently stir to combine. Drizzle with the oil to serve.

Per Serving
Calories: 181 | fat: 10g | protein: 15g | carbs: 8g | fiber: 1g | sodium: 788mg

Fig and Ricotta Toast with Walnuts and Honey

Prep time: 5 minutes | Cook time: 0 minutes | Serves 2

¼ cup ricotta cheese
2 pieces whole-wheat bread, toasted
4 figs, halved
2 tablespoons walnuts, chopped
1 teaspoon honey

1. Spread 2 tablespoons of ricotta cheese on each piece of toast. Add 4 fig halves to each piece of toast, pressing firmly to keep the figs in the ricotta. 2. Sprinkle 1 tablespoon of walnuts and drizzle ½ teaspoon of honey on each piece of toast.

Per Serving
Calories: 215 | fat:10 g | protein: 7g | carbs: 26g | fiber:3 g | sodium: 125mg

Jalapeño Popper Egg Cups

Prep time: 10 minutes | Cook time: 10 minutes | Serves 2

4 large eggs
¼ cup chopped pickled jalapeños
2 ounces (57 g) full-fat cream cheese
½ cup shredded sharp Cheddar cheese

1. In a medium bowl, beat the eggs, then pour into four silicone muffin cups. 2. In a large microwave-safe bowl, place jalapeños, cream cheese, and Cheddar. Microwave for 30 seconds and stir. Take a spoonful, approximately ¼ of the mixture, and place it in the center of one of the egg cups. Repeat with remaining mixture. 3. Place egg cups into the air fryer basket. 4. Adjust the temperature to 320ºF (160ºC) and bake for 10 minutes. 5. Serve warm.

Per Serving
Calories: 375 | fat: 30g | protein: 23g | carbs: 3g | fiber: 0g | sodium: 445mg

Spinach and Feta Egg Bake

Prep time: 7 minutes | Cook time: 23 to 25 minutes | Serves 2

Avocado oil spray
⅓ cup diced red onion
1 cup frozen chopped spinach, thawed and drained
4 large eggs
¼ cup heavy (whipping) cream

Sea salt and freshly ground black pepper, to taste
¼ teaspoon cayenne pepper
½ cup crumbled feta cheese
¼ cup shredded Parmesan cheese

1. Spray a deep pan with oil. Put the onion in the pan, and place the pan in the air fryer basket. Set the air fryer to 350°F (177°C) and bake for 7 minutes. 2. Sprinkle the spinach over the onion. 3. In a medium bowl, beat the eggs, heavy cream, salt, black pepper, and cayenne. Pour this mixture over the vegetables. 4. Top with the feta and Parmesan cheese. Bake for 16 to 18 minutes, until the eggs are set and lightly brown.

Per Serving
Calories: 366 | fat: 26g | protein: 25g | carbs: 8g | fiber: 3g | sodium: 520mg

Berry Warming Smoothie

Prep time: 5 minutes | Cook time: 0 minutes | Serves 1

⅔ cup plain kefir or plain yogurt
½ cup frozen mixed berries
½ cup baby spinach
½ cup cucumber, chopped
2 tablespoons unsweetened shredded coconut

¼ teaspoon grated ginger
¼ teaspoon ground cinnamon
¼ teaspoon ground nutmeg
⅛ teaspoon ground cardamom
¼ teaspoon vanilla extract (optional)

1. In a blender or Vitamix, add all the ingredients. Blend to combine.

Per Serving
Calories: 165 | fat: 7g | protein: 7g | carbs: 20g | fiber: 4g | sodium: 100mg

Mediterranean-Inspired White Smoothie

Prep time: 5 minutes | Cook time: 0 minutes | Serves 1

½ medium apple (any variety), peeled, halved, and seeded
5 roasted almonds
½ medium frozen banana, sliced (be sure to peel the

banana before freezing)
¼ cup full-fat Greek yogurt
½ cup low-fat 1% milk
¼ teaspoon ground cinnamon
½ teaspoon honey

1. Combine all the ingredients in a blender. Process until smooth. 2. Pour into a glass and serve promptly. (This recipe is best consumed fresh.)

Per Serving
Calories: 236 | fat: 7g | protein: 8g | carbs: 40g | fiber: 5g | sodium: 84mg

Egg in a "Pepper Hole" with Avocado

Prep time: 15 minutes | Cook time: 5 minutes | Serves 4

4 bell peppers, any color
1 tablespoon extra-virgin olive oil
8 large eggs
¾ teaspoon kosher salt, divided
¼ teaspoon freshly ground

black pepper, divided
1 avocado, peeled, pitted, and diced
¼ cup red onion, diced
¼ cup fresh basil, chopped
Juice of ½ lime

1. Stem and seed the bell peppers. Cut 2 (2-inch-thick) rings from each pepper. Chop the remaining bell pepper into small dice, and set aside. 2. Heat the olive oil in a large skillet over medium heat. Add 4 bell pepper rings, then crack 1 egg in the middle of each ring. Season with ¼ teaspoon of the salt and ⅛ teaspoon of the black pepper. Cook until the egg whites are mostly set but the yolks are still runny, 2 to 3 minutes. Gently flip and cook 1 additional minute for over easy. Move the egg-bell pepper rings to a platter or onto plates, and repeat with the remaining 4 bell pepper rings. 3. In a medium bowl, combine the avocado, onion, basil, lime juice, reserved diced bell pepper, the remaining ¼ teaspoon kosher salt, and the remaining ⅛ teaspoon black pepper. Divide among the 4 plates.

Per Serving 2 egg-pepper rings:
Calories: 270 | fat: 19g | protein: 15g | carbs: 12g | fiber: 5g | sodium: 360mg

Summer Day Fruit Salad

Prep time: 5 minutes | Cook time: 0 minutes | Serves 8

2 cups cubed honeydew melon
2 cups cubed cantaloupe
2 cups red seedless grapes
1 cup sliced fresh strawberries
1 cup fresh blueberries
Zest and juice of 1 large lime

½ cup unsweetened toasted coconut flakes
¼ cup honey
¼ teaspoon sea salt
½ cup extra-virgin olive oil

1. Combine all of the fruits, the lime zest, and the coconut flakes in a large bowl and stir well to blend. Set aside. 2. In a blender, combine the lime juice, honey, and salt and blend on low. Once the honey is incorporated, slowly add the olive oil and blend until opaque. 3. Pour the dressing over the fruit and mix well. Cover and refrigerate for at least 4 hours before serving, stirring a few times to distribute the dressing.

Per Serving
Calories: 249 | fat: 15g | protein: 1g | carbs: 30g | fiber: 3g | sodium: 104mg

Avocado Toast with Smoked Trout

Prep time: 10 minutes | Cook time: 0 minutes | Serves 2

1 avocado, peeled and pitted
2 teaspoons lemon juice, plus more for serving
¾ teaspoon ground cumin
¼ teaspoon kosher salt

¼ teaspoon red pepper flakes, plus more for sprinkling
¼ teaspoon lemon zest
2 pieces whole-wheat bread, toasted
1 (3.75-ounce / 106-g) can smoked trout

1. In a medium bowl, mash together the avocado, lemon juice, cumin, salt, red pepper flakes, and lemon zest. 2. Spread half the avocado mixture on each piece of toast. Top each piece of toast with half the smoked trout. Garnish with a pinch of red pepper flakes (if desired), and/or a sprinkle of lemon juice (if desired).
Per Serving
Calories: 300 | fat: 20g | protein: 11g | carbs: 21g | fiber: 6g | sodium: 390mg

Almond Butter Banana Chocolate Smoothie

Prep time: 5 minutes | Cook time: 0 minutes | Serves 1

¾ cup almond milk
½ medium banana, preferably frozen
¼ cup frozen blueberries

1 tablespoon almond butter
1 tablespoon unsweetened cocoa powder
1 tablespoon chia seeds

1. In a blender or Vitamix, add all the ingredients. Blend to combine.
Per Serving
Calories: 300 | fat: 16g | protein: 8g | carbs: 37g | fiber: 10g | sodium: 125mg

Chapter 6 Desserts

Pomegranate-Quinoa Dark Chocolate Bark

Prep time: 10 minutes |Cook time: 10 minutes| Serves: 6

Nonstick cooking spray	8 ounces (227 g) dark
½ cup uncooked tricolor or	chocolate or 1 cup dark
regular quinoa	chocolate chips
½ teaspoon kosher or sea salt	½ cup fresh pomegranate seeds

1. In a medium saucepan coated with nonstick cooking spray over medium heat, toast the uncooked quinoa for 2 to 3 minutes, stirring frequently. Do not let the quinoa burn. Remove the pan from the stove, and mix in the salt. Set aside 2 tablespoons of the toasted quinoa to use for the topping. 2. Break the chocolate into large pieces, and put it in a gallon-size zip-top plastic bag. Using a metal ladle or a meat pounder, pound the chocolate until broken into smaller pieces. (If using chocolate chips, you can skip this step.) Dump the chocolate out of the bag into a medium, microwave-safe bowl and heat for 1 minute on high in the microwave. Stir until the chocolate is completely melted. Mix the toasted quinoa (except the topping you set aside) into the melted chocolate. 3. Line a large, rimmed baking sheet with parchment paper. Pour the chocolate mixture onto the sheet and spread it evenly until the entire pan is covered. Sprinkle the remaining 2 tablespoons of quinoa and the pomegranate seeds on top. Using a spatula or the back of a spoon, press the quinoa and the pomegranate seeds into the chocolate. 4. Freeze the mixture for 10 to 15 minutes, or until set. Remove the bark from the freezer, and break it into about 2-inch jagged pieces. Store in a sealed container or zip-top plastic bag in the refrigerator until ready to serve.

Per Serving
Calories: 290 | fat: 17g | protein: 5g | carbs: 29g | fiber: 6g | sodium: 202mg

Grilled Pineapple Dessert

Prep time: 5 minutes | Cook time: 12 minutes | Serves 4

Oil for misting or cooking	¼ teaspoon brandy
spray	2 tablespoons slivered
4½-inch-thick slices fresh	almonds, toasted
pineapple, core removed	Vanilla frozen yogurt or
1 tablespoon honey	coconut sorbet

1. Spray both sides of pineapple slices with oil or cooking spray. Place into air fryer basket. 2. Air fry at 390°F (199°C) for 6 minutes. Turn slices over and cook for an additional 6 minutes. 3. Mix together the honey and brandy. 4. Remove cooked pineapple slices from air fryer, sprinkle with toasted almonds, and drizzle with honey mixture. 5. Serve with a scoop of frozen yogurt or sorbet on the side.

Per Serving
Calories: 65 | fat: 2g | protein: 1g | carbs: 11g | fiber: 1g | sodium: 1mg

Chocolate Lava Cakes

Prep time: 5 minutes | Cook time: 15 minutes | Serves 2

2 large eggs, whisked	½ teaspoon vanilla extract
¼ cup blanched finely ground	2 ounces (57 g) low-carb
almond flour	chocolate chips, melted

1. In a medium bowl, mix eggs with flour and vanilla. Fold in chocolate until fully combined. 2. Pour batter into two ramekins greased with cooking spray. Place ramekins into air fryer basket. Adjust the temperature to 320°F (160°C) and bake for 15 minutes. Cakes will be set at the edges and firm in the center when done. Let cool 5 minutes before serving.

Per Serving
Calories: 313 | fat: 23g | protein: 11g | carbs: 16g | fiber: 5g | sodium: 77mg

Tortilla Fried Pies

Prep time: 10 minutes | Cook time: 5 minutes per batch | Makes 12 pies

12 small flour tortillas (4-inch	2 tablespoons shredded,
diameter)	unsweetened coconut
½ cup fig preserves	Oil for misting or cooking
¼ cup sliced almonds	spray

1. Wrap refrigerated tortillas in damp paper towels and heat in microwave 30 seconds to warm. 2. Working with one tortilla at a time, place 2 teaspoons fig preserves, 1 teaspoon sliced almonds, and ½ teaspoon coconut in the center of each. 3. Moisten outer edges of tortilla all around. 4. Fold one side of tortilla over filling to make a half-moon shape and press down lightly on center. Using the tines of a fork, press down firmly on edges of tortilla to seal in filling. 5. Mist both sides with oil or cooking spray. 6. Place hand pies in air fryer basket close but not overlapping. It's fine to lean some against the sides and corners of the basket. You may need to cook in 2 batches. 7. Air fry at 390°F (199°C) for 5 minutes or until lightly browned. Serve hot. 8. Refrigerate any leftover pies in a closed container. To serve later, toss them back in the air fryer basket and cook for 2 or 3 minutes to reheat.

Per Serving (1 pie)
Calories: 137 | fat: 4g | protein: 4g | carbs: 22g | fiber: 2g | sodium: 279mg

S'mores

Prep time: 5 minutes | Cook time: 30 seconds | Makes 8 s' mores

Oil, for spraying
8 graham cracker squares
2 (1½-ounce / 43-g) chocolate

bars
4 large marshmallows

1. Line the air fryer basket with parchment and spray lightly with oil. 2. Place 4 graham cracker squares in the prepared basket. 3. Break the chocolate bars in half and place 1 piece on top of each graham cracker. Top with 1 marshmallow. 4. Air fry at 370°F (188°C) for 30 seconds, or until the marshmallows are puffed and golden brown and slightly melted. 5. Top with the remaining graham cracker squares and serve.

Per Serving
Calories: 154 | fat: 7g | protein: 2g | carbs: 22g | fiber: 2g | sodium: 75mg

Chocolate Pudding

Prep time: 10 minutes | Cook time: 0 minutes | Serves 4

2 ripe avocados, halved and pitted
¼ cup unsweetened cocoa powder
¼ cup heavy whipping cream, plus more if needed
2 teaspoons vanilla extract

1 to 2 teaspoons liquid stevia or monk fruit extract (optional)
½ teaspoon ground cinnamon (optional)
¼ teaspoon salt
Whipped cream, for serving (optional)

1. Using a spoon, scoop out the ripe avocado into a blender or large bowl, if using an immersion blender. Mash well with a fork. 2. Add the cocoa powder, heavy whipping cream, vanilla, sweetener (if using), cinnamon (if using), and salt. Blend well until smooth and creamy, adding additional cream, 1 tablespoon at a time, if the mixture is too thick. 3. Cover and refrigerate for at least 1 hour before serving. Serve chilled with additional whipped cream, if desired.

Per Serving
Calories: 205 | fat: 18g | protein: 3g | carbs: 12g | fiber: 9g | sodium: 156mg

Olive Oil Ice Cream

Prep time: 5 minutes | Cook time: 25 minutes | Serves 8

4 large egg yolks
⅓ cup powdered sugar-free sweetener (such as stevia or monk fruit extract)
2 cups half-and-half or 1 cup heavy whipping cream and 1

cup whole milk
1 teaspoon vanilla extract
⅛ teaspoon salt
¼ cup light fruity extra-virgin olive oil

1. Freeze the bowl of an ice cream maker for at least 12 hours or overnight. 2. In a large bowl, whisk together the egg yolks and sugar-free sweetener. 3. In a small saucepan, heat the half-and-half over medium heat until just below a boil. Remove from the heat and allow to cool slightly. 4. Slowly pour the warm half-and-half into the egg mixture, whisking constantly to avoid cooking the eggs. Return the eggs and cream to the saucepan over low heat. 5. Whisking constantly, cook over low heat until thickened, 15 to 20 minutes. Remove from the heat and stir in the vanilla extract and salt. Whisk in the olive oil and transfer to a glass bowl. Allow to cool, cover, and refrigerate for at least 6 hours. 6. Freeze custard in an ice cream maker according to manufacturer's directions.

Per Serving
Calories: 168 | fat: 15g | protein: 2g | carbs: 8g | fiber: 0g | sodium: 49mg

Nut Butter Cup Fat Bomb

Prep time: 5 minutes | Cook time: 0 minutes | Serves 8

½ cup crunchy almond butter (no sugar added)
½ cup light fruity extra-virgin olive oil
¼ cup ground flaxseed
2 tablespoons unsweetened

cocoa powder
1 teaspoon vanilla extract
1 teaspoon ground cinnamon (optional)
1 to 2 teaspoons sugar-free sweetener of choice (optional)

1. In a mixing bowl, combine the almond butter, olive oil, flaxseed, cocoa powder, vanilla, cinnamon (if using), and sweetener (if using) and stir well with a spatula to combine. Mixture will be a thick liquid. 2. Pour into 8 mini muffin liners and freeze until solid, at least 12 hours. Store in the freezer to maintain their shape.

Per Serving
Calories: 239 | fat: 24g | protein: 4g | carbs: 5g | fiber: 3g | sodium: 3mg

Strawberry Panna Cotta

Prep time: 10 minutes | Cook time: 10 minutes | Serves 4

2 tablespoons warm water
2 teaspoons gelatin powder
2 cups heavy cream
1 cup sliced strawberries, plus more for garnish
1 to 2 tablespoons sugar-free

sweetener of choice (optional)
1½ teaspoons pure vanilla extract
4 to 6 fresh mint leaves, for garnish (optional)

1. Pour the warm water into a small bowl. Sprinkle the gelatin over the water and stir well to dissolve. Allow the mixture to sit for 10 minutes. 2. In a blender or a large bowl, if using an immersion blender, combine the cream, strawberries, sweetener (if using), and vanilla. Blend until the mixture is smooth and the strawberries are well puréed. 3. Transfer the mixture to a saucepan and heat over medium-low heat until just below a simmer. Remove from the heat and cool for 5 minutes. 4. Whisking constantly, add in the gelatin mixture until smooth. Divide the custard between ramekins or small glass bowls, cover and refrigerate until set, 4 to 6 hours. 5. Serve chilled, garnishing with additional sliced strawberries or mint leaves (if using).

Per Serving
Calories: 229 | fat: 22g | protein: 3g | carbs: 5g | fiber: 1g | sodium: 26mg

Red-Wine Poached Pears

Prep time: 10 minutes | Cook time: 20 minutes | Serves 2

2 cups red wine, such as Merlot or Zinfandel, more if necessary
2 firm pears, peeled
2 to 3 cardamom pods, split
1 cinnamon stick
2 peppercorns
1 bay leaf

1. Put all ingredients in a large pot and bring to a boil. Make sure the pears are submerged in the wine. 2. Reduce heat and simmer for 15–20 minutes until the pears are tender when poked with a fork. 3. Remove the pears from the wine, and allow to cool. 4. Bring the wine to a boil, and cook until it reduces to a syrup. 5. Strain and drizzle the pears with the warmed syrup before serving.

Per Serving
Calories: 268 | fat: 0g | protein: 1g | carbs: 22g | fiber: 6g | sodium: 0mg

Crispy Apple Phyllo Tart

Prep time: 15 minutes | Cook time: 30 minutes | Serves 4

5 teaspoons extra virgin olive oil
2 teaspoons fresh lemon juice
¼ teaspoon ground cinnamon
1½ teaspoons granulated sugar, divided
1 large apple (any variety), peeled and cut into ⅛-inch thick slices
5 phyllo sheets, defrosted
1 teaspoon all-purpose flour
1½ teaspoons apricot jam

1. Preheat the oven to 350°F (180°C). Line a baking sheet with parchment paper, and pour the olive oil into a small dish. Set aside. 2. In a separate small bowl, combine the lemon juice, cinnamon, 1 teaspoon of the sugar, and the apple slices. Mix well to ensure the apple slices are coated in the seasonings. Set aside. 3. On a clean working surface, stack the phyllo sheets one on top of the other. Place a large bowl with an approximate diameter of 15 inches on top of the sheets, then draw a sharp knife around the edge of the bowl to cut out a circle through all 5 sheets. Discard the remaining phyllo. 4. Working quickly, place the first sheet on the lined baking sheet and then brush with the olive oil. Repeat the process by placing a second sheet on top of the first sheet, then brushing the second sheet with olive oil. Repeat until all the phyllo sheets are in a single stack. 5. Sprinkle the flour and remaining sugar over the top of the sheets. Arrange the apples in overlapping circles 4 inches from the edge of the phyllo. 6. Fold the edges of the phyllo in and then twist them all around the apple filling to form a crust edge. Brush the edge with the remaining olive oil. Bake for 30 minutes or until the crust is golden and the apples are browned on the edges. 7. While the tart is baking, heat the apricot jam in a small sauce pan over low heat until it's melted. 8. When the tart is done baking, brush the apples with the jam sauce. Slice the tart into 4 equal servings and serve warm. Store at room temperature, covered in plastic wrap, for up to 2 days.

Per Serving
Calories: 165 | fat: 7g | protein: 2g | carbs: 24g | fiber: 2g | sodium: 116mg

Orange–Olive Oil Cupcakes

Prep time: 15 minutes | Cook time: 20 minutes | Makes 6 cupcakes

1 large egg
2 tablespoons powdered sugar-free sweetener (such as stevia or monk fruit extract)
½ cup extra-virgin olive oil
1 teaspoon almond extract
Zest of 1 orange
1 cup almond flour
¾ teaspoon baking powder
⅛ teaspoon salt
1 tablespoon freshly squeezed orange juice

1. Preheat the oven to 350°F (180°C). Place muffin liners into 6 cups of a muffin tin. 2. In a large bowl, whisk together the egg and powdered sweetener. Add the olive oil, almond extract, and orange zest and whisk to combine well. 3. In a small bowl, whisk together the almond flour, baking powder, and salt. Add to wet ingredients along with the orange juice and stir until just combined. 4. Divide the batter evenly into 6 muffin cups and bake until a toothpick inserted in the center of the cupcake comes out clean, 15 to 18 minutes. 5. Remove from the oven and cool for 5 minutes in the tin before transferring to a wire rack to cool completely.

Per Serving (1 cupcake)
Calories: 280 | fat: 27g | protein: 4g | carbs: 8g | fiber: 2g | sodium: 65mg

Pumpkin-Ricotta Cheesecake

Prep time: 25 minutes | Cook time: 45 minutes | Serves 10 to 12

1 cup almond flour
½ cup butter, melted
1 (14½-ounce / 411-g) can pumpkin purée
8 ounces (227 g) cream cheese, at room temperature
½ cup whole-milk ricotta cheese
½ to ¾ cup sugar-free sweetener
4 large eggs
2 teaspoons vanilla extract
2 teaspoons pumpkin pie spice
Whipped cream, for garnish (optional)

1. Preheat the oven to 350°F (180°C). Line the bottom of a 9-inch springform pan with parchment paper. 2. In a small bowl, combine the almond flour and melted butter with a fork until well combined. Using your fingers, press the mixture into the bottom of the prepared pan. 3. In a large bowl, beat together the pumpkin purée, cream cheese, ricotta, and sweetener using an electric mixer on medium. 4. Add the eggs, one at a time, beating after each addition. Stir in the vanilla and pumpkin pie spice until just combined. 5. Pour the mixture over the crust and bake until set, 40 to 45 minutes. 6. Allow to cool to room temperature. Refrigerate for at least 6 hours before serving. 7. Serve chilled, garnishing with whipped cream, if desired.

Per Serving
Calories: 230 | fat: 21g | protein: 6g | carbs: 5g | fiber: 1g | sodium: 103mg

Grilled Stone Fruit with Whipped Ricotta

Prep time: 10 minutes |Cook time: 10 minutes| Serves: 4

Nonstick cooking spray
4 peaches or nectarines (or 8 apricots or plums), halved and pitted
2 teaspoons extra-virgin olive oil
¾ cup whole-milk ricotta cheese
1 tablespoon honey
¼ teaspoon freshly grated nutmeg
4 sprigs mint, for garnish (optional)

1. Spray the cold grill or a grill pan with nonstick cooking spray. Heat the grill or grill pan to medium heat. 2. Place a large, empty bowl in the refrigerator to chill. 3. Brush the fruit all over with the oil. Place the fruit cut-side down on the grill or pan and cook for 3 to 5 minutes, or until grill marks appear. (If you're using a grill pan, cook in two batches.) Using tongs, turn the fruit over. Cover the grill (or the grill pan with aluminum foil) and cook for 4 to 6 minutes, until the fruit is easily pierced with a sharp knife. Set aside to cool. 4. Remove the bowl from the refrigerator and add the ricotta. Using an electric beater, beat the ricotta on high for 2 minutes. Add the honey and nutmeg and beat for 1 more minute. Divide the warm (or room temperature) fruit among 4 serving bowls, top with the ricotta mixture, and a sprig of mint (if using) and serve.

Per Serving
Calories: 180 | fat: 9g | protein: 7g | carbs: 21g | fiber: 3g | sodium: 39mg

Honey-Vanilla Apple Pie with Olive Oil Crust

Prep time: 10 minutes | Cook time: 45 minutes | Serves 8

For the Crust:
¼ cup olive oil
1½ cups whole-wheat flour
½ teaspoon sea salt
2 tablespoons ice water
For the Filling:
4 large apples of your choice,
peeled, cored, and sliced
Juice of 1 lemon
1 tablespoon pure vanilla extract
1 tablespoon honey
½ teaspoon sea salt
Olive oil

Make the Crust: 1. Put the olive oil, flour, and sea salt in a food processor and process until dough forms. 2. Slowly add the water and pulse until you have a stiff dough. 3. Form the dough into 2 equal-sized balls, wrap in plastic wrap, and put in the refrigerator while you make the filling. Make the Filling: 1. Combine the apples, lemon juice, vanilla, honey, and sea salt in a large bowl. 2. Stir and allow to sit for at least 10 minutes. Preheat oven to 400°F (205°C). 3. Roll 1 crust out on a lightly floured surface. Transfer to a 9-inch pie plate and top with filling. 4. Roll the other ball of dough out and put on top of the pie. Cut a few slices in the top to vent the pie, and lightly brush the top of the pie with olive oil. 5. Bake for 45 minutes, or until top is browned and apples are bubbly. 6. Allow to cool completely before slicing and serving with your favorite frozen yogurt.

Per Serving
Calories: 208 | fat: 8g | protein: 3g | carbs: 34g | fiber: 5g | sodium: 293mg

Roasted Honey-Cinnamon Apples

Prep time: 15 minutes | Cook time: 20 minutes | Serves 2

1 teaspoon extra-virgin olive oil
4 firm apples, peeled, cored, and sliced
½ teaspoon salt
1½ teaspoons ground cinnamon, divided
2 tablespoons low-fat milk
2 tablespoons honey

1. Preheat the oven to 375°F (190°C). Grease a small casserole dish with the olive oil. 2. In a medium bowl, toss the apple slices with the salt and ½ teaspoon of the cinnamon. Spread the apples in the baking dish and bake for 20 minutes. 3. Meanwhile, in a small saucepan, heat the milk, honey, and remaining 1 teaspoon cinnamon over medium heat, stirring frequently. When it reaches a simmer, remove the pan from the heat and cover to keep warm. 4. Divide the apple slices between 2 dessert plates and pour the sauce over the apples. Serve warm.

Per Serving
Calories: 285 | fat: 3g | protein: 2g | carbs: 70g | fiber: 10g | sodium: 593mg

Cretan Cheese Pancakes

Prep time: 15 minutes | Cook time: 25 minutes | Serves 4

2 cups all-purpose flour, plus extra for kneading
½ cup water
2 tablespoons olive oil, plus extra for frying
1 tablespoon freshly squeezed lemon juice
1 tablespoon brandy
1 teaspoon sea salt
5 tablespoons crumbled feta cheese
2 tablespoons olive oil
½ cup chopped nuts of your choice
⅛ to ¼ teaspoon ground cinnamon, for topping
1 tablespoon honey, for drizzling

1. In a large bowl, stir together the flour, water, olive oil, lemon juice, brandy, and salt until a ball of dough forms. Turn the dough out onto a lightly floured surface and knead for 10 minutes. If the dough is too wet, add a little more flour. If it's too dry, add some water. 2. Divide the dough into 5 equal pieces and roll each piece into a ball. Place a dough ball on a lightly floured surface and roll it out into a 6-inch-wide circle about ¼ inch thick. Place 1 tablespoon of the feta in the center, fold the dough over, and knead the dough and cheese together. Once the cheese is well incorporated, roll the dough out flat to the same size. Repeat with the remaining balls of dough. 3. In a large skillet, heat the oil over medium-high heat. Place one round of dough in the skillet and cook for 5 to 6 minutes on each side, until golden brown. Transfer the cooked pancake to a paper towel–lined plate to drain. Repeat to cook the remaining dough pancakes. 4. Sprinkle the pancakes evenly with the nuts and cinnamon, drizzle with the honey, and serve.

Per Serving
Calories: 480 | fat: 24g | protein: 11g | carbs: 57g | fiber: 3g | sodium: 396mg

Olive Oil Greek Yogurt Brownies

Prep time: 5 minutes | Cook time: 25 minutes | Serves 9

¼ cup extra virgin olive oil
¾ cup granulated sugar
1 teaspoon pure vanilla extract
2 eggs
¼ cup 2% Greek yogurt
½ cup all-purpose flour
⅓ cup unsweetened cocoa powder
¼ teaspoon salt
¼ teaspoon baking powder
⅓ cup chopped walnuts

1. Preheat the oven to 350ºF (180ºC) and line a 9-inch (22cm) square baking pan with wax paper. 2. In a small bowl, combine the olive oil and sugar. Stir until well combined, then add the vanilla extract and mix well. 3. In another small bowl, beat the eggs and then add them to the olive oil mixture. Mix well. Add the yogurt and mix again. 4. In medium bowl, combine the flour, cocoa powder, salt, and baking powder, then mix well. Add the olive oil mixture to the dry ingredients and mix well, then add the walnuts and mix again. 5. Carefully pour the brownie mixture into the prepared pan and use a spatula to smooth the top. Transfer to the oven and bake for 25 minutes. 6. Set the brownies aside to cool completely. Lift the wax paper to remove the brownies from the pan. Remove the paper and cut the brownies into 9 squares. Store at room temperature in an airtight container for up to 2 days.

Per Serving
Calories: 198 | fat: 10g | protein: 4g | carbs: 25g | fiber: 2g | sodium: 85mg

Cranberry-Orange Cheesecake Pears

Prep time: 10 minutes | Cook time: 30 minutes | Serves 5

5 firm pears
1 cup unsweetened cranberry juice
1 cup freshly squeezed orange juice
1 tablespoon pure vanilla extract
½ teaspoon ground cinnamon
½ cup low-fat cream cheese, softened
¼ teaspoon ground ginger
¼ teaspoon almond extract
¼ cup dried, unsweetened cranberries
¼ cup sliced almonds, toasted

1. Peel the pears and slice off the bottoms so they sit upright. Remove the inside cores, and put the pears in a wide saucepan. 2. Add the cranberry and orange juice, as well as the vanilla and cinnamon extract. 3. Bring to a boil, and reduce to a simmer. 4. Cover and simmer on low heat for 25–30 minutes, until pears are soft but not falling apart. 5. Beat the cream cheese with the ginger and almond extract. 6. Stir the cranberries and almonds into the cream cheese mixture. 7. Once the pears have cooled, spoon the cream cheese into them. 8. Boil the remaining juices down to a syrup, and drizzle over the top of the filled pears.

Per Serving
Calories: 187 | fat: 6g | protein: 4g | carbs: 29g | fiber: 6g | sodium: 88mg

Greek Island Almond Cocoa Bites

Prep time: 5 minutes | Cook time: 0 minutes | Serves 6

½ cup roasted, unsalted whole almonds (with skins)
3 tablespoons granulated sugar, divided
1½ teaspoons unsweetened
cocoa powder
1¼ tablespoons unseasoned breadcrumbs
¾ teaspoon pure vanilla extract
1½ teaspoons orange juice

1. Place the almonds in a food processor and process until you have a coarse ground texture. 2. In a medium bowl, combine the ground almonds, 2 tablespoons sugar, the cocoa powder, and the breadcrumbs. Mix well. 3. In a small bowl, combine the vanilla extract and orange juice. Stir and then add the mixture to the almond mixture. Mix well. 4. Measure out a teaspoon of the mixture. Squeeze the mixture with your hand to make the dough stick together, then mold the dough into a small ball. 5. Add the remaining tablespoon of the sugar to a shallow bowl. Roll the balls in the sugar until covered, then transfer the bites to an airtight container. Store covered at room temperature for up to 1 week.

Per Serving
Calories: 102 | fat: 6g | protein: 3g | carbs: 10g | fiber: 2g | sodium: 11mg

Pears Poached in Pomegranate and Wine

Prep time: 5 minutes | Cook time: 60 minutes | Serves 4

4 ripe, firm Bosc pears, peeled, left whole, and stems left intact
1½ cups pomegranate juice
1 cup sweet, white dessert
wine, such as vin santo
½ cup pomegranate seeds (seeds from about ½ whole fruit)

1. Slice off a bit of the bottom of each pear to create a flat surface so that the pears can stand upright. If desired, use an apple corer to remove the cores of the fruit, working from the bottom. 2. Lay the pears in a large saucepan on their sides and pour the juice and wine over the top. Set over medium-high heat and bring to a simmer. Cover the pan, reduce the heat, and let the pears simmer, turning twice, for about 40 minutes, until the pears are tender. Transfer the pears to a shallow bowl, leaving the cooking liquid in the saucepan. 3. Turn the heat under the saucepan to high and bring the poaching liquid to a boil. Cook, stirring frequently, for about 15 to 20 minutes, until the liquid becomes thick and syrupy and is reduced to about ½ cup. 4. Spoon a bit of the syrup onto each of 4 serving plates and top each with a pear, sitting it upright. Drizzle a bit more of the sauce over the pears and garnish with the pomegranate seeds. Serve immediately.

Per Serving
Calories: 208 | fat: 0g | protein: 1g | carbs: 46g | fiber: 7g | sodium: 7mg

Apricot and Mint No-Bake Parfait

Prep time: 10 minutes | Cook time: 0 minutes | Serves 6

4 ounces (113 g) Neufchâtel or other light cream cheese
1 (7-ounce / 198-g) container 2% Greek yogurt
½ cup plus 2 tablespoons sugar
2 teaspoons vanilla extract
1 tablespoon fresh lemon juice

1 pound (454 g) apricots, rinsed, pitted, and cut into bite-size pieces
2 tablespoons finely chopped fresh mint, plus whole leaves for garnish if desired

1. In the bowl of a stand mixer fitted with the paddle attachment, beat the Neufchâtel cheese and yogurt on low speed until well combined, about 2 minutes, scraping down the bowl as needed. Add ½ cup of the sugar, the vanilla, and the lemon juice. Mix until smooth and free of lumps, 2 to 3 minutes; set aside. 2. In a medium bowl, combine the apricots, mint, and remaining 2 tablespoons sugar. Stir occasionally, waiting to serve until after the apricots have released their juices and have softened. 3. Line up six 6-to 8-ounce (170- to 227-g) glasses. Using an ice cream scoop, spoon 3 to 4 tablespoons of the cheesecake mixture evenly into the bottom of each glass. (Alternatively, transfer the cheesecake mixture to a piping bag or a small zip-top bag with one corner snipped and pipe the mixture into the glasses.) Add a layer of the same amount of apricots to each glass. Repeat so you have two layers of cheesecake mixture and two layers of the apricots, ending with the apricots.) Garnish with the mint, if desired, and serve.

Per Serving
Calories: 132 | fat: 2g | protein: 5g | carbs: 23g | fiber: 2g | sodium: 35mg

Chocolate-Dipped Fruit Bites

Prep time: 10 minutes | Cook time: 0 minutes | Serves 4 to 6

½ cup semisweet chocolate chips
¼ cup low-fat milk
½ teaspoon pure vanilla extract
½ teaspoon ground nutmeg
¼ teaspoon salt

2 kiwis, peeled and sliced
1 cup honeydew melon chunks (about 2-inch chunks)
1 pound (454 g) whole strawberries

1. Place the chocolate chips in a small bowl. 2. In another small bowl, microwave the milk until hot, about 30 seconds. Pour the milk over the chocolate chips and let sit for 1 minute, then whisk until the chocolate is melted and smooth. Stir in the vanilla, nutmeg, and salt and allow to cool for 5 minutes. 3. Line a baking sheet with wax paper. Dip each piece of fruit halfway into the chocolate, tap gently to remove excess chocolate, and place the fruit on the baking sheet. 4. Once all the fruit has been dipped, allow to sit until dry, about 30 minutes. Arrange on a platter and serve.

Per Serving
Calories: 125 | fat: 5g | protein: 2g | carbs: 21g | fiber: 3g | sodium: 110mg

Poached Apricots and Pistachios with Greek Yogurt

Prep time: 2 minutes | Cook time: 18 minutes | Serves 4

½ cup orange juice
2 tablespoons brandy
2 tablespoons honey
¾ cup water
1 cinnamon stick
12 dried apricots

⅓ cup 2% Greek yogurt
2 tablespoons mascarpone cheese
2 tablespoons shelled pistachios

1. Place a saucepan over medium heat and add the orange juice, brandy, honey, and water. Stir to combine, then add the cinnamon stick. 2. Once the honey has dissolved, add the apricots. Bring the mixture to a boil, then cover, reduce the heat to low, and simmer for 15 minutes. 3. While the apricots are simmering, combine the Greek yogurt and mascarpone cheese in a small serving bowl. Stir until smooth, then set aside. 4. When the cooking time for the apricots is complete, uncover, add the pistachios, and continue simmering for 3 more minutes. Remove the pan from the heat. 5. To serve, divide the Greek yogurt–mascarpone cheese mixture into 4 serving bowls and top each serving with 3 apricots, a few pistachios, and 1 teaspoon of the syrup. The apricots and syrup can be stored in a jar at room temperature for up to 1 month.

Per Serving
Calories: 146 | fat: 3g | protein: 4g | carbs: 28g | fiber: 4g | sodium: 62mg

Mediterranean Orange Yogurt Cake

Prep time: 10 minutes | Cook time: 3 to 5 hours | Serves 4 to 6

Nonstick cooking spray
¾ cup all-purpose flour
¾ cup whole-wheat flour
2 teaspoons baking powder
¼ teaspoon salt
1 cup coconut palm sugar
½ cup plain Greek yogurt

½ cup mild-flavored, extra-virgin olive oil
3 large eggs
2 teaspoons vanilla extract
Grated zest of 1 orange
Juice of 1 orange

1. Generously coat a slow cooker with cooking spray, or line the bottom and sides with parchment paper or aluminum foil. 2. In a large bowl, whisk together the all-purpose and whole-wheat flours, baking powder, and salt. 3. In another large bowl, whisk together the sugar, yogurt, olive oil, eggs, vanilla, orange zest, and orange juice until smooth. 4. Add the dry ingredients to the wet ingredients and mix together until well-blended. Pour the batter into the prepared slow cooker. 5. Cover the cooker and cook for 3 to 5 hours on Low heat, or until the middle has set and a knife inserted into it comes out clean.

Per Serving
Calories: 544 | fat: 33g | protein: 11g | carbs: 53g | fiber: 4g | sodium: 482mg

Lightened-Up Baklava Rolls

Prep time: 2 minutes | Cook time: 1 hour 15 minutes | Serves 12

4 ounces (113 g) shelled walnuts
1¼ teaspoons ground cinnamon
1½ teaspoons granulated sugar
5 teaspoons unseasoned breadcrumbs
1 teaspoon extra virgin olive

oil plus 2 tablespoons for brushing
6 phyllo sheets, defrosted
Syrup:
¼ cup water
½ cup granulated sugar
1½ tablespoons fresh lemon juice

1. Preheat the oven to 350ºF (180ºC). 2. Make the syrup by combining the water and sugar in a small pan placed over medium heat. Bring to a boil, cook for 2 minutes, then remove the pan from the heat. Add the lemon juice, and stir. Set aside to cool. 3. In a food processor, combine the walnuts, cinnamon, sugar, breadcrumbs, and 1 teaspoon of the olive oil. Pulse until combined and grainy, but not chunky. 4. Place 1 phyllo sheet on a clean working surface and brush with the olive oil. Place a second sheet on top of the first sheet, brush with olive oil, and repeat the process with a third sheet. Cut the sheets in half crosswise, and then cut each half into 3 pieces crosswise. 5. Scatter 1 tablespoon of the walnut mixture over the phyllo sheet. Start rolling the phyllo and filling into a log shape while simultaneously folding the sides in (like a burrito) until the filling is encased in each piece of dough. The rolls should be about 3½ inches long. Place the rolls one next to the other in a large baking pan, then repeat the process with the remaining 3 phyllo sheets. You should have a total of 12 rolls. 6. Lightly brush the rolls with the remaining olive oil. Place in the oven to bake for 30 minutes or until the rolls turn golden brown, then remove from the oven and promptly drizzle the cold syrup over the top. 7. Let the rolls sit for 20 minutes, then flip them over and let them sit for an additional 20 minutes. Turn them over once more and sprinkle any remining walnut mixture over the rolls before serving. Store uncovered at room temperature for 2 days (to retain crispiness) and then cover with plastic wrap and store at room temperature for up to 10 days.
Per Serving
Calories: 148 | fat: 9g | protein: 2g | carbs: 16g | fiber: 1g | sodium: 53mg

Grilled Pineapple and Melon

Prep time: 10 minutes | Cook time: 7 minutes | Serves 4

8 fresh pineapple rings, rind removed
8 watermelon triangles, with rind

1 tablespoon honey
½ teaspoon freshly ground black pepper

1. Preheat an outdoor grill or a grill pan over high heat. 2. Drizzle the fruit slices with honey and sprinkle one side of each piece with pepper. Grill for 5 minutes, turn, and grill for another 2 minutes. Serve.
Per Serving
Calories: 244 | fat: 1g | protein: 4g | carbs: 62g | fiber: 4g | sodium: 7mg

Strawberry-Pomegranate Molasses Sauce

Prep time: 10 minutes | Cook time: 5 minutes | Serves 6

3 tablespoons olive oil
¼ cup honey
2 pints strawberries, hulled and halved
1 to 2 tablespoons pomegranate

molasses
2 tablespoons chopped fresh mint
Greek yogurt, for serving

1. In a medium saucepan, heat the olive oil over medium heat. Add the strawberries; cook until their juices are released. Stir in the honey and cook for 1 to 2 minutes. Stir in the molasses and mint. Serve warm over Greek yogurt.
Per Serving
Calories: 189 | fat: 7g | protein: 4g | carbs: 24g | fiber: 3g | sodium: 12mg

Red Grapefruit Granita

Prep time: 5 minutes | Cook time: 0 minutes | Serves 4 to 6

3 cups red grapefruit sections
1 cup freshly squeezed red grapefruit juice
¼ cup honey

1 tablespoon freshly squeezed lime juice
Fresh basil leaves for garnish

1. Remove as much pith (white part) and membrane as possible from the grapefruit segments. 2. Combine all ingredients except the basil in a blender or food processor and pulse just until smooth. 3. Pour the mixture into a shallow glass baking dish and place in the freezer for 1 hour. Stir with a fork and freeze for another 30 minutes, then repeat. To serve, scoop into small dessert glasses and garnish with fresh basil leaves.
Per Serving
Calories: 94 | fat: 0g | protein: 1g | carbs: 24g | fiber: 1g | sodium: 1mg

Fruit with Mint and Crème Fraîche

Prep time: 10 minutes | Cook time: 0 minutes | Serves 4

4 cups chopped fresh fruit (such as strawberries, honeydew, cantaloupe, watermelon, and blueberries)
1 cup crème fraîche

1 teaspoon sugar (optional)
¼ cup chopped fresh mint leaves, plus mint sprigs for garnish

1. Evenly divide the fruit among four bowls. 2. In a small bowl, mix the crème fraîche and sugar, if desired. Top the fruit with a generous spoonful or two of the crème fraîche. 3. Sprinkle the mint over each bowl, garnish with 1 to 2 whole sprigs of mint, and serve.
Per Serving
Calories: 164 | fat: 12g | protein: 2g | carbs: 14g | fiber: 3g | sodium: 29mg

Banana Cream Pie Parfaits

Prep time: 10 minutes | Cook time: 0 minutes | Serves 2

1 cup nonfat vanilla pudding
2 low-sugar graham crackers, crushed

1 banana, peeled and sliced
¼ cup walnuts, chopped
Honey for drizzling

1. In small parfait dishes or glasses, layer the ingredients, starting with the pudding and ending with chopped walnuts. 2. You can repeat the layers, depending on the size of the glass and your preferences. 3. Drizzle with the honey. Serve chilled.

Per Serving

Calories: 312 | fat: 11g | protein: 7g | carbs: 50g | fiber: 3g | sodium: 273mg

Cocoa and Coconut Banana Slices

Prep time: 10 minutes | Cook time: 0 minutes | Serves 1

1 banana, peeled and sliced
2 tablespoons unsweetened, shredded coconut

1 tablespoon unsweetened cocoa powder
1 teaspoon honey

1. Lay the banana slices on a parchment-lined baking sheet in a single layer. Put in the freezer for about 10 minutes, until firm but not frozen solid. Mix the coconut with the cocoa powder in a small bowl. 2. Roll the banana slices in honey, followed by the coconut mixture. 3. You can either eat immediately or put back in the freezer for a frozen, sweet treat.

Per Serving

Calories: 187 | fat: 4g | protein: 3g | carbs: 41g | fiber: 6g | sodium: 33mg

Almond Rice Pudding

Prep time: 5 minutes | Cook time: 45 minutes | Serves 8

1 cup Arborio rice
¼ teaspoon kosher salt
5 cups unsweetened almond milk
2 tablespoons chopped preserved lemon or dried

lemons
½ cup sugar
2 teaspoons vanilla extract
2 tablespoons slivered almonds, toasted (optional)

1. In a medium saucepan, combine the rice, salt, and 2 cups water. Bring to a boil. Reduce the heat to low-medium, cover the pan with the lid ajar, and cook until the water has been almost completely absorbed, 6 to 8 minutes, stirring occasionally. 2. Stir in the almond milk, sugar, dried or preserved lemon, and vanilla. Bring the mixture to a simmer, stirring occasionally, and cook until the rice is tender and the mixture has thickened, 30 to 35 minutes. Let cool slightly before serving. 3. Serve warm, topped with toasted almonds, if desired.

Per Serving

Calories: 203 | fat: 10g | protein: 9g | carbs: 23g | fiber: 4g | sodium: 146mg

Cucumber-Lime Popsicles

Prep time: 5 minutes | Cook time: 0 minutes | Serves 4 to 6

2 cups cold water
1 cucumber, peeled

¼ cup honey
Juice of 1 lime

1. In a blender, purée the water, cucumber, honey, and lime juice. Pour into popsicle molds, freeze, and enjoy on a hot summer day!

Per Serving

Calories: 49 | fat: 0g | protein: 0g | carbs: 13g | fiber: 0g | sodium: 3mg

Fresh Figs with Chocolate Sauce

Prep time: 5 minutes | Cook time: 0 minutes | Serves 4

¼ cup honey
2 tablespoons cocoa powder

8 fresh figs

1. Combine the honey and cocoa powder in a small bowl, and mix well to form a syrup. 2. Cut the figs in half and place cut side up. Drizzle with the syrup and serve.

Per Serving

Calories: 112 | fat: 1g | protein: 1g | carbs: 30g | fiber: 3g | sodium: 3mg

Frozen Raspberry Delight

Prep time: 10 minutes | Cook time: 0 minutes | Serves 2

3 cups frozen raspberries
1 peach, peeled and pitted

1 mango, peeled and pitted
1 teaspoon honey

1. Add all ingredients to a blender and purée, only adding enough water to keep the mixture moving and your blender from overworking itself. Freeze for 10 minutes to firm up if desired.

Per Serving

Calories: 237 | fat: 2g | protein: 4g | carbs: 57g | fiber: 16g | sodium: 4mg

Grilled Stone Fruit

Prep time: 15 minutes | Cook time: 6 minutes | Serves 2

2 peaches, halved and pitted
2 plums, halved and pitted
3 apricots, halved and pitted

½ cup low-fat ricotta cheese
2 tablespoons honey

1. Heat grill to medium heat. 2. Oil the grates or spray with cooking spray. 3. Place the fruit cut side down on the grill, and grill for 2–3 minutes per side, until lightly charred and soft. 4. Serve warm with the ricotta and drizzle with honey.

Per Serving

Calories: 263 | fat: 6g | protein: 10g | carbs: 48g | fiber: 4g | sodium: 63mg

Pears with Blue Cheese and Walnuts

Prep time: 10 minutes | Cook time: 0 minutes | Serves 1

1 to 2 pears, cored and sliced into 12 slices
¼ cup blue cheese crumbles
12 walnut halves
1 tablespoon honey

1. Lay the pear slices on a plate, and top with the blue cheese crumbles. Top each slice with 1 walnut, and drizzle with honey.
2. Serve and enjoy!

Per Serving
Calories: 420 | fat: 29g | protein: 12g | carbs: 35g | fiber: 6g | sodium: 389mg

Slow-Cooked Fruit Medley

Prep time: 10 minutes | Cook time: 3 to 5 hours | Serves 4 to 6

Nonstick cooking spray
1 pound (454 g) fresh or frozen fruit of your choice, stemmed and chopped as needed
⅓ cup almond milk or low-sugar fruit juice of your choice
½ cup honey

1. Generously coat a slow cooker with cooking spray, or line the bottom and sides with parchment paper or aluminum foil.
2. In a slow cooker, combine the fruit and milk. Gently stir to mix. 3. Drizzle the fruit with the honey. 4. Cover the cooker and cook for 3 to 5 hours on Low heat.

Per Serving
Calories: 192 | fat: 0g | protein: 1g | carbs: 50g | fiber: 3g | sodium: 27mg

Ricotta with Balsamic Cherries and Black Pepper

Prep time: 10 minutes | Cook time: 0 minutes | Serves 4

1 cup (8 ounces / 227 g) ricotta
2 tablespoons honey
1 teaspoon vanilla extract
3 cups pitted sweet cherries (thawed if frozen), halved
1½ teaspoons aged balsamic vinegar
Pinch of freshly ground black pepper

1. In a food processor, combine the ricotta, honey, and vanilla and process until smooth. Transfer the mixture to a medium bowl, cover, and refrigerate for 1 hour. 2. In a small bowl, combine the cherries, vinegar, and pepper and stir to mix well. Chill along with the ricotta mixture. 3. To serve, spoon the ricotta mixture into 4 serving bowls or glasses. Top with the cherries, dividing them equally and spooning a bit of the accumulated juice over the top of each bowl. Serve chilled.

Per Serving
Calories: 236 | fat: 5g | protein: 7g | carbs: 42g | fiber: 1g | sodium: 93mg

Greek Yogurt with Honey and Pomegranates

Prep time: 5 minutes | Cook time: 0 minutes | Serves 4

4 cups plain full-fat Greek yogurt
½ cup pomegranate seeds
¼ cup honey
Sugar, for topping (optional)

1. Evenly divide the yogurt among four bowls. Evenly divide the pomegranate seeds among the bowls and drizzle each with the honey. 2. Sprinkle each bowl with a pinch of sugar, if desired, and serve.

Per Serving
Calories: 232 | fat: 8g | protein: 9g | carbs: 33g | fiber: 1g | sodium: 114mg

Toasted Almonds with Honey

Prep time: 15 minutes | Cook time: 5 minutes | Serves 4

½ cup raw almonds
3 tablespoons good-quality
honey, plus more if desired

1. Fill a medium saucepan three-quarters full with water and bring to a boil over high heat. Add the almonds and cook for 1 minute. Drain the almonds in a fine-mesh sieve and rinse them under cold water to cool and stop the cooking. Remove the skins from the almonds by rubbing them in a clean kitchen towel. Place the almonds on a paper towel to dry. 2. In the same saucepan, combine the almonds and honey and cook over medium heat until the almonds get a little golden, 4 to 5 minutes. Remove from the heat and let cool completely, about 15 minutes, before serving or storing.

Per Serving
Calories: 151 | fat: 9g | protein: 4g | carbs: 17g | fiber: 2g | sodium: 1mg

Grilled Peaches with Greek Yogurt

Prep time: 5 minutes | Cook time: 30 minutes | Serves 4

4 ripe peaches, halved and pitted
2 tablespoons olive oil
1 teaspoon ground cinnamon,
plus extra for topping
2 cups plain full-fat Greek yogurt
¼ cup honey, for drizzling

1. Preheat the oven to 350°F (180°C). 2. Place the peaches in a baking dish, cut-side up. 3. In a small bowl, stir together the olive oil and cinnamon, then brush the mixture over the peach halves. 4. Bake the peaches for about 30 minutes, until they are soft. 5. Top the peaches with the yogurt and drizzle them with the honey, then serve.

Per Serving
Calories: 259 | fat: 11g | protein: 6g | carbs: 38g | fiber: 3g | sodium: 57mg

Strawberry Ricotta Parfaits

Prep time: 10 minutes | Cook time: 0 minutes | Serves 4

2 cups ricotta cheese
¼ cup honey
2 cups sliced strawberries
1 teaspoon sugar

Toppings such as sliced almonds, fresh mint, and lemon zest (optional)

1. In a medium bowl, whisk together the ricotta and honey until well blended. Place the bowl in the refrigerator for a few minutes to firm up the mixture. 2. In a medium bowl, toss together the strawberries and sugar. 3. In each of four small glasses, layer 1 tablespoon of the ricotta mixture, then top with a layer of the strawberries and finally another layer of the ricotta. 4. Finish with your preferred toppings, if desired, then serve.

Per Serving

Calories: 311 | fat: 16g | protein: 14g | carbs: 29g | fiber: 2g | sodium: 106mg

Figs with Mascarpone and Honey

Prep time: 5 minutes | Cook time: 5 minutes | Serves 4

⅓ cup walnuts, chopped
8 fresh figs, halved
¼ cup mascarpone cheese

1 tablespoon honey
¼ teaspoon flaked sea salt

1. In a skillet over medium heat, toast the walnuts, stirring often, 3 to 5 minutes. 2. Arrange the figs cut-side up on a plate or platter. Using your finger, make a small depression in the cut side of each fig and fill with mascarpone cheese. Sprinkle with a bit of the walnuts, drizzle with the honey, and add a tiny pinch of sea salt.

Per Serving

Calories: 200 | fat: 13g | protein: 3g | carbs: 24g | fiber: 3g | sodium: 105mg

Greek Yogurt Chocolate "Mousse" with Berries

Prep time: 15 minutes | Cook time: 0 minutes | Serves 4

2 cups plain Greek yogurt
¼ cup heavy cream
¼ cup pure maple syrup
3 tablespoons unsweetened cocoa powder

2 teaspoons vanilla extract
¼ teaspoon kosher salt
1 cup fresh mixed berries
¼ cup chocolate chips

1. Place the yogurt, cream, maple syrup, cocoa powder, vanilla, and salt in the bowl of a stand mixer or use a large bowl with an electric hand mixer. Mix at medium-high speed until fluffy, about 5 minutes. 2. Spoon evenly among 4 bowls and put in the refrigerator to set for at least 15 minutes. 3. Serve each bowl with ¼ cup mixed berries and 1 tablespoon chocolate chips.

Per Serving

Calories: 300 | fat: 11g | protein: 16g | carbs: 35g | fiber: 3g | sodium: 60mg

Ricotta Cheesecake

Prep time: 2 minutes | Cook time: 45 to 50 minutes | Serves 12

2 cups skim or fat-free ricotta cheese (one 15-ounce / 425-g container)
1¼ cups sugar

1 teaspoon vanilla extract
6 eggs
Zest of 1 orange

1. Preheat the oven to 375ºF (190ºC). Grease an 8-inch square baking pan with butter or cooking spray. 2. In a medium bowl, stir together the ricotta and sugar. Add the eggs one at a time until well incorporated. Stir in the vanilla and orange zest. 3. Pour the batter into the prepared pan. Bake for 45 to 50 minutes, until set. Let cool in the pan for 20 minutes. Serve warm.

Per Serving

Calories: 160 | fat: 5g | protein: 12g | carbs: 15g | fiber: 0g | sodium: 388mg

Whipped Greek Yogurt with Chocolate

Prep time: 10 minutes | Cook time: 0 minutes | Serves 4

4 cups plain full-fat Greek yogurt
½ cup heavy (whipping) cream

2 ounces (57 g) dark chocolate (at least 70% cacao), grated, for topping

1. In the bowl of a stand mixer fitted with the whisk attachment or in a large bowl using a handheld mixer, whip the yogurt and cream for about 5 minutes, or until peaks form. 2. Evenly divide the whipped yogurt mixture among bowls and top with the grated chocolate. Serve.

Per Serving

Calories: 337 | fat: 25g | protein: 10g | carbs: 19g | fiber: 2g | sodium: 127mg

Honey Ricotta with Espresso and Chocolate Chips

Prep time: 5 minutes | Cook time: 0 minutes | Serves 2

8 ounces (227 g) ricotta cheese
2 tablespoons honey
2 tablespoons espresso, chilled

or room temperature
1 teaspoon dark chocolate chips or chocolate shavings

1. In a medium bowl, whip together the ricotta cheese and honey until light and smooth, 4 to 5 minutes. 2. Spoon the ricotta cheese-honey mixture evenly into 2 dessert bowls. Drizzle 1 tablespoon espresso into each dish and sprinkle with chocolate chips or shavings.

Per Serving

Calories: 235 | fat: 10g | protein: 13g | carbs: 25g | fiber: 0g | sodium: 115mg

Minty Cantaloupe Granita

Prep time: 10 minutes | Cook time: 5 minutes | Serves 4

½ cup plus 2 tablespoons honey
¼ cup water
2 tablespoons fresh mint leaves, plus more for garnish

1 medium cantaloupe (about 4 pounds / 1.8 kg) peeled, seeded, and cut into 1-inch chunks

1. In a small saucepan set over low heat, combine the honey and water and cook, stirring, until the honey has fully dissolved. Stir in the mint and remove from the heat. Set aside to cool. 2. In a food processor, process the cantaloupe until very smooth. Transfer to a medium bowl. Remove the mint leaves from the syrup and discard them. Pour the syrup into the cantaloupe purée and stir to mix. 3. Transfer the mixture into a 7-by-12-inch glass baking dish and freeze, stirring with a fork every 30 minutes, for 3 to 4 hours, until it is frozen, but still grainy. Serve chilled, scooped into glasses and garnished with mint leaves.

Per Serving
Calories: 174 | fat: 0g | protein: 1g | carbs: 47g | fiber: 1g | sodium: 9mg

Date and Honey Almond Milk Ice Cream

Prep time: 10 minutes | Cook time: 5 minutes | Serves 4

¾ cup (about 4 ounces / 113 g) pitted dates
¼ cup honey
½ cup water

2 cups cold unsweetened almond milk
2 teaspoons vanilla extract

1. Combine the dates and water in a small saucepan and bring to a boil over high heat. Remove the pan from the heat, cover, and let stand for 15 minutes. 2. In a blender, combine the almond milk, dates, the date soaking water, honey, and the vanilla and process until very smooth. 3. Cover the blender jar and refrigerate the mixture until cold, at least 1 hour. 4. Transfer the mixture to an electric ice cream maker and freeze according to the manufacturer's instructions. 5. Serve immediately or transfer to a freezer-safe storage container and freeze for 4 hours (or longer). Serve frozen.

Per Serving
Calories: 106 | fat: 2g | protein: 1g | carbs: 23g | fiber: 3g | sodium: 92mg

Roasted Plums with Nut Crumble

Prep time: 5 minutes | Cook time: 25 minutes | Serves 4

¼ cup honey
¼ cup freshly squeezed orange juice
4 large plums, halved and pitted
¼ cup whole-wheat pastry flour

1 tablespoon pure maple sugar
1 tablespoon nuts, coarsely chopped (your choice; I like almonds, pecans, and walnuts)
1½ teaspoons canola oil
½ cup plain Greek yogurt

1. Preheat the oven to 400°F (205°C). Combine the honey and orange juice in a square baking dish. Place the plums, cut-side down, in the dish. Roast about 15 minutes, and then turn the plums over and roast an additional 10 minutes, or until tender and juicy. 2. In a medium bowl, combine the flour, maple sugar, nuts, and canola oil and mix well. Spread on a small baking sheet and bake alongside the plums, tossing once, until golden brown, about 5 minutes. Set aside until the plums have finished cooking. 3. Serve the plums drizzled with pan juices and topped with the nut crumble and a dollop of yogurt.

Per Serving
Calories: 175 | fat: 3g | protein: 4g | carbs: 36g | fiber: 2g | sodium: 10mg

Greek Yogurt Ricotta Mousse

Prep time: 1 hour 5 minutes | Cook time: 0 minutes | Serves 4

9 ounces (255 g) full-fat ricotta cheese
4½ ounces (128 g) 2% Greek yogurt

3 teaspoons fresh lemon juice
½ teaspoon pure vanilla extract
2 tablespoons granulated sugar

1. Combine all of the ingredients in a food processor. Blend until smooth, about 1 minute. 2. Divide the mousse between 4 serving glasses. Cover and transfer to the refrigerator to chill for 1 hour before serving. Store covered in the refrigerator for up to 4 days.

Per Serving
Calories: 156 | fat: 8g | protein: 10g | carbs: 10g | fiber: 0g | sodium: 65mg

Chapter 7 Fish and Seafood

Chilean Sea Bass with Olive Relish

Prep time: 10 minutes | Cook time: 10 minutes | Serves 2

Olive oil spray
2 (6-ounce / 170-g) Chilean sea bass fillets or other firm-fleshed white fish
3 tablespoons extra-virgin olive oil
½ teaspoon ground cumin
½ teaspoon kosher salt
½ teaspoon black pepper
⅓ cup pitted green olives, diced
¼ cup finely diced onion
1 teaspoon chopped capers

1. Spray the air fryer basket with the olive oil spray. Drizzle the fillets with the olive oil and sprinkle with the cumin, salt, and pepper. Place the fish in the air fryer basket. Set the air fryer to 325°F (163°C) for 10 minutes, or until the fish flakes easily with a fork. 2. Meanwhile, in a small bowl, stir together the olives, onion, and capers. 3. Serve the fish topped with the relish.

Per Serving
Calories: 379 | fat: 26g | protein: 32g | carbs: 3g | fiber: 1g | sodium: 581mg

Black Cod with Grapes and Kale

Prep time: 10 minutes | Cook time: 15 minutes | Serves 2

2 (6- to 8-ounce / 170- to 227-g) fillets of black cod
Salt and freshly ground black pepper, to taste
Olive oil
1 cup grapes, halved
1 small bulb fennel, sliced
¼-inch thick
½ cup pecans
3 cups shredded kale
2 teaspoons white balsamic vinegar or white wine vinegar
2 tablespoons extra-virgin olive oil

1. Preheat the air fryer to 400°F (204°C). 2. Season the cod fillets with salt and pepper and drizzle, brush or spray a little olive oil on top. Place the fish, presentation side up (skin side down), into the air fryer basket. Air fry for 10 minutes. 3. When the fish has finished cooking, remove the fillets to a side plate and loosely tent with foil to rest. 4. Toss the grapes, fennel and pecans in a bowl with a drizzle of olive oil and season with salt and pepper. Add the grapes, fennel and pecans to the air fryer basket and air fry for 5 minutes at 400°F (204°C), shaking the basket once during the cooking time. 5. Transfer the grapes, fennel and pecans to a bowl with the kale. Dress the kale with the balsamic vinegar and olive oil, season to taste with salt and pepper and serve along side the cooked fish.

Per Serving
Calories: 509 | fat: 33g | protein: 31g | carbs: 28g | fiber: 8g | sodium: 587mg

Tuna Steaks with Olive Tapenade

Prep time: 10 minutes | Cook time: 10 minutes | Serves 4

4 (6-ounce / 170-g) ahi tuna steaks
1 tablespoon olive oil
Salt and freshly ground black pepper, to taste
½ lemon, sliced into 4 wedges
Olive Tapenade:
½ cup pitted kalamata olives
1 tablespoon olive oil
1 tablespoon chopped fresh parsley
1 clove garlic
2 teaspoons red wine vinegar
1 teaspoon capers, drained

1. Preheat the air fryer to 400°F (204°C). 2. Drizzle the tuna steaks with the olive oil and sprinkle with salt and black pepper. Arrange the tuna steaks in a single layer in the air fryer basket. Pausing to turn the steaks halfway through the cooking time, air fry for 10 minutes until the fish is firm. 3. To make the tapenade: In a food processor fitted with a metal blade, combine the olives, olive oil, parsley, garlic, vinegar, and capers. Pulse until the mixture is finely chopped, pausing to scrape down the sides of the bowl if necessary. Spoon the tapenade over the top of the tuna steaks and serve with lemon wedges.

Per Serving
Calories: 269 | fat: 9g | protein: 42g | carbs: 2g | fiber: 1g | sodium: 252mg

Marinated Swordfish Skewers

Prep time: 30 minutes | Cook time: 6 to 8 minutes | Serves 4

1 pound (454 g) filleted swordfish
¼ cup avocado oil
2 tablespoons freshly squeezed lemon juice
1 tablespoon minced fresh
parsley
2 teaspoons Dijon mustard
Sea salt and freshly ground black pepper, to taste
3 ounces (85 g) cherry tomatoes

1. Cut the fish into 1½-inch chunks, picking out any remaining bones. 2. In a large bowl, whisk together the oil, lemon juice, parsley, and Dijon mustard. Season to taste with salt and pepper. Add the fish and toss to coat the pieces. Cover and marinate the fish chunks in the refrigerator for 30 minutes. 3. Remove the fish from the marinade. Thread the fish and cherry tomatoes on 4 skewers, alternating as you go. 4. Set the air fryer to 400°F (204°C). Place the skewers in the air fryer basket and air fry for 3 minutes. Flip the skewers and cook for 3 to 5 minutes longer, until the fish is cooked through and an instant-read thermometer reads 140°F (60°C).

Per Serving
Calories: 291 | fat: 21g | protein: 23g | carbs: 2g | fiber: 0g | sodium: 121mg

Salmon with Garlicky Broccoli Rabe and White Beans

Prep time: 20 minutes | Cook time: 10 minutes | Serves 4

2 tablespoons extra-virgin olive oil, plus extra for drizzling
4 garlic cloves, sliced thin
½ cup chicken or vegetable broth
¼ teaspoon red pepper flakes
1 lemon, sliced ¼ inch thick, plus lemon wedges for serving
4 (6-ounce / 170-g) skinless salmon fillets, 1½ inches thick
½ teaspoon table salt
¼ teaspoon pepper
1 pound (454 g) broccoli rabe, trimmed and cut into 1-inch pieces
1 (15-ounce / 425-g) can cannellini beans, rinsed

1. Using highest sauté function, cook oil and garlic in Instant Pot until garlic is fragrant and light golden brown, about 3 minutes. Using slotted spoon, transfer garlic to paper towel–lined plate and season with salt to taste; set aside for serving. Turn off Instant Pot, then stir in broth and pepper flakes. 2. Fold sheet of aluminum foil into 16 by 6-inch sling. Arrange lemon slices widthwise in 2 rows across center of sling. Sprinkle flesh side of salmon with salt and pepper, then arrange skinned side down on top of lemon slices. Using sling, lower salmon into Instant Pot; allow narrow edges of sling to rest along sides of insert. Lock lid in place and close pressure release valve. Select high pressure cook function and cook for 3 minutes. 3. Turn off Instant Pot and quick-release pressure. Carefully remove lid, allowing steam to escape away from you. Using sling, transfer salmon to large plate. Tent with foil and let rest while preparing broccoli rabe mixture. 4. Stir broccoli rabe and beans into cooking liquid, partially cover, and cook, using highest sauté function, until broccoli rabe is tender, about 5 minutes. Season with salt and pepper to taste. Gently lift and tilt salmon fillets with spatula to remove lemon slices. Serve salmon with broccoli rabe mixture and lemon wedges, sprinkling individual portions with garlic chips and drizzling with extra oil.

Per Serving
Calories: 510 | fat: 30g | protein: 43g | carbs: 15g | fiber: 6g | sodium: 650mg

Sesame-Crusted Tuna Steak

Prep time: 5 minutes | Cook time: 8 minutes | Serves 2

2 (6-ounce / 170-g) tuna steaks
1 tablespoon coconut oil, melted
½ teaspoon garlic powder
2 teaspoons white sesame seeds
2 teaspoons black sesame seeds

1. Brush each tuna steak with coconut oil and sprinkle with garlic powder. 2. In a large bowl, mix sesame seeds and then press each tuna steak into them, covering the steak as completely as possible. Place tuna steaks into the air fryer basket. 3. Adjust the temperature to 400°F (204°C) and air fry for 8 minutes. 4. Flip the steaks halfway through the cooking time. Steaks will be well-done at 145°F (63°C) internal temperature. Serve warm.

Per Serving
Calories: 281 | fat: 11g | protein: 43g | carbs: 1g | fiber: 1g | sodium: 80mg

Braised Striped Bass with Zucchini and Tomatoes

Prep time: 20 minutes | Cook time: 16 minutes | Serves 4

2 tablespoons extra-virgin olive oil, divided, plus extra for drizzling
3 zucchini (8 ounces / 227 g each), halved lengthwise and sliced ¼ inch thick
1 onion, chopped
¾ teaspoon table salt, divided
3 garlic cloves, minced
1 teaspoon minced fresh oregano or ¼ teaspoon dried
¼ teaspoon red pepper flakes
1 (28-ounce / 794-g) can whole peeled tomatoes, drained with juice reserved, halved
1½ pounds (680 g) skinless striped bass, 1½ inches thick, cut into 2-inch pieces
¼ teaspoon pepper
2 tablespoons chopped pitted kalamata olives
2 tablespoons shredded fresh mint

1. Using highest sauté function, heat 1 tablespoon oil in Instant Pot for 5 minutes (or until just smoking). Add zucchini and cook until tender, about 5 minutes; transfer to bowl and set aside. 2. Add remaining 1 tablespoon oil, onion, and ¼ teaspoon salt to now-empty pot and cook, using highest sauté function, until onion is softened, about 5 minutes. Stir in garlic, oregano, and pepper flakes and cook until fragrant, about 30 seconds. Stir in tomatoes and reserved juice. 3. Sprinkle bass with remaining ½ teaspoon salt and pepper. Nestle bass into tomato mixture and spoon some of cooking liquid on top of pieces. Lock lid in place and close pressure release valve. Select high pressure cook function and set cook time for 0 minutes. Once Instant Pot has reached pressure, immediately turn off pot and quick-release pressure. Carefully remove lid, allowing steam to escape away from you. 4. Transfer bass to plate, tent with aluminum foil, and let rest while finishing vegetables. Stir zucchini into pot and let sit until heated through, about 5 minutes. Stir in olives and season with salt and pepper to taste. Serve bass with vegetables, sprinkling individual portions with mint and drizzling with extra oil.

Per Serving
Calories: 302 | fat: 12g | protein: 34g | carbs: 15g | fiber: 6g | sodium: 618mg

Blackened Red Snapper

Prep time: 13 minutes | Cook time: 8 to 10 minutes | Serves 4

1½ teaspoons black pepper
¼ teaspoon thyme
¼ teaspoon garlic powder
⅛ teaspoon cayenne pepper
1 teaspoon olive oil
4 (4-ounce / 113-g) red snapper fillet portions, skin on
4 thin slices lemon
Cooking spray

1. Mix the spices and oil together to make a paste. Rub into both sides of the fish. 2. Spray the air fryer basket with nonstick cooking spray and lay snapper steaks in basket, skin-side down. 3. Place a lemon slice on each piece of fish. 4. Roast at 390°F (199°C) for 8 to 10 minutes. The fish will not flake when done, but it should be white through the center.

Per Serving
Calories: 128 | fat: 3g | protein: 23g | carbs: 1g | fiber: 1g | sodium: 73mg

Honey-Balsamic Salmon

Prep time: 5 minutes | Cook time: 8 minutes | Serves 2

Oil, for spraying
2 (6-ounce / 170-g) salmon fillets
¼ cup balsamic vinegar
2 tablespoons honey
2 teaspoons red pepper flakes
2 teaspoons olive oil
½ teaspoon salt
¼ teaspoon freshly ground black pepper

1. Line the air fryer basket with parchment and spray lightly with oil. 2. Place the salmon in the prepared basket. 3. In a small bowl, whisk together the balsamic vinegar, honey, red pepper flakes, olive oil, salt, and black pepper. Brush the mixture over the salmon. 4. Roast at 390°F (199°C) for 7 to 8 minutes, or until the internal temperature reaches 145°F (63°C). Serve immediately.

Per Serving
Calories: 353 | fat: 12g | protein: 35g | carbs: 24g | fiber: 1g | sodium: 590mg

Shrimp and Asparagus Risotto

Prep time: 15 minutes | Cook time: 20 minutes | Serves 4

¼ cup extra-virgin olive oil, divided
8 ounces (227 g) asparagus, trimmed and cut on bias into 1-inch lengths
½ onion, chopped fine
¼ teaspoon table salt
1½ cups Arborio rice
3 garlic cloves, minced
½ cup dry white wine
3 cups chicken or vegetable broth, plus extra as needed
1 pound (454 g) large shrimp (26 to 30 per pound), peeled and deveined
2 ounces (57 g) Parmesan cheese, grated (1 cup)
1 tablespoon lemon juice
1 tablespoon minced fresh chives

1. Using highest sauté function, heat 1 tablespoon oil in Instant Pot until shimmering. Add asparagus, partially cover, and cook until just crisp-tender, about 4 minutes. Using slotted spoon, transfer asparagus to bowl; set aside. 2. Add onion, 2 tablespoons oil, and salt to now-empty pot and cook, using highest sauté function, until onion is softened, about 5 minutes. Stir in rice and garlic and cook until grains are translucent around edges, about 3 minutes. Stir in wine and cook until nearly evaporated, about 1 minute. 3. Stir in broth, scraping up any rice that sticks to bottom of pot. Lock lid in place and close pressure release valve. Select high pressure cook function and cook for 7 minutes. 4. Turn off Instant Pot and quick-release pressure. Carefully remove lid, allowing steam to escape away from you. Stir shrimp and asparagus into risotto, cover, and let sit until shrimp are opaque throughout, 5 to 7 minutes. Add Parmesan and remaining 1 tablespoon oil, and stir vigorously until risotto becomes creamy. Adjust consistency with extra hot broth as needed. Stir in lemon juice and season with salt and pepper to taste. Sprinkle individual portions with chives before serving.

Per Serving
Calories: 707 | fat: 24g | protein: 45g | carbs: 76g | fiber: 5g | sodium: 360mg

Maple Balsamic Glazed Salmon

Prep time: 5 minutes | Cook time: 10 minutes | Serves 4

4 (6-ounce / 170-g) fillets of salmon
Salt and freshly ground black pepper, to taste
Vegetable oil
¼ cup pure maple syrup
3 tablespoons balsamic vinegar
1 teaspoon Dijon mustard

1. Preheat the air fryer to 400°F (204°C). 2. Season the salmon well with salt and freshly ground black pepper. Spray or brush the bottom of the air fryer basket with vegetable oil and place the salmon fillets inside. Air fry the salmon for 5 minutes. 3. While the salmon is air frying, combine the maple syrup, balsamic vinegar and Dijon mustard in a small saucepan over medium heat and stir to blend well. Let the mixture simmer while the fish is cooking. It should start to thicken slightly, but keep your eye on it so it doesn't burn. 4. Brush the glaze on the salmon fillets and air fry for an additional 5 minutes. The salmon should feel firm to the touch when finished and the glaze should be nicely browned on top. Brush a little more glaze on top before removing and serving with rice and vegetables, or a nice green salad.

Per Serving
Calories: 279 | fat: 8g | protein: 35g | carbs: 15g | fiber: 0g | sodium: 146mg

Spicy Trout over Sautéed Mediterranean Salad

Prep time: 10 minutes | Cook time: 30 minutes | Serves 4

2 pounds (907 g) rainbow trout fillets (about 6 fillets)
Salt
Ground white pepper
1 tablespoon extra-virgin olive oil
1 pound (454 g) asparagus
4 medium golden potatoes, thinly sliced
1 scallion, thinly sliced, green and white parts separated
1 garlic clove, finely minced
1 large carrot, thinly sliced
2 Roma tomatoes, chopped
8 pitted kalamata olives, chopped
¼ cup ground cumin
2 tablespoons dried parsley
2 tablespoons paprika
1 tablespoon vegetable bouillon seasoning
½ cup dry white wine

1. Lightly season the fish with salt and white pepper and set aside. 2. In a large sauté pan or skillet, heat the oil over medium heat. Add and stir in the asparagus, potatoes, the white part of the scallions, and garlic to the hot oil. Cook and stir for 5 minutes, until fragrant. Add the carrot, tomatoes, and olives; continue to cook for 5 to 7 minutes, until the carrots are slightly tender. 3. Sprinkle the cumin, parsley, paprika, and vegetable bouillon seasoning over the pan. Season with salt. Stir to incorporate. Put the trout on top of the vegetables and add the wine to cover the vegetables. 4. Reduce the heat to low, cover, and cook for 5 to 7 minutes, until the fish flakes easily with a fork and juices run clear. Top with scallion greens and serve.

Per Serving
Calories: 493 | fat: 19g | protein: 40g | carbs: 41g | fiber: 7g | sodium: 736mg

Cucumber and Salmon Salad

Prep time: 10 minutes | Cook time: 8 to 10 minutes | Serves 2

1 pound (454 g) salmon fillet
1½ tablespoons olive oil, divided
1 tablespoon sherry vinegar
1 tablespoon capers, rinsed and drained
1 seedless cucumber, thinly

sliced
¼ Vidalia onion, thinly sliced
2 tablespoons chopped fresh parsley
Salt and freshly ground black pepper, to taste

1. Preheat the air fryer to 400°F (204°C). 2. Lightly coat the salmon with ½ tablespoon of the olive oil. Place skin-side down in the air fryer basket and air fry for 8 to 10 minutes until the fish is opaque and flakes easily with a fork. Transfer the salmon to a plate and let cool to room temperature. Remove the skin and carefully flake the fish into bite-size chunks. 3. In a small bowl, whisk the remaining 1 tablespoon olive oil and the vinegar until thoroughly combined. Add the flaked fish, capers, cucumber, onion, and parsley. Season to taste with salt and freshly ground black pepper. Toss gently to coat. Serve immediately or cover and refrigerate for up to 4 hours.

Per Serving

Calories: 399 | fat: 20g | protein: 47g | carbs: 4g | fiber: 1g | sodium: 276mg

Salmon with Lemon-Garlic Mashed Cauliflower

Prep time: 15 minutes | Cook time: 10 minutes | Serves 4

2 tablespoons extra-virgin olive oil
4 garlic cloves, peeled and smashed
½ cup chicken or vegetable broth
¾ teaspoon table salt, divided
1 large head cauliflower (3 pounds / 1.4 kg), cored and cut

into 2-inch florets
4 (6-ounce / 170-g) skinless salmon fillets, 1½ inches thick
½ teaspoon ras el hanout
½ teaspoon grated lemon zest
3 scallions, sliced thin
1 tablespoon sesame seeds, toasted

1. Using highest sauté function, cook oil and garlic in Instant Pot until garlic is fragrant and light golden brown, about 3 minutes. Turn off Instant Pot, then stir in broth and ¼ teaspoon salt. Arrange cauliflower in pot in even layer. 2. Fold sheet of aluminum foil into 16 by 6-inch sling. Sprinkle flesh side of salmon with ras el hanout and remaining ½ teaspoon salt, then arrange skinned side down in center of sling. Using sling, lower salmon into Instant Pot on top of cauliflower; allow narrow edges of sling to rest along sides of insert. Lock lid in place and close pressure release valve. Select high pressure cook function and cook for 2 minutes. 3. Turn off Instant Pot and quick-release pressure. Carefully remove lid, allowing steam to escape away from you. Using sling, transfer salmon to large plate. Tent with foil and let rest while finishing cauliflower. 4. Using potato masher, mash cauliflower mixture until no large chunks remain. Using highest sauté function, cook cauliflower, stirring often, until slightly thickened, about 3 minutes. Stir in lemon zest and season with salt and pepper to taste. Serve

salmon with cauliflower, sprinkling individual portions with scallions and sesame seeds.

Per Serving

Calories: 480 | fat: 31g | protein: 38g | carbs: 9g | fiber: 3g | sodium: 650mg

Salmon with Tarragon-Dijon Sauce

Prep time: 5 minutes | Cook time: 15 minutes | Serves 4

1¼ pounds (567 g) salmon fillet (skin on or removed), cut into 4 equal pieces
¼ cup avocado oil mayonnaise
¼ cup Dijon or stone-ground mustard
Zest and juice of ½ lemon
2 tablespoons chopped fresh

tarragon or 1 to 2 teaspoons dried tarragon
½ teaspoon salt
¼ teaspoon freshly ground black pepper
4 tablespoons extra-virgin olive oil, for serving

1. Preheat the oven to 425°F (220°C). Line a baking sheet with parchment paper. 2. Place the salmon pieces, skin-side down, on a baking sheet. 3. In a small bowl, whisk together the mayonnaise, mustard, lemon zest and juice, tarragon, salt, and pepper. Top the salmon evenly with the sauce mixture. 4. Bake until slightly browned on top and slightly translucent in the center, 10 to 12 minutes, depending on the thickness of the salmon. Remove from the oven and leave on the baking sheet for 10 minutes. Drizzle each fillet with 1 tablespoon olive oil before serving.

Per Serving

Calories: 343 | fat: 23g | protein: 30g | carbs: 4g | fiber: 1g | sodium: 585mg

Shrimp in Creamy Pesto over Zoodles

Prep time: 10 minutes | Cook time: 10 minutes | Serves 4

1 pound (454 g) peeled and deveined fresh shrimp
Salt
Freshly ground black pepper
2 tablespoons extra-virgin olive oil
½ small onion, slivered
8 ounces (227 g) store-bought

jarred pesto
¾ cup crumbled goat or feta cheese, plus more for serving
6 cups zucchini noodles (from about 2 large zucchini), for serving
¼ cup chopped flat-leaf Italian parsley, for garnish

1. In a bowl, season the shrimp with salt and pepper and set aside. 2. In a large skillet, heat the olive oil over medium-high heat. Sauté the onion until just golden, 5 to 6 minutes. 3. Reduce the heat to low and add the pesto and cheese, whisking to combine and melt the cheese. Bring to a low simmer and add the shrimp. Reduce the heat back to low and cover. Cook until the shrimp is cooked through and pink, another 3 to 4 minutes. 4. Serve warm over zucchini noodles, garnishing with chopped parsley and additional crumbled cheese, if desired.

Per Serving

Calories: 608 | fat: 49g | protein: 37g | carbs: 9g | fiber: 3g | sodium: 564mg

Mediterranean-Style Cod

Prep time: 5 minutes | Cook time: 12 minutes | Serves 4

4 (6-ounce / 170-g) cod fillets	¼ teaspoon salt
3 tablespoons fresh lemon juice	6 cherry tomatoes, halved
1 tablespoon olive oil	¼ cup pitted and sliced kalamata olives

1. Place cod into an ungreased round nonstick baking dish. Pour lemon juice into dish and drizzle cod with olive oil. Sprinkle with salt. Place tomatoes and olives around baking dish in between fillets. 2. Place dish into air fryer basket. Adjust the temperature to 350°F (177°C) and bake for 12 minutes, carefully turning cod halfway through cooking. Fillets will be lightly browned, easily flake, and have an internal temperature of at least 145°F (63°C) when done. Serve warm.

Per Serving

Calories: 186 | fat: 5g | protein: 31g | carbs: 2g | fiber: 1g | sodium: 300mg

Crushed Marcona Almond Swordfish

Prep time: 25 minutes | Cook time: 15 minutes | Serves 4

½ cup almond flour	chopped
¼ cup crushed Marcona almonds	1 lemon, juiced
½ to 1 teaspoon salt, divided	1 tablespoon Spanish paprika
2 pounds (907 g) Swordfish, preferably 1 inch thick	5 medium baby portobello mushrooms, chopped (optional)
1 large egg, beaten (optional)	4 or 5 chopped scallions, both green and white parts
¼ cup pure apple cider	
¼ cup extra-virgin olive oil, plus more for frying	3 to 4 garlic cloves, peeled
3 to 4 sprigs flat-leaf parsley,	¼ cup chopped pitted kalamata olives

1. On a dinner plate, spread the flour and crushed Marcona almonds and mix in the salt. Alternately, pour the flour, almonds, and ¼ teaspoon of salt into a large plastic food storage bag. Add the fish and coat it with the flour mixture. If a thicker coat is desired, repeat this step after dipping the fish in the egg (if using). 2. In a measuring cup, combine the apple cider, ¼ cup of olive oil, parsley, lemon juice, paprika, and ¼ teaspoon of salt. Mix well and set aside. 3. In a large, heavy-bottom sauté pan or skillet, pour the olive oil to a depth of ⅛ inch and heat on medium heat. Once the oil is hot, add the fish and brown for 3 to 5 minutes, then turn the fish over and add the mushrooms (If using), scallions, garlic, and olives. Cook for an additional 3 minutes. Once the other side of the fish is brown, remove the fish from the pan and set aside. 4. Pour the cider mixture into the skillet and mix well with the vegetables. Put the fried fish into the skillet on top of the mixture and cook with sauce on medium-low heat for 10 minutes, until the fish flakes easily with a fork. Carefully remove the fish from the pan and plate. Spoon the sauce over the fish. Serve with white rice or home-fried potatoes.

Per Serving

Calories: 620 | fat: 37g | protein: 63g | carbs: 10g | fiber: 5g | sodium: 644mg

Weeknight Sheet Pan Fish Dinner

Prep time: 10 minutes |Cook time: 10 minutes| Serves: 4

Nonstick cooking spray	such as cod or tilapia (½ inch thick)
2 tablespoons extra-virgin olive oil	
1 tablespoon balsamic vinegar	2½ cups green beans
4 (4-ounce / 113-g) fish fillets,	1 pint cherry or grape tomatoes (about 2 cups)

1. Preheat the oven to 400°F (205°C). Coat two large, rimmed baking sheets with nonstick cooking spray. 2. In a small bowl, whisk together the oil and vinegar. Set aside. 3. Place two pieces of fish on each baking sheet. 4. In a large bowl, combine the beans and tomatoes. Pour in the oil and vinegar, and toss gently to coat. Pour half of the green bean mixture over the fish on one baking sheet, and the remaining half over the fish on the other. Turn the fish over, and rub it in the oil mixture to coat. Spread the vegetables evenly on the baking sheets so hot air can circulate around them. 5. Bake for 5 to 8 minutes, until the fish is just opaque and not translucent. The fish is done and ready to serve when it just begins to separate into flakes (chunks) when pressed gently with a fork.

Per Serving

Calories: 190 | fat: 8g | protein: 22g | carbs: 8g | fiber: 3g | sodium: 70mg

Salmon Burgers with Creamy Broccoli Slaw

Prep time: 15 minutes | Cook time: 10 minutes | Serves 4

Salmon Burgers:	Broccoli Slaw:
1 pound (454 g) salmon fillets, bones and skin removed	3 cups chopped or shredded broccoli
1 egg	½ cup shredded carrots
¼ cup fresh dill, chopped	¼ cup sunflower seeds
1 cup whole wheat bread crumbs	2 garlic cloves, minced
½ teaspoon salt	½ teaspoon salt
½ teaspoon cayenne pepper	2 tablespoons apple cider vinegar
2 garlic cloves, minced	1 cup nonfat plain Greek yogurt
4 whole wheat buns	

Make the Salmon Burgers: 1. Preheat the air fryer to 360°F (182°C). 2. In a food processor, pulse the salmon fillets until they are finely chopped. 3. In a large bowl, combine the chopped salmon, egg, dill, bread crumbs, salt, cayenne, and garlic until it comes together. 4. Form the salmon into 4 patties. Place them into the air fryer basket, making sure that they don't touch each other. 5. Bake for 5 minutes. Flip the salmon patties and bake for 5 minutes more. Make the Broccoli Slaw: 6. In a large bowl, combine all of the ingredients for the broccoli slaw. Mix well. 7. Serve the salmon burgers on toasted whole wheat buns, and top with a generous portion of broccoli slaw.

Per Serving

Calories: 504 | fat: 14g | protein: 40g | carbs: 54g | fiber: 5g | sodium: 631mg

Cod with Warm Tabbouleh Salad

Prep time: 10 minutes | Cook time: 6 minutes | Serves 4

1 cup medium-grind bulgur, rinsed
1 teaspoon table salt, divided
1 lemon, sliced ¼ inch thick, plus 2 tablespoons juice
4 (6-ounce / 170-g) skinless cod fillets, 1½ inches thick
3 tablespoons extra-virgin

olive oil, divided, plus extra for drizzling
¼ teaspoon pepper
1 small shallot, minced
10 ounces (283 g) cherry tomatoes, halved
1 cup chopped fresh parsley
½ cup chopped fresh mint

1. Arrange trivet included with Instant Pot in base of insert and add ½ cup water. Fold sheet of aluminum foil into 16 by 6-inch sling, then rest 1½-quart round soufflé dish in center of sling. Combine 1 cup water, bulgur, and ½ teaspoon salt in dish. Using sling, lower soufflé dish into pot and onto trivet; allow narrow edges of sling to rest along sides of insert. 2. Lock lid in place and close pressure release valve. Select high pressure cook function and cook for 3 minutes. Turn off Instant Pot and quick-release pressure. Carefully remove lid, allowing steam to escape away from you. Using sling, transfer soufflé dish to wire rack; set aside to cool. Remove trivet; do not discard sling or water in pot. 3. Arrange lemon slices widthwise in 2 rows across center of sling. Brush cod with 1 tablespoon oil and sprinkle with remaining ½ teaspoon salt and pepper. Arrange cod skinned side down in even layer on top of lemon slices. Using sling, lower cod into Instant Pot; allow narrow edges of sling to rest along sides of insert. Lock lid in place and close pressure release valve. Select high pressure cook function and cook for 3 minutes. 4. Meanwhile, whisk remaining 2 tablespoons oil, lemon juice, and shallot together in large bowl. Add bulgur, tomatoes, parsley, and mint, and gently toss to combine. Season with salt and pepper to taste. 5. Turn off Instant Pot and quick-release pressure. Carefully remove lid, allowing steam to escape away from you. Using sling, transfer cod to large plate. Gently lift and tilt fillets with spatula to remove lemon slices. Serve cod with salad, drizzling individual portions with extra oil.

Per Serving

Calories: 380 | fat: 12g | protein: 36g | carbs: 32g | fiber: 6g | sodium: 690mg

Mussels with Fennel and Leeks

Prep time: 20 minutes | Cook time: 6 minutes | Serves 4

1 tablespoon extra-virgin olive oil, plus extra for drizzling
1 fennel bulb, 1 tablespoon fronds minced, stalks discarded, bulb halved, cored, and sliced thin
1 leek, ends trimmed, leek halved lengthwise, sliced

1 inch thick, and washed thoroughly
4 garlic cloves, minced
3 sprigs fresh thyme
¼ teaspoon red pepper flakes
½ cup dry white wine
3 pounds (1.4 kg) mussels, scrubbed and debearded

1. Using highest sauté function, heat oil in Instant Pot until shimmering. Add fennel and leek and cook until softened, about 5 minutes. Stir in garlic, thyme sprigs, and pepper flakes and cook until fragrant, about 30 seconds. Stir in wine, then

add mussels. 2. Lock lid in place and close pressure release valve. Select high pressure cook function and set cook time for 0 minutes. Once Instant Pot has reached pressure, immediately turn off pot and quick-release pressure. Carefully remove lid, allowing steam to escape away from you. 3. Discard thyme sprigs and any mussels that have not opened. Transfer mussels to individual serving bowls, sprinkle with fennel fronds, and drizzle with extra oil. Serve.

Per Serving

Calories: 384 | fat: 11g | protein: 42g | carbs: 23g | fiber: 2g | sodium: 778mg

Baked Salmon and Tomato Pockets

Prep time: 5 minutes | Cook time: 25 minutes | Serves 4

1 pint (2 cups) cherry tomatoes
3 tablespoons extra-virgin olive oil
3 tablespoons lemon juice
1 teaspoon oregano

3 tablespoons unsalted butter, melted
½ teaspoon salt
4 (5-ounce / 142-g) salmon fillets

1. Preheat the oven to 400ºF (205ºC). 2. Cut the tomatoes in half and put them in a bowl. 3. Add the olive oil, lemon juice, oregano, melted butter, and salt to the tomatoes and toss to combine. 4. Cut 4 pieces of foil, about 12-by-12 inches each. 5. Place the salmon in the middle of each piece of foil. 6. Divide the tomato mixture evenly over the 4 pieces of salmon. Bring the ends of the foil together and seal to form a closed pocket. 7. Place the 4 pockets on a baking sheet. Cook for 25 minutes. 8. To serve, place each pocket on a plate and let your guests open to reveal the baked salmon and tomatoes.

Per Serving

Calories: 410 | fat: 32g | protein: 30g | carbs: 4g | fiber: 1g | sodium: 370mg

Whitefish with Lemon and Capers

Prep time: 5 minutes | Cook time: 20 minutes | Serves 4

4 (4- to 5-ounce / 113- to 142-g) cod fillets (or any whitefish)
1 tablespoon extra-virgin olive oil
1 teaspoon salt, divided
4 tablespoons (½ stick)

unsalted butter
2 tablespoons capers, drained
3 tablespoons lemon juice
½ teaspoon freshly ground black pepper

1. Preheat the oven to 450ºF (235ºC). Put the cod in a large baking dish and drizzle with the olive oil and ½ teaspoon of salt. Bake for 15 minutes. 2. Right before the fish is done cooking, melt the butter in a small saucepan over medium heat. Add the capers, lemon juice, remaining ½ teaspoon of salt, and pepper; simmer for 30 seconds. 3. Place the fish in a serving dish once it is done baking; spoon the caper sauce over the fish and serve.

Per Serving

Calories: 255 | fat: 16g | protein: 26g | carbs: 1g | fiber: 0g | sodium: 801mg

Salmon Poached in Red Wine

Prep time: 15 minutes | Cook time: 16 minutes | Serves 6

1 medium onion, peeled and quartered
2 cloves garlic, peeled and smashed
1 stalk celery, diced
1 bay leaf
½ teaspoon dried thyme
3½ cups water
2 cups dry red wine
2 tablespoons red wine vinegar
½ teaspoon salt
½ teaspoon black peppercorns
1 (2½-pound / 1.1-kg) center-cut salmon roast
1 medium lemon, cut into wedges

1. Add all ingredients except salmon and lemon to the Instant Pot®. Close lid, set steam release to Sealing, press the Manual button, and set time to 10 minutes. When the timer beeps, quick-release the pressure until the float valve drops and open lid. Press the Cancel button. 2. Set the rack in the pot and put steamer basket on rack. Wrap salmon in cheesecloth, leaving ends long enough to extend about 3". Use two sets of tongs to hold on to the 3" cheesecloth extensions and place the salmon on the rack. Close lid, set steam release to Sealing, press the Manual button, and set time to 6 minutes. When the timer beeps, let pressure release naturally for 20 minutes. 3. Quick-release any remaining pressure until the float valve drops and open lid. Use tongs to hold on to the 3" cheesecloth extensions to lift salmon out of the Instant Pot®. Set in a metal colander to allow extra moisture to drain away. When salmon is cool enough to handle, unwrap the cheesecloth. Peel away and discard any skin. 4. Transfer salmon to a serving platter. Garnish with lemon wedges.

Per Serving
Calories: 435 | fat: 24g | protein: 43g | carbs: 4g | fiber: 0g | sodium: 213mg

Steamed Cod with Garlic and Swiss Chard

Prep time: 5 minutes | Cook time: 12 minutes | Serves 4

1 teaspoon salt
½ teaspoon dried oregano
½ teaspoon dried thyme
½ teaspoon garlic powder
4 cod fillets
½ white onion, thinly sliced
2 cups Swiss chard, washed, stemmed, and torn into pieces
¼ cup olive oil
1 lemon, quartered

1. Preheat the air fryer to 380°F (193°C). 2. In a small bowl, whisk together the salt, oregano, thyme, and garlic powder. 3. Tear off four pieces of aluminum foil, with each sheet being large enough to envelop one cod fillet and a quarter of the vegetables. 4. Place a cod fillet in the middle of each sheet of foil, then sprinkle on all sides with the spice mixture. 5. In each foil packet, place a quarter of the onion slices and ½ cup Swiss chard, then drizzle 1 tablespoon olive oil and squeeze ¼ lemon over the contents of each foil packet. 6. Fold and seal the sides of the foil packets and then place them into the air fryer basket. Steam for 12 minutes. 7. Remove from the basket, and carefully open each packet to avoid a steam burn.

Per Serving
Calories: 324 | fat: 15g | protein: 42g | carbs: 4g | fiber: 1g | sodium: 746mg

Parmesan Mackerel with Coriander

Prep time: 10 minutes | Cook time: 7 minutes | Serves 2

12 ounces (340 g) mackerel fillet
2 ounces (57 g) Parmesan,
grated
1 teaspoon ground coriander
1 tablespoon olive oil

1. Sprinkle the mackerel fillet with olive oil and put it in the air fryer basket. 2. Top the fish with ground coriander and Parmesan. 3. Cook the fish at 390°F (199°C) for 7 minutes.

Per Serving
Calories: 522 | fat: 39g | protein: 42g | carbs: 1g | fiber: 0g | sodium: 544mg

Salmon with Wild Rice and Orange Salad

Prep time: 20 minutes | Cook time: 18 minutes | Serves 4

1 cup wild rice, picked over and rinsed
3 tablespoons extra-virgin olive oil, divided
1½ teaspoon table salt, for cooking rice
2 oranges, plus ⅛ teaspoon grated orange zest
4 (6-ounce / 170-g) skinless
salmon fillets, 1½ inches thick
1 teaspoon ground dried Aleppo pepper
½ teaspoon table salt
1 small shallot, minced
1 tablespoon red wine vinegar
2 teaspoons Dijon mustard
1 teaspoon honey
2 carrots, peeled and shredded
¼ cup chopped fresh mint

1. Combine 6 cups water, rice, 1 tablespoon oil, and 1½ teaspoons salt in Instant Pot. Lock lid in place and close pressure release valve. Select high pressure cook function and cook for 15 minutes. Turn off Instant Pot and let pressure release naturally for 15 minutes. Quick-release any remaining pressure, then carefully remove lid, allowing steam to escape away from you. Drain rice and set aside to cool slightly. Wipe pot clean with paper towels. 2. Add ½ cup water to now-empty Instant Pot. Fold sheet of aluminum foil into 16 by 6-inch sling. Slice 1 orange ¼ inch thick and shingle widthwise in 3 rows across center of sling. Sprinkle flesh side of salmon with Aleppo pepper and ½ teaspoon salt, then arrange skinned side down on top of orange slices. Using sling, lower salmon into Instant Pot; allow narrow edges of sling to rest along sides of insert. Lock lid in place and close pressure release valve. Select high pressure cook function and cook for 3 minutes. 3. Meanwhile, cut away peel and pith from remaining 1 orange. Quarter orange, then slice crosswise into ¼-inch pieces. Whisk remaining 2 tablespoons oil, shallot, vinegar, mustard, honey, and orange zest together in large bowl. Add rice, orange pieces, carrots, and mint, and gently toss to combine. Season with salt and pepper to taste. 4. Turn off Instant Pot and quick-release pressure. Carefully remove lid, allowing steam to escape away from you. Using sling, transfer salmon to large plate. Gently lift and tilt fillets with spatula to remove orange slices. Serve salmon with salad.

Per Serving
Calories: 690 | fat: 34g | protein: 43g | carbs: 51g | fiber: 5g | sodium: 770mg

Moroccan Crusted Sea Bass

Prep time: 15 minutes | Cook time: 40 minutes | Serves 4

1½ teaspoons ground turmeric, divided
¾ teaspoon saffron
½ teaspoon ground cumin
¼ teaspoon kosher salt
¼ teaspoon freshly ground black pepper
1½ pounds (680 g) sea bass fillets, about ½ inch thick
8 tablespoons extra-virgin olive oil, divided
8 garlic cloves, divided (4 minced cloves and 4 sliced)
6 medium baby portobello mushrooms, chopped
1 large carrot, sliced on an angle
2 sun-dried tomatoes, thinly sliced (optional)
2 tablespoons tomato paste
1 (15-ounce / 425-g) can chickpeas, drained and rinsed
1½ cups low-sodium vegetable broth
¼ cup white wine
1 tablespoon ground coriander (optional)
1 cup sliced artichoke hearts marinated in olive oil
½ cup pitted kalamata olives
½ lemon, juiced
½ lemon, cut into thin rounds
4 to 5 rosemary sprigs or 2 tablespoons dried rosemary
Fresh cilantro, for garnish

1. In a small mixing bowl, combine 1 teaspoon turmeric and the saffron and cumin. Season with salt and pepper. Season both sides of the fish with the spice mixture. Add 3 tablespoons of olive oil and work the fish to make sure it's well coated with the spices and the olive oil. 2. In a large sauté pan or skillet, heat 2 tablespoons of olive oil over medium heat until shimmering but not smoking. Sear the top side of the sea bass for about 1 minute, or until golden. Remove and set aside. 3. In the same skillet, add the minced garlic and cook very briefly, tossing regularly, until fragrant. Add the mushrooms, carrot, sun-dried tomatoes (if using), and tomato paste. Cook for 3 to 4 minutes over medium heat, tossing frequently, until fragrant. Add the chickpeas, broth, wine, coriander (if using), and the sliced garlic. Stir in the remaining ½ teaspoon ground turmeric. Raise the heat, if needed, and bring to a boil, then lower heat to simmer. Cover part of the way and let the sauce simmer for about 20 minutes, until thickened. 4. Carefully add the seared fish to the skillet. Ladle a bit of the sauce on top of the fish. Add the artichokes, olives, lemon juice and slices, and rosemary sprigs. Cook another 10 minutes or until the fish is fully cooked and flaky. Garnish with fresh cilantro.

Per Serving
Calories: 696 | fat: 41g | protein: 48g | carbs: 37g | fiber: 9g | sodium: 810mg

Baked Grouper with Tomatoes and Garlic

Prep time: 5 minutes | Cook time: 12 minutes | Serves 4

4 grouper fillets
½ teaspoon salt
3 garlic cloves, minced
1 tomato, sliced
¼ cup sliced Kalamata olives
¼ cup fresh dill, roughly chopped
Juice of 1 lemon
¼ cup olive oil

1. Preheat the air fryer to 380°F (193°C). 2. Season the grouper fillets on all sides with salt, then place into the air fryer basket and top with the minced garlic, tomato slices, olives, and fresh dill. 3. Drizzle the lemon juice and olive oil over the top of the grouper, then bake for 10 to 12 minutes, or until the internal temperature reaches 145°F (63°C).

Per Serving
Calories: 379 | fat: 17g | protein: 51g | carbs: 3g | fiber: 1g | sodium: 492mg

Almond-Encrusted Salmon

Prep time: 10 minutes | Cook time: 12 minutes | Serves 4

¼ cup olive oil
1 tablespoon honey
¼ cup breadcrumbs
½ cup finely chopped almonds, lightly toasted
½ teaspoon dried thyme
Sea salt and freshly ground pepper, to taste
4 salmon steaks

1. Preheat the oven to 350°F (180°C). 2. Combine the olive oil with the honey. (Soften the honey in the microwave for 15 seconds, if necessary, for easier blending.) 3. In a shallow dish, combine the breadcrumbs, almonds, thyme, sea salt, and freshly ground pepper. 4. Coat the salmon steaks with the olive oil mixture, then the almond mixture. 5. Place on a baking sheet brushed with olive oil and bake 8–12 minutes, or until the almonds are lightly browned and the salmon is firm.

Per Serving
Calories: 634 | fat: 34g | protein: 69g | carbs: 12g | fiber: 2g | sodium: 289mg

Shrimp Pasta with Basil and Mushrooms

Prep time: 10 minutes | Cook time: 10 minutes | Serves 6

1 pound (454 g) small shrimp, peeled and deveined
¼ cup plus 1 tablespoon olive oil, divided
¼ teaspoon garlic powder
¼ teaspoon cayenne
1 pound (454 g) whole grain pasta
5 garlic cloves, minced
8 ounces (227 g) baby bella mushrooms, sliced
½ cup Parmesan, plus more for serving (optional)
1 teaspoon salt
½ teaspoon black pepper
½ cup fresh basil

1. Preheat the air fryer to 380°F (193°C). 2. In a small bowl, combine the shrimp, 1 tablespoon olive oil, garlic powder, and cayenne. Toss to coat the shrimp. 3. Place the shrimp into the air fryer basket and roast for 5 minutes. Remove the shrimp and set aside. 4. Cook the pasta according to package directions. Once done cooking, reserve ½ cup pasta water, then drain. 5. Meanwhile, in a large skillet, heat ¼ cup of olive oil over medium heat. Add the garlic and mushrooms and cook down for 5 minutes. 6. Pour the pasta, reserved pasta water, Parmesan, salt, pepper, and basil into the skillet with the vegetable-and-oil mixture, and stir to coat the pasta. 7. Toss in the shrimp and remove from heat, then let the mixture sit for 5 minutes before serving with additional Parmesan, if desired.

Per Serving
Calories: 428 | fat: 11g | protein: 22g | carbs: 62g | fiber: 9g | sodium: 483mg

Sea Bass with Roasted Root Vegetables

Prep time: 10 minutes | Cook time: 15 minutes | Serves 4

1 carrot, diced small
1 parsnip, diced small
1 rutabaga, diced small
¼ cup olive oil
1 teaspoon salt, divided

4 sea bass fillets
½ teaspoon onion powder
2 garlic cloves, minced
1 lemon, sliced, plus additional wedges for serving

1. Preheat the air fryer to 380°F (193°C). 2. In a small bowl, toss the carrot, parsnip, and rutabaga with olive oil and 1 teaspoon salt. 3. Lightly season the sea bass with the remaining 1 teaspoon of salt and the onion powder, then place it into the air fryer basket in a single layer. 4. Spread the garlic over the top of each fillet, then cover with lemon slices. 5. Pour the prepared vegetables into the basket around and on top of the fish. Roast for 15 minutes. 6. Serve with additional lemon wedges if desired.

Per Serving
Calories: 295 | fat: 16g | protein: 25g | carbs: 12g | fiber: 3g | sodium: 687mg

Shrimp with Marinara Sauce

Prep time: 15 minutes | Cook time: 6 to 7 hours | Serves 4

1 (15-ounce / 425-g) can diced tomatoes, with the juice
1 (6-ounce / 170-g) can tomato paste
1 clove garlic, minced
2 tablespoons minced fresh flat-leaf parsley
½ teaspoon dried basil
1 teaspoon dried oregano

1 teaspoon garlic powder
1½ teaspoons sea salt
¼ teaspoon black pepper
1 pound (454 g) cooked shrimp, peeled and deveined
2 cups hot cooked spaghetti or linguine, for serving
½ cup grated parmesan cheese, for serving

1. Combine the tomatoes, tomato paste, and minced garlic in the slow cooker. Sprinkle with the parsley, basil, oregano, garlic powder, salt, and pepper. 2. Cover and cook on low for 6 to 7 hours. 3. Turn up the heat to high, stir in the cooked shrimp, and cover and cook on high for about 15 minutes longer. 4. Serve hot over the cooked pasta. Top with Parmesan cheese.

Per Serving
Calories: 313 | fat: 5g | protein: 39g | carbs: 32g | fiber: 7g | sodium: 876mg

Steamed Shrimp and Asparagus

Prep time: 15 minutes | Cook time: 1 minute | Serves 4

1 cup water
1 bunch asparagus, trimmed
½ teaspoon salt, divided
1 pound (454 g) shrimp, peeled

and deveined
1½ tablespoons lemon juice
2 tablespoons olive oil

1. Pour water into the Instant Pot®. Insert rack and place steamer basket onto rack. 2. Spread asparagus on the bottom of the steamer basket. Sprinkle with ¼ teaspoon salt. Add shrimp. Drizzle with lemon juice and sprinkle with remaining ¼ teaspoon salt. Drizzle olive oil over shrimp. 3. Close lid, set steam release to Sealing, press the Manual button, and set time to 1 minute. When the timer beeps, quick-release the pressure until the float valve drops and open lid. 4. Transfer shrimp and asparagus to a platter and serve.

Per Serving
Calories: 145 | fat: 8g | protein: 19g | carbs: 1g | fiber: 0g | sodium: 295mg

Steamed Cod with Capers and Lemon

Prep time: 10 minutes | Cook time: 3 minutes | Serves 4

1 cup water
4 (4-ounce / 113-g) cod fillets, rinsed and patted dry
½ teaspoon ground black pepper
1 small lemon, thinly sliced

2 tablespoons extra-virgin olive oil
¼ cup chopped fresh parsley
2 tablespoons capers
1 tablespoon chopped fresh chives

1. Add water to the Instant Pot® and place the rack inside. 2. Season fish fillets with pepper. Top each fillet with three slices of lemon. Place fillets on rack. Close lid, set steam release to Sealing, press the Steam button, and set time to 3 minutes. 3. While fish cooks, combine olive oil, parsley, capers, and chives in a small bowl and mix well. Set aside. 4. When the timer beeps, quick-release the pressure until the float valve drops. Press the Cancel button and open lid. Place cod fillets on a serving platter. Remove and discard lemon slices and drizzle fish with olive oil mixture, making sure each fillet has herbs and capers on top. Serve immediately.

Per Serving
Calories: 140 | fat: 10g | protein: 14g | carbs: 0g | fiber: 0g | sodium: 370mg

Moroccan-Style Grilled Tuna

Prep time: 10 minutes | Cook time: 6 to 8 minutes | Serves 4

2 tablespoons finely chopped cilantro
2 tablespoons finely chopped parsley
6 cloves garlic, minced
½ teaspoon unrefined sea salt or salt

½ teaspoon paprika
1 lemon, juiced and zested
3 tablespoons extra-virgin olive oil
4 tuna steaks (4 ounces / 113 g each)

1. In a medium bowl, mix the cilantro, parsley, garlic, salt, paprika, and lemon juice and zest together. Whisk in the olive oil. 2. Place the fish in a glass baking dish and pour half of the chermoula sauce over the top. Cover with plastic wrap and allow to marinate for 1 hour. 3. Preheat grill to medium-high heat. 4. Grill the fish, turning once, until firm, 6 to 8 minutes. Transfer to a platter, spread with the remaining chermoula sauce, and let stand for 5 minutes to absorb the flavors.

Per Serving
Calories: 217 | fat: 11g | protein: 25g | carbs: 3g | fiber: 0g | sodium: 335mg

Salmon with Provolone Cheese

Prep time: 5 minutes | Cook time: 15 minutes | Serves 4

1 pound (454 g) salmon fillet, chopped
2 ounces (57 g) Provolone, grated
1 teaspoon avocado oil
¼ teaspoon ground paprika

1. Sprinkle the salmon fillets with avocado oil and put in the air fryer. 2. Then sprinkle the fish with ground paprika and top with Provolone cheese. 3. Cook the fish at 360°F (182°C) for 15 minutes.

Per Serving
Calories: 204 | fat: 10g | protein: 27g | carbs: 0g | fiber: 0g | sodium: 209mg

Cod with Warm Beet and Arugula Salad

Prep time: 15 minutes | Cook time: 8 minutes | Serves 4

¼ cup extra-virgin olive oil, divided, plus extra for drizzling
1 shallot, sliced thin
2 garlic cloves, minced
1½ pounds (680 g) small beets, scrubbed, trimmed, and cut into ½-inch wedges
½ cup chicken or vegetable broth
1 tablespoon dukkah, plus extra for sprinkling
¼ teaspoon table salt
4 (6-ounce / 170-g) skinless cod fillets, 1½ inches thick
1 tablespoon lemon juice
2 ounces (57 g) baby arugula

1. Using highest sauté function, heat 1 tablespoon oil in Instant Pot until shimmering. Add shallot and cook until softened, about 2 minutes. Stir in garlic and cook until fragrant, about 30 seconds. Stir in beets and broth. Lock lid in place and close pressure release valve. Select high pressure cook function and cook for 3 minutes. Turn off Instant Pot and quick-release pressure. Carefully remove lid, allowing steam to escape away from you. 2. Fold sheet of aluminum foil into 16 by 6-inch sling. Combine 2 tablespoons oil, dukkah, and salt in bowl, then brush cod with oil mixture. Arrange cod skinned side down in center of sling. Using sling, lower cod into Instant Pot; allow narrow edges of sling to rest along sides of insert. Lock lid in place and close pressure release valve. Select high pressure cook function and cook for 2 minutes. 3. Turn off Instant Pot and quick-release pressure. Carefully remove lid, allowing steam to escape away from you. Using sling, transfer cod to large plate. Tent with foil and let rest while finishing beet salad. 4. Combine lemon juice and remaining 1 tablespoon oil in large bowl. Using slotted spoon, transfer beets to bowl with oil mixture. Add arugula and gently toss to combine. Season with salt and pepper to taste. Serve cod with salad, sprinkling individual portions with extra dukkah and drizzling with extra oil.

Per Serving
Calories: 340 | fat: 16g | protein: 33g | carbs: 14g | fiber: 4g | sodium: 460mg

Mussels with Tomatoes and Herbs

Prep time: 15 minutes | Cook time: 7 minutes | Serves 6

2 tablespoons light olive oil
1 medium white onion, peeled and chopped
2 cloves garlic, peeled and minced
2 tablespoons chopped fresh dill
2 tablespoons chopped fresh tarragon
½ teaspoon ground fennel
½ teaspoon ground black pepper
3 pounds (1.4 kg) mussels, scrubbed and beards removed
½ cup vegetable broth
1 (14½-ounce / 411-g) can diced tomatoes, drained

1. Press the Sauté button on the Instant Pot® and heat oil. Add onion and cook until tender, about 3 minutes. Add garlic, dill, tarragon, fennel, and pepper, and cook until garlic is fragrant, about 30 seconds. Press the Cancel button. 2. Add mussels, broth, and tomatoes. Stir to combine. Close lid, set steam release to Sealing, press the Manual button, and set time to 3 minutes. When the timer beeps, quick-release the pressure until the float valve drops and open lid. Discard any mussels that haven't opened. Serve immediately.

Per Serving
Calories: 162 | fat: 7g | protein: 14g | carbs: 10g | fiber: 2g | sodium: 435mg

Shrimp with White Beans and Feta

Prep time: 15 minutes | Cook time: 15 minutes | Serves 4

3 tablespoons lemon juice, divided
2 tablespoons extra-virgin olive oil, divided
½ teaspoon kosher salt, divided
1 pound (454 g) shrimp, peeled and deveined
1 large shallot, diced
¼ cup no-salt-added vegetable stock
1 (15-ounce / 425-g) can no-salt-added or low-sodium cannellini beans, rinsed and drained
¼ cup fresh mint, chopped
1 teaspoon lemon zest
1 tablespoon white wine vinegar
¼ teaspoon freshly ground black pepper
¼ cup crumbled feta cheese, for garnish

1. In a small bowl, whisk together 1 tablespoon of the lemon juice, 1 tablespoon of the olive oil, and ¼ teaspoon of the salt. Add the shrimp and set aside. 2. Heat the remaining 1 tablespoon olive oil in a large skillet or sauté pan over medium heat. Add the shallot and sauté until translucent, about 2 to 3 minutes. Add the vegetable stock and deglaze the pan, scraping up any brown bits, and bring to a boil. Add the beans and shrimp. Reduce the heat to low, cover, and simmer until the shrimp are cooked through, about 3 to 4 minutes. 3. Turn off the heat and add the mint, lemon zest, vinegar, and black pepper. Stir gently to combine. Garnish with the feta.

Per Serving
Calories: 340 | fat: 11g | protein: 32g | carbs: 28g | fiber: 6g | sodium: 415mg

Italian Halibut with Grapes and Olive Oil

Prep time: 15 minutes | Cook time: 20 minutes | Serves 4

¼ cup extra-virgin olive oil
4 boneless halibut fillets, 4 ounces (113 g) each
4 cloves garlic, roughly chopped
1 small red chile pepper, finely chopped

2 cups seedless green grapes
A handful of fresh basil leaves, roughly torn
½ teaspoon unrefined sea salt or salt
Freshly ground black pepper

1. Heat the olive oil in a large, heavy-bottomed skillet over medium-high heat. Add the halibut, followed by the garlic, chile pepper, grapes, basil, and the salt and pepper. Pour in 1 ¾ cups (410 ml) of water, turn the heat down to medium-low, cover, and cook the fish until opaque, or for 7 minutes on each side. 2. Remove the fish from the pan and place on a large serving dish. Raise the heat, cook the sauce for 30 seconds to concentrate the flavors slightly. Taste and adjust salt and pepper. Pour sauce over the fish.

Per Serving
Calories: 389 | fat: 29g | protein: 17g | carbs: 15g | fiber: 1g | sodium: 384mg

Olive Oil–Poached Fish over Citrus Salad

Prep time: 10 minutes | Cook time: 25 minutes | Serves 4

Fish
4 skinless white fish fillets (1¼ to 1½ pounds / 567 to 680 g total), such as halibut, sole, or cod, ¾'–1' thick
¼ teaspoon kosher salt
¼ teaspoon ground black pepper
5–7 cups olive oil
1 lemon, thinly sliced
Salad
¼ cup white wine vinegar
1 Earl Grey tea bag
2 blood oranges or tangerines

1 ruby red grapefruit or pomelo
6 kumquats, thinly sliced, or 2 clementines, peeled and sectioned
4 cups baby arugula
½ cup pomegranate seeds
¼ cup extra-virgin olive oil
2 teaspoons minced shallot
½ teaspoon kosher salt
¼ teaspoon ground black pepper
¼ cup mint leaves, coarsely chopped

1. Make the Fish: Season the fish with the salt and pepper and set aside for 30 minutes. 2. Preheat the oven to 225°F (107°C). 3. In a large high-sided ovenproof skillet or roasting pan over medium heat, warm 1' to 1½' of the oil and the lemon slices until the temperature reaches 120°F (49°C). Add the fish fillets to the oil, without overlapping, making sure they're completely submerged. 4. Transfer the skillet or pan to the oven, uncovered. Bake for 25 minutes. Transfer the fish to a rack to drain for 5 minutes. 5. Make the Salad: In a small saucepan, heat the vinegar until almost boiling. Add the tea bag and set aside to steep for 10 minutes. 6. Meanwhile, with a paring knife, cut off enough of the top and bottom of 1 of the oranges or tangerines to reveal the flesh. Cut along the inside of the peel, between the pith and the flesh, taking off as much pith as possible. Over a large bowl, hold the orange in 1 hand. With the paring knife, cut along the membranes between each section, allowing the fruit to fall into the bowl. Once all the fruit segments have been released, squeeze the remaining membranes over a small bowl. Repeat with the second orange and the grapefruit or pomelo. 7. In the large bowl with the segmented fruit, add the kumquats or clementines, arugula, and pomegranate seeds. Gently toss to distribute. 8. Remove the tea bag from the vinegar and squeeze out as much liquid as possible. Discard the bag and add the vinegar to the small bowl with the citrus juice. Slowly whisk in the oil, shallot, salt, and pepper. Drizzle 3 to 4 tablespoons over the salad and gently toss. (Store the remaining vinaigrette in the refrigerator for up to 1 week.) 9. Sprinkle the salad with the mint and serve with the fish.

Per Serving
Calories: 280 | fat: 7g | protein: 29g | carbs: 25g | fiber: 6g | sodium: 249mg

Flounder with Tomatoes and Basil

Prep time: 10 minutes | Cook time: 20 minutes | Serves 4

1 pound (454 g) cherry tomatoes
4 garlic cloves, sliced
2 tablespoons extra-virgin olive oil
2 tablespoons lemon juice
2 tablespoons basil, cut into

ribbons
½ teaspoon kosher salt
¼ teaspoon freshly ground black pepper
4 (5- to 6-ounce / 142- to 170-g) flounder fillets

1. Preheat the oven to 425°F (220°C). 2. In a baking dish, combine the tomatoes, garlic, olive oil, lemon juice, basil, salt, and black pepper; mix well. Bake for 5 minutes. 3. Remove the baking dish from the oven and arrange the flounder on top of the tomato mixture. Bake until the fish is opaque and begins to flake, about 10 to 15 minutes, depending on thickness.

Per Serving
Calories: 215 | fat: 9g | protein: 28g | carbs: 6g | fiber: 2g | sodium: 261mg

Citrus–Marinated Scallops

Prep time: 10 minutes | Cook time: 10 minutes | Serves 4

Juice and zest of 2 lemons
¼ cup extra-virgin olive oil
Unrefined sea salt or salt, to taste
Freshly ground black pepper,

to taste
1 clove garlic, minced
1½ pounds (680 g) dry scallops, side muscle removed

1. In a large shallow bowl or baking dish, combine the lemon juice and zest, olive oil, salt, pepper, and garlic. Mix well to combine. Add the scallops to the marinade; cover and refrigerate 1 hour. 2. Heat a large skillet over medium-high heat. Drain the scallops and place them in skillet. Cook 4 to 5 minutes per side, until cooked through.

Per Serving
Calories: 243 | fat: 14g | protein: 21g | carbs: 7g | fiber: 0g | sodium: 567mg

Trout Cooked in Parchment

Prep time: 10 minutes | Cook time: 10 minutes | Serves 4

4 (4 ounces / 113 g each) trout fillets
3 cloves garlic, finely chopped
8 fresh sage leaves, finely chopped
½ cup finely chopped fresh parsley
Zest and juice of 1 lemon

⅓ cup extra-virgin olive oil
1 teaspoon unrefined sea salt or salt
Freshly ground pepper
Lemon wedges

1. Preheat the oven to 425°F (220°C). Combine the garlic, sage, parsley, lemon zest and juice, olive oil, salt, and pepper in a small bowl. Cut four pieces of parchment paper—each more than double the size of the trout. 2. Place 1 trout on top of each piece of parchment and equally distribute ¼ of garlic herb mixture on each fish. Brush any remaining garlic herb mixture over the fish and fold the parchment over the fish. Fold and crimp the edges to seal tightly and place in a baking dish. 3. Bake about 10 minutes, until fish is cooked through. Remove from the oven, and serve with lemon wedges, allowing guests to open their own individual packages at the table.

Per Serving
Calories: 339 | fat: 26g | protein: 24g | carbs: 3g | fiber: 1g | sodium: 646mg

Citrus–Marinated Salmon with Fennel Cream

Prep time: 15 minutes | Cook time: 25 minutes | Serves 4

2 tablespoons extra-virgin olive oil
¼ cup orange juice
½ teaspoon unrefined sea salt or salt
Freshly ground pepper
4 salmon fillets (4 ounces / 113 g each), skin-on

1 fennel bulb, thinly sliced (reserve fronds)
½ sweet onion, thinly sliced
1 cup plain Greek yogurt
2 oranges, 1 zested, 1 thinly sliced

1. In a small bowl, whisk the olive oil, orange juice, salt, and pepper together until emulsified. 2. Place the salmon fillets in a glass baking dish and pour marinade over the top. Allow to marinate for 1 hour. 3. Preheat the oven to 400°F (205°C). 4. Scatter fennel and onion around the sides of the salmon, and cover the baking dish with aluminum foil. Bake until the fish flakes easily with a fork and is opaque in color, 20 to 25 minutes. 5. While the fish is baking, combine the Greek yogurt with 2 tablespoons fennel fronds, finely chopped, and orange zest. 6. Remove the fish from oven and place on a serving plate. Dollop each with about ¼ of yogurt mixture and garnish with orange slices.

Per Serving
Calories: 312 | fat: 14g | protein: 27g | carbs: 20g | fiber: 4g | sodium: 438mg

Rosemary-Lemon Snapper Baked in Parchment

Prep time: 15 minutes | Cook time: 15 minutes | Serves 4

1¼ pounds (567 g) fresh red snapper fillet, cut into two equal pieces
2 lemons, thinly sliced
6 to 8 sprigs fresh rosemary, stems removed or 1 to 2 tablespoons dried rosemary

½ cup extra-virgin olive oil
6 garlic cloves, thinly sliced
1 teaspoon salt
½ teaspoon freshly ground black pepper

1. Preheat the oven to 425°F (220°C). 2. Place two large sheets of parchment (about twice the size of each piece of fish) on the counter. Place 1 piece of fish in the center of each sheet. 3. Top the fish pieces with lemon slices and rosemary leaves. 4. In a small bowl, combine the olive oil, garlic, salt, and pepper. Drizzle the oil over each piece of fish. 5. Top each piece of fish with a second large sheet of parchment and starting on a long side, fold the paper up to about 1 inch from the fish. Repeat on the remaining sides, going in a clockwise direction. Fold in each corner once to secure. 6. Place both parchment pouches on a baking sheet and bake until the fish is cooked through, 10 to 12 minutes.

Per Serving
Calories: 399 | fat: 29g | protein: 30g | carbs: 5g | fiber: 1g | sodium: 584mg

Chapter 8 Pasta

Creamy Spring Vegetable Linguine

Prep time: 10 minutes | Cook time: 10 minutes | Serves 4 to 6

1 pound (454 g) linguine
5 cups water, plus extra as needed
1 tablespoon extra-virgin olive oil
1 teaspoon table salt
1 cup jarred whole baby artichokes packed in water, quartered
1 cup frozen peas, thawed
4 ounces (113 g) finely grated Pecorino Romano (2 cups), plus extra for serving
½ teaspoon pepper
2 teaspoons grated lemon zest
2 tablespoons chopped fresh tarragon

1. Loosely wrap half of pasta in dish towel, then press bundle against corner of counter to break noodles into 6-inch lengths; repeat with remaining pasta. 2. Add pasta, water, oil, and salt to Instant Pot, making sure pasta is completely submerged. Lock lid in place and close pressure release valve. Select high pressure cook function and cook for 4 minutes. Turn off Instant Pot and quick-release pressure. Carefully remove lid, allowing steam to escape away from you. 3. Stir artichokes and peas into pasta, cover, and let sit until heated through, about 3 minutes. Gently stir in Pecorino and pepper until cheese is melted and fully combined, 1 to 2 minutes. Adjust consistency with extra hot water as needed. Stir in lemon zest and tarragon, and season with salt and pepper to taste. Serve, passing extra Pecorino separately.

Per Serving
Calories: 390 | fat: 8g | protein: 17g | carbs: 59g | fiber: 4g | sodium: 680mg

Toasted Orzo with Shrimp and Feta

Prep time: 10 minutes | Cook time: 15 minutes | Serves 4 to 6

1 pound (454 g) large shrimp (26 to 30 per pound), peeled and deveined
1 tablespoon grated lemon zest plus 1 tablespoon juice
¼ teaspoon table salt
¼ teaspoon pepper
2 tablespoons extra-virgin olive oil, plus extra for serving
1 onion, chopped fine
2 garlic cloves, minced
2 cups orzo
2 cups chicken broth, plus extra as needed
1¼ cups water
½ cup pitted kalamata olives, chopped coarse
1 ounce (28 g) feta cheese, crumbled (¼ cup), plus extra for serving
1 tablespoon chopped fresh dill

1. Toss shrimp with lemon zest, salt, and pepper in bowl; refrigerate until ready to use. 2. Using highest sauté function, heat oil in Instant Pot until shimmering. Add onion and cook until softened, about 5 minutes. Stir in garlic and cook until fragrant, about 30 seconds. Add orzo and cook, stirring frequently, until orzo is coated with oil and lightly browned, about 5 minutes. Stir in broth and water, scraping up any browned bits. 3. Lock lid in place and close pressure release valve. Select high pressure cook function and cook for 2 minutes. Turn off Instant Pot and quick-release pressure. Carefully remove lid, allowing steam to escape away from you. 4. Stir shrimp, olives, and feta into orzo. Cover and let sit until shrimp are opaque throughout, 5 to 7 minutes. Adjust consistency with extra hot broth as needed. Stir in dill and lemon juice, and season with salt and pepper to taste. Sprinkle individual portions with extra feta and drizzle with extra oil before serving.

Per Serving
Calories: 320 | fat: 8g | protein: 18g | carbs: 46g | fiber: 2g | sodium: 670mg

Neapolitan Pasta and Zucchini

Prep time: 5 minutes | Cook time: 28 minutes | Serves 3

⅓ cup extra virgin olive oil
1 large onion (any variety), diced
1 teaspoon fine sea salt, divided
2 large zucchini, quartered lengthwise and cut into ½-inch pieces
10 ounces (283 g) uncooked
spaghetti, broken into 1-inch pieces
2 tablespoons grated Parmesan cheese
2 ounces (57 g) grated or shaved Parmesan cheese for serving
½ teaspoon freshly ground black pepper

1. Add the olive oil to a medium pot over medium heat. When the oil begins to shimmer, add the onions and ¼ teaspoon of the sea salt. Sauté for 3 minutes, add the zucchini, and continue sautéing for 3 more minutes. 2. Add 2 cups of hot water to the pot or enough to just cover the zucchini (the amount of water may vary depending on the size of the pot). Cover, reduce the heat to low, and simmer for 10 minutes. 3. Add the pasta to the pot, stir, then add 2 more cups of hot water. Continue simmering, stirring occasionally, until the pasta is cooked and the mixture has thickened, about 12 minutes. (If the pasta appears to be dry or undercooked, add small amounts of hot water to the pot to ensure the pasta is covered in the water.). When the pasta is cooked, remove the pot from the heat. Add 2 tablespoons of the grated Parmesan and stir. 4. Divide the pasta into three servings and then top each with 1 ounce (28 g) of the grated or shaved Parmesan. Sprinkle the remaining sea salt and black pepper over the top of each serving. Store covered in the refrigerator for up to 3 days.

Per Serving
Calories: 718 | fat: 33g | protein: 24g | carbs: 83g | fiber: 6g | sodium: 815mg

Roasted Asparagus Caprese Pasta

Prep time: 10 minutes |Cook time: 15 minutes| Serves: 6

8 ounces (227 g) uncooked small pasta, like orecchiette (little ears) or farfalle (bow ties)	2 tablespoons extra-virgin olive oil
1½ pounds (680 g) fresh asparagus, ends trimmed and stalks chopped into 1-inch pieces (about 3 cups)	¼ teaspoon freshly ground black pepper
	¼ teaspoon kosher or sea salt
	2 cups fresh mozzarella, drained and cut into bite-size pieces (about 8 ounces / 227 g)
1 pint grape tomatoes, halved (about 1½ cups)	⅓ cup torn fresh basil leaves
	2 tablespoons balsamic vinegar

1. Preheat the oven to 400°F (205°C). 2. In a large stockpot, cook the pasta according to the package directions. Drain, reserving about ¼ cup of the pasta water. 3. While the pasta is cooking, in a large bowl, toss the asparagus, tomatoes, oil, pepper, and salt together. Spread the mixture onto a large, rimmed baking sheet and bake for 15 minutes, stirring twice as it cooks. 4. Remove the vegetables from the oven, and add the cooked pasta to the baking sheet. Mix with a few tablespoons of pasta water to help the sauce become smoother and the saucy vegetables stick to the pasta. 5. Gently mix in the mozzarella and basil. Drizzle with the balsamic vinegar. Serve from the baking sheet or pour the pasta into a large bowl. 6. If you want to make this dish ahead of time or to serve it cold, follow the recipe up to step 4, then refrigerate the pasta and vegetables. When you are ready to serve, follow step 5 either with the cold pasta or with warm pasta that's been gently reheated in a pot on the stove.

Per Serving

Calories: 317 | fat: 12g | protein: 16g | carbs: 38g | fiber: 7g | sodium: 110mg

Zucchini with Bow Ties

Prep time: 5 minutes |Cook time: 25 minutes| Serves: 4

3 tablespoons extra-virgin olive oil	¼ teaspoon ground nutmeg
2 garlic cloves, minced (about 1 teaspoon)	8 ounces (227 g) uncooked farfalle (bow ties) or other small pasta shape
3 large or 4 medium zucchini, diced (about 4 cups)	½ cup grated Parmesan or Romano cheese (about 2 ounces / 57 g)
½ teaspoon freshly ground black pepper	1 tablespoon freshly squeezed lemon juice (from ½ medium lemon)
¼ teaspoon kosher or sea salt	
½ cup 2% milk	

1. In a large skillet over medium heat, heat the oil. Add the garlic and cook for 1 minute, stirring frequently. Add the zucchini, pepper, and salt. Stir well, cover, and cook for 15 minutes, stirring once or twice. 2. In a small, microwave-safe bowl, warm the milk in the microwave on high for 30 seconds. Stir the milk and nutmeg into the skillet and cook uncovered for another 5 minutes, stirring occasionally. 3. While the zucchini is cooking, in a large stockpot, cook the pasta according to the package directions. 4. Drain the pasta in a colander, saving about 2 tablespoons of pasta water. Add the pasta and pasta water to the skillet. Mix everything together and remove from the heat. Stir in the cheese and lemon juice and serve.

Per Serving

Calories: 405 | fat: 16g | protein: 12g | carbs: 57g | fiber: 9g | sodium: 407mg

Penne with Broccoli and Anchovies

Prep time: 10 minutes | Cook time: 10 minutes | Serves 4

¼ cup olive oil	in olive oil
1 pound (454 g) whole-wheat pasta	2 cloves garlic, sliced
½ pound (227 g) broccoli or broccoli rabe cut into 1-inch florets	Pinch red pepper flakes
	¼ cup freshly grated, lowfat Parmesan
3 to 4 anchovy fillets, packed	Sea salt and freshly ground pepper, to taste

1. Heat the olive oil in a deep skillet on medium heat. 2. In the meantime, prepare the pasta al dente, according to the package directions. 3. Fry the broccoli, anchovies, and garlic in the oil until the broccoli is almost tender and the garlic is slightly browned, about 5 minutes or so. 4. Rinse and drain the pasta, and add it to the broccoli mixture. Stir to coat the pasta with the garlic oil. Transfer to a serving dish, toss with red pepper flakes and Parmesan, and season.

Per Serving

Calories: 568 | fat: 17g | protein: 21g | carbs: 89g | fiber: 11g | sodium: 203mg

Rigatoni with Lamb Meatballs

Prep time: 15 minutes | Cook time: 3 to 5 hours | Serves 4

8 ounces (227 g) dried rigatoni pasta	1 pound (454 g) raw ground lamb
2 (28-ounce / 794-g) cans no-salt-added crushed tomatoes or no-salt-added diced tomatoes	1 large egg
	2 tablespoons bread crumbs
1 small onion, diced	1 tablespoon dried parsley
1 bell pepper, any color, seeded and diced	1 teaspoon dried oregano
	1 teaspoon sea salt
3 garlic cloves, minced, divided	½ teaspoon freshly ground black pepper

1. In a slow cooker, combine the pasta, tomatoes, onion, bell pepper, and 1 clove of garlic. Stir to mix well. 2. In a large bowl, mix together the ground lamb, egg, bread crumbs, the remaining 2 garlic cloves, parsley, oregano, salt, and black pepper until all of the ingredients are evenly blended. Shape the meat mixture into 6 to 9 large meatballs. Nestle the meatballs into the pasta and tomato sauce. 3. Cover the cooker and cook for 3 to 5 hours on Low heat, or until the pasta is tender.

Per Serving

Calories: 653 | fat: 29g | protein: 32g | carbs: 69g | fiber: 10g | sodium: 847mg

No-Drain Pasta alla Norma

Prep time: 5 minutes |Cook time: 25 minutes| Serves: 6

1 medium globe eggplant (about 1 pound / 454 g), cut into ¾-inch cubes
1 tablespoon extra-virgin olive oil
1 cup chopped onion (about ½ medium onion)
8 ounces (227 g) uncooked thin spaghetti
1 (15-ounce / 425-g) container

part-skim ricotta cheese
3 Roma tomatoes, chopped (about 2 cups)
2 garlic cloves, minced (about 1 teaspoon)
¼ teaspoon kosher or sea salt
½ cup loosely packed fresh basil leaves
Grated Parmesan cheese, for serving (optional)

1. Lay three paper towels on a large plate, and pile the cubed eggplant on top. (Don't cover the eggplant.) Microwave the eggplant on high for 5 minutes to dry and partially cook it. 2. In a large stockpot over medium-high heat, heat the oil. Add the eggplant and the onion and cook for 5 minutes, stirring occasionally. 3. Add the spaghetti, ricotta, tomatoes, garlic, and salt. Cover with water by a ½ inch (about 4 cups of water). Cook uncovered for 12 to 15 minutes, or until the pasta is just al dente (tender with a bite), stirring occasionally to prevent the pasta from sticking together or sticking to the bottom of the pot. 4. Remove the pot from the heat and let the pasta stand for 3 more minutes to absorb more liquid while you tear the basil into pieces. Sprinkle the basil over the pasta and gently stir. Serve with Parmesan cheese, if desired.

Per Serving
Calories: 299 | fat: 9g | protein: 15g | carbs: 41g | fiber: 5g | sodium: 174mg

Mediterranean Pasta Salad

Prep time: 20 minutes | Cook time: 15 minutes | Serves 4

4 cups dried farfalle (bow-tie) pasta
1 cup canned chickpeas, drained and rinsed
⅔ cup water-packed artichoke hearts, drained and diced
½ red onion, thinly sliced
1 cup packed baby spinach
½ red bell pepper, diced

1 Roma (plum) tomato, diced
½ English cucumber, quartered lengthwise and cut into ½-inch pieces
⅓ cup extra-virgin olive oil
Juice of ½ lemon
Sea salt
Freshly ground black pepper
½ cup crumbled feta cheese

1. Fill a large saucepan three-quarters full with water and bring to a boil over high heat. Add the pasta and cook according to the package directions until al dente, about 15 minutes. Drain the pasta and run it under cold water to stop the cooking process and cool. 2. While the pasta is cooking, in a large bowl, mix the chickpeas, artichoke hearts, onion, spinach, bell pepper, tomato, and cucumber. 3. Add the pasta to the bowl with the vegetables. Add the olive oil and lemon juice and season with salt and black pepper. Mix well. 4. Top the salad with the feta and serve.

Per Serving
Calories: 702 | fat: 25g | protein: 22g | carbs: 99g | fiber: 10g | sodium: 207mg

Greek Chicken Pasta Casserole

Prep time: 15 minutes | Cook time: 4 to 6 hours | Serves 4

2 pounds (907 g) boneless, skinless chicken thighs or breasts, cut into 1-inch pieces
8 ounces (227 g) dried rotini pasta
7 cups low-sodium chicken broth
½ red onion, diced
3 garlic cloves, minced
¼ cup whole Kalamata olives,

pitted
3 Roma tomatoes, diced
2 tablespoons red wine vinegar
1 teaspoon extra-virgin olive oil
2 teaspoons dried oregano
1 teaspoon sea salt
½ teaspoon freshly ground black pepper
¼ cup crumbled feta cheese

1. In a slow cooker, combine the chicken, pasta, chicken broth, onion, garlic, olives, tomatoes, vinegar, olive oil, oregano, salt, and pepper. Stir to mix well. 2. Cover the cooker and cook for 4 to 6 hours on Low heat. 3. Garnish with the feta cheese for serving.

Per Serving
Calories: 608 | fat: 17g | protein: 59g | carbs: 55g | fiber: 8g | sodium: 775mg

Pasta with Chickpeas and Cabbage

Prep time: 20 minutes | Cook time: 30 minutes | Serves 8

1 pound (454 g) rotini pasta
8 cups water, divided
2 tablespoons olive oil, divided
1 stalk celery, thinly sliced
1 medium red onion, peeled and sliced
1 small head savoy cabbage, cored and shredded
⅔ cup dried chickpeas, soaked

overnight and drained
8 ounces (227 g) button mushrooms, sliced
½ teaspoon salt
¾ teaspoon ground black pepper
½ cup grated Pecorino Romano cheese

1. Add pasta, 4 cups water, and 1 tablespoon oil to the Instant Pot®. Close lid, set steam release to Sealing, press the Manual button, and set time to 4 minutes. When the timer beeps, quick-release the pressure until the float valve drops, open lid, and drain pasta. Press the Cancel button. Set aside. 2. Press the Sauté button and heat remaining 1 tablespoon oil. Add celery and onion, and cook until just tender, about 4 minutes. Stir in cabbage and cook until wilted, about 2 minutes. Add chickpeas, mushrooms, and remaining 4 cups water. Stir well, then press the Cancel button. 3. Close lid, set steam release to Sealing, press the Manual button, and set time to 20 minutes. When the timer beeps, let pressure release naturally, about 25 minutes. 4. Open lid and stir well. Season with salt and pepper. Use a fork to mash some of the chickpeas to thicken sauce. Pour sauce over pasta and top with cheese. Serve hot.

Per Serving
Calories: 301 | fat: 5g | protein: 9g | carbs: 49g | fiber: 3g | sodium: 207mg

Quick Shrimp Fettuccine

Prep time: 10 minutes | Cook time: 10 minutes | Serves 4 to 6

8 ounces (227 g) fettuccine pasta
¼ cup extra-virgin olive oil
3 tablespoons garlic, minced
1 pound (454 g) large shrimp (21-25), peeled and deveined
⅓ cup lemon juice
1 tablespoon lemon zest
½ teaspoon salt
½ teaspoon freshly ground black pepper

1. Bring a large pot of salted water to a boil. Add the fettuccine and cook for 8 minutes. 2. In a large saucepan over medium heat, cook the olive oil and garlic for 1 minute. 3. Add the shrimp to the saucepan and cook for 3 minutes on each side. Remove the shrimp from the pan and set aside. 4. Add the lemon juice and lemon zest to the saucepan, along with the salt and pepper. 5. Reserve ½ cup of the pasta water and drain the pasta. 6. Add the pasta water to the saucepan with the lemon juice and zest and stir everything together. Add the pasta and toss together to evenly coat the pasta. Transfer the pasta to a serving dish and top with the cooked shrimp. Serve warm.

Per Serving
Calories: 615 | fat: 17g | protein: 33g | carbs: 89g | fiber: 4g | sodium: 407mg

Pine Nut and Currant Couscous with Butternut Squash

Prep time: 10 minutes | Cook time: 50 minutes | Serves 4

3 tablespoons olive oil
1 medium onion, chopped
3 cloves garlic, minced
6 canned plum tomatoes, crushed
1 cinnamon stick
1 teaspoon ground coriander
1 teaspoon ground cumin
1 teaspoon salt, divided
¼ teaspoon red pepper flakes
1½ pounds (680 g) diced butternut squash
1 (16-ounce / 454-g) can chickpeas, drained and rinsed
4½ cups vegetable broth, divided
1-inch strip lemon zest
½ cup currants
4 cups (about 5 ounces / 142 g) chopped spinach
Juice of ½ lemon
¼ teaspoon pepper
1 cup whole-wheat couscous
¼ cup toasted pine nuts

1. Heat the olive oil in a medium saucepan set over medium heat. Add the onion and cook, stirring frequently, until softened and lightly browned, about 10 minutes. Stir in the garlic, tomatoes, cinnamon stick, coriander, cumin, ½ teaspoon of the salt, and the red pepper flakes and cook for about 3 minutes more, until the tomatoes begin to break down. Stir in the butternut squash, chickpeas, 3 cups broth, lemon zest, and currants and bring to a simmer. 2. Partially cover the pan and cook for about 25 minutes, until the squash is tender. Add the spinach and cook, stirring, for 2 or 3 more minutes, until the spinach is wilted. Stir in the lemon juice. 3. While the vegetables are cooking, prepare the couscous. Combine the remaining 1½ cups broth, the remaining ½ teaspoon of salt, and the pepper in a small saucepan and bring to a boil. Remove the pan from the heat and stir in the couscous. Cover immediately and let sit for about 5 minutes, until the liquid has been fully absorbed. Fluff with a fork. 4. Spoon the couscous into serving bowls, top with the vegetable and chickpea mixture, and sprinkle some of the pine nuts over the top of each bowl. Serve immediately.

Per Serving
Calories: 549 | fat: 19g | protein: 16g | carbs: 84g | fiber: 14g | sodium: 774mg

Creamy Chicken Pasta

Prep time: 10 minutes | Cook time: 4 to 6 hours | Serves 4

¼ cup water
2 tablespoons arrowroot flour
2 pounds (907 g) boneless, skinless chicken breasts or thighs
1 (28-ounce / 794-g) can no-salt-added diced tomatoes, plus more as needed
1 green or red bell pepper, seeded and diced
1 small red onion, diced
2 garlic cloves, minced
1 teaspoon dried oregano
1 teaspoon dried parsley
1 teaspoon sea salt
½ teaspoon freshly ground black pepper
8 ounces (227 g) dried pasta
1 cup low-sodium chicken broth (optional)

1. In a small bowl, whisk together the water and arrowroot flour until the flour dissolves. 2. In a slow cooker, combine the chicken, tomatoes, bell pepper, onion, garlic, oregano, parsley, salt, black pepper, and arrowroot mixture. Stir to mix well. 3. Cover the cooker and cook for 4 to 6 hours on Low heat. 4. Stir in the pasta, making sure it is completely submerged. If it is not, add an additional 1 cup of diced tomatoes or 1 cup of chicken broth. Replace the cover on the cooker and cook for 15 to 30 minutes on Low heat, or until the pasta is tender.

Per Serving
Calories: 555 | fat: 12g | protein: 52g | carbs: 61g | fiber: 11g | sodium: 623mg

Tahini Soup

Prep time: 5 minutes | Cook time: 4 minutes | Serves 6

2 cups orzo
8 cups water
1 tablespoon olive oil
1 teaspoon salt
½ teaspoon ground black pepper
½ cup tahini
¼ cup lemon juice

1. Add pasta, water, oil, salt, and pepper to the Instant Pot®. Close lid, set steam release to Sealing, press the Manual button, and set time to 4 minutes. When the timer beeps, quick-release the pressure until the float valve drops, and open lid. Set aside. 2. Add tahini to a small mixing bowl and slowly add lemon juice while whisking constantly. Once lemon juice has been incorporated, take about ½ cup hot broth from the pot and slowly add to tahini mixture while whisking, until creamy smooth. 3. Pour mixture into the soup and mix well. Serve immediately.

Per Serving
Calories: 338 | fat: 13g | protein: 12g | carbs: 49g | fiber: 5g | sodium: 389mg

Spicy Broccoli Pasta Salad

Prep time: 10 minutes | Cook time: 10 minutes | Serves 2

8 ounces (227 g) whole-wheat pasta	¼ cup plain Greek yogurt
2 cups broccoli florets	Juice of 1 lemon
1 cup carrots, peeled and shredded	1 teaspoon red pepper flakes
	Sea salt and freshly ground pepper, to taste

1. Cook the pasta according to the package directions for al dente and drain well. 2. When the pasta is cool, combine it with the veggies, yogurt, lemon juice, and red pepper flakes in a large bowl, and stir thoroughly to combine. 3. Taste for seasoning, and add sea salt and freshly ground pepper as needed. 4. This dish can be served at room temperature or chilled.

Per Serving

Calories: 473 | fat: 2g | protein: 22g | carbs: 101g | fiber: 13g | sodium: 101mg

Linguine with Avocado Pesto

Prep time: 10 minutes | Cook time: 10 minutes | Serves 4

1 pound (454 g) dried linguine	1 tablespoon packed sun-dried tomatoes
2 avocados, coarsely chopped	⅛ teaspoon Italian seasoning
½ cup olive oil	⅛ teaspoon red pepper flakes
½ cup packed fresh basil	Sea salt
½ cup pine nuts	Freshly ground black pepper
Juice of 1 lemon	
3 garlic cloves	

1. Fill a large stockpot three-quarters full with water and bring to a boil over high heat. Add the pasta and cook according to the package instructions until al dente, about 15 minutes. 2. While the pasta is cooking, in a food processor, combine the avocados, olive oil, basil, pine nuts, lemon juice, garlic, sun-dried tomatoes, Italian seasoning, and red pepper flakes and process until a paste forms. Taste and season with salt and black pepper. 3. When the pasta is done, drain it and return it to the pot. Add half the pesto and mix. Add more pesto as desired and serve.

Per Serving

Calories: 694 | fat: 29g | protein: 17g | carbs: 93g | fiber: 8g | sodium: 11mg

Shrimp with Angel Hair Pasta

Prep time: 10 minutes | Cook time: 5 minutes | Serves 4

1 pound (454 g) dried angel hair pasta	Zest of ½ lemon
2 tablespoons olive oil	¼ cup chopped fresh Italian parsley
3 garlic cloves, minced	¼ teaspoon red pepper flakes (optional)
1 pound (454 g) large shrimp, peeled and deveined	

1. Fill a large stockpot three-quarters full with water and bring to a boil over high heat. Add the pasta and cook according to the package instructions until al dente, about 5 minutes. Drain the pasta and set aside. 2. In the same pot, heat the olive oil over medium heat. Add the garlic and sauté until fragrant, about 3 minutes. Add the shrimp and cook for about 2 minutes on each side, until pink and fully cooked. 3. Turn off the heat and return the pasta to the pot. Add the lemon zest and mix well. 4. Serve garnished with the parsley and red pepper flakes, if desired.

Per Serving

Calories: 567 | fat: 10g | protein: 31g | carbs: 87g | fiber: 4g | sodium: 651mg

Bowtie Pesto Pasta Salad

Prep time: 5 minutes | Cook time: 4 minutes | Serves 8

1 pound (454 g) whole-wheat bowtie pasta	2 cups baby spinach
4 cups water	½ cup chopped fresh basil
1 tablespoon extra-virgin olive oil	½ cup prepared pesto
2 cups halved cherry tomatoes	½ teaspoon ground black pepper
	½ cup grated Parmesan cheese

1. Add pasta, water, and olive oil to the Instant Pot®. Close lid, set steam release to Sealing, press the Manual button, and set time to 4 minutes. 2. When the timer beeps, quick-release the pressure until the float valve drops and open lid. Drain off any excess liquid. Allow pasta to cool to room temperature, about 30 minutes. Stir in tomatoes, spinach, basil, pesto, pepper, and cheese. Refrigerate for 2 hours. Stir well before serving.

Per Serving

Calories: 360 | fat: 13g | protein: 16g | carbs: 44g | fiber: 7g | sodium: 372mg

Penne with Tuna and Green Olives

Prep time: 5 minutes | Cook time: 5 minutes | Serves 4

2 tablespoons olive oil	oil)
3 garlic cloves, minced	½ teaspoon wine vinegar
½ cup green olives	12 ounces (340 g) penne pasta, cooked according to package directions
½ teaspoon salt	
¼ teaspoon freshly ground black pepper	2 tablespoons chopped flat-leaf parsley
2 (6-ounce / 170-g) cans tuna in olive oil (don't drain off the	

1. Heat the olive oil in a medium skillet over medium heat. Add the garlic and cook, stirring, 2 to 3 minutes, just until the garlic begins to brown. Add the olives, salt, pepper, and the tuna along with its oil. Cook, stirring, for a minute or two to heat the ingredients through. Remove from the heat and stir in the vinegar. 2. Add the cooked pasta to the skillet and toss to combine the pasta with the sauce. Serve immediately, garnished with the parsley.

Per Serving

Calories: 511 | fat: 22g | protein: 31g | carbs: 52g | fiber: 1g | sodium: 826mg

Whole-Wheat Spaghetti à la Puttanesca

Prep time: 5 minutes | Cook time: 20 minutes | Serves 6

1 pound (454 g) dried whole-wheat spaghetti
⅓ cup olive oil
5 garlic cloves, minced or pressed
4 anchovy fillets, chopped
½ teaspoon red pepper flakes
1 teaspoon salt
½ teaspoon freshly ground black pepper
1 (28-ounce / 794-g) can tomato purée
1 pint cherry tomatoes, halved
½ cup pitted green olives, halved
2 tablespoons drained capers
¾ cup coarsely chopped basil

1. Cook the pasta according to the package instructions. 2. Meanwhile, heat the oil in a large skillet over medium-high heat. Add the garlic, anchovies, red pepper flakes, salt, and pepper. Cook, stirring frequently, until the garlic just begins to turn golden brown, 2 to 3 minutes. Add the tomato purée, olives, cherry tomatoes, and capers and let the mixture simmer, reducing the heat if necessary, and stirring occasionally, until the pasta is done, about 10 minutes. 3. Drain the pasta in a colander and then add it to the sauce, tossing with tongs until the pasta is well coated. Serve hot, garnished with the basil.

Per Serving
Calories: 464 | fat: 17g | protein: 12g | carbs: 70g | fiber: 12g | sodium: 707mg

Rotini with Walnut Pesto, Peas, and Cherry Tomatoes

Prep time: 10 minutes | Cook time: 4 minutes | Serves 8

1 cup packed fresh basil leaves
⅓ cup chopped walnuts
¼ cup grated Parmesan cheese
¼ cup plus 1 tablespoon extra-virgin olive oil, divided
1 clove garlic, peeled
1 tablespoon lemon juice
¼ teaspoon salt
1 pound (454 g) whole-wheat rotini pasta
4 cups water
1 pint cherry tomatoes
1 cup fresh or frozen green peas
½ teaspoon ground black pepper

1. In a food processor, add basil and walnuts. Pulse until finely chopped, about 12 pulses. Add cheese, ¼ cup oil, garlic, lemon juice, and salt, and pulse until a rough paste forms, about 10 pulses. Refrigerate until ready to use. 2. Add pasta, water, and remaining 1 tablespoon oil to the Instant Pot®. Close lid, set steam release to Sealing, press the Manual button, and set time to 4 minutes. 3. When the timer beeps, quick-release the pressure until the float valve drops and open lid. Drain off any excess liquid. Allow pasta to cool to room temperature, about 30 minutes. Stir in basil mixture until pasta is well coated. Add tomatoes, peas, and pepper and toss to coat. Refrigerate for 2 hours. Stir well before serving.

Per Serving
Calories: 371 | fat: 15g | protein: 12g | carbs: 47g | fiber: 7g | sodium: 205mg

Pasta with Marinated Artichokes and Spinach

Prep time: 10 minutes | Cook time: 5 minutes | Serves 6

1 pound (454 g) whole-wheat spaghetti, broken in half
3½ cups water
4 tablespoons extra-virgin olive oil, divided
¼ teaspoon salt
2 cups baby spinach
1 cup drained marinated artichoke hearts
2 tablespoons chopped fresh oregano
2 tablespoons chopped fresh flat-leaf parsley
1 teaspoon ground black pepper
½ cup grated Parmesan cheese

1. Add pasta, water, 2 tablespoons oil, and salt to the Instant Pot®. Close lid, set steam release to Sealing, press the Manual button, and set time to 5 minutes. 2. When the timer beeps, quick-release the pressure until the float valve drops and open lid. Drain off any excess liquid. Stir in remaining 2 tablespoons oil and spinach. Toss until spinach is wilted. Stir in artichokes, oregano, and parsley until well mixed. Sprinkle with pepper and cheese, and serve immediately.

Per Serving
Calories: 414 | fat: 16g | protein: 16g | carbs: 56g | fiber: 9g | sodium: 467mg

Greek Spaghetti with Meat Sauce

Prep time: 10 minutes | Cook time: 17 minutes | Serves 6

1 pound (454 g) spaghetti
4 cups water
3 tablespoons olive oil, divided
1 medium white onion, peeled and diced
½ pound (227 g) lean ground veal
½ teaspoon salt
¼ teaspoon ground black pepper
¼ cup white wine
½ cup tomato sauce
1 cinnamon stick
2 bay leaves
1 clove garlic, peeled
¼ cup grated aged myzithra or Parmesan cheese

1. Add pasta, water, and 1 tablespoon oil to the Instant Pot®. Close lid, set steam release to Sealing, press the Manual button, and set time to 4 minutes. When the timer beeps, quick-release the pressure until the float valve drops, open lid, and drain. Press the Cancel button. Set aside. 2. Press the Sauté button and heat remaining 2 tablespoons oil. Add onion and cook until soft, about 3 minutes. Add veal and crumble well. Keep stirring until meat is browned, about 5 minutes. Add salt, pepper, wine, and tomato sauce, and mix well. 3. Stir in cinnamon stick, bay leaves, and garlic. Press the Cancel button. Close lid, set steam release to Sealing, press the Manual button, and set time to 5 minutes. When the timer beeps, quick-release the pressure until the float valve drops and open lid. Remove and discard cinnamon stick and bay leaves. 4. Place pasta in a large bowl. Sprinkle with cheese and spoon meat sauce over top. Serve immediately.

Per Serving
Calories: 447 | fat: 15g | protein: 18g | carbs: 60g | fiber: 4g | sodium: 394mg

Spaghetti with Fresh Mint Pesto and Ricotta Salata

Prep time: 5 minutes | Cook time: 15 minutes | Serves 4

1 pound (454 g) spaghetti	lemon
¼ cup slivered almonds	⅓ cup olive oil
2 cups packed fresh mint leaves, plus more for garnish	¼ teaspoon freshly ground black pepper
3 medium garlic cloves	½ cup freshly grated ricotta salata, plus more for garnish
1 tablespoon lemon juice and ½ teaspoon lemon zest from 1	

1. Set a large pot of salted water over high heat to boil for the pasta. 2. In a food processor, combine the almonds, mint leaves, garlic, lemon juice and zest, olive oil, and pepper and pulse to a smooth paste. Add the cheese and pulse to combine. 3. When the water is boiling, add the pasta and cook according to the package instructions. Drain the pasta and return it to the pot. Add the pesto to the pasta and toss until the pasta is well coated. Serve hot, garnished with additional mint leaves and cheese, if desired.

Per Serving
Calories: 619 | fat: 31g | protein: 21g | carbs: 70g | fiber: 4g | sodium: 113mg

Rotini with Spinach, Cherry Tomatoes, and Feta

Prep time: 5 minutes | Cook time: 30 minutes | Serves 2

6 ounces (170 g) uncooked rotini pasta (penne pasta will also work)	9 ounces (255 g) baby leaf spinach, washed and chopped
1 garlic clove, minced	1½ ounces (43 g) crumbled feta, divided
3 tablespoons extra virgin olive oil, divided	Kosher salt, to taste
1½ cups cherry tomatoes, halved and divided	Freshly ground black pepper, to taste

1. Cook the pasta according to the package instructions, reserving ½ cup of the cooking water. Drain and set aside. 2. While the pasta is cooking, combine the garlic with 2 tablespoons of the olive oil in a small bowl. Set aside. 3. Add the remaining tablespoon of olive oil to a medium pan placed over medium heat and then add 1 cup of the tomatoes. Cook for 2–3 minutes, then use a fork to mash lightly. 4. Add the spinach to the pan and continue cooking, stirring occasionally, until the spinach is wilted and the liquid is absorbed, about 4–5 minutes. 5. Transfer the cooked pasta to the pan with the spinach and tomatoes. Add 3 tablespoons of the pasta water, the garlic and olive oil mixture, and 1 ounce (28 g) of the crumbled feta. Increase the heat to high and cook for 1 minute. 6. Top with the remaining cherry tomatoes and feta, and season to taste with kosher salt and black pepper. Store covered in the refrigerator for up to 2 days.

Per Serving
Calories: 602 | fat: 27g | protein: 19g | carbs: 74g | fiber: 7g | sodium: 307mg

Mixed Vegetable Couscous

Prep time: 20 minutes | Cook time: 10 minutes | Serves 8

1 tablespoon light olive oil	oregano
1 medium zucchini, trimmed and chopped	2 cups Israeli couscous
1 medium yellow squash, chopped	3 cups vegetable broth
1 large red bell pepper, seeded and chopped	½ cup crumbled feta cheese
1 large orange bell pepper, seeded and chopped	¼ cup red wine vinegar
2 tablespoons chopped fresh	¼ cup extra-virgin olive oil
	½ teaspoon ground black pepper
	¼ cup chopped fresh basil

1. Press the Sauté button on the Instant Pot® and heat light olive oil. Add zucchini, squash, bell peppers, and oregano, and sauté 8 minutes. Press the Cancel button. Transfer to a serving bowl and set aside to cool. 2. Add couscous and broth to the Instant Pot® and stir well. Close lid, set steam release to Sealing, press the Manual button, and set time to 2 minutes. When the timer beeps, let pressure release naturally for 5 minutes, then quick-release the remaining pressure and open lid. 3. Fluff with a fork and stir in cooked vegetables, cheese, vinegar, extra-virgin olive oil, black pepper, and basil. Serve warm.

Per Serving
Calories: 355 | fat: 9g | protein: 14g | carbs: 61g | fiber: 7g | sodium: 588mg

Toasted Orzo Salad

Prep time: 15 minutes | Cook time: 8 minutes | Serves 6

2 tablespoons light olive oil	1 medium red bell pepper, seeded and diced
1 clove garlic, peeled and crushed	¼ cup crumbled feta cheese
2 cups orzo	1 tablespoon extra-virgin olive oil
3 cups vegetable broth	1 tablespoon red wine vinegar
½ cup sliced black olives	½ teaspoon ground black pepper
3 scallions, thinly sliced	¼ teaspoon salt
1 medium Roma tomato, seeded and diced	

1. Press the Sauté button on the Instant Pot® and heat light olive oil. Add garlic and orzo and cook, stirring frequently, until orzo is light golden brown, about 5 minutes. Press the Cancel button. 2. Add broth and stir. Close lid, set steam release to Sealing, press the Manual button, and set time to 3 minutes. When the timer beeps, let pressure release naturally for 5 minutes, then quick-release the remaining pressure until the float valve drops and open lid. 3. Transfer orzo to a medium bowl, then set aside to cool to room temperature, about 30 minutes. Add olives, scallions, tomato, bell pepper, feta, extra-virgin olive oil, vinegar, black pepper, and salt, and stir until combined. Serve at room temperature or refrigerate for at least 2 hours.

Per Serving
Calories: 120 | fat: 4g | protein: 4g | carbs: 17g | fiber: 1g | sodium: 586mg

Israeli Pasta Salad

Prep time: 15 minutes | Cook time: 4 minutes | Serves 6

½ pound (227 g) whole-wheat penne pasta	½ medium red onion, peeled and chopped
4 cups water	½ cup crumbled feta cheese
1 tablespoon plus ¼ cup extra-virgin olive oil, divided	1 teaspoon fresh thyme leaves
1 cup quartered cherry tomatoes	1 teaspoon chopped fresh oregano
½ English cucumber, chopped	½ teaspoon ground black pepper
½ medium orange bell pepper, seeded and chopped	¼ cup lemon juice

1. Add pasta, water, and 1 tablespoon oil to the Instant Pot®. Close lid, set steam release to Sealing, press the Manual button, and set time to 4 minutes. 2. When the timer beeps, quick-release the pressure until the float valve drops and open lid. Drain and set aside to cool for 30 minutes. Stir in tomatoes, cucumber, bell pepper, onion, feta, thyme, oregano, black pepper, lemon juice, and remaining ¼ cup oil. Refrigerate for 2 hours.

Per Serving
Calories: 243 | fat: 16g | protein: 7g | carbs: 20g | fiber: 3g | sodium: 180mg

Toasted Couscous with Feta, Cucumber, and Tomato

Prep time: 15 minutes | Cook time: 10 minutes | Serves 8

1 tablespoon plus ¼ cup light olive oil, divided	1 medium red onion, peeled and chopped
2 cups Israeli couscous	½ cup crumbled feta cheese
3 cups vegetable broth	¼ cup red wine vinegar
2 large tomatoes, seeded and diced	½ teaspoon ground black pepper
1 large English cucumber, diced	¼ cup chopped flat-leaf parsley
	¼ cup chopped fresh basil

1. Press the Sauté button on the Instant Pot® and heat 1 tablespoon oil. Add couscous and cook, stirring frequently, until couscous is light golden brown, about 7 minutes. Press the Cancel button. 2. Add broth and stir. Close lid, set steam release to Sealing, press the Manual button, and set time to 2 minutes. When the timer beeps, let pressure release naturally for 5 minutes, then quick-release the remaining pressure until the float valve drops and open lid. 3. Fluff couscous with a fork, then transfer to a medium bowl and set aside to cool to room temperature, about 30 minutes. Add remaining ¼ cup oil, tomatoes, cucumber, onion, feta, vinegar, pepper, parsley, and basil, and stir until combined. Serve at room temperature or refrigerate for at least 2 hours.

Per Serving
Calories: 286 | fat: 11g | protein: 9g | carbs: 38g | fiber: 3g | sodium: 438mg

Pasta Salad with Tomato, Arugula, and Feta

Prep time: 10 minutes | Cook time: 4 minutes | Serves 8

1 pound (454 g) rotini	seeded and diced
4 cups water	2 tablespoons white wine vinegar
3 tablespoons extra-virgin olive oil, divided	5 ounces (142 g) baby arugula
2 medium Roma tomatoes, diced	1 cup crumbled feta cheese
2 cloves garlic, peeled and minced	½ teaspoon salt
1 medium red bell pepper,	½ teaspoon ground black pepper

1. Add pasta, water, and 1 tablespoon oil to the Instant Pot®. Close lid, set steam release to Sealing, press the Manual button, and set time to 4 minutes. When the timer beeps, quick-release the pressure until the float valve drops, open lid, drain pasta, then rinse with cold water. Set aside. 2. In a large bowl, mix remaining 2 tablespoons oil, tomatoes, garlic, bell pepper, vinegar, arugula, and cheese. Stir in pasta and season with salt and pepper. Cover and refrigerate for 2 hours before serving.

Per Serving
Calories: 332 | fat: 12g | protein: 12g | carbs: 44g | fiber: 3g | sodium: 480mg

Chilled Pearl Couscous Salad

Prep time: 15 minutes | Cook time: 10 minutes | Serves 6

3 tablespoons olive oil, divided	¼ cup slivered almonds
1 cup pearl couscous	¼ cup chopped fresh mint leaves
1 cup water	
1 cup orange juice	2 tablespoons lemon juice
1 small cucumber, seeded and diced	1 teaspoon grated lemon zest
1 small yellow bell pepper, seeded and diced	¼ cup crumbled feta cheese
	¼ teaspoon fine sea salt
2 small Roma tomatoes, seeded and diced	1 teaspoon smoked paprika
	1 teaspoon garlic powder

1. Press the Sauté button and heat 1 tablespoon oil. Add couscous and cook for 2–4 minutes until couscous is slightly browned. Add water and orange juice. Press the Cancel button. 2. Close lid, set steam release to Sealing, press the Manual button, and set time to 5 minutes. When the timer beeps, let pressure release naturally for 5 minutes. Quick-release any remaining pressure until the float valve drops and open lid. Drain any liquid and set aside to cool for 20 minutes. 3. Combine remaining 2 tablespoons oil, cucumber, bell pepper, tomatoes, almonds, mint, lemon juice, lemon zest, cheese, salt, paprika, and garlic powder in a medium bowl. Add couscous and toss ingredients together. Cover and refrigerate overnight before serving.

Per Serving
Calories: 177 | fat: 11g | protein: 5g | carbs: 12g | fiber: 1g | sodium: 319mg

Couscous with Tomatoes and Olives

Prep time: 5 minutes | Cook time: 3 minutes | Serves 4

1 tablespoon tomato paste
2 cups vegetable broth
1 cup couscous
1 cup halved cherry tomatoes
½ cup halved mixed olives
¼ cup minced fresh flat-leaf parsley
2 tablespoons minced fresh

oregano
2 tablespoons minced fresh chives
1 tablespoon extra-virgin olive oil
1 tablespoon red wine vinegar
½ teaspoon ground black pepper

1. Pour tomato paste and broth into the Instant Pot® and stir until completely dissolved. Stir in couscous. Close lid, set steam release to Sealing, press the Manual button, and set time to 3 minutes. When the timer beeps, let pressure release naturally for 10 minutes, then quick-release the remaining pressure and open lid. 2. Fluff couscous with a fork. Add tomatoes, olives, parsley, oregano, chives, oil, vinegar, and pepper, and stir until combined. Serve warm or at room temperature.

Per Serving
Calories: 232 | fat: 5g | protein: 7g | carbs: 37g | fiber: 2g | sodium: 513mg

Avgolemono

Prep time: 10 minutes | Cook time: 3 minutes | Serves 6

6 cups chicken stock
½ cup orzo
1 tablespoon olive oil
12 ounces (340 g) cooked chicken breast, shredded
½ teaspoon salt
½ teaspoon ground black

pepper
¼ cup lemon juice
2 large eggs
2 tablespoons chopped fresh dill
1 tablespoon chopped fresh flat-leaf parsley

1. Add stock, orzo, and olive oil to the Instant Pot®. Close lid, set steam release to Sealing, press the Manual button, and set time to 3 minutes. When the timer beeps, quick-release the pressure until the float valve drops. Open lid and stir in chicken, salt, and pepper. 2. In a medium bowl, combine lemon juice and eggs, then slowly whisk in hot cooking liquid from the pot, ¼ cup at a time, until 1 cup of liquid has been added. Immediately add egg mixture to soup and stir well. Let stand on the Keep Warm setting, stirring occasionally, for 10 minutes. Add dill and parsley. Serve immediately.

Per Serving
Calories: 193 | fat: 5g | protein: 21g | carbs: 15g | fiber: 1g | sodium: 552mg

Couscous with Crab and Lemon

Prep time: 10 minutes | Cook time: 7 minutes | Serves 4

1 cup couscous
1 clove garlic, peeled and minced
2 cups water

3 tablespoons extra-virgin olive oil, divided
¼ cup minced fresh flat-leaf parsley

1 tablespoon minced fresh dill
8 ounces (227 g) jumbo lump crabmeat
3 tablespoons lemon juice

½ teaspoon ground black pepper
¼ cup grated Parmesan cheese

1. Place couscous, garlic, water, and 1 tablespoon oil in the Instant Pot® and stir well. Close lid, set steam release to Sealing, press the Manual button, and set time to 7 minutes. When the timer beeps, let pressure release naturally for 10 minutes, then quick-release the remaining pressure and open lid. 2. Fluff couscous with a fork. Add parsley, dill, crabmeat, lemon juice, pepper, and remaining 2 tablespoons oil, and stir until combined. Top with cheese and serve immediately.

Per Serving
Calories: 360 | fat: 15g | protein: 22g | carbs: 34g | fiber: 2g | sodium: 388mg

Puglia-Style Pasta with Broccoli Sauce

Prep time: 15 minutes | Cook time: 25 minutes | Serves 3

1 pound (454 g) fresh broccoli, washed and cut into small florets
7 ounces (198 g) uncooked rigatoni pasta
2 tablespoons extra virgin olive oil, plus 1½ tablespoons for serving
3 garlic cloves, thinly sliced
2 tablespoons pine nuts

4 canned packed-in-oil anchovies
½ teaspoon kosher salt
3 teaspoons fresh lemon juice
3 ounces (85 g) grated or shaved Parmesan cheese, divided
½ teaspoon freshly ground black pepper

1. Place the broccoli in a large pot filled with enough water to cover the broccoli. Bring the pot to a boil and cook for 12 minutes or until the stems can be easily pierced with a fork. Use a slotted spoon to transfer the broccoli to a plate, but do not discard the cooking water. Set the broccoli aside. 2. Add the pasta to the pot with the broccoli water and cook according to package instructions. 3. About 3 minutes before the pasta is ready, place a large, deep pan over medium heat and add 2 tablespoons of the olive oil. When the olive oil is shimmering, add the garlic and sauté for 1 minute, stirring continuously, until the garlic is golden, then add the pine nuts and continue sautéing for 1 more minute. 4. Stir in the anchovies, using a wooden spoon to break them into smaller pieces, then add the broccoli. Continue cooking for 1 additional minute, stirring continuously and using the spoon to break the broccoli into smaller pieces. 5. When the pasta is ready, remove the pot from the heat and drain, reserving ¼ cup of the cooking water. 6. Add the pasta and 2 tablespoons of the cooking water to the pan, stirring until all the ingredients are well combined. Cook for 1 minute, then remove the pan from the heat. 7. Promptly divide the pasta among three plates. Top each serving with a pinch of kosher salt, 1 teaspoon of the lemon juice, 1 ounce (28 g) of the Parmesan, 1½ teaspoons of the remaining olive oil, and a pinch of fresh ground pepper. Store covered in the refrigerator for up to 3 days.

Per Serving
Calories: 610 | fat: 31g | protein: 24g | carbs: 66g | fiber: 12g | sodium: 654mg

Yogurt and Dill Pasta Salad

Prep time: 10 minutes | Cook time: 4 minutes | Serves 8

½ cup low-fat plain Greek yogurt
1 tablespoon apple cider vinegar
2 tablespoons chopped fresh dill
1 teaspoon honey
1 pound (454 g) whole-wheat elbow macaroni
4 cups water
1 tablespoon extra-virgin olive oil
1 medium red bell pepper, seeded and chopped
1 medium sweet onion, peeled and diced
1 stalk celery, diced
½ teaspoon ground black pepper

1. In a small bowl, combine yogurt and vinegar. Add dill and honey, and mix well. Refrigerate until ready to use. 2. Place pasta, water, and olive oil to the Instant Pot®. Close lid, set steam release to Sealing, press the Manual button, and set time to 4 minutes. 3. When the timer beeps, quick-release the pressure until the float valve drops and open lid. Drain off any excess liquid. Cool pasta to room temperature, about 30 minutes. Add prepared dressing and toss until pasta is well coated. Add bell pepper, onion, celery, and black pepper, and toss to coat. Refrigerate for 2 hours. Stir well before serving.

Per Serving
Calories: 295 | fat: 5g | protein: 19g | carbs: 47g | fiber: 8g | sodium: 51mg

Rotini with Red Wine Marinara

Prep time: 10 minutes | Cook time: 25 minutes | Serves 6

1 pound (454 g) rotini
4 cups water
1 tablespoon olive oil
½ medium yellow onion, peeled and diced
3 cloves garlic, peeled and minced
1 (15-ounce / 425-g) can
crushed tomatoes
½ cup red wine
1 teaspoon sugar
2 tablespoons chopped fresh basil
½ teaspoon salt
¼ teaspoon ground black pepper

1. Add pasta and water to the Instant Pot®. Close lid, set steam release to Sealing, press the Manual button, and set time to 4 minutes. When the timer beeps, quick-release the pressure until the float valve drops and open the lid. Press the Cancel button. Drain pasta and set aside. 2. Clean pot and return to machine. Press the Sauté button and heat oil. Add onion and cook until it begins to caramelize, about 10 minutes. Add garlic and cook 30 seconds. Add tomatoes, red wine, and sugar, and simmer for 10 minutes. Add basil, salt, pepper, and pasta. Serve immediately.

Per Serving
Calories: 320 | fat: 4g | protein: 10g | carbs: 59g | fiber: 4g | sodium: 215mg

Orzo with Feta and Marinated Peppers

Prep time:1 hour 25 minutes | Cook time: 37 minutes | Serves 2

2 medium red bell peppers
¼ cup extra virgin olive oil
1 tablespoon balsamic vinegar plus 1 teaspoon for serving
¼ teaspoon ground cumin
Pinch of ground cinnamon
Pinch of ground cloves
¼ teaspoon fine sea salt plus a
pinch for the orzo
1 cup uncooked orzo
3 ounces (85 g) crumbled feta
1 tablespoon chopped fresh basil
¼ teaspoon freshly ground black pepper

1. Preheat the oven at 350ºF (180ºC). Place the peppers on a baking pan and roast in the oven for 25 minutes or until they're soft and can be pierced with a fork. Set aside to cool for 10 minutes. 2. While the peppers are roasting, combine the olive oil, 1 tablespoon of the balsamic vinegar, cumin, cinnamon, cloves, and ¼ teaspoon of the sea salt. Stir to combine, then set aside. 3. Peel the cooled peppers, remove the seeds, and then chop into large pieces. Place the peppers in the olive oil and vinegar mixture and then toss to coat, ensuring the peppers are covered in the marinade. Cover and place in the refrigerator to marinate for 20 minutes. 4. While the peppers are marinating, prepare the orzo by bringing 3 cups of water and a pinch of salt to a boil in a large pot over high heat. When the water is boiling, add the orzo, reduce the heat to medium, and cook, stirring occasionally, for 10–12 minutes or until soft, then drain and transfer to a serving bowl. 5. Add the peppers and marinade to the orzo, mixing well, then place in the refrigerator and to cool for at least 1 hour. 6. To serve, top with the feta, basil, black pepper, and 1 teaspoon of the balsamic vinegar. Mix well, and serve promptly. Store covered in the refrigerator for up to 3 days.

Per Serving
Calories: 600 | fat: 37g | protein: 15g | carbs: 51g | fiber: 4g | sodium: 690mg

Chapter 9 Pizzas, Wraps, and Sandwiches

Mexican Pizza

Prep time: 10 minutes | Cook time: 7 to 9 minutes | Serves 4

¾ cup refried beans (from a 16-ounce / 454-g can)
½ cup salsa
10 frozen precooked beef meatballs, thawed and sliced
1 jalapeño pepper, sliced
4 whole-wheat pita breads
1 cup shredded pepper Jack cheese
½ cup shredded Colby cheese
⅓ cup sour cream

1. In a medium bowl, combine the refried beans, salsa, meatballs, and jalapeño pepper. 2. Preheat the air fryer for 3 to 4 minutes or until hot. 3. Top the pitas with the refried bean mixture and sprinkle with the cheeses. 4. Bake at 370°F (188°C) for 7 to 9 minutes or until the pizza is crisp and the cheese is melted and starts to brown. 5. Top each pizza with a dollop of sour cream and serve warm.
Per Serving
Calories: 484 | fat: 30g | protein: 24g | carbs: 32g | fiber: 7g | sodium: 612mg

Greek Salad Wraps

Prep time: 15 minutes |Cook time: 0 minutes| Serves: 4

1½ cups seedless cucumber, peeled and chopped (about 1 large cucumber)
1 cup chopped tomato (about 1 large tomato)
½ cup finely chopped fresh mint
1 (2¼-ounce / 64-g) can sliced black olives (about ½ cup), drained
¼ cup diced red onion (about ¼ onion)
2 tablespoons extra-virgin olive oil
1 tablespoon red wine vinegar
¼ teaspoon freshly ground black pepper
¼ teaspoon kosher or sea salt
½ cup crumbled goat cheese (about 2 ounces / 57 g)
4 whole-wheat flatbread wraps or soft whole-wheat tortillas

1. In a large bowl, mix together the cucumber, tomato, mint, olives, and onion until well combined. 2. In a small bowl, whisk together the oil, vinegar, pepper, and salt. Drizzle the dressing over the salad, and mix gently. 3. With a knife, spread the goat cheese evenly over the four wraps. Spoon a quarter of the salad filling down the middle of each wrap. 4. Fold up each wrap: Start by folding up the bottom, then fold one side over and fold the other side over the top. Repeat with the remaining wraps and serve.
Per Serving
Calories: 217 | fat: 14g | protein: 7g | carbs: 17g | fiber: 3g | sodium: 329mg

Mediterranean Tuna Salad Sandwiches

Prep time: 10 minutes | Cook time: 5 minutes | Serves 2

1 can white tuna, packed in water or olive oil, drained
1 roasted red pepper, diced
½ small red onion, diced
10 low-salt olives, pitted and finely chopped
¼ cup plain Greek yogurt
1 tablespoon flat-leaf parsley, chopped
Juice of 1 lemon
Sea salt and freshly ground pepper, to taste
4 whole-grain pieces of bread

1. In a small bowl, combine all of the ingredients except the bread, and mix well. 2. Season with sea salt and freshly ground pepper to taste. Toast the bread or warm in a pan. 3. Make the sandwich and serve immediately.
Per Serving
Calories: 307 | fat: 7g | protein: 30g | carbs: 31g | fiber: 5g | sodium: 564mg

Open-Faced Eggplant Parmesan Sandwich

Prep time: 10 minutes | Cook time: 10 minutes | Serves 2

1 small eggplant, sliced into ¼-inch rounds
Pinch sea salt
2 tablespoons olive oil
Sea salt and freshly ground pepper, to taste
2 slices whole-grain bread, thickly cut and toasted
1 cup marinara sauce (no added sugar)
¼ cup freshly grated, low-fat Parmesan cheese

1. Preheat broiler to high heat. 2. Salt both sides of the sliced eggplant, and let sit for 20 minutes to draw out the bitter juices. 3. Rinse the eggplant and pat dry with a paper towel. 4. Brush the eggplant with the olive oil, and season with sea salt and freshly ground pepper. 5. Lay the eggplant on a sheet pan, and broil until crisp, about 4 minutes. Flip over and crisp the other side. 6. Lay the toasted bread on a sheet pan. Spoon some marinara sauce on each slice of bread, and layer the eggplant on top. 7. Sprinkle half of the cheese on top of the eggplant and top with more marinara sauce. 8. Sprinkle with remaining cheese. 9. Put the sandwiches under the broiler until the cheese has melted, about 2 minutes. 10. Using a spatula, transfer the sandwiches to plates and serve.
Per Serving
Calories: 355 | fat: 19g | protein: 10g | carbs: 38g | fiber: 13g | sodium: 334mg

Turkish Pizza

Prep time: 20 minutes | Cook time: 10 minutes | Serves 4

4 ounces (113 g) ground lamb or 85% lean ground beef
¼ cup finely chopped green bell pepper
¼ cup chopped fresh parsley
1 small plum tomato, seeded and finely chopped
2 tablespoons finely chopped yellow onion
1 garlic clove, minced
2 teaspoons tomato paste
¼ teaspoon sweet paprika
¼ teaspoon ground cumin
⅛ to ¼ teaspoon red pepper flakes
⅛ teaspoon ground allspice
⅛ teaspoon kosher salt
⅛ teaspoon black pepper
4 (6-inch) flour tortillas
For Serving:
Chopped fresh mint
Extra-virgin olive oil
Lemon wedges

1. In a medium bowl, gently mix the ground lamb, bell pepper, parsley, chopped tomato, onion, garlic, tomato paste, paprika, cumin, red pepper flakes, allspice, salt, and black pepper until well combined. 2. Divide the meat mixture evenly among the tortillas, spreading it all the way to the edge of each tortilla. 3. Place 1 tortilla in the air fryer basket. Set the air fryer to 400ºF (204ºC) for 10 minutes, or until the meat topping has browned and the edge of the tortilla is golden. Transfer to a plate and repeat to cook the remaining tortillas. 4. Serve the pizzas warm, topped with chopped fresh mint and a drizzle of extra-virgin olive oil and with lemon wedges alongside.

Per Serving
Calories: 172 | fat: 8g | protein: 8g | carbs: 18g | fiber: 2g | sodium: 318mg

Beans and Greens Pizza

Prep time: 11 minutes | Cook time: 14 to 19 minutes | Serves 4

¾ cup whole-wheat pastry flour
½ teaspoon low-sodium baking powder
1 tablespoon olive oil, divided
1 cup chopped kale
2 cups chopped fresh baby spinach
1 cup canned no-salt-added cannellini beans, rinsed and drained
½ teaspoon dried thyme
1 piece low-sodium string cheese, torn into pieces

1. In a small bowl, mix the pastry flour and baking powder until well combined. 2. Add ¼ cup of water and 2 teaspoons of olive oil. Mix until a dough forms. 3. On a floured surface, press or roll the dough into a 7-inch round. Set aside while you cook the greens. 4. In a baking pan, mix the kale, spinach, and remaining teaspoon of the olive oil. Air fry at 350ºF (177ºC) for 3 to 5 minutes, until the greens are wilted. Drain well. 5. Put the pizza dough into the air fryer basket. Top with the greens, cannellini beans, thyme, and string cheese. Air fry for 11 to 14 minutes, or until the crust is golden brown and the cheese is melted. Cut into quarters to serve.

Per Serving
Calories: 181 | fat: 6g | protein: 8g | carbs: 27g | fiber: 6g | sodium: 103mg

Pesto Chicken Mini Pizzas

Prep time: 5 minutes | Cook time: 10 minutes | Serves 4

2 cups shredded cooked chicken
¾ cup pesto
4 English muffins, split
2 cups shredded Mozzarella cheese

1. In a medium bowl, toss the chicken with the pesto. Place one-eighth of the chicken on each English muffin half. Top each English muffin with ¼ cup of the Mozzarella cheese. 2. Put four pizzas at a time in the air fryer and air fry at 350ºF (177ºC) for 5 minutes. Repeat this process with the other four pizzas.

Per Serving
Calories: 617 | fat: 36g | protein: 45g | carbs: 29g | fiber: 3g | sodium: 544mg

Turkey and Provolone Panini with Roasted Peppers and Onions

Prep time: 15 minutes | Cook time: 1 hour 5 minutes | Serves 4

For the Peppers And Onions:
2 red bell pepper, seeded and quartered
2 red onions, peeled and quartered
2 tablespoons olive oil
½ teaspoon salt
½ teaspoon freshly ground
black pepper
For the Panini:
2 tablespoons olive oil
8 slices whole-wheat bread
8 ounces (227 g) thinly sliced provolone cheese
8 ounces (227 g) sliced roasted turkey or chicken breast

1. Preheat the oven to 375ºF (190ºC). 2. To roast the peppers and onions, toss them together with the olive oil, salt, and pepper on a large, rimmed baking sheet. Spread them out in a single layer and then bake in the preheated oven for 45 to 60 minutes, turning occasionally, until they are tender and beginning to brown. Remove the peppers and onions from the oven and let them cool for a few minutes until they are cool enough to handle. Skin the peppers and thinly slice them. Thinly slice the onions. 3. Preheat a skillet or grill pan over medium-high heat. 4. To make the panini, brush one side of each of the 8 slices of bread with olive oil. Place 4 of the bread slices, oiled side down, on your work surface. Top each with ¼ of the cheese and ¼ of the turkey, and top with some of the roasted peppers and onions. Place the remaining 4 bread slices on top of the sandwiches, oiled side up. 5. Place the sandwiches in the skillet or grill pan (you may have to cook them in two batches), cover the pan, and cook until the bottoms have golden brown grill marks and the cheese is beginning to melt, about 2 minutes. Turn the sandwiches over and cook, covered, until the second side is golden brown and the cheese is melted, another 2 minutes or so. Cut each sandwich in half and serve immediately.

Per Serving
Calories: 603 | fat: 32g | protein: 41g | carbs: 37g | fiber: 6g | sodium: 792mg

Bocadillo with Herbed Tuna and Piquillo Peppers

Prep time: 5 minutes | Cook time: 20 minutes | Serves 4

2 tablespoons olive oil, plus more for brushing
1 medium onion, finely chopped
2 leeks, white and tender green parts only, finely chopped
1 teaspoon chopped thyme
½ teaspoon dried marjoram
½ teaspoon salt
¼ teaspoon freshly ground black pepper
3 tablespoons sherry vinegar
1 carrot, finely diced
2 (8-ounce / 227-g) jars Spanish tuna in olive oil
4 crusty whole-wheat sandwich rolls, split
1 ripe tomato, grated on the large holes of a box grater
4 piquillo peppers, cut into thin strips

1. Heat 2 tablespoons olive oil in a medium skillet over medium heat. Add the onion, leeks, thyme, marjoram, salt, and pepper. Stir frequently until the onions are softened, about 10 minutes. Stir in the vinegar and carrot and cook until the liquid has evaporated, 5 minutes. Transfer the mixture to a bowl and let cool to room temperature or refrigerate for 15 minutes or so. 2. In a medium bowl, combine the tuna, along with its oil, with the onion mixture, breaking the tuna chunks up with a fork. 3. Brush the rolls lightly with oil and toast under the broiler until lightly browned, about 2 minutes. Spoon the tomato pulp onto the bottom half of each roll, dividing equally and spreading it with the back of the spoon. Divide the tuna mixture among the rolls and top with the piquillo pepper slices. Serve immediately.
Per Serving
Calories: 416 | fat: 18g | protein: 35g | carbs: 30g | fiber: 5g | sodium: 520mg

Classic Margherita Pizza

Prep time: 10 minutes | Cook time: 10 minutes | Serves 4

All-purpose flour, for dusting
1 pound (454 g) premade pizza dough
1 (15-ounce / 425-g) can crushed San Marzano tomatoes, with their juices
2 garlic cloves
1 teaspoon Italian seasoning
Pinch sea salt, plus more as needed
1½ teaspoons olive oil, for drizzling
10 slices mozzarella cheese
12 to 15 fresh basil leaves

1. Preheat the oven to 475°F (245°C). 2. On a floured surface, roll out the dough to a 12-inch round and place it on a lightly floured pizza pan or baking sheet. 3. In a food processor, combine the tomatoes with their juices, garlic, Italian seasoning, and salt and process until smooth. Taste and adjust the seasoning. 4. Drizzle the olive oil over the pizza dough, then spoon the pizza sauce over the dough and spread it out evenly with the back of the spoon, leaving a 1-inch border. Evenly distribute the mozzarella over the pizza. 5. Bake until the crust is cooked through and golden, 8 to 10 minutes. Remove from the oven and let sit for 1 to 2 minutes. Top with the basil right before serving.
Per Serving
Calories: 570 | fat: 21g | protein: 28g | carbs: 66g | fiber: 4g | sodium: 570mg

Sautéed Mushroom, Onion, and Pecorino Romano Panini

Prep time: 10 minutes | Cook time: 20 minutes | Serves 4

3 tablespoons olive oil, divided
1 small onion, diced
10 ounces (283 g) button or cremini mushrooms, sliced
½ teaspoon salt
¼ teaspoon freshly ground black pepper
4 crusty Italian sandwich rolls
4 ounces (113 g) freshly grated Pecorino Romano

1. Heat 1 tablespoon of the olive oil in a skillet over medium-high heat. Add the onion and cook, stirring, until it begins to soften, about 3 minutes. Add the mushrooms, season with salt and pepper, and cook, stirring, until they soften and the liquid they release evaporates, about 7 minutes. 2. To make the panini, heat a skillet or grill pan over high heat and brush with 1 tablespoon olive oil. Brush the inside of the rolls with the remaining 1 tablespoon olive oil. Divide the mushroom mixture evenly among the rolls and top each with ¼ of the grated cheese. 3. Place the sandwiches in the hot pan and place another heavy pan, such as a cast-iron skillet, on top to weigh them down. Cook for about 3 to 4 minutes, until crisp and golden on the bottom, and then flip over and repeat on the second side, cooking for an additional 3 to 4 minutes until golden and crisp. Slice each sandwich in half and serve hot.
Per Serving
Calories: 348 | fat: 20g | protein: 14g | carbs: 30g | fiber: 2g | sodium: 506mg

Herbed Focaccia Panini with Anchovies and Burrata

Prep time: 5 minutes | Cook time: 8 minutes | Serves 4

8 ounces (227 g) burrata cheese, chilled and sliced
1 pound (454 g) whole-wheat herbed focaccia, cut crosswise into 4 rectangles and split horizontally
1 can anchovy fillets packed in oil, drained
8 slices tomato, sliced
2 cups arugula
1 tablespoon olive oil

1. Divide the cheese evenly among the bottom halves of the focaccia rectangles. Top each with 3 or 4 anchovy fillets, 2 slices of tomato, and ½ cup arugula. Place the top halves of the focaccia on top of the sandwiches. 2. To make the panini, heat a skillet or grill pan over high heat and brush with the olive oil. 3. Place the sandwiches in the hot pan and place another heavy pan, such as a cast-iron skillet, on top to weigh them down. Cook for about 3 to 4 minutes, until crisp and golden on the bottom, and then flip over and repeat on the second side, cooking for an additional 3 to 4 minutes until golden and crisp. Slice each sandwich in half and serve hot.
Per Serving
Calories: 596 | fat: 30g | protein: 27g | carbs: 58g | fiber: 5g | sodium: 626mg

Margherita Open-Face Sandwiches

Prep time: 10 minutes |Cook time: 5 minutes| Serves: 4

2 (6- to 7-inch) whole-wheat submarine or hoagie rolls, sliced open horizontally
1 tablespoon extra-virgin olive oil
1 garlic clove, halved
1 large ripe tomato, cut into 8 slices
¼ teaspoon dried oregano

1 cup fresh mozzarella (about 4 ounces / 113 g), patted dry and sliced
¼ cup lightly packed fresh basil leaves, torn into small pieces
¼ teaspoon freshly ground black pepper

1. Preheat the broiler to high with the rack 4 inches under the heating element. 2. Place the sliced bread on a large, rimmed baking sheet. Place under the broiler for 1 minute, until the bread is just lightly toasted. Remove from the oven. 3. Brush each piece of the toasted bread with the oil, and rub a garlic half over each piece. 4. Place the toasted bread back on the baking sheet. Evenly distribute the tomato slices on each piece, sprinkle with the oregano, and layer the cheese on top. 5. Place the baking sheet under the broiler. Set the timer for 1½ minutes, but check after 1 minute. When the cheese is melted and the edges are just starting to get dark brown, remove the sandwiches from the oven (this can take anywhere from 1½ to 2 minutes). 6. Top each sandwich with the fresh basil and pepper.
Per Serving
Calories: 176 | fat: 9g | protein: 10g | carbs: 14g | fiber: 2g | sodium: 119mg

Jerk Chicken Wraps

Prep time: 30 minutes | Cook time: 15 minutes | Serves 4

1 pound (454 g) boneless, skinless chicken tenderloins
1 cup jerk marinade
Olive oil
4 large low-carb tortillas

1 cup julienned carrots
1 cup peeled cucumber ribbons
1 cup shredded lettuce
1 cup mango or pineapple chunks

1. In a medium bowl, coat the chicken with the jerk marinade, cover, and refrigerate for 1 hour. 2. Spray the air fryer basket lightly with olive oil. 3. Place the chicken in the air fryer basket in a single layer and spray lightly with olive oil. You may need to cook the chicken in batches. Reserve any leftover marinade. 4. Air fry at 375°F (191°C) for 8 minutes. Turn the chicken over and brush with some of the remaining marinade. Cook until the chicken reaches an internal temperature of at least 165°F (74°C), an additional 5 to 7 minutes. 5. To assemble the wraps, fill each tortilla with ¼ cup carrots, ¼ cup cucumber, ¼ cup lettuce, and ¼ cup mango. Place one quarter of the chicken tenderloins on top and roll up the tortilla. These are great served warm or cold.
Per Serving
Calories: 241 | fat: 4g | protein: 28g | carbs: 23g | fiber: 4g | sodium: 85mg

Vegetable Pita Sandwiches

Prep time: 15 minutes | Cook time: 9 to 12 minutes | Serves 4

1 baby eggplant, peeled and chopped
1 red bell pepper, sliced
½ cup diced red onion
½ cup shredded carrot

1 teaspoon olive oil
⅓ cup low-fat Greek yogurt
½ teaspoon dried tarragon
2 low-sodium whole-wheat pita breads, halved crosswise

1. In a baking pan, stir together the eggplant, red bell pepper, red onion, carrot, and olive oil. Put the vegetable mixture into the air fryer basket and roast at 390°F (199°C) for 7 to 9 minutes, stirring once, until the vegetables are tender. Drain if necessary. 2. In a small bowl, thoroughly mix the yogurt and tarragon until well combined. 3. Stir the yogurt mixture into the vegetables. Stuff one-fourth of this mixture into each pita pocket. 4. Place the sandwiches in the air fryer and cook for 2 to 3 minutes, or until the bread is toasted. Serve immediately.
Per Serving
Calories: 115 | fat: 2g | protein: 4g | carbs: 22g | fiber: 6g | sodium: 90mg

Roasted Vegetable Bocadillo with Romesco Sauce

Prep time: 10 minutes | Cook time: 20 minutes | Serves 4

2 small yellow squash, sliced lengthwise
2 small zucchini, sliced lengthwise
1 medium red onion, thinly sliced
4 large button mushrooms, sliced
2 tablespoons olive oil
1 teaspoon salt, divided
½ teaspoon freshly ground black pepper, divided

2 roasted red peppers from a jar, drained
2 tablespoons blanched almonds
1 tablespoon sherry vinegar
1 small clove garlic
4 crusty multigrain rolls
4 ounces (113 g) goat cheese, at room temperature
1 tablespoon chopped fresh basil

1. Preheat the oven to 400°F (205°C). 2. In a medium bowl, toss the yellow squash, zucchini, onion, and mushrooms with the olive oil, ½ teaspoon salt, and ¼ teaspoon pepper. Spread on a large baking sheet. Roast the vegetables in the oven for about 20 minutes, until softened. 3. Meanwhile, in a food processor, combine the roasted peppers, almonds, vinegar, garlic, the remaining ½ teaspoon salt, and the remaining ¼ teaspoon pepper and process until smooth. 4. Split the rolls and spread ¼ of the goat cheese on the bottom of each. Place the roasted vegetables on top of the cheese, dividing equally. Top with chopped basil. Spread the top halves of the rolls with the roasted red pepper sauce and serve immediately.
Per Serving
Calories: 379 | fat: 21g | protein: 17g | carbs: 32g | fiber: 4g | sodium: 592mg

Mediterranean-Pita Wraps

Prep time: 5 minutes | Cook time: 14 minutes | Serves 4

1 pound (454 g) mackerel fish fillets
2 tablespoons olive oil
1 tablespoon Mediterranean seasoning mix
½ teaspoon chili powder
Sea salt and freshly ground black pepper, to taste
2 ounces (57 g) feta cheese, crumbled
4 tortillas

1. Toss the fish fillets with the olive oil; place them in the lightly oiled air fryer basket. 2. Air fry the fish fillets at 400°F (204°C) for about 14 minutes, turning them over halfway through the cooking time. 3. Assemble your pitas with the chopped fish and remaining ingredients and serve warm.

Per Serving
Calories: 275 | fat: 13g | protein: 27g | carbs: 13g | fiber: 2g | sodium: 322mg

Grilled Eggplant and Chopped Greek Salad Wraps

Prep time: 10 minutes | Cook time: 20 minutes | Serves 4

15 small tomatoes, such as cherry or grape tomatoes, halved
10 pitted Kalamata olives, chopped
1 medium red onion, halved and thinly sliced
¾ cup crumbled feta cheese (about 4 ounces / 113 g)
2 tablespoons balsamic vinegar
1 tablespoon chopped fresh parsley
1 clove garlic, minced
2 tablespoons olive oil, plus 2 teaspoons, divided
¾ teaspoon salt, divided
1 medium cucumber, peeled, halved lengthwise, seeded, and diced
1 large eggplant, sliced ½-inch thick
½ teaspoon freshly ground black pepper
4 whole-wheat sandwich wraps or whole-wheat flour tortillas

1. In a medium bowl, toss together the tomatoes, olives, onion, cheese, vinegar, parsley, garlic, 2 teaspoons olive oil, and ¼ teaspoon of salt. Let sit at room temperature for 20 minutes. Add the cucumber, toss to combine, and let sit another 10 minutes. 2. While the salad is resting, grill the eggplant. Heat a grill or grill pan to high heat. Brush the remaining 2 tablespoons olive oil onto both sides of the eggplant slices. Grill for about 8 to 10 minutes per side, until grill marks appear and the eggplant is tender and cooked through. Transfer to a plate and season with the remaining ½ teaspoon of salt and the pepper. 3. Heat the wraps in a large, dry skillet over medium heat just until warm and soft, about 1 minute on each side. Place 2 or 3 eggplant slices down the center of each wrap. Spoon some of the salad mixture on top of the eggplant, using a slotted spoon so that any excess liquid is drained off. Fold in the sides of the wrap and roll up like a burrito. Serve immediately.

Per Serving
Calories: 233 | fat: 10g | protein: 8g | carbs: 29g | fiber: 7g | sodium: 707mg

Dill Salmon Salad Wraps

Prep time: 10 minutes |Cook time: 10 minutes| Serves:6

1 pound (454 g) salmon filet, cooked and flaked, or 3 (5-ounce / 142-g) cans salmon
½ cup diced carrots (about 1 carrot)
½ cup diced celery (about 1 celery stalk)
3 tablespoons chopped fresh dill
3 tablespoons diced red onion (a little less than ⅛ onion)
2 tablespoons capers
1½ tablespoons extra-virgin olive oil
1 tablespoon aged balsamic vinegar
½ teaspoon freshly ground black pepper
¼ teaspoon kosher or sea salt
4 whole-wheat flatbread wraps or soft whole-wheat tortillas

1. In a large bowl, mix together the salmon, carrots, celery, dill, red onion, capers, oil, vinegar, pepper, and salt. 2. Divide the salmon salad among the flatbreads. Fold up the bottom of the flatbread, then roll up the wrap and serve.

Per Serving
Calories: 185 | fat: 8g | protein: 17g | carbs: 12g | fiber: 2g | sodium: 237mg

Croatian Double-Crust Pizza with Greens and Garlic

Prep time: 15 minutes | Cook time: 20 minutes | Serves 4

4½ cups all-purpose flour
1¼ teaspoons salt, divided
1½ cups olive oil, plus 3 tablespoons, divided
1 cup warm water
1 pound (454 g) Swiss chard or kale, tough center ribs
removed, leaves julienned
¼ small head of green cabbage, thinly sliced
¼ teaspoon freshly ground black pepper
4 cloves garlic, minced

1. In a medium bowl, combine the flour and 1 teaspoon salt. Add 1½ cups olive oil and the warm water and stir with a fork until the mixture comes together and forms a ball. Wrap the ball in plastic wrap and refrigerate for at least 30 minutes. 2. While the dough is chilling, in a large bowl, toss together the greens, cabbage, 2 tablespoons olive oil, the remaining ¼ teaspoon salt, and the pepper. 3. Preheat the oven to 400°F (205°C). 4. Halve the dough and place the halves on two sheets of lightly floured parchment paper. Roll or pat the dough out into two ¼-inch-thick, 11-inch-diameter rounds. 5. Spread the greens mixture over one of the dough rounds, leaving about an inch clear around the edge. Place the second dough round over the greens and fold the edges together to seal the two rounds together. Bake in the preheated oven until the crust is golden brown, about 20 minutes. 6. While the pizza is in the oven, combine 1 tablespoon of olive oil with the garlic. When the pizza is done, remove it from the oven and immediately brush the garlic-oil mixture over the crust. Cut into wedges and serve hot.

Per Serving
Calories: 670 | fat: 45g | protein: 10g | carbs: 62g | fiber: 5g | sodium: 504mg

Barbecue Chicken Pita Pizza

Prep time: 5 minutes | Cook time: 5 to 7 minutes per batch | Makes 4 pizzas

1 cup barbecue sauce, divided
4 pita breads
2 cups shredded cooked chicken
2 cups shredded Mozzarella

cheese
½ small red onion, thinly sliced
2 tablespoons finely chopped fresh cilantro

1. Measure ½ cup of the barbecue sauce in a small measuring cup. Spread 2 tablespoons of the barbecue sauce on each pita. 2. In a medium bowl, mix together the remaining ½ cup of barbecue sauce and chicken. Place ½ cup of the chicken on each pita. Top each pizza with ½ cup of the Mozzarella cheese. Sprinkle the tops of the pizzas with the red onion. 3. Place one pizza in the air fryer. Air fry at 400°F (204°C) for 5 to 7 minutes. Repeat this process with the remaining pizzas. 4. Top the pizzas with the cilantro.

Per Serving
Calories: 530 | fat: 19g | protein: 40g | carbs: 47g | fiber: 2g | sodium: 672mg

Moroccan Lamb Wrap with Harissa

Prep time: 10 minutes | Cook time: 10 minutes | Serves 4

1 clove garlic, minced
2 teaspoons ground cumin
2 teaspoons chopped fresh thyme
¼ cup olive oil, divided
1 lamb leg steak, about 12 ounces (340 g)
4 (8-inch) pocketless pita rounds or naan, preferably whole-wheat

1 medium eggplant, sliced ½-inch thick
1 medium zucchini, sliced lengthwise into 4 slices
1 bell pepper (any color), roasted and skinned
6 to 8 Kalamata olives, sliced
Juice of 1 lemon
2 to 4 tablespoons harissa
2 cups arugula

1. In a large bowl, combine the garlic, cumin, thyme, and 1 tablespoon of the olive oil. Add the lamb, turn to coat, cover, refrigerate, and marinate for at least an hour. 2. Preheat the oven to 400°F (205°C). 3. Heat a grill or grill pan to high heat. Remove the lamb from the marinade and grill for about 4 minutes per side, until medium-rare. Transfer to a plate and let rest for about 10 minutes before slicing thinly across the grain. 4. While the meat is resting, wrap the bread rounds in aluminum foil and heat in the oven for about 10 minutes. 5. Meanwhile, brush the eggplant and zucchini slices with the remaining olive oil and grill until tender, about 3 minutes. Dice them and the bell pepper. Toss in a large bowl with the olives and lemon juice. 6. Spread some of the harissa onto each warm flatbread round and top each evenly with roasted vegetables, a few slices of lamb, and a handful of the arugula. 7. Roll up the wraps, cut each in half crosswise, and serve immediately.

Per Serving
Calories: 553 | fat: 24g | protein: 33g | carbs: 53g | fiber: 11g | sodium: 531mg

Moroccan Lamb Flatbread with Pine Nuts, Mint, and Ras Al Hanout

Prep time: 10 minutes | Cook time: 20 minutes | Serves 4

1⅓ cups plain Greek yogurt
Juice of 1½ lemons, divided
1¼ teaspoons salt, divided
1 pound (454 g) ground lamb
1 medium red onion, diced
1 clove garlic, minced
1 tablespoon ras al hanout
¼ cup chopped fresh mint

leaves
Freshly ground black pepper
4 Middle Eastern-style flatbread rounds
2 tablespoons toasted pine nuts
16 cherry tomatoes, halved
2 tablespoons chopped cilantro

1. Preheat the oven to 450°F (235°C). 2. In a small bowl, stir together the yogurt, the juice of ½ lemon, and ¼ teaspoon salt. 3. Heat a large skillet over medium-high heat. Add the lamb and cook, stirring frequently, until browned, about 5 minutes. Drain any excess rendered fat from the pan and then stir in the onion and garlic and cook, stirring, until softened, about 3 minutes more. Stir in the ras al hanout, mint, the remaining teaspoon of salt, and pepper. 4. Place the flatbread rounds on a baking sheet (or two if necessary) and top with the lamb mixture, pine nuts, and tomatoes, dividing equally. Bake in the preheated oven until the crust is golden brown and the tomatoes have softened, about 10 minutes. Scatter the cilantro over the flatbreads and squeeze the remaining lemon juice over them. Cut into wedges and serve dolloped with the yogurt sauce.

Per Serving
Calories: 463 | fat: 22g | protein: 34g | carbs: 34g | fiber: 3g | sodium: 859mg

Turkey Burgers with Feta and Dill

Prep time: 5 minutes | Cook time: 15 minutes | Serves 4

1 pound (454 g) ground turkey breast
1 small red onion, ½ finely chopped, ½ sliced
½ cup crumbled feta cheese
¼ cup chopped fresh dill
1 clove garlic, minced

½ teaspoon kosher salt
¼ teaspoon ground black pepper
4 whole grain hamburger rolls
4 thick slices tomato
4 leaves lettuce

1. Coat a grill rack or grill pan with olive oil and prepare to medium-high heat. 2. In a large bowl, use your hands to combine the turkey, chopped onion, cheese, dill, garlic, salt, and pepper. Do not overmix. Divide into 4 patties, 4' in diameter. 3. Grill the patties, covered, until a thermometer inserted in the center registers 165°F (74°C), 5 to 6 minutes per side. 4. Serve each patty on a roll with the sliced onion, 1 slice of the tomato, and 1 leaf of the lettuce.

Per Serving
Calories: 305 | fat: 7g | protein: 35g | carbs: 26g | fiber: 3g | sodium: 708mg

Za'atar Pizza

Prep time: 10 minutes | Cook time: 15 minutes | Serves 4 to 6

1 sheet puff pastry
¼ cup extra-virgin olive oil
⅓ cup za'atar seasoning

1. Preheat the oven to 350°F (180°C). 2. Put the puff pastry on a parchment-lined baking sheet. Cut the pastry into desired slices. 3. Brush the pastry with olive oil. Sprinkle with the za'atar. 4. Put the pastry in the oven and bake for 10 to 12 minutes or until edges are lightly browned and puffed up. Serve warm or at room temperature.
Per Serving
Calories: 374 | fat: 30g | protein: 3g | carbs: 20g | fiber: 1g | sodium: 166mg

Grilled Eggplant and Feta Sandwiches

Prep time: 10 minutes | Cook time: 8 minutes | Serves 2

1 medium eggplant, sliced into ½-inch-thick slices
2 tablespoons olive oil
Sea salt and freshly ground pepper, to taste
5 to 6 tablespoons hummus
4 slices whole-wheat bread, toasted
1 cup baby spinach leaves
2 ounces (57 g) feta cheese, softened

1. Preheat a gas or charcoal grill to medium-high heat. 2. Salt both sides of the sliced eggplant, and let sit for 20 minutes to draw out the bitter juices. 3. Rinse the eggplant and pat dry with a paper towel. 4. Brush the eggplant slices with olive oil and season with sea salt and freshly ground pepper. 5. Grill the eggplant until lightly charred on both sides but still slightly firm in the middle, about 3–4 minutes a side. 6. Spread the hummus on the bread and top with the spinach leaves, feta, and eggplant. Top with the other slice of bread and serve warm.
Per Serving
Calories: 516 | fat: 27g | protein: 14g | carbs: 59g | fiber: 14g | sodium: 597mg

Avocado and Asparagus Wraps

Prep time: 10 minutes | Cook time: 10 minutes | Serves 6

12 spears asparagus
1 ripe avocado, mashed slightly
Juice of 1 lime
2 cloves garlic, minced
2 cups brown rice, cooked and chilled
3 tablespoons Greek yogurt
Sea salt and freshly ground pepper, to taste
3 (8-inch) whole-grain tortillas
½ cup cilantro, diced
2 tablespoons red onion, diced

1. Steam asparagus in microwave or stove top steamer until tender. Mash the avocado, lime juice, and garlic in a medium mixing bowl. In a separate bowl, mix the rice and yogurt. 2. Season both mixtures with sea salt and freshly ground pepper to taste. Heat the tortillas in a dry nonstick skillet. 3. Spread each tortilla with the avocado mixture, and top with the rice,

cilantro, and onion, followed by the asparagus. 4. Fold up both sides of the tortilla, and roll tightly to close. Cut in half diagonally before serving.
Per Serving
Calories: 361 | fat: 9g | protein: 9g | carbs: 63g | fiber: 7g | sodium: 117mg

Greek Salad Pita

Prep time: 15 minutes | Cook time: 0 minutes | Serves 4

1 cup chopped romaine lettuce
1 tomato, chopped and seeded
½ cup baby spinach leaves
½ small red onion, thinly sliced
½ small cucumber, chopped and deseeded
2 tablespoons olive oil
1 tablespoon crumbled feta cheese
½ tablespoon red wine vinegar
1 teaspoon Dijon mustard
Sea salt and freshly ground pepper, to taste
1 whole-wheat pita

1. Combine everything except the sea salt, freshly ground pepper, and pita bread in a medium bowl. 2. Toss until the salad is well combined. 3. Season with sea salt and freshly ground pepper to taste. Fill the pita with the salad mixture, serve, and enjoy!
Per Serving
Calories: 123 | fat: 8g | protein: 3g | carbs: 12g | fiber: 2g | sodium: 125mg

Flatbread Pizza with Roasted Cherry Tomatoes, Artichokes, and Feta

Prep time: 5 minutes | Cook time: 20 minutes | Serves 4

1½ pounds (680 g) cherry or grape tomatoes, halved
3 tablespoons olive oil, divided
½ teaspoon salt
½ teaspoon freshly ground black pepper
4 Middle Eastern–style flatbread rounds
1 can artichoke hearts, rinsed, well drained, and cut into thin wedges
8 ounces (227 g) crumbled feta cheese
¼ cup chopped fresh Greek oregano

1. Preheat the oven to 500°F (260°C). 2. In a medium bowl, toss the tomatoes with 1 tablespoon olive oil, the salt, and the pepper. Spread out on a large baking sheet. Roast in the preheated oven until the tomato skins begin to blister and crack, about 10 to 12 minutes. Remove the tomatoes from the oven and reduce the heat to 450°F (235°C). 3. Place the flatbreads on a large baking sheet (or two baking sheets if necessary) and brush the tops with the remaining 2 tablespoons of olive oil. Top with the artichoke hearts, roasted tomatoes, and cheese, dividing equally. 4. Bake the flatbreads in the oven for about 8 to 10 minutes, until the edges are lightly browned and the cheese is melted. Sprinkle the oregano over the top and serve immediately.
Per Serving
Calories: 436 | fat: 27g | protein: 16g | carbs: 34g | fiber: 6g | sodium: 649mg

Cucumber Basil Sandwiches

Prep time: 10 minutes | Cook time: 0 minutes | Serves 2

4 slices whole-grain bread
¼ cup hummus

1 large cucumber, thinly sliced
4 whole basil leaves

1. Spread the hummus on 2 slices of bread, and layer the cucumbers onto it. Top with the basil leaves and close the sandwiches. 2. Press down lightly and serve immediately.

Per Serving
Calories: 209 | fat: 5g | protein: 9g | carbs: 32g | fiber: 6g | sodium: 275mg

Chicken and Goat Cheese Pizza

Prep time: 10 minutes | Cook time: 10 minutes | Serves 4

All-purpose flour, for dusting
1 pound (454 g) premade pizza dough
2 tablespoons olive oil
1 cup shredded cooked chicken

3 ounces (85 g) goat cheese, crumbled
Sea salt
Freshly ground black pepper

1. Preheat the oven to 475ºF (245ºC). 2. On a floured surface, roll out the dough to a 12-inch round and place it on a lightly floured pizza pan or baking sheet. Drizzle the dough with the olive oil and spread it out evenly. Top the dough with the chicken and goat cheese. 3. Bake the pizza for 8 to 10 minutes, until the crust is cooked through and golden. 4. Season with salt and pepper and serve.

Per Serving
Calories: 555 | fat: 23g | protein: 24g | carbs: 60g | fiber: 2g | sodium: 660mg

Grilled Chicken Salad Pita

Prep time: 15 minutes | Cook time: 16 minutes | Serves 1

1 boneless, skinless chicken breast
Sea salt and freshly ground pepper, to taste
1 cup baby spinach
1 roasted red pepper, sliced
1 tomato, chopped
½ small red onion, thinly sliced

½ small cucumber, chopped
1 tablespoon olive oil
Juice of 1 lemon
1 whole-wheat pita pocket
2 tablespoons crumbled feta cheese

1. Preheat a gas or charcoal grill to medium-high heat. 2. Season the chicken breast with sea salt and freshly ground pepper, and grill until cooked through, about 7–8 minutes per side. 3. Allow chicken to rest for 5 minutes before slicing into strips. 4. While the chicken is cooking, put all the chopped vegetables into a medium-mixing bowl and season with sea salt and freshly ground pepper. 5. Chop the chicken into cubes and add to salad. Add the olive oil and lemon juice and toss well. 6. Stuff the mixture onto a pita pocket and top with the feta cheese. Serve immediately.

Per Serving
Calories: 653 | fat: 26g | protein: 71g | carbs: 34g | fiber: 6g | sodium: 464mg

South Indian Pepper Chicken

Prep time: 30 minutes | Cook time: 15 minutes | Serves 4

Spice Mix:
1 dried red chile, or ½ teaspoon dried red pepper flakes
1-inch piece cinnamon or cassia bark
1½ teaspoons coriander seeds
1 teaspoon fennel seeds
1 teaspoon cumin seeds
1 teaspoon black peppercorns
½ teaspoon cardamom seeds

¼ teaspoon ground turmeric
1 teaspoon kosher salt
Chicken:
1 pound (454 g) boneless, skinless chicken thighs, cut crosswise into thirds
2 medium onions, cut into ½-inch-thick slices
¼ cup olive oil
Cauliflower rice, steamed rice, or naan bread, for serving

1. For the spice mix: Combine the dried chile, cinnamon, coriander, fennel, cumin, peppercorns, and cardamom in a clean coffee or spice grinder. Grind, shaking the grinder lightly so all the seeds and bits get into the blades, until the mixture is broken down to a fine powder. Stir in the turmeric and salt. 2. For the chicken: Place the chicken and onions in resealable plastic bag. Add the oil and 1½ tablespoons of the spice mix. Seal the bag and massage until the chicken is well coated. Marinate at room temperature for 30 minutes or in the refrigerator for up to 24 hours. 3. Place the chicken and onions in the air fryer basket. Set the air fryer to 350ºF (177ºC) for 10 minutes, stirring once halfway through the cooking time. Increase the temperature to 400ºF (204ºC) for 5 minutes. Use a meat thermometer to ensure the chicken has reached an internal temperature of 165ºF (74ºC). 4. Serve with steamed rice, cauliflower rice, or naan.
Per Serving
Calories: 295 | fat: 19g | protein: 24g | carbs: 9g | fiber: 3g | sodium: 694mg

Za'atar Chicken Tenders

Prep time: 5 minutes | Cook time: 15 minutes | Serves 4

Olive oil cooking spray
1 pound (454 g) chicken tenders
1½ tablespoons za'atar

½ teaspoon kosher salt
¼ teaspoon freshly ground black pepper

1. Preheat the oven to 450ºF (235ºC). Line a baking sheet with parchment paper or foil and lightly spray with olive oil cooking spray. 2. In a large bowl, combine the chicken, za'atar, salt, and black pepper. Mix together well, covering the chicken tenders fully. Arrange in a single layer on the baking sheet and bake for 15 minutes, turning the chicken over once halfway through the cooking time.
Per Serving
Calories: 145 | fat: 4g | protein: 26g | carbs: 0g | fiber: 0g | sodium: 190mg

Coconut Chicken Meatballs

Prep time: 10 minutes | Cook time: 14 minutes | Serves 4

1 pound (454 g) ground chicken
2 scallions, finely chopped
1 cup chopped fresh cilantro leaves
¼ cup unsweetened shredded coconut

1 tablespoon hoisin sauce
1 tablespoon soy sauce
2 teaspoons Sriracha or other hot sauce
1 teaspoon toasted sesame oil
½ teaspoon kosher salt
1 teaspoon black pepper

1. In a large bowl, gently mix the chicken, scallions, cilantro, coconut, hoisin, soy sauce, Sriracha, sesame oil, salt, and pepper until thoroughly combined (the mixture will be wet and sticky). 2. Place a sheet of parchment paper in the air fryer basket. Using a small scoop or teaspoon, drop rounds of the mixture in a single layer onto the parchment paper. 3. Set the air fryer to 350ºF (177ºC) for 10 minutes, turning the meatballs halfway through the cooking time. Raise the air fryer temperature to 400ºF (204ºC) and cook for 4 minutes more to brown the outsides of the meatballs. Use a meat thermometer to ensure the meatballs have reached an internal temperature of 165ºF (74ºC). 4. Transfer the meatballs to a serving platter. Repeat with any remaining chicken mixture.
Per Serving
Calories: 213 | fat: 13g | protein: 21g | carbs: 4g | fiber: 1g | sodium: 501mg

Cornish Hens with Honey-Lime Glaze

Prep time: 15 minutes | Cook time: 25 to 30 minutes | Serves 2 to 3

1 Cornish game hen (1½ to 2 pounds / 680 to 907 g)
1 tablespoon honey
1 tablespoon lime juice

1 teaspoon poultry seasoning
Salt and pepper, to taste
Cooking spray

1. To split the hen into halves, cut through breast bone and down one side of the backbone. 2. Mix the honey, lime juice, and poultry seasoning together and brush or rub onto all sides of the hen. Season to taste with salt and pepper. 3. Spray the air fryer basket with cooking spray and place hen halves in the basket, skin-side down. 4. Air fry at 330ºF (166ºC) for 25 to 30 minutes. Hen will be done when juices run clear when pierced at leg joint with a fork. Let hen rest for 5 to 10 minutes before cutting.
Per Serving
Calories: 287 | fat: 8g | protein: 46g | carbs: 7g | fiber: 0g | sodium: 155mg

Crispy Dill Chicken Strips

Prep time: 30 minutes | Cook time: 10 minutes | Serves 4

2 whole boneless, skinless chicken breasts (about 1 pound / 454 g each), halved lengthwise
1 cup Italian dressing
3 cups finely crushed potato chips
1 tablespoon dried dill weed
1 tablespoon garlic powder
1 large egg, beaten
1 to 2 tablespoons oil

1. In a large resealable bag, combine the chicken and Italian dressing. Seal the bag and refrigerate to marinate at least 1 hour. 2. In a shallow dish, stir together the potato chips, dill, and garlic powder. Place the beaten egg in a second shallow dish. 3. Remove the chicken from the marinade. Roll the chicken pieces in the egg and the potato chip mixture, coating thoroughly. 4. Preheat the air fryer to 325ºF (163ºC). Line the air fryer basket with parchment paper. 5. Place the coated chicken on the parchment and spritz with oil. 6. Cook for 5 minutes. Flip the chicken, spritz it with oil, and cook for 5 minutes more until the outsides are crispy and the insides are no longer pink.

Per Serving
Calories: 349 | fat: 16g | protein: 30g | carbs: 20g | fiber: 2g | sodium: 92mg

Harissa-Rubbed Cornish Game Hens

Prep time: 30 minutes | Cook time: 21 minutes | Serves 4

Harissa:
½ cup olive oil
6 cloves garlic, minced
2 tablespoons smoked paprika
1 tablespoon ground coriander
1 tablespoon ground cumin
1 teaspoon ground caraway
1 teaspoon kosher salt
½ to 1 teaspoon cayenne pepper
Hens:
½ cup yogurt
2 Cornish game hens, any giblets removed, split in half lengthwise

1. For the harissa: In a medium microwave-safe bowl, combine the oil, garlic, paprika, coriander, cumin, caraway, salt, and cayenne. Microwave on high for 1 minute, stirring halfway through the cooking time. (You can also heat this on the stovetop until the oil is hot and bubbling. Or, if you must use your air fryer for everything, cook it in the air fryer at 350ºF (177ºC) for 5 to 6 minutes, or until the paste is heated through.) 2. For the hens: In a small bowl, combine 1 to 2 tablespoons harissa and the yogurt. Whisk until well combined. Place the hen halves in a resealable plastic bag and pour the marinade over. Seal the bag and massage until all of the pieces are thoroughly coated. Marinate at room temperature for 30 minutes or in the refrigerator for up to 24 hours. 3. Arrange the hen halves in a single layer in the air fryer basket. (If you have a smaller air fryer, you may have to cook this in two batches.) Set the air fryer to 400ºF (204ºC) for 20 minutes. Use a meat thermometer to ensure the game hens have reached an internal temperature of 165ºF (74ºC).

Per Serving
Calories: 421 | fat: 33g | protein: 26g | carbs: 6g | fiber: 2g | sodium: 683mg

Pecan Turkey Cutlets

Prep time: 10 minutes | Cook time: 10 to 12 minutes per batch | Serves 4

¾ cup panko bread crumbs
¼ teaspoon salt
¼ teaspoon pepper
¼ teaspoon dry mustard
¼ teaspoon poultry seasoning
½ cup pecans
¼ cup cornstarch
1 egg, beaten
1 pound (454 g) turkey cutlets, ½-inch thick
Salt and pepper, to taste
Oil for misting or cooking spray

1. Place the panko crumbs, ¼ teaspoon salt, ¼ teaspoon pepper, mustard, and poultry seasoning in food processor. Process until crumbs are finely crushed. Add pecans and process in short pulses just until nuts are finely chopped. Go easy so you don't overdo it! 2. Preheat the air fryer to 360ºF (182ºC). 3. Place cornstarch in one shallow dish and beaten egg in another. Transfer coating mixture from food processor into a third shallow dish. 4. Sprinkle turkey cutlets with salt and pepper to taste. 5. Dip cutlets in cornstarch and shake off excess. Then dip in beaten egg and roll in crumbs, pressing to coat well. Spray both sides with oil or cooking spray. 6. Place 2 cutlets in air fryer basket in a single layer and cook for 10 to 12 minutes or until juices run clear. 7. Repeat step 6 to cook remaining cutlets.

Per Serving
Calories: 340 | fat: 13g | protein: 31g | carbs: 24g | fiber: 4g | sodium: 447mg

Brazilian Tempero Baiano Chicken Drumsticks

Prep time: 30 minutes | Cook time: 20 minutes | Serves 4

1 teaspoon cumin seeds
1 teaspoon dried oregano
1 teaspoon dried parsley
1 teaspoon ground turmeric
½ teaspoon coriander seeds
1 teaspoon kosher salt
½ teaspoon black peppercorns
½ teaspoon cayenne pepper
¼ cup fresh lime juice
2 tablespoons olive oil
1½ pounds (680 g) chicken drumsticks

1. In a clean coffee grinder or spice mill, combine the cumin, oregano, parsley, turmeric, coriander seeds, salt, peppercorns, and cayenne. Process until finely ground. 2. In a small bowl, combine the ground spices with the lime juice and oil. Place the chicken in a resealable plastic bag. Add the marinade, seal, and massage until the chicken is well coated. Marinate at room temperature for 30 minutes or in the refrigerator for up to 24 hours. 3. When you are ready to cook, place the drumsticks skin side up in the air fryer basket. Set the air fryer to 400ºF (204ºC) for 20 to 25 minutes, turning the legs halfway through the cooking time. Use a meat thermometer to ensure that the chicken has reached an internal temperature of 165ºF (74ºC). 4. Serve with plenty of napkins.

Per Serving
Calories: 267 | fat: 13g | protein: 33g | carbs: 2g | fiber: 1g | sodium: 777mg

Honey-Glazed Chicken Thighs

Prep time: 5 minutes | Cook time: 14 minutes | Serves 4

Oil, for spraying
4 boneless, skinless chicken thighs, fat trimmed
3 tablespoons soy sauce
1 tablespoon balsamic vinegar
2 teaspoons honey
2 teaspoons minced garlic
1 teaspoon ground ginger

1. Preheat the air fryer to 400°F (204°C). Line the air fryer basket with parchment and spray lightly with oil. 2. Place the chicken in the prepared basket. 3. Cook for 7 minutes, flip, and cook for another 7 minutes, or until the internal temperature reaches 165°F (74°C) and the juices run clear. 4. In a small saucepan, combine the soy sauce, balsamic vinegar, honey, garlic, and ginger and cook over low heat for 1 to 2 minutes, until warmed through. 5. Transfer the chicken to a serving plate and drizzle with the sauce just before serving.

Per Serving
Calories: 286 | fat: 10g | protein: 39g | carbs: 7g | fiber: 0g | sodium: 365mg

Chicken and Olives with Couscous

Prep time: 15 minutes | Cook time: 1 hour | Serves 6

2 tablespoons olive oil, divided
8 bone-in, skin-on chicken thighs
½ teaspoon kosher salt
¼ teaspoon ground black pepper
2 cloves garlic, chopped
1 small red onion, chopped
1 red bell pepper, seeded and chopped
1 green bell pepper, seeded and chopped
1 tablespoon fresh thyme leaves
2 teaspoons fresh oregano leaves
1 (28-ounce / 794-g) can no-salt-added diced tomatoes
1 cup low-sodium chicken broth
1 cup pitted green olives, coarsely chopped
2 cups whole wheat couscous
Chopped flat-leaf parsley, for garnish

1. Preheat the oven to 350°F (180°C). 2. In a large ovenproof or cast-iron skillet over medium heat, warm 1 tablespoon of the oil. Pat the chicken thighs dry with a paper towel, season with the salt and black pepper, and cook, turning once, until golden and crisp, 8 to 10 minutes per side. Remove the chicken from the skillet and set aside. 3. Add the remaining 1 tablespoon oil to the skillet. Cook the garlic, onion, bell peppers, thyme, and oregano until softened, about 5 minutes. Add the tomatoes and broth and bring to a boil. Return the chicken to the skillet, add the olives, cover, and place the skillet in the oven. Roast until the chicken is tender and a thermometer inserted in the thickest part registers 165°F (74°C), 40 to 50 minutes. 4. While the chicken is cooking, prepare the couscous according to package directions. 5. To serve, pile the couscous on a serving platter and nestle the chicken on top. Pour the vegetables and any pan juices over the chicken and couscous. Sprinkle with the parsley and serve.

Per Serving
Calories: 481 | fat: 15g | protein: 29g | carbs: 61g | fiber: 11g | sodium: 893mg

Southward Pesto Stuffed Peppers

Prep time: 20 minutes | Cook time: 15 minutes | Serves 4 to 6

Nonstick cooking spray
3 large bell peppers, halved
2 tablespoons extra-virgin olive oil, plus more to garnish
¼ cup cooked chickpeas
½ shredded carrot
2 garlic cloves, minced
1 pound (454 g) ground turkey or chicken
Salt
Freshly ground black pepper
1 cup cooked brown rice
½ cup halved cherry tomatoes
½ zucchini, chopped
1 tablespoon dried Italian herb medley
2 tablespoons chopped black olives
6 tablespoons prepared pesto
½ cup shredded Italian cheese blend

1. Preheat the oven to 350°F (180°C). Lightly spray a medium-size casserole or glass baking dish with cooking spray. 2. Bring a medium pot of water to a boil and reduce to a steady simmer. Using tongs to lower the peppers in the water, simmer each pepper half for about 3 minutes, just to soften. Remove from the water and drain in a colander. 3. In a large sauté pan or skillet, heat the olive oil over medium-high heat and sauté the chickpeas and carrot for about 5 minutes, until tender. Add the garlic and sauté for 1 minute, until fragrant. Then add the turkey, season with salt and pepper, and toss to cook evenly. 4. Just before the turkey is cooked through, add the rice, cherry tomatoes, zucchini, and herbs, and sauté an additional 5 to 7 minutes, until cooked through. 5. Remove from the heat and stir in the olives. Place the prepared pepper halves in the greased casserole dish. 6. Divide the filling evenly among the peppers. Top each pepper with 1 tablespoon of pesto and a sprinkle of Italian cheese. Bake the peppers for 7 to 10 minutes, until heated through. Allow the peppers to rest for 10 minutes before serving. Drizzle with a dash of your favorite olive oil and enjoy!

Per Serving
Calories: 546 | fat: 38g | protein: 26g | carbs: 28g | fiber: 5g | sodium: 493mg

Yogurt-Marinated Chicken Kebabs

Prep time: 10 minutes | Cook time: 20 minutes | Serves 4

½ cup plain Greek yogurt
1 tablespoon lemon juice
½ teaspoon ground cumin
½ teaspoon ground coriander
½ teaspoon kosher salt
¼ teaspoon cayenne pepper
1½ pounds (680 g) skinless, boneless chicken breast, cut into 1-inch cubes

1. In a large bowl or zip-top bag, combine the yogurt, lemon juice, cumin, coriander, salt, and cayenne pepper. Mix together thoroughly and then add the chicken. Marinate for at least 30 minutes, and up to overnight in the refrigerator. 2. Preheat the oven to 425°F (220°C). Line a baking sheet with parchment paper or foil. Remove the chicken from the marinade and thread it on 4 bamboo or metal skewers. 3. Bake for 20 minutes, turning the chicken over once halfway through the cooking time.

Per Serving
Calories: 170 | fat: 4g | protein: 31g | carbs: 1g | fiber: 0g | sodium: 390mg

Greek Roasted Lemon Chicken with Potatoes

Prep time: 10 minutes | Cook time: 1 hour 20 minutes | Serves 4

2 pounds (907 g) potatoes (russet or white varieties), peeled
1½ pounds (680 g) chicken pieces (breasts, thighs, legs)
1 cup wine (any variety), for rinsing
1½ teaspoons freshly ground black pepper, divided
2 tablespoons dried oregano, divided
1 teaspoon salt, divided
½ cup extra virgin olive oil
2 tablespoons fresh lemon juice
2 to 3 allspice berries
2 to 3 cloves
2 garlic cloves, cut into quarters

1. Preheat the oven to 375ºF (190ºC). Place the peeled potatoes in a large bowl and cover them with cold water. Set aside. 2. Rinse the chicken pieces with the wine, pat dry with paper towels, and transfer to a large plate. In a small bowl, mix 1 teaspoon of black pepper, 1 tablespoon of oregano, and ½ teaspoon of salt to make a rub. Apply the rub to the chicken pieces and then set aside. 3. Remove the potatoes from the water. Rinse and pat dry the potatoes, then cut them into wedges and then cut again into half wedges. Place them in a large bowl. 4. Add the olive oil, lemon juice, remaining tablespoon of the oregano, remaining ½ teaspoon of the black pepper, and remaining ½ teaspoon of salt to the potatoes. Mix until all the potatoes are coated with the spices and olive oil. 5. Transfer the potatoes to a large baking dish and spread them into a single layer. Place the chicken pieces on top of the potatoes and then scatter the allspice berries, cloves, and garlic around the chicken. 6. Add hot water to one corner of the dish and then tilt the dish until the water is distributed throughout and fills about ¼ of the depth of the dish. (Do not pour the water directly over the potatoes because it will rinse off the olive oil and spices.) 7. Transfer to the oven and roast for 20 minutes, then reduce the oven temperature to 350ºF (180ºC) and roast for 1 more hour or until the potatoes and chicken are done. (If the water in the dish evaporates too quickly, add more hot water, ¼ cup at a time.) The potatoes are done when they have a golden color and a knife can be inserted easily. Serve hot. Store in the refrigerator for up to 3 days.

Per Serving
Calories: 629 | fat: 34g | protein: 38g | carbs: 43g | fiber: 3g | sodium: 761mg

Deconstructed Greek Chicken Kebabs

Prep time: 20 minutes | Cook time: 6 to 8 hours | Serves 4

2 pounds (907 g) boneless, skinless chicken thighs, cut into 1-inch cubes
2 zucchini (nearly 1 pound / 454 g), cut into 1-inch pieces
1 green bell pepper, seeded and cut into 1-inch pieces
1 red bell pepper, seeded and cut into 1-inch pieces
1 large red onion, chopped
2 tablespoons extra-virgin olive oil
2 tablespoons freshly squeezed lemon juice
1 tablespoon red wine vinegar
2 garlic cloves, minced
1 teaspoon sea salt
1 teaspoon dried oregano
½ teaspoon dried basil
½ teaspoon dried thyme
¼ teaspoon freshly ground black pepper

1. In a slow cooker, combine the chicken, zucchini, green and red bell peppers, onion, olive oil, lemon juice, vinegar, garlic, salt, oregano, basil, thyme, and black pepper. Stir to mix well. 2. Cover the cooker and cook for 6 to 8 hours on Low heat.

Per Serving
Calories: 372 | fat: 17g | protein: 47g | carbs: 8g | fiber: 2g | sodium: 808mg

Whole-Roasted Spanish Chicken

Prep time: 1 hour | Cook time: 55 minutes | Serves 4

4 tablespoons (½ stick) unsalted butter, softened
2 tablespoons lemon zest
2 tablespoons smoked paprika
2 tablespoons garlic, minced
1½ teaspoons salt
1 teaspoon freshly ground black pepper
1 (5-pound / 2.3-kg) whole chicken

1. In a small bowl, combine the butter with the lemon zest, paprika, garlic, salt, and pepper. 2. Pat the chicken dry using a paper towel. Using your hands, rub the seasoned butter all over the chicken. Refrigerate the chicken for 30 minutes. 3. Preheat the oven to 425ºF (220ºC). Take the chicken out of the fridge and let it sit out for 20 minutes. 4. Put the chicken in a baking dish in the oven and let it cook for 20 minutes. Turn the temperature down to 350ºF (180ºC) and let the chicken cook for another 35 minutes. 5. Take the chicken out of the oven and let it stand for 10 minutes before serving.

Per Serving
Calories: 705 | fat: 17g | protein: 126g | carbs: 4g | fiber: 1g | sodium: 880mg

Simply Terrific Turkey Meatballs

Prep time: 10 minutes | Cook time: 7 to 10 minutes | Serves 4

1 red bell pepper, seeded and coarsely chopped
2 cloves garlic, coarsely chopped
¼ cup chopped fresh parsley
1½ pounds (680 g) 85% lean ground turkey
1 egg, lightly beaten
½ cup grated Parmesan cheese
1 teaspoon salt
½ teaspoon freshly ground black pepper

1. Preheat the air fryer to 400ºF (204ºC). 2. In a food processor fitted with a metal blade, combine the bell pepper, garlic, and parsley. Pulse until finely chopped. Transfer the vegetables to a large mixing bowl. 3. Add the turkey, egg, Parmesan, salt, and black pepper. Mix gently until thoroughly combined. Shape the mixture into 1¼-inch meatballs. 4. Working in batches if necessary, arrange the meatballs in a single layer in the air fryer basket; coat lightly with olive oil spray. Pausing halfway through the cooking time to shake the basket, air fry for 7 to 10 minutes, until lightly browned and a thermometer inserted into the center of a meatball registers 165ºF (74ºC).

Per Serving
Calories: 388 | fat: 25g | protein: 34g | carbs: 5g | fiber: 1g | sodium: 527mg

Harissa Yogurt Chicken Thighs

Prep time: 5 minutes | Cook time: 25 minutes | Serves 4

½ cup plain Greek yogurt
2 tablespoons harissa
1 tablespoon lemon juice
½ teaspoon kosher salt

¼ teaspoon freshly ground black pepper
1½ pounds (680 g) boneless, skinless chicken thighs

1. In a bowl, combine the yogurt, harissa, lemon juice, salt, and black pepper. Add the chicken and mix together. Marinate for at least 15 minutes, and up to 4 hours in the refrigerator. 2. Preheat the oven to 425°F (220°C). Line a baking sheet with parchment paper or foil. Remove the chicken thighs from the marinade and arrange in a single layer on the baking sheet. Roast for 20 minutes, turning the chicken over halfway. 3. Change the oven temperature to broil. Broil the chicken until golden brown in spots, 2 to 3 minutes.

Per Serving

Calories: 190 | fat: 10g | protein: 24g | carbs: 1g | fiber: 0g | sodium: 230mg

Chicken Cutlets with Greek Salsa

Prep time: 15 minutes | Cook time: 15 minutes | Serves 2

2 tablespoons olive oil, divided
¼ teaspoon salt, plus additional to taste
Zest of ½ lemon
Juice of ½ lemon
8 ounces (227 g) chicken cutlets, or chicken breast sliced through the middle to make 2 thin pieces
1 cup cherry or grape tomatoes, halved or quartered (about 4 ounces / 113 g)
½ cup minced red onion (about ⅓ medium onion)
1 medium cucumber, peeled,

seeded and diced (about 1 cup)
5 to 10 pitted Greek olives, minced (more or less depending on size and your taste)
1 tablespoon minced fresh parsley
1 tablespoon minced fresh oregano
1 tablespoon minced fresh mint
1 ounce (28 g) crumbled feta cheese
1 tablespoon red wine vinegar

1. In a medium bowl, combine 1 tablespoon of olive oil, the salt, lemon zest, and lemon juice. Add the chicken and let it marinate while you make the salsa. 2. In a small bowl, combine the tomatoes, onion, cucumber, olives, parsley, oregano, mint, feta cheese, and red wine vinegar, and toss lightly. Cover and let rest in the refrigerator for at least 30 minutes. Taste the salsa before serving and add a pinch of salt or extra herbs if desired. 3. To cook the chicken, heat the remaining 1 tablespoon of olive oil in a large nonstick skillet over medium-high heat. Add the chicken pieces and cook for 3 to 6 minutes on each side, depending on the thickness. If the chicken sticks to the pan, it's not quite ready to flip. 4. When chicken is cooked through, top with the salsa and serve.

Per Serving

Calories: 357 | fat: 23g | protein: 31g | carbs: 8g | fiber: 2g | sodium: 202mg

Chicken and Vegetable Fajitas

Prep time: 15 minutes | Cook time: 23 minutes | Serves 6

Chicken:
1 pound (454 g) boneless, skinless chicken thighs, cut crosswise into thirds
1 tablespoon vegetable oil
4½ teaspoons taco seasoning
Vegetables:
1 cup sliced onion
1 cup sliced bell pepper
1 or 2 jalapeños, quartered

lengthwise
1 tablespoon vegetable oil
½ teaspoon kosher salt
½ teaspoon ground cumin
For Serving:
Tortillas
Sour cream
Shredded cheese
Guacamole
Salsa

1. For the chicken: In a medium bowl, toss together the chicken, vegetable oil, and taco seasoning to coat. 2. For the vegetables: In a separate bowl, toss together the onion, bell pepper, jalapeño(s), vegetable oil, salt, and cumin to coat. 3. Place the chicken in the air fryer basket. Set the air fryer to 375°F (191°C) for 10 minutes. Add the vegetables to the basket, toss everything together to blend the seasonings, and set the air fryer for 13 minutes more. Use a meat thermometer to ensure the chicken has reached an internal temperature of 165°F (74°C). 4. Transfer the chicken and vegetables to a serving platter. Serve with tortillas and the desired fajita fixings.

Per Serving

Calories: 151 | fat: 8g | protein: 15g | carbs: 4g | fiber: 1g | sodium: 421mg

Turkish Chicken Kebabs

Prep time: 30 minutes | Cook time: 15 minutes | Serves 4

¼ cup plain Greek yogurt
1 tablespoon minced garlic
1 tablespoon tomato paste
1 tablespoon fresh lemon juice
1 tablespoon vegetable oil
1 teaspoon kosher salt
1 teaspoon ground cumin
1 teaspoon sweet Hungarian

paprika
½ teaspoon ground cinnamon
½ teaspoon black pepper
½ teaspoon cayenne pepper
1 pound (454 g) boneless, skinless chicken thighs, quartered crosswise

1. In a large bowl, combine the yogurt, garlic, tomato paste, lemon juice, vegetable oil, salt, cumin, paprika, cinnamon, black pepper, and cayenne. Stir until the spices are blended into the yogurt. 2. Add the chicken to the bowl and toss until well coated. Marinate at room temperature for 30 minutes, or cover and refrigerate for up to 24 hours. 3. Arrange the chicken in a single layer in the air fryer basket. Set the air fryer to 375°F (191°C) for 10 minutes. Turn the chicken and cook for 5 minutes more. Use a meat thermometer to ensure the chicken has reached an internal temperature of 165°F (74°C).

Per Serving

Calories: 188 | fat: 8g | protein: 24g | carbs: 4g | fiber: 1g | sodium: 705mg

Sumac Chicken with Cauliflower and Carrots

Prep time: 15 minutes | Cook time: 40 minutes | Serves 4

3 tablespoons extra-virgin olive oil
1 tablespoon ground sumac
1 teaspoon kosher salt
½ teaspoon ground cumin
¼ teaspoon freshly ground black pepper
1½ pounds (680 g) bone-in chicken thighs and drumsticks
1 medium cauliflower, cut into 1-inch florets
2 carrots, peeled and cut into 1-inch rounds
1 lemon, cut into ¼-inch-thick slices
1 tablespoon lemon juice
¼ cup fresh parsley, chopped
¼ cup fresh mint, chopped

1. Preheat the oven to 425ºF (220ºC). Line a baking sheet with parchment paper or foil. 2. In a large bowl, whisk together the olive oil, sumac, salt, cumin, and black pepper. Add the chicken, cauliflower, and carrots and toss until thoroughly coated with the oil and spice mixture. 3. Arrange the cauliflower, carrots, and chicken in a single layer on the baking sheet. Top with the lemon slices. Roast for 40 minutes, tossing the vegetables once halfway through. Sprinkle the lemon juice over the chicken and vegetables and garnish with the parsley and mint.

Per Serving
Calories: 510 | fat: 38g | protein: 31g | carbs: 13g | fiber: 4g | sodium: 490mg

Lemon Chicken with Artichokes and Crispy Kale

Prep time: 15 minutes | Cook time: 35 minutes | Serves 4

3 tablespoons extra-virgin olive oil, divided
2 tablespoons lemon juice
Zest of 1 lemon
2 garlic cloves, minced
2 teaspoons dried rosemary
½ teaspoon kosher salt
¼ teaspoon freshly ground
black pepper
1½ pounds (680 g) boneless, skinless chicken breast
2 (14-ounce / 397-g) cans artichoke hearts, drained
1 bunch (about 6 ounces / 170 g) lacinato kale, stemmed and torn or chopped into pieces

1. In a large bowl or zip-top bag, combine 2 tablespoons of the olive oil, the lemon juice, lemon zest, garlic, rosemary, salt, and black pepper. Mix well and then add the chicken and artichokes. Marinate for at least 30 minutes, and up to 4 hours in the refrigerator. 2. Preheat the oven to 350ºF (180ºC). Line a baking sheet with parchment paper or foil. Remove the chicken and artichokes from the marinade and spread them in a single layer on the baking sheet. Roast for 15 minutes, turn the chicken over, and roast another 15 minutes. Remove the baking sheet and put the chicken, artichokes, and juices on a platter or large plate. Tent with foil to keep warm. 3. Change the oven temperature to broil. In a large bowl, combine the kale with the remaining 1 tablespoon of the olive oil. Arrange the kale on the baking sheet and broil until golden brown in spots and as crispy as you like, about 3 to 5 minutes. Place the kale on top of the chicken and artichokes.

Per Serving
Calories: 430 | fat: 16g | protein: 46g | carbs: 29g | fiber: 19g | sodium: 350mg

Pesto Chicken and Potatoes

Prep time: 15 minutes | Cook time: 6 to 8 hours | Serves 6

For the Pesto:
1 cup fresh basil leaves
1 garlic clove, crushed
¼ cup pine nuts
¼ cup grated Parmesan cheese
2 tablespoons extra-virgin olive oil, plus more as needed
1 teaspoon sea salt
½ teaspoon freshly ground
black pepper
For the Chicken:
Nonstick cooking spray
2 pounds (907 g) red potatoes, quartered
3 pounds (1.4 kg) boneless, skinless chicken thighs
½ cup low-sodium chicken broth

Make the Pesto: In a food processor, combine the basil, garlic, pine nuts, Parmesan cheese, olive oil, salt, and pepper. Pulse until smooth, adding more olive oil ½ teaspoon at a time if needed until any clumps are gone. Set aside. Make the Chicken: 1. Coat a slow-cooker insert with cooking spray and put the potatoes into the prepared slow cooker. 2. Place the chicken on top of the potatoes. 3. In a medium bowl, whisk together the pesto and broth until combined and pour the mixture over the chicken. 4. Cover the cooker and cook for 6 to 8 hours on Low heat.

Per Serving
Calories: 467 | fat: 24g | protein: 38g | carbs: 25g | fiber: 3g | sodium: 819mg

Chicken with Lemon Asparagus

Prep time: 10 minutes | Cook time: 13 minutes | Serves 4

2 tablespoons olive oil
4 (6-ounce / 170-g) boneless, skinless chicken breasts
½ teaspoon ground black pepper
¼ teaspoon salt
¼ teaspoon smoked paprika
2 cloves garlic, peeled and minced
2 sprigs thyme
2 sprigs oregano
1 tablespoon grated lemon zest
¼ cup lemon juice
¼ cup low-sodium chicken broth
1 bunch asparagus, trimmed
¼ cup chopped fresh parsley
1lemon wedges

1. Press Sauté on the Instant Pot® and heat oil. Season chicken with pepper, salt, and smoked paprika. Brown chicken on both sides, about 4 minutes per side. Add garlic, thyme, oregano, lemon zest, lemon juice, and chicken broth. Press the Cancel button. 2. Close lid, set steam release to Sealing, press the Manual button, and set time to 5 minutes. 3. When the timer beeps, quick-release the pressure until the float valve drops. Press the Cancel button and open lid. Transfer chicken breasts to a serving platter. Tent with foil to keep warm. 4. Add asparagus to the Instant Pot®. Close lid, set steam release to Sealing, press the Manual button, and set time to 0. When the timer beeps, quick-release the pressure until the float valve drops. Open lid and remove asparagus. Arrange asparagus around chicken and garnish with parsley and lemon wedges. Serve immediately.

Per Serving
Calories: 227 | fat: 11g | protein: 35g | carbs: 0g | fiber: 0g | sodium: 426mg

Bruschetta Chicken Burgers

Prep time: 15 minutes | Cook time: 15 minutes | Serves 2

1 tablespoon olive oil
3 tablespoons finely minced onion
2 garlic cloves, minced
1 teaspoon dried basil
¼ teaspoon salt
3 tablespoons minced sun-dried tomatoes packed in olive oil
8 ounces (227 g) ground chicken breast
3 pieces small mozzarella balls (ciliegine), minced

1. Heat the grill to high heat (about 400°F / 205°C) and oil the grill grates. Alternatively, you can cook these in a nonstick skillet. 2. Heat the olive oil in a small skillet over medium-high heat. Add the onion and garlic and sauté for 5 minutes, until softened. Stir in the basil. Remove from the heat and place in a medium bowl. 3. Add the salt, sun-dried tomatoes, and ground chicken and stir to combine. Mix in the mozzarella balls. 4. Divide the chicken mixture in half and form into two burgers, each about ¾-inch thick. 5. Place the burgers on the grill and cook for five minutes, or until golden on the bottom. Flip the burgers over and grill for another five minutes, or until they reach an internal temperature of 165°F (74°C). 6. If cooking the burgers in a skillet on the stovetop, heat a nonstick skillet over medium-high heat and add the burgers. Cook them for 5 to 6 minutes on the first side, or until golden brown on the bottom. Flip the burgers and cook for an additional 5 minutes, or until they reach an internal temperature of 165°F (74°C).

Per Serving
Calories: 301 | fat: 17g | protein: 32g | carbs: 6g | fiber: 1g | sodium: 725mg

Rosemary Baked Chicken Thighs

Prep time: 20 minutes | Cook time: 20 minutes | Serves 4 to 6

5 tablespoons extra-virgin olive oil, divided
3 medium shallots, diced
4 garlic cloves, peeled and crushed
1 rosemary sprig
2 to 2½ pounds (907 g to 1.1 kg) bone-in, skin-on chicken thighs (about 6 pieces)
2 teaspoons kosher salt
¼ teaspoon freshly ground black pepper
1 lemon, juiced and zested
⅓ cup low-sodium chicken broth

1. In a large sauté pan or skillet, heat 3 tablespoons of olive oil over medium heat. Add the shallots and garlic and cook for about a minute, until fragrant. Add the rosemary sprig. 2. Season the chicken with salt and pepper. Place it in the skillet, skin-side down, and brown for 3 to 5 minutes. 3. Once it's cooked halfway through, turn the chicken over and add lemon juice and zest. 4. Add the chicken broth, cover the pan, and continue to cook for 10 to 15 more minutes, until cooked through and juices run clear. Serve.

Per Serving
Calories: 294 | fat: 18g | protein: 30g | carbs: 3g | fiber: 1g | sodium: 780mg

Chicken with Dates and Almonds

Prep time: 15 minutes | Cook time: 6 to 8 hours | Serves 4

1 onion, sliced
1 (15-ounce / 425-g) can reduced-sodium chickpeas, drained and rinsed
2½ pounds (1.1 kg) bone-in, skin-on chicken thighs
½ cup low-sodium chicken broth
2 garlic cloves, minced
1 teaspoon sea salt
1 teaspoon ground cumin
½ teaspoon ground ginger
½ teaspoon ground coriander
¼ teaspoon ground cinnamon
¼ teaspoon freshly ground black pepper
½ cup dried dates
¼ cup sliced almonds

1. In a slow cooker, gently toss together the onion and chickpeas. 2. Place the chicken on top of the chickpea mixture and pour the chicken broth over the chicken. 3. In a small bowl, stir together the garlic, salt, cumin, ginger, coriander, cinnamon, and pepper. Sprinkle the spice mix over everything. 4. Top with the dates and almonds. 5. Cover the cooker and cook for 6 to 8 hours on Low heat.

Per Serving
Calories: 841 | fat: 48g | protein: 57g | carbs: 41g | fiber: 9g | sodium: 812mg

Mediterranean Roasted Turkey Breast

Prep time: 15 minutes | Cook time: 6 to 8 hours | Serves 4

3 garlic cloves, minced
1 teaspoon sea salt
1 teaspoon dried oregano
½ teaspoon freshly ground black pepper
½ teaspoon dried basil
½ teaspoon dried parsley
½ teaspoon dried rosemary
½ teaspoon dried thyme
¼ teaspoon dried dill
¼ teaspoon ground nutmeg
2 tablespoons extra-virgin olive oil
2 tablespoons freshly squeezed lemon juice
1 (4- to 6-pound / 1.8- to 2.7-kg) boneless or bone-in turkey breast
1 onion, chopped
½ cup low-sodium chicken broth
4 ounces (113 g) whole Kalamata olives, pitted
1 cup sun-dried tomatoes (packaged, not packed in oil), chopped

1. In a small bowl, stir together the garlic, salt, oregano, pepper, basil, parsley, rosemary, thyme, dill, and nutmeg. 2. Drizzle the olive oil and lemon juice all over the turkey breast and generously season it with the garlic-spice mix. 3. In a slow cooker, combine the onion and chicken broth. Place the seasoned turkey breast on top of the onion. Top the turkey with the olives and sun-dried tomatoes. 4. Cover the cooker and cook for 6 to 8 hours on Low heat. 5. Slice or shred the turkey for serving.

Per Serving
Calories: 676 | fat: 19g | protein: 111g | carbs: 14g | fiber: 3g | sodium: 626mg

Bomba Chicken with Chickpeas

Prep time: 10 minutes | Cook time: 30 minutes | Serves 4

2 pounds (907 g) boneless, skinless chicken thighs
Sea salt
Freshly ground black pepper
2 tablespoons olive oil, divided
1 onion, chopped
3 garlic cloves, minced
1 cup chicken broth
1 tablespoon bomba sauce or harissa
2 (15-ounce / 425-g) cans chickpeas, drained and rinsed
¼ cup chopped fresh Italian parsley

1. Season the chicken thighs generously with salt and pepper. 2. In a large skillet, heat 1 tablespoon of olive oil over medium-high heat. Add the chicken and cook until browned, 2 to 3 minutes per side. Transfer the chicken to a plate and set aside. 3. In the same skillet, heat the remaining 1 tablespoon of olive oil. Add the onion and garlic and sauté for 4 to 5 minutes, until softened. Return the chicken to the skillet, then add the broth and bomba sauce. Bring to a boil, reduce the heat to low, cover, and simmer for 15 minutes, or until the chicken is cooked through. 4. Add the chickpeas and simmer for 5 minutes more. 5. Garnish with the parsley and serve.

Per Serving
Calories: 552 | fat: 19g | protein: 56g | carbs: 37g | fiber: 10g | sodium: 267mg

Chicken and Shrimp Paella

Prep time: 20 minutes | Cook time: 40 minutes | Serves 6

3 tablespoons olive oil
1 onion, chopped (about 2 cups)
5 garlic cloves, minced
1 pound (454 g) chicken breasts, cut into 1-inch pieces
1 cup Arborio rice
1 teaspoon ground cumin
1 teaspoon smoked paprika
½ teaspoon ground turmeric
1½ cups low-sodium chicken broth
1 (14½-ounce / 411-g) can
diced tomatoes, with their juices
Zest and juice of 1 lemon
½ teaspoon salt
1 cup thawed frozen peas
1 medium zucchini, cut into cubes (about 2 cups)
8 ounces (227 g) uncooked shrimp, thawed, peeled, and deveined
2 tablespoons chopped fresh parsley

1. In a large saucepan, heat 2 tablespoons of the olive oil over medium heat. Add the onion and cook, occasionally stirring, for 5 minutes, or until softened. Add the garlic, chicken, rice, and remaining 1 tablespoon olive oil. Stir until the rice is coated with the oil. 2. Add the cumin, smoked paprika, turmeric, broth, tomatoes with their juices, lemon zest, lemon juice, and salt. Spread the rice mixture evenly in the pan. Bring to a boil. Reduce the heat to medium-low, cover, and cook for 25 minutes—do not stir. 3. Remove the lid and stir in the peas and zucchini. Add the shrimp, nestling them into the rice. Cover and cook for 8 to 10 minutes. Remove from the heat and let stand for 10 minutes. 4. Top with the parsley and serve.

Per Serving
Calories: 310 | fat: 18g | protein: 26g | carbs: 18g | fiber: 7g | sodium: 314mg

Herb–Marinated Chicken Breasts

Prep time: 10 minutes | Cook time: 10 minutes | Serves 4

½ cup fresh lemon juice
¼ cup extra-virgin olive oil
4 cloves garlic, minced
2 tablespoons chopped fresh basil
1 tablespoon chopped fresh oregano
1 tablespoon chopped fresh
mint
2 pounds (907 g) chicken breast tenders
½ teaspoon unrefined sea salt or salt
¼ teaspoon freshly ground black pepper

1. In a small bowl, whisk the lemon juice, olive oil, garlic, basil, oregano, and mint well to combine. Place the chicken breasts in a large shallow bowl or glass baking pan, and pour dressing over the top. 2. Cover, place in the refrigerator, and allow to marinate for 1 to 2 hours. Remove from the refrigerator, and season with salt and pepper. 3. Heat a large, wide skillet over medium-high heat. Using tongs, place chicken tenders evenly in the bottom of the skillet. Pour the remaining marinade over the chicken. 4. Allow to cook for 3 to 5 minutes each side, or until chicken is golden, juices have been absorbed, and meat is cooked to an internal temperature of 160ºF (71ºC).
Per Serving
Calories: 521 | fat: 35g | protein: 48g | carbs: 3g | fiber: 0g | sodium: 435mg

Garlic Chicken with Couscous

Prep time: 10 minutes | Cook time: 3½ hours | Serves 4

1 whole chicken, 3½ to 4 pounds (1.6 to 1.8 kg), cut into 6 to 8 pieces and patted dry
Coarse sea salt
Black pepper
1 tablespoon extra-virgin olive oil
1 medium yellow onion,
halved and thinly sliced
6 cloves garlic, halved
2 teaspoons dried thyme
1 cup dry white wine
⅓ cup all-purpose flour
1 cup uncooked couscous
¼ chopped fresh parsley

1. Season the chicken with salt and pepper. 2. In a large skillet, heat the oil over medium-high heat. Add the chicken skin-side down and cook in batches until the skin is golden brown, about 4 minutes. Turn and cook an additional 2 minutes. 3. Add the onion, garlic, and thyme to the slow cooker. 4. Top the contents of slow cooker with chicken, skin-side up, in a tight layer. 5. In a small bowl, whisk together the wine and the flour until smooth, and add to the slow cooker. 6. Cover and cook until the chicken is tender, about 3½ hours on high or 7 hours on low. 7. Cook the couscous according to package instructions. 8. Serve the chicken and sauce hot over the couscous, sprinkled with parsley.

Per Serving
Calories: 663 | fat: 38g | protein: 46g | carbs: 21g | fiber: 1g | sodium: 166mg

Bell Pepper and Tomato Chicken

Prep time: 15 minutes | Cook time: 5 hours | Serves 6 to 8

1 medium yellow onion, sliced thickly
1 bell pepper, any color, cored, seeded, and sliced thickly
4 cloves garlic, minced
6 ounces (170 g) pitted black olives, drained
1 (28-ounce / 794-g) can stewed tomatoes
1 (15-ounce / 425-g) can stewed tomatoes
1 (6-ounce / 170-g) can tomato paste
1 cup red or white wine
2 tablespoons lemon juice
4 to 6 boneless, skinless chicken breasts, cut in half
¼ cup chopped fresh parsley, or 2 tablespoons dried parsley
1 tablespoon dried basil
½ teaspoon ground nutmeg
Sea salt
Black pepper
1 tablespoon red pepper flakes (optional)

1. Place the onion, bell pepper, garlic, and olives in slow cooker. 2. Add the stewed tomatoes, tomato paste, wine, and lemon juice. Stir to combine. 3. Place the chicken pieces in the slow cooker. Make sure all the pieces are covered with the liquid. 4. Sprinkle with the parsley, basil, and nutmeg. Season with salt and black pepper, and add the red pepper flakes, if using. Cover and cook on high for 5 hours or on low for 8 hours. Make sure the chicken is cooked thoroughly. 5. Serve hot over cooked pasta of your choice or cooked spaghetti squash.

Per Serving
Calories: 280 | fat: 7g | protein: 34g | carbs: 15g | fiber: 5g | sodium: 423mg

Greek-Style Roast Turkey Breast

Prep time: 10 minutes | Cook time: 7½ hours | Serves 8

1 (4-pound / 1.8-kg) turkey breast, trimmed of fat
½ cup chicken stock
2 tablespoons fresh lemon juice
2 cups chopped onions
½ cup pitted kalamata olives
½ cup oil-packed sun-dried tomatoes, drained and thinly sliced
1 clove garlic, minced
1 teaspoon dried oregano
½ teaspoon ground cinnamon
½ teaspoon ground dill
¼ teaspoon ground nutmeg
¼ teaspoon cayenne pepper
1 teaspoon sea salt
¼ teaspoon black pepper
3 tablespoons all-purpose flour

1. Place the turkey breast, ¼ cup of the chicken stock, lemon juice, onions, Kalamata olives, garlic, and sun-dried tomatoes into the slow cooker. Sprinkle with the oregano, cinnamon, dill, nutmeg, cayenne pepper, salt, and black pepper. Cover and cook on low for 7 hours. 2. Combine the remaining ¼ cup chicken stock and the flour in a small bowl. Whisk until smooth. Stir into the slow cooker. Cover and cook on low for an additional 30 minutes. 3. Serve hot over rice, pasta, potatoes, or another starch of your choice.

Per Serving
Calories: 386 | fat: 7g | protein: 70g | carbs: 8g | fiber: 2g | sodium: 601mg

Spanish Sautéed Lemon and Garlic Chicken

Prep time: 10 minutes | Cook time: 15 minutes | Serves 3

2 large boneless, skinless chicken breasts
¼ cup extra virgin olive oil
3 garlic cloves, finely chopped
5 tablespoons fresh lemon juice
Zest of 1 lemon
½ cup chopped fresh parsley
¼ teaspoon fine sea salt
Pinch of freshly ground black pepper

1. Slice the chicken crosswise into very thin slices, each about ¼-inch thick. 2. In a pan large enough to hold the chicken in a single layer, heat the olive oil over medium heat. When the olive oil starts to shimmer, add the garlic and sauté for about 30 seconds, then add the chicken. Reduce the heat to medium-low and sauté for about 12 minutes, tossing the chicken breasts periodically until they begin to brown on the edges. 3. Add the lemon zest and lemon juice. Increase the heat to medium and bring to a boil. Cook for about 2 minutes while using a wooden spatula to scrape any browned bits from the bottom of the pan. 4. Add the parsley, stir, then remove the pan from the heat. 5. Transfer the chicken along with any juices to a platter. Season with the sea salt and black pepper, then serve promptly. Store in an airtight container in the refrigerator for up to 2 days.

Per Serving
Calories: 358 | fat: 22g | protein: 35g | carbs: 4g | fiber: 1g | sodium: 269mg

Skillet Greek Turkey and Rice

Prep time: 20 minutes | Cook time: 30 minutes | Serves 2

1 tablespoon olive oil
½ medium onion, minced
2 garlic cloves, minced
8 ounces (227 g) ground turkey breast
½ cup roasted red peppers, chopped (about 2 jarred peppers)
¼ cup sun-dried tomatoes,
minced
1 teaspoon dried oregano
½ cup brown rice
1¼ cups low-sodium chicken stock
Salt
2 cups lightly packed baby spinach

1. Heat the olive oil in a sauté pan over medium heat. Add the onion and sauté for 5 minutes. Add the garlic and cook for another 30 seconds. 2. Add the turkey breast and cook for 7 minutes, breaking the turkey up with a spoon, until no longer pink. 3. Add the roasted red peppers, sun-dried tomatoes, and oregano and stir to combine. Add the rice and chicken stock and bring the mixture to a boil. 4. Cover the pan and reduce the heat to medium-low. Simmer for 30 minutes, or until the rice is cooked and tender. Season with salt. 5. Add the spinach to the pan and stir until it wilts slightly.

Per Serving
Calories: 446 | fat: 17g | protein: 30g | carbs: 49g | fiber: 5g | sodium: 663mg

Pesto-Glazed Chicken Breasts

Prep time: 5 minutes | Cook time: 20 minutes | Serves 4

¼ cup plus 1 tablespoon extra-virgin olive oil, divided
4 boneless, skinless chicken breasts
½ teaspoon salt
¼ teaspoon freshly ground
black pepper
1 packed cup fresh basil leaves
1 garlic clove, minced
¼ cup grated Parmesan cheese
¼ cup pine nuts

1. In a large, heavy skillet, heat 1 tablespoon of the olive oil over medium-high heat. 2. Season the chicken breasts on both sides with salt and pepper and place in the skillet. Cook for 10 minutes on the first side, then turn and cook for 5 minutes. 3. Meanwhile, in a blender or food processor, combine the basil, garlic, Parmesan cheese, and pine nuts, and blend on high. Gradually pour in the remaining ¼ cup olive oil and blend until smooth. 4. Spread 1 tablespoon pesto on each chicken breast, cover the skillet, and cook for 5 minutes. Serve the chicken pesto side up.

Per Serving
Calories: 531 | fat: 28g | protein: 64g | carbs: 2g | fiber: 0g | sodium: 572mg

Herb-Roasted Whole Chicken

Prep time: 5 minutes | Cook time: 50 to 60 minutes | Serves 6

1 (3 to 3½-pound / 1.4- to 1.6-kg) roasting chicken
1 tablespoon extra-virgin olive oil
4 rosemary sprigs
6 thyme sprigs
4 fresh sage leaves
1 bay leaf
1 teaspoon freshly squeezed lemon juice
1 teaspoon salt
½ teaspoon freshly ground black pepper

1. Preheat the oven to 400°F (205°C). Place a rack inside a large roasting pan. 2. Rub the olive oil all over the chicken. As you do, gently loosen the skin over the breast to form a pocket. 3. Slide half of the rosemary and thyme sprigs underneath the skin over the breast, and put the sage leaves, bay leaf, and remaining sprigs inside the cavity. 4. Rub with the lemon juice and season with salt and pepper. 5. Roast until an instant-read thermometer inserted into the thigh registers 165°F (74°C), 50 to 60 minutes. Remove from the oven and allow to rest for 10 minutes before carving.

Per Serving
Calories: 273 | fat: 8g | protein: 46g | carbs: 0g | fiber: 0g | sodium: 558mg

Crispy Mediterranean Chicken Thighs

Prep time: 5 minutes | Cook time: 30 to 35 minutes | Serves 6

2 tablespoons extra-virgin olive oil
2 teaspoons dried rosemary
1½ teaspoons ground cumin
1½ teaspoons ground coriander
¾ teaspoon dried oregano
⅛ teaspoon salt
6 bone-in, skin-on chicken
thighs (about 3 pounds / 1.4 kg)

1. Preheat the oven to 450°F (235°C). Line a baking sheet with parchment paper. 2. Place the olive oil and spices into a large bowl and mix together, making a paste. Add the chicken and mix together until evenly coated. Place on the prepared baking sheet. 3. Bake for 30 to 35 minutes, or until golden brown and the chicken registers an internal temperature of 165°F (74°C).

Per Serving
Calories: 440 | fat: 34g | protein: 30g | carbs: 1g | fiber: 0g | sodium: 180mg

Braised Duck with Fennel Root

Prep time: 10 minutes | Cook time: 50 minutes | Serves 6

¼ cup olive oil
1 whole duck, cleaned
3 teaspoon fresh rosemary
2 garlic cloves, minced
Sea salt and freshly ground pepper, to taste
3 fennel bulbs, cut into chunks
½ cup sherry

1. Preheat the oven to 375°F (190°C) 2. Heat the olive oil in a large stew pot or Dutch oven. 3. Season the duck, including the cavity, with the rosemary, garlic, sea salt, and freshly ground pepper. 4. Place the duck in the oil, and cook it for 10–15 minutes, turning as necessary to brown all sides. 5. Add the fennel bulbs and cook an additional 5 minutes. 6. Pour the sherry over the duck and fennel, cover the pot, and cook in the oven for 30–45 minutes, or until internal temperature of the duck is 150°F (66°C) at its thickest part. 7. Allow duck to sit for 15 minutes before serving.

Per Serving
Calories: 308 | fat: 23g | protein: 17g | carbs: 9g | fiber: 4g | sodium: 112mg

Turkey Breast in Yogurt Sauce

Prep time: 10 minutes | Cook time: 16 minutes | Serves 6

1 cup plain low-fat yogurt
1 teaspoon ground turmeric
1 teaspoon ground cumin
1 teaspoon yellow mustard seeds
¼ teaspoon salt
½ teaspoon ground black pepper
1 pound (454 g) boneless turkey breast, cut into bite-sized pieces
1 tablespoon olive oil
1 (1-pound / 454-g) bag frozen baby peas and pearl onions, thawed

1. In a large bowl, mix together yogurt, turmeric, cumin, mustard seeds, salt, and pepper. Stir in in turkey. Cover and refrigerate for 4 hours. 2. Press the Sauté button on the Instant Pot® and heat oil. Add turkey and yogurt mixture. Press the Cancel button, close lid, set steam release to Sealing, press the Manual button, and set time to 8 minutes. When the timer beeps, quick-release the pressure and open lid. 3. Stir in peas and onions. Press the Cancel button, then press the Sauté button and simmer until sauce is thickened, about 8 minutes. Serve hot.

Per Serving
Calories: 146 | fat: 6g | protein: 17g | carbs: 7g | fiber: 1g | sodium: 554mg

Chapter 11 Salads

Powerhouse Arugula Salad

Prep time: 10 minutes | Cook time: 0 minutes | Serves 4

4 tablespoons extra-virgin olive oil
Zest and juice of 2 clementines or 1 orange (2 to 3 tablespoons)
1 tablespoon red wine vinegar
½ teaspoon salt
¼ teaspoon freshly ground black pepper
8 cups baby arugula
1 cup coarsely chopped walnuts
1 cup crumbled goat cheese
½ cup pomegranate seeds

1. In a small bowl, whisk together the olive oil, zest and juice, vinegar, salt, and pepper and set aside. 2. To assemble the salad for serving, in a large bowl, combine the arugula, walnuts, goat cheese, and pomegranate seeds. Drizzle with the dressing and toss to coat.

Per Serving
Calories: 448 | fat: 41g | protein: 11g | carbs: 13g | fiber: 4g | sodium: 647mg

Chopped Greek Antipasto Salad

Prep time: 20 minutes |Cook time: 0 minutes| Serves: 6

For the Salad:
1 head Bibb lettuce or ½ head romaine lettuce, chopped (about 2½ cups)
¼ cup loosely packed chopped basil leaves
1 (15-ounce / 425-g) can chickpeas, drained and rinsed
1 (14-ounce / 397-g) can artichoke hearts, drained and halved
1 pint grape tomatoes, halved (about 1½ cups)
1 seedless cucumber, peeled and chopped (about 1½ cups)
½ cup cubed feta cheese (about
2 ounces / 57 g)
1 (2¼-ounce / 35-g) can sliced black olives (about ½ cup)
For the Dressing:
3 tablespoons extra-virgin olive oil
1 tablespoon red wine vinegar
1 tablespoon freshly squeezed lemon juice (from about ½ small lemon)
1 tablespoon chopped fresh oregano or ½ teaspoon dried oregano
1 teaspoon honey
¼ teaspoon freshly ground black pepper

1. In a medium bowl, toss the lettuce and basil together. Spread out on a large serving platter or in a large salad bowl. Arrange the chickpeas, artichoke hearts, tomatoes, cucumber, feta, and olives in piles next to each other on top of the lettuce layer. 2. In a small pitcher or bowl, whisk together the oil, vinegar, lemon juice, oregano, honey, and pepper. Serve on the side with the salad, or drizzle over all the ingredients right before serving.

Per Serving
Calories: 267 | fat: 13g | protein: 11g | carbs: 31g | fiber: 11g | sodium: 417mg

Mediterranean Potato Salad

Prep time: 10 minutes |Cook time: 20 minutes| Serves: 6

2 pounds (907 g) Yukon Gold baby potatoes, cut into 1-inch cubes
3 tablespoons freshly squeezed lemon juice (from about 1 medium lemon)
3 tablespoons extra-virgin olive oil
1 tablespoon olive brine
¼ teaspoon kosher or sea salt
1 (2¼-ounce / 35-g) can sliced olives (about ½ cup)
1 cup sliced celery (about 2 stalks) or fennel
2 tablespoons chopped fresh oregano
2 tablespoons torn fresh mint

1. In a medium saucepan, cover the potatoes with cold water until the waterline is one inch above the potatoes. Set over high heat, bring the potatoes to a boil, then turn down the heat to medium-low. Simmer for 12 to 15 minutes, until the potatoes are just fork tender. 2. While the potatoes are cooking, in a small bowl, whisk together the lemon juice, oil, olive brine, and salt. 3. Drain the potatoes in a colander and transfer to a serving bowl. Immediately pour about 3 tablespoons of the dressing over the potatoes. Gently mix in the olives and celery. 4. Before serving, gently mix in the oregano, mint, and the remaining dressing.

Per Serving
Calories: 192 | fat: 8g | protein: 3g | carbs: 28g | fiber: 4g | sodium: 195mg

Tuscan Kale Salad with Anchovies

Prep time: 15 minutes | Cook time: 0 minutes | Serves 4

1 large bunch lacinato or dinosaur kale
¼ cup toasted pine nuts
1 cup shaved or coarsely shredded fresh Parmesan cheese
¼ cup extra-virgin olive oil
8 anchovy fillets, roughly chopped
2 to 3 tablespoons freshly squeezed lemon juice (from 1 large lemon)
2 teaspoons red pepper flakes (optional)

1. Remove the rough center stems from the kale leaves and roughly tear each leaf into about 4-by-1-inch strips. Place the torn kale in a large bowl and add the pine nuts and cheese. 2. In a small bowl, whisk together the olive oil, anchovies, lemon juice, and red pepper flakes (if using). Drizzle over the salad and toss to coat well. Let sit at room temperature 30 minutes before serving, tossing again just prior to serving.

Per Serving
Calories: 333 | fat: 27g | protein: 16g | carbs: 12g | fiber: 4g | sodium: 676mg

Israeli Salad with Nuts and Seeds

Prep time: 15 minutes | Cook time: 0 minutes | Serves 4

¼ cup pine nuts
¼ cup shelled pistachios
¼ cup coarsely chopped walnuts
¼ cup shelled pumpkin seeds
¼ cup shelled sunflower seeds
2 large English cucumbers, unpeeled and finely chopped
1 pint cherry tomatoes, finely chopped
½ small red onion, finely

chopped
½ cup finely chopped fresh flat-leaf Italian parsley
¼ cup extra-virgin olive oil
2 to 3 tablespoons freshly squeezed lemon juice (from 1 lemon)
1 teaspoon salt
¼ teaspoon freshly ground black pepper
4 cups baby arugula

1. In a large dry skillet, toast the pine nuts, pistachios, walnuts, pumpkin seeds, and sunflower seeds over medium-low heat until golden and fragrant, 5 to 6 minutes, being careful not to burn them. Remove from the heat and set aside. 2. In a large bowl, combine the cucumber, tomatoes, red onion, and parsley. 3. In a small bowl, whisk together olive oil, lemon juice, salt, and pepper. Pour over the chopped vegetables and toss to coat. 4. Add the toasted nuts and seeds and arugula and toss with the salad to blend well. Serve at room temperature or chilled.

Per Serving

Calories: 404 | fat: 36g | protein: 10g | carbs: 16g | fiber: 5g | sodium: 601mg

Roasted Cauliflower Salad with Tahini-Yogurt Dressing

Prep time: 10 minutes | Cook time: 35 minutes | Serves 8 to 10

10 cups cauliflower florets (1- to 2-inch florets, from 1 to 2 heads)
1½ tablespoons olive oil
¾ teaspoon kosher salt, divided
½ cup walnuts
½ cup yogurt

¼ cup tahini, at room temperature
¼ cup lemon juice, plus more to taste
¼ cup water
1 tablespoon honey
¼ cup chopped fresh dill
1 tablespoon minced shallot

1. Preheat the oven to 450ºF (235ºC). 2. On a large baking sheet, toss the cauliflower with the olive oil and ¼ teaspoon of the salt. Spread the cauliflower out in a single layer and roast in the preheated oven for about 30 minutes, until it is tender and browned on the bottom. Place the cooked cauliflower in a large bowl and set aside to cool while you prepare the rest of the salad. 3. Toast the walnuts in a skillet over medium heat until fragrant and golden, about 5 minutes. Chop and set aside. 4. In a blender or food processor, combine the yogurt, tahini, lemon juice, water, and honey and process until smooth. If the mixture is too thick, add a tablespoon or two of additional water. 5. Add the dill, shallot, and the remaining ½ teaspoon of salt to the cauliflower and toss to combine. Add the dressing and toss again to coat well. 6. Serve the salad at room temperature, garnished with the toasted walnuts.

Per Serving

Calories: 153 | fat: 10g | protein: 6g | carbs: 12g | fiber: 4g | sodium: 249mg

Roasted Broccoli Panzanella Salad

Prep time: 10 minutes |Cook time: 20 minutes| Serves: 4

1 pound (454 g) broccoli (about 3 medium stalks), trimmed, cut into 1-inch florets and ½-inch stem slices
3 tablespoons extra-virgin olive oil, divided
1 pint cherry or grape tomatoes (about 1½ cups)
1½ teaspoons honey, divided
3 cups cubed whole-grain

crusty bread
1 tablespoon balsamic vinegar
½ teaspoon freshly ground black pepper
¼ teaspoon kosher or sea salt
Grated Parmesan cheese (or other hard cheese) and chopped fresh oregano leaves, for serving (optional)

1. Place a large, rimmed baking sheet in the oven. Preheat the oven to 450ºF (235ºC) with the pan inside. 2. Put the broccoli in a large bowl, and drizzle with 1 tablespoon of the oil. Toss to coat. 3. Carefully remove the hot baking sheet from the oven and spoon the broccoli onto it, leaving some oil in the bottom of the bowl. Add the tomatoes to the same bowl, and toss to coat with the leftover oil (don't add any more oil). Toss the tomatoes with 1 teaspoon of honey, and scrape them onto the baking sheet with the broccoli. 4. Roast for 15 minutes, stirring halfway through. Remove the sheet from the oven, and add the bread cubes. Roast for 3 more minutes. The broccoli is ready when it appears slightly charred on the tips and is tender-crisp when poked with a fork. 5. Spoon the vegetable mixture onto a serving plate or into a large, flat bowl. 6. In a small bowl, whisk the remaining 2 tablespoons of oil together with the vinegar, the remaining ½ teaspoon of honey, and the pepper and salt. Pour over the salad, and toss gently. Sprinkle with cheese and oregano, if desired, and serve.

Per Serving

Calories: 197 | fat: 12g | protein: 7g | carbs: 19g | fiber: 5g | sodium: 296mg

Easy Greek Salad

Prep time: 10 minutes | Cook time: 0 minutes | Serves 4 to 6

1 head iceberg lettuce
1 pint (2 cups) cherry tomatoes
1 large cucumber
1 medium onion
½ cup extra-virgin olive oil
¼ cup lemon juice

1 teaspoon salt
1 clove garlic, minced
1 cup Kalamata olives, pitted
1 (6-ounce / 170-g) package feta cheese, crumbled

1. Cut the lettuce into 1-inch pieces and put them in a large salad bowl. 2. Cut the tomatoes in half and add them to the salad bowl. 3. Slice the cucumber into bite-size pieces and add them to the salad bowl. 4. Thinly slice the onion and add it to the salad bowl. 5. In another small bowl, whisk together the olive oil, lemon juice, salt, and garlic. Pour the dressing over the salad and gently toss to evenly coat. 6. Top the salad with the Kalamata olives and feta cheese and serve.

Per Serving

Calories: 297 | fat: 27g | protein: 6g | carbs: 11g | fiber: 3g | sodium: 661mg

Orange-Tarragon Chicken Salad Wrap

Prep time: 15 minutes | Cook time: 0 minutes | Serves 4

½ cup plain whole-milk Greek yogurt
2 tablespoons Dijon mustard
2 tablespoons extra-virgin olive oil
2 tablespoons chopped fresh tarragon or 1 teaspoon dried tarragon
½ teaspoon salt
¼ teaspoon freshly ground

black pepper
2 cups cooked shredded chicken
½ cup slivered almonds
4 to 8 large Bibb lettuce leaves, tough stem removed
2 small ripe avocados, peeled and thinly sliced
Zest of 1 clementine, or ½ small orange (about 1 tablespoon)

1. In a medium bowl, combine the yogurt, mustard, olive oil, tarragon, orange zest, salt, and pepper and whisk until creamy. 2. Add the shredded chicken and almonds and stir to coat. 3. To assemble the wraps, place about ½ cup chicken salad mixture in the center of each lettuce leaf and top with sliced avocados.

Per Serving

Calories: 491 | fat: 38g | protein: 28g | carbs: 14g | fiber: 9g | sodium: 454mg

Caprese Salad with Fresh Mozzarella

Prep time: 10 minutes | Cook time: 0 minutes | Serves 6 to 8

For the Pesto:
2 cups (packed) fresh basil leaves, plus more for garnish
⅓ cup pine nuts
3 garlic cloves, minced
½ cup (about 2 ounces / 57 g) freshly grated Parmesan cheese
½ cup extra-virgin olive oil
Salt

Freshly ground black pepper
For the Salad:
4 to 6 large, ripe tomatoes, cut into thick slices
1 pound (454 g) fresh mozzarella, cut into thick slices
3 tablespoons balsamic vinegar
Salt
Freshly ground black pepper

1. To make the pesto, in a food processor combine the basil, pine nuts, and garlic and pulse several times to chop. Add the Parmesan cheese and pulse again until well combined. With the food processor running, add the olive oil in a slow, steady stream. Transfer to a small bowl, taste, and add salt and pepper as needed. Slice, quarter, or halve the tomatoes, based on your preferred salad presentation. 2. To make the salad, on a large serving platter arrange the tomato slices and cheese slices, stacking them like fallen dominoes. 3. Dollop the pesto decoratively on top of the tomato and cheese slices. (You will likely have extra pesto. Refrigerate the extra in a tightly sealed container and use within 3 days, or freeze it for up to 3 months.) 4. Drizzle the balsamic vinegar over the top, garnish with basil leaves, sprinkle with salt and pepper to taste, and serve immediately.

Per Serving

Calories: 398 | fat: 32g | protein: 23g | carbs: 8g | fiber: 1g | sodium: 474mg

Traditional Greek Salad

Prep time: 10 minutes | Cook time: 0 minutes | Serves 4

2 large English cucumbers
4 Roma tomatoes, quartered
1 green bell pepper, cut into 1- to 1½-inch chunks
¼ small red onion, thinly sliced
4 ounces (113 g) pitted Kalamata olives
¼ cup extra-virgin olive oil

2 tablespoons freshly squeezed lemon juice
1 tablespoon red wine vinegar
1 tablespoon chopped fresh oregano or 1 teaspoon dried oregano
¼ teaspoon freshly ground black pepper
4 ounces (113 g) crumbled traditional feta cheese

1. Cut the cucumbers in half lengthwise and then into ½-inch-thick half-moons. Place in a large bowl. 2. Add the quartered tomatoes, bell pepper, red onion, and olives. 3. In a small bowl, whisk together the olive oil, lemon juice, vinegar, oregano, and pepper. Drizzle over the vegetables and toss to coat. 4. Divide between salad plates and top each with 1 ounce (28 g) of feta.

Per Serving

Calories: 256 | fat: 22g | protein: 6g | carbs: 11g | fiber: 3g | sodium: 476mg

Spinach Salad with Pomegranate, Lentils, and Pistachios

Prep time: 10 minutes | Cook time: 30 minutes | Serves 4

1 tablespoon extra-virgin olive oil
1 shallot, finely chopped
1 small red chile pepper, such as a Fresno, finely chopped (wear plastic gloves when handling)
½ teaspoon ground cumin
¼ teaspoon ground coriander seeds
¼ teaspoon ground cinnamon
Pinch of kosher salt
1 cup French green lentils,

rinsed
3 cups water
6 cups baby spinach
½ cup pomegranate seeds
¼ cup chopped fresh cilantro
¼ cup chopped fresh flat-leaf parsley
¼ cup chopped pistachi os
2 tablespoons fresh lemon juice
1 teaspoon finely grated lemon peel
Ground black pepper, to taste

1. In a medium saucepan over medium heat, warm the oil until shimmering. Cook the shallot and chile pepper, stirring, until the shallot is translucent, about 8 minutes. Stir in the cumin, coriander, cinnamon, and salt until fragrant, about 1 minute. Add the lentils and water and bring to a boil. Cover and reduce the heat to a simmer. Cook, stirring occasionally, until the lentils are completely tender and the liquid has been absorbed, about 30 minutes. 2. In a large bowl, toss the lentils with the spinach, pomegranate seeds, cilantro, parsley, pistachios, lemon juice, lemon peel, and pepper to taste.

Per Serving

Calories: 279 | fat: 7g | protein: 15g | carbs: 39g | fiber: 10g | sodium: 198mg

Pistachio-Parmesan Kale-Arugula Salad

Prep time: 20 minutes |Cook time: 0 minutes| Serves: 6

6 cups raw kale, center ribs removed and discarded, leaves coarsely chopped
¼ cup extra-virgin olive oil
2 tablespoons freshly squeezed lemon juice (from about 1 small lemon)
½ teaspoon smoked paprika
2 cups arugula
⅓ cup unsalted shelled pistachios
6 tablespoons grated Parmesan or Pecorino Romano cheese

1. In a large salad bowl, combine the kale, oil, lemon juice, and smoked paprika. With your hands, gently massage the leaves for about 15 seconds or so, until all are thoroughly coated. Let the kale sit for 10 minutes. 2. When you're ready to serve, gently mix in the arugula and pistachios. Divide the salad among six serving bowls, sprinkle 1 tablespoon of grated cheese over each, and serve.

Per Serving
Calories: 150 | fat: 14g | protein: 4g | carbs: 5g | fiber: 1g | sodium: 99mg

Zucchini and Ricotta Salad

Prep time: 5 minutes | Cook time: 2 minutes | Serves 1

2 teaspoons raw pine nuts
5 ounces (142 g) whole-milk ricotta cheese
1 tablespoon chopped fresh mint
1 teaspoon chopped fresh basil
1 tablespoon chopped fresh parsley
Pinch of fine sea salt
1 medium zucchini, very thinly sliced horizontally with
a mandoline slicer
Pinch of freshly ground black pepper
For the Dressing:
1½ tablespoons extra virgin olive oil
1 tablespoon fresh lemon juice
Pinch of fine sea salt
Pinch of freshly ground black pepper

1. Add the pine nuts to a small pan placed over medium heat. Toast the nuts, turning them frequently, for 2 minutes or until golden. Set aside. 2. In a food processor, combine the ricotta, mint, basil, parsley, and a pinch of sea salt. Process until smooth and then set aside. 3. Make the dressing by combining the olive oil and lemon juice in a small bowl. Use a fork to stir rapidly until the mixture thickens, then add a pinch of sea salt and a pinch of black pepper. Stir again. 4. Place the sliced zucchini in a medium bowl. Add half of the dressing, and toss to coat the zucchini. 5. To serve, place half of the ricotta mixture in the center of a serving plate, then layer the zucchini in a circle, covering the cheese. Add the rest of the cheese in the center and on top of the zucchini, then sprinkle the toasted pine nuts over the top. Drizzle the remaining dressing over the top, and finish with a pinch of black pepper. Store covered in the refrigerator for up to 1 day.

Per Serving
Calories: 504 | fat: 43g | protein: 19g | carbs: 13g | fiber: 3g | sodium: 136mg

Melon Caprese Salad

Prep time: 20 minutes |Cook time: 0 minutes| Serves: 6

1 cantaloupe, quartered and seeded
½ small seedless watermelon
1 cup grape tomatoes
2 cups fresh mozzarella balls (about 8 ounces / 227 g)
⅓ cup fresh basil or mint
leaves, torn into small pieces
2 tablespoons extra-virgin olive oil
1 tablespoon balsamic vinegar
¼ teaspoon freshly ground black pepper
¼ teaspoon kosher or sea salt

1. Using a melon baller or a metal, teaspoon-size measuring spoon, scoop balls out of the cantaloupe. You should get about 2½ to 3 cups from one cantaloupe. (If you prefer, cut the melon into bite-size pieces instead of making balls.) Put them in a large colander over a large serving bowl. 2. Using the same method, ball or cut the watermelon into bite-size pieces; you should get about 2 cups. Put the watermelon balls in the colander with the cantaloupe. 3. Let the fruit drain for 10 minutes. Pour the juice from the bowl into a container to refrigerate and save for drinking or adding to smoothies. Wipe the bowl dry, and put in the cut fruit. 4. Add the tomatoes, mozzarella, basil, oil, vinegar, pepper, and salt to the fruit mixture. Gently mix until everything is incorporated and serve.

Per Serving
Calories: 297 | fat: 12g | protein: 14g | carbs: 39g | fiber: 3g | sodium: 123mg

Greek Salad with Lemon-Oregano Vinaigrette

Prep time: 15 minutes | Cook time: 15 minutes | Serves 8

½ red onion, thinly sliced
¼ cup extra-virgin olive oil
3 tablespoons fresh lemon juice or red wine vinegar
1 clove garlic, minced
1 teaspoon chopped fresh oregano or ½ teaspoon dried
½ teaspoon ground black pepper
¼ teaspoon kosher salt
4 tomatoes, cut into large chunks
1 large English cucumber, peeled, seeded (if desired), and diced
1 large yellow or red bell pepper, chopped
½ cup pitted kalamata or Niçoise olives, halved
¼ cup chopped fresh flat-leaf parsley
4 ounces (113 g) Halloumi or feta cheese, cut into ½' cubes

1. In a medium bowl, soak the onion in enough water to cover for 10 minutes. 2. In a small bowl, combine the oil, lemon juice or vinegar, garlic, oregano, black pepper, and salt. 3. Drain the onion and add to a large bowl with the tomatoes, cucumber, bell pepper, olives, and parsley. Gently toss to mix the vegetables. 4. Pour the vinaigrette over the salad. Add the cheese and toss again to distribute. 5. Serve immediately, or chill for up to 30 minutes.

Per Serving
Calories: 190 | fat: 16g | protein: 5g | carbs: 8g | fiber: 2g | sodium: 554mg

Classic Tabouli

Prep time: 30 minutes | Cook time: 0 minutes | Serves 8 to 10

1 cup bulgur wheat, grind
4 cups Italian parsley, finely chopped
2 cups ripe tomato, finely diced
1 cup green onion, finely

chopped
½ cup lemon juice
½ cup extra-virgin olive oil
1½ teaspoons salt
1 teaspoon dried mint

1. Before you chop the vegetables, put the bulgur in a small bowl. Rinse with water, drain, and let stand in the bowl while you prepare the other ingredients. 2. Put the parsley, tomatoes, green onion, and bulgur into a large bowl. 3. In a small bowl, whisk together the lemon juice, olive oil, salt, and mint. 4. Pour the dressing over the tomato, onion, and bulgur mixture, tossing everything together. Add additional salt to taste. Serve immediately or store in the fridge for up to 2 days.

Per Serving
Calories: 207 | fat: 14g | protein: 4g | carbs: 20g | fiber: 5g | sodium: 462mg

Yellow and White Hearts of Palm Salad

Prep time: 10 minutes | Cook time: 0 minutes | Serves 4

2 (14-ounce / 397-g) cans hearts of palm, drained and cut into ½-inch-thick slices
1 avocado, cut into ½-inch pieces
1 cup halved yellow cherry tomatoes
½ small shallot, thinly sliced
¼ cup coarsely chopped flat-

leaf parsley
2 tablespoons low-fat mayonnaise
2 tablespoons extra-virgin olive oil
¼ teaspoon salt
⅛ teaspoon freshly ground black pepper

1. In a large bowl, toss the hearts of palm, avocado, tomatoes, shallot, and parsley. 2. In a small bowl, whisk the mayonnaise, olive oil, salt, and pepper, then mix into the large bowl.

Per Serving
Calories: 192 | fat: 15g | protein: 5g | carbs: 14g | fiber: 7g | sodium: 841mg

Mediterranean Quinoa and Garbanzo Salad

Prep time: 10 minutes | Cook time: 30 minutes | Serves 8

4 cups water
2 cups red or yellow quinoa
2 teaspoons salt, divided
1 cup thinly sliced onions (red or white)
1 (16-ounce / 454-g) can

garbanzo beans, rinsed and drained
⅓ cup extra-virgin olive oil
¼ cup lemon juice
1 teaspoon freshly ground black pepper

1. In a 3-quart pot over medium heat, bring the water to a boil.

2. Add the quinoa and 1 teaspoon of salt to the pot. Stir, cover, and let cook over low heat for 15 to 20 minutes. 3. Turn off the heat, fluff the quinoa with a fork, cover again, and let stand for 5 to 10 more minutes. 4. Put the cooked quinoa, onions, and garbanzo beans in a large bowl. 5. In a separate small bowl, whisk together the olive oil, lemon juice, remaining 1 teaspoon of salt, and black pepper. 6. Add the dressing to the quinoa mixture and gently toss everything together. Serve warm or cold.

Per Serving
Calories: 318 | fat: 13g | protein: 9g | carbs: 43g | fiber: 6g | sodium: 585mg

Spanish Potato Salad

Prep time: 10 minutes | Cook time: 10 minutes | Serves 6 to 8

4 russet potatoes, peeled and chopped
3 large hard-boiled eggs, chopped
1 cup frozen mixed vegetables, thawed
½ cup plain, unsweetened, full-fat Greek yogurt
5 tablespoons pitted Spanish

olives
½ teaspoon freshly ground black pepper
½ teaspoon dried mustard seed
½ tablespoon freshly squeezed lemon juice
½ teaspoon dried dill
Salt
Freshly ground black pepper

1. Boil potatoes for 5 to 7 minutes, until just fork-tender, checking periodically for doneness. You don't want to overcook them. 2. While the potatoes are cooking, in a large bowl, mix the eggs, vegetables, yogurt, olives, pepper, mustard, lemon juice, and dill. Season with salt and pepper. Once the potatoes are cooled somewhat, add them to the large bowl, then mix well and serve.

Per Serving
Calories: 192 | fat: 5g | protein: 9g | carbs: 30g | fiber: 2g | sodium: 59mg

No-Mayo Florence Tuna Salad

Prep time: 10 minutes | Cook time: 0 minutes | Serves 4

4 cups spring mix greens
1 (15-ounce / 425-g) can cannellini beans, drained
2 (5-ounce / 142-g) cans water-packed, white albacore tuna, drained (I prefer Wild Planet brand)
⅔ cup crumbled feta cheese
½ cup thinly sliced sun-dried tomatoes
¼ cup sliced pitted kalamata

olives
¼ cup thinly sliced scallions, both green and white parts
3 tablespoons extra-virgin olive oil
½ teaspoon dried cilantro
2 or 3 leaves thinly chopped fresh sweet basil
1 lime, zested and juiced
Kosher salt
Freshly ground black pepper

1. In a large bowl, combine greens, beans, tuna, feta, tomatoes, olives, scallions, olive oil, cilantro, basil, and lime juice and zest. Season with salt and pepper, mix, and enjoy!

Per Serving 1 cup:
Calories: 355 | fat: 19g | protein: 22g | carbs: 25g | fiber: 8g | sodium: 744mg

Wild Greens Salad with Fresh Herbs

Prep time: 10 minutes | Cook time: 20 minutes | Serves 6 to 8

¼ cup olive oil
2 pounds (907 g) dandelion greens, tough stems removed and coarsely chopped
1 small bunch chicory, trimmed and coarsely chopped
1 cup chopped fresh flat-leaf parsley, divided
1 cup chopped fresh mint, divided
½ cup water
2 tablespoons red wine vinegar or apple cider vinegar

1 tablespoon fresh thyme, chopped
2 cloves garlic, minced
½ teaspoon kosher salt
½ teaspoon ground black pepper
¼ cup almonds or walnuts, coarsely chopped
2 tablespoons chopped fresh chives or scallion greens
1 tablespoon chopped fresh dill

1. In a large pot over medium heat, warm the oil. Add the greens, half of the parsley, half of the mint, the water, vinegar, thyme, garlic, salt, and pepper. Reduce the heat to a simmer and cook until the greens are very tender, about 20 minutes. 2. Meanwhile, in a small skillet over medium heat, toast the nuts until golden and fragrant, 5 to 8 minutes. Remove from the heat. 3. If serving immediately, stir the chives or scallion greens, dill, and the remaining parsley and mint into the pot. If serving as a cool or cold salad, allow to come to room temperature or refrigerate until cold before stirring in the fresh herbs. Top with the toasted nuts before serving.
Per Serving
Calories: 190 | fat: 13g | protein: 6g | carbs: 17g | fiber: 7g | sodium: 279mg

Tomato and Pepper Salad

Prep time: 10 minutes | Cook time: 0 minutes | Serves 6

3 large yellow peppers
¼ cup olive oil
1 small bunch fresh basil leaves
2 cloves garlic, minced

4 large tomatoes, seeded and diced
Sea salt and freshly ground pepper, to taste

1. Preheat broiler to high heat and broil the peppers until blackened on all sides. 2. Remove from heat and place in a paper bag. Seal and allow peppers to cool. 3. Once cooled, peel the skins off the peppers, then seed and chop them. 4. Add half of the peppers to a food processor along with the olive oil, basil, and garlic, and pulse several times to make the dressing. 5. Combine the rest of the peppers with the tomatoes and toss with the dressing. Season the salad with sea salt and freshly ground pepper. Allow salad to come to room temperature before serving.
Per Serving
Calories: 129 | fat: 9g | protein: 2g | carbs: 11g | fiber: 2g | sodium: 8mg

Mediterranean No-Mayo Potato Salad

Prep time: 5 minutes | Cook time: 15 minutes | Serves 4

2 pounds (907 g) potatoes (white or Yukon Gold varieties), peeled and cut into 1½-inch chunks
¼ cup extra virgin olive oil

3 tablespoons red wine vinegar
½ medium red onion, chopped
2 tablespoons dried oregano
½ teaspoon fine sea salt

1. Fill a medium pot with water and place it over high heat. When the water comes to a boil, carefully place the potatoes in the water, reduce the heat to medium, and simmer for 12–15 minutes or until the potatoes can be pierced with a fork but are not falling apart. Use a slotted spoon to transfer the potatoes to a colander, rinse briefly with cold water, then set aside to drain. 2. In a small bowl, whisk the olive oil and red wine vinegar. 3. Transfer the potatoes to a large bowl. Add the olive oil and vinegar mixture to the potatoes and toss gently and then add the onions. Rub the oregano between your fingers to release the aroma, then sprinkle it over the potatoes and toss again. Add the sea salt and toss once more. Store in an airtight container in the refrigerator for up to 3 days.
Per Serving
Calories: 347 | fat: 14g | protein: 5g | carbs: 50g | fiber: 6g | sodium: 309mg

Citrus Avocado Salad

Prep time: 5 minutes | Cook time: 0 minutes | Serves 2

½ medium orange (any variety), peeled and cut into bite-sized chunks
1 medium tangerine, peeled and sectioned
½ medium white grapefruit, peeled and cut into bite-sized chunks
2 thin slices red onion
1 medium avocado, peeled, pitted, and sliced

Pinch of freshly ground black pepper
For the Dressing:
3 tablespoons extra virgin olive oil
1 tablespoon fresh lemon juice
½ teaspoon ground cumin
½ teaspoon coarse sea salt
Pinch of freshly ground black pepper

1. Make the dressing by combining the olive oil, lemon juice, cumin, sea salt, and black pepper in a small jar or bowl. Whisk or shake to combine. 2. Toss the orange, tangerine, and grapefruit in a medium bowl, then place the sliced onion on top. Drizzle half the dressing over the salad. 3. Fan the avocado slices over the top of the salad. Drizzle the remaining dressing over the salad and then sprinkle a pinch of black pepper over the top. 4. Toss gently before serving. (This salad is best eaten fresh, but can be stored in the refrigerator for up to 1 day.)
Per Serving
Calories: 448 | fat: 36g | protein: 4g | carbs: 35g | fiber: 11g | sodium: 595mg

Superfood Salmon Salad Bowl

Prep time: 5 minutes | Cook time: 10 minutes | Serves 2

Salmon:
2 fillets wild salmon
Salt and black pepper, to taste
2 teaspoons extra-virgin avocado oil
Dressing:
1 tablespoon capers
1 teaspoon Dijon or whole-grain mustard
1 tablespoon apple cider vinegar or fresh lemon juice
3 tablespoons extra-virgin olive oil
1 teaspoon coconut aminos
Salt and black pepper, to taste

Salad:
½ medium cucumber, diced
1 cup sugar snap peas, sliced into matchsticks
½ small red bell pepper, sliced
⅓ cup pitted Kalamata olives, halved
2 sun-dried tomatoes, chopped
1 medium avocado, diced
3 tablespoons chopped fresh herbs, such as dill, chives, parsley, and/or basil
1 tablespoon pumpkin seeds
1 tablespoon sunflower seeds

1. To make the salmon: Season the salmon with salt and pepper. Heat a pan greased with the avocado oil over medium heat. Add the salmon, skin-side down, and cook for 4 to 5 minutes. Flip and cook for 1 to 2 minutes or until cooked through. Remove from the heat and transfer to a plate to cool. Remove the skin from the salmon and flake into chunks. 2. To make the dressing: Mix all the dressing ingredients together in a small bowl. Set aside. 3. To make the salad: Place the cucumber, sugar snap peas, bell pepper, olives, sun-dried tomatoes, avocado, and herbs in a mixing bowl, and combine well. Add the flaked salmon. Dry-fry the seeds in a pan placed over medium-low heat until lightly golden. Allow to cool, then add to the bowl. Drizzle with the prepared dressing and serve. This salad can be stored in the fridge for up to 1 day.

Per Serving
Calories: 660 | fat: 54g | protein: 31g | carbs: 18g | fiber: 9g | sodium: 509mg

Greek Village Salad

Prep time: 10 minutes | Cook time: 0 minutes | Serves 4

5 large tomatoes, cut into medium chunks
2 red onions, cut into medium chunks or sliced
1 English cucumber, peeled and cut into medium chunks
2 green bell peppers, cut into medium chunks
¼ cup extra-virgin olive oil,

plus extra for drizzling
1 cup kalamata olives, for topping
¼ teaspoon dried oregano, plus extra for garnish
¼ lemon
4 ounces (113 g) Greek feta cheese, sliced

1. In a large bowl, mix the tomatoes, onions, cucumber, bell peppers, olive oil, olives, and oregano. 2. Divide the vegetable mixture evenly among four bowls and top each with a squirt of lemon juice and 1 slice of feta. Drizzle with olive oil, garnish with oregano, and serve.

Per Serving
Calories: 315 | fat: 24g | protein: 8g | carbs: 21g | fiber: 6g | sodium: 524mg

Toasted Pita Bread Salad

Prep time: 10 minutes | Cook time: 0 minutes | Serves 4

For the Dressing:
½ cup lemon juice
½ cup olive oil
1 small clove garlic, minced
1 teaspoon salt
½ teaspoon ground sumac
¼ teaspoon freshly ground black pepper
For the Salad:
2 cups shredded romaine lettuce
1 large or 2 small cucumbers, seeded and diced

2 medium tomatoes, diced
½ cup chopped fresh flat-leaf parsley leaves
¼ cup chopped fresh mint leaves
1 small green bell pepper, diced
1 bunch scallions, thinly sliced
2 whole-wheat pita bread rounds, toasted and broken into quarter-sized pieces
Ground sumac for garnish

1. To make the dressing, whisk together the lemon juice, olive oil, garlic, salt, sumac, and pepper in a small bowl. 2. To make the salad, in a large bowl, combine the lettuce, cucumber, tomatoes, parsley, mint, bell pepper, scallions, and pita bread. Toss to combine. Add the dressing and toss again to coat well. 3. Serve immediately sprinkled with sumac.

Per Serving
Calories: 359 | fat: 27g | protein: 6g | carbs: 29g | fiber: 6g | sodium: 777mg

Mediterranean Salad with Bulgur

Prep time: 27 minutes | Cook time: 12 minutes | Serves 4

1 cup water
½ cup dried bulgur
1 (9-ounce / 255-g) bag chopped romaine lettuce
1 English cucumber, cut into ¼-inch-thick slices
1 red bell pepper, chopped
½ cup raw hulled pumpkin seeds

20 kalamata olives, pitted and halved lengthwise
¼ cup extra-virgin olive oil
Juice of 1 small orange
Juice of 1 small lemon
¼ teaspoon dried oregano
Sea salt
Freshly ground black pepper

1. In a medium saucepan, combine the water and bulgur and bring to a boil over medium heat. Reduce the heat to low, cover, and cook until the bulgur is tender, about 12 minutes. Drain off any excess liquid, fluff the bulgur with a fork, and set aside. 2. In a medium bowl, toss together the lettuce, cucumber, bell pepper, bulgur, pumpkin seeds, and olives and set aside. 3. In a small bowl, stir together the olive oil, orange juice, lemon juice, and oregano. Season with salt and black pepper. 4. Add 3 tablespoons of the dressing to the salad and toss to coat. Taste, add more dressing and season with additional salt and/or black pepper if needed, then serve.

Per Serving
Calories: 322 | fat: 23g | protein: 8g | carbs: 24g | fiber: 6g | sodium: 262mg

Roasted Cauliflower "Steak" Salad

Prep time: 10 minutes | Cook time: 50 minutes | Serves 4

2 tablespoons olive oil, divided
2 large heads cauliflower (about 3 pounds / 1.4 kg each), trimmed of outer leaves
2 teaspoons za'atar
1½ teaspoons kosher salt, divided
1¼ teaspoons ground black pepper, divided
1 teaspoon ground cumin
2 large carrots
8 ounces (227 g) dandelion greens, tough stems removed
½ cup low-fat plain Greek yogurt
2 tablespoons tahini
2 tablespoons fresh lemon juice
1 tablespoon water
1 clove garlic, minced

1. Preheat the oven to 450°F (235°C). Brush a large baking sheet with some of the oil. 2. Place the cauliflower on a cutting board, stem side down. Cut down the middle, through the core and stem, and then cut two 1'-thick "steaks" from the middle. Repeat with the other cauliflower head. Set aside the remaining cauliflower for another use. Brush both sides of the steaks with the remaining oil and set on the baking sheet. 3. Combine the za'atar, 1 teaspoon of the salt, 1 teaspoon of the pepper, and the cumin. Sprinkle on the cauliflower steaks. Bake until the bottom is deeply golden, about 30 minutes. Flip and bake until tender, 10 to 15 minutes. 4. Meanwhile, set the carrots on a cutting board and use a vegetable peeler to peel them into ribbons. Add to a large bowl with the dandelion greens. 5. In a small bowl, combine the yogurt, tahini, lemon juice, water, garlic, the remaining ½ teaspoon salt, and the remaining ¼ teaspoon pepper. 6. Dab 3 tablespoons of the dressing onto the carrot-dandelion mix. With a spoon or your hands, massage the dressing into the mix for 5 minutes. 7. Remove the steaks from the oven and transfer to individual plates. Drizzle each with 2 tablespoons of the dressing and top with 1 cup of the salad.

Per Serving
Calories: 214 | fat: 12g | protein: 9g | carbs: 21g | fiber: 7g | sodium: 849mg

Grain-Free Kale Tabbouleh

Prep time: 15 minutes | Cook time: 0 minutes | Serves 8

2 plum tomatoes, seeded and chopped
½ cup finely chopped fresh parsley
4 scallions (green onions), finely chopped
1 head kale, finely chopped (about 2 cups)
1 cup finely chopped fresh
mint
1 small Persian cucumber, peeled, seeded, and diced
3 tablespoons extra-virgin olive oil
2 tablespoons fresh lemon juice
Coarsely ground black pepper (optional)

1. Place the tomatoes in a strainer set over a bowl and set aside to drain as much liquid as possible. 2. In a large bowl, stir to combine the parsley, scallions, kale, and mint. 3. Shake any remaining liquid from the tomatoes and add them to the kale mixture. Add the cucumber. 4. Add the olive oil and lemon juice and toss to combine. Season with pepper, if desired.

Per Serving 1 cup:
Calories: 65 | fat: 5g | protein: 1g | carbs: 4g | fiber: 1g | sodium: 21mg

Beets with Goat Cheese and Chermoula

Prep time: 10 minutes | Cook time: 40 minutes | Serves 4

6 beets, trimmed
Chermoula:

1 cup fresh cilantro leaves
1 cup fresh flat-leaf parsley leaves
¼ cup fresh lemon juice
3 cloves garlic, minced
2 teaspoons ground cumin
1 teaspoon smoked paprika
½ teaspoon kosher salt
¼ teaspoon chili powder (optional)
¼ cup extra-virgin olive oil
2 ounces (57 g) goat cheese, crumbled

1. Preheat the oven to 400°F (205°C). 2. Wrap the beets in a piece of foil and place on a baking sheet. Roast until the beets are tender enough to be pierced with a fork, 30 to 40 minutes. When cool enough to handle, remove the skins and slice the beets into ¼' rounds. Arrange the beet slices on a large serving platter. 3. To make the chermoula: In a food processor, pulse the cilantro, parsley, lemon juice, garlic, cumin, paprika, salt, and chili powder (if using) until the herbs are just coarsely chopped and the ingredients are combined. Stir in the oil. 4. To serve, dollop the chermoula over the beets and scatter the cheese on top.

Per Serving
Calories: 249 | fat: 19g | protein: 6g | carbs: 15g | fiber: 5g | sodium: 472mg

Arugula Salad with Grapes, Goat Cheese, and Za'atar Croutons

Prep time: 10 minutes | Cook time: 10 minutes | Serves 4

Croutons:
2 slices whole wheat bread, cubed
2 teaspoons olive oil, divided
1 teaspoon za'atar
Vinaigrette:
2 tablespoons olive oil
1 tablespoon red wine vinegar
½ teaspoon chopped fresh rosemary
¼ teaspoon kosher salt
⅛ teaspoon ground black pepper
Salad:
4 cups baby arugula
1 cup grapes, halved
½ red onion, thinly sliced
2 ounces (57 g) goat cheese, crumbled

1. Make the Croutons: Toss the bread cubes with 1 teaspoon of the oil and the za'atar. In a medium skillet over medium heat, warm the remaining 1 teaspoon oil. Cook the bread cubes, stirring frequently, until browned and crispy, 8 to 10 minutes. 2. Make the Vinaigrette: In a small bowl, whisk together the oil, vinegar, rosemary, salt, and pepper. 3. Make the Salad: In a large bowl, toss the arugula, grapes, and onion with the vinaigrette. Top with the cheese and croutons.

Per Serving
Calories: 204 | fat: 14g | protein: 6g | carbs: 15g | fiber: 2g | sodium: 283mg

Bacalhau and Black-Eyed Pea Salad

Prep time: 10 minutes | Cook time: 10 minutes | Serves 4

1 pound (454 g) bacalhau (salt cod) fillets
¼ cup olive oil, plus 1 tablespoon, divided
3 tablespoons white wine vinegar
1 teaspoon salt
¼ teaspoon freshly ground black pepper

1 (15-ounce / 425-g) can black-eyed peas, drained and rinsed
1 small yellow onion, halved and thinly sliced crosswise
1 small clove garlic, minced
¼ cup chopped fresh flat-leaf parsley leaves, divided

1. Rinse the cod under cold running water to remove any surface salt. Place the fish pieces in a large nonreactive pot, cover with water and refrigerate (covered) for 24 hours, changing the water several times. 2. Pour off the water, refill the pot with clean water and gently boil the cod until it flakes easily with a fork, about 7 to 10 minutes (or longer), depending on the thickness. Drain and set aside to cool. 3. To make the dressing, whisk together the oil, vinegar, salt, and pepper in a small bowl. 4. In a large bowl, combine the beans, onion, garlic, and ¾ of the parsley. Add the dressing and mix to coat well. Stir in the salt cod, cover, and chill in the refrigerator for at least 2 hours to let the flavors meld. Let sit on the countertop for 30 minutes before serving. 5. Serve garnished with the remaining parsley.

Per Serving

Calories: 349 | fat: 18g | protein: 32g | carbs: 16g | fiber: 4g | sodium: 8mg

Turkish Shepherd'S Salad

Prep time: 15 minutes | Cook time: 0 minutes | Serves 6

¼ cup extra-virgin olive oil
2 tablespoons apple cider vinegar
2 tablespoons lemon juice
½ teaspoon kosher salt
¼ teaspoon ground black pepper
3 plum tomatoes, seeded and chopped
2 cucumbers, seeded and chopped
1 red bell pepper, seeded and

chopped
1 green bell pepper, seeded and chopped
1 small red onion, chopped
⅓ cup pitted black olives (such as kalamata), halved
½ cup chopped fresh flat-leaf parsley
¼ cup chopped fresh mint
¼ cup chopped fresh dill
6 ounces (170 g) feta cheese, cubed

1. In a small bowl, whisk together the oil, vinegar, lemon juice, salt, and black pepper. 2. In a large serving bowl, combine the tomatoes, cucumber, bell peppers, onion, olives, parsley, mint, and dill. Pour the dressing over the salad, toss gently, and sprinkle with the cheese.

Per Serving

Calories: 238 | fat: 20g | protein: 6g | carbs: 10g | fiber: 2g | sodium: 806mg

Italian Summer Vegetable Barley Salad

Prep time: 1 minutes | Cook time: 25 to 45 minutes | Serves 4

1 cup uncooked barley (hulled or pearl)
3 cups water
¾ teaspoon fine sea salt, divided
1 teaspoon plus 3 tablespoons extra virgin olive oil, divided
3 tablespoons fresh lemon juice

2 medium zucchini, washed and chopped
15 Kalamata olives, pitted and sliced or chopped
¼ cup chopped fresh parsley
¼ cup chopped fresh basil
1 cup cherry tomatoes, halved
½ teaspoon freshly ground black pepper

1. Place the barley in a medium pot and add 3 cups of water and ¼ teaspoon of the sea salt. Bring to a boil over high heat, then reduce the heat to low. Simmer for 25–40 minutes, depending on the type of barley you're using, adding small amounts of hot water if the barley appears to be drying out. Cook until the barley is soft but still chewy, then transfer to a mesh strainer and rinse with cold water. 2. Empty the rinsed barley into a large bowl, drizzle 1 teaspoon of the olive oil over the top, fluff with a fork, and then set aside. 3. In a small bowl, combine the remaining 3 tablespoons of olive oil and the lemon juice. Whisk until the dressing thickens. 4. In a large bowl, combine the barley, zucchini, olives, parsley, and basil. Toss and then add the cherry tomatoes, remaining ½ teaspoon of sea salt, and black pepper. Toss gently, drizzle the dressing over the top, and continue tossing until the ingredients are coated with the dressing. Serve promptly. Store covered in the refrigerator for up to 3 days.

Per Serving

Calories: 308 | fat: 13g | protein: 7g | carbs: 45g | fiber: 10g | sodium: 614mg

Valencia-Inspired Salad

Prep time: 5 minutes | Cook time: 0 minutes | Serves 4

2 small oranges, peeled, thinly sliced, and pitted
1 small blood orange, peeled, thinly sliced, and pitted
1 (7-ounce / 198-g) bag butter lettuce
½ English cucumber, thinly sliced into rounds
1 (6-ounce / 170-g) can pitted black olives, halved

1 small shallot, thinly sliced (optional)
¼ cup raw hulled pumpkin seeds
8 slices Manchego cheese, roughly broken
2 to 3 tablespoons extra-virgin olive oil
Juice of 1 orange

1. In a large bowl, toss together the oranges, lettuce, cucumber, olives, shallot (if desired), pumpkin seeds, and cheese until well mixed. Evenly divide the mixture among four plates. 2. Drizzle the salads with the olive oil and orange juice. Serve.

Per Serving

Calories: 419 | fat: 31g | protein: 17g | carbs: 22g | fiber: 5g | sodium: 513mg

Italian Tuna and Olive Salad

Prep time : 5 minutes | Cook time: 0 minutes | Serves 4

¼ cup olive oil
3 tablespoons white wine vinegar
1 teaspoon salt
1 cup pitted green olives
1 medium red bell pepper,
seeded and diced
1 small clove garlic, minced
2 (6-ounce / 170-g) cans or jars tuna in olive oil, well drained
Several leaves curly green or red lettuce

1. In a large bowl, whisk together the olive oil, vinegar, and salt. 2. Add the olives, bell pepper, and garlic to the dressing and toss to coat. Stir in the tuna, cover, and chill in the refrigerator for at least 1 hour to let the flavors meld. 3. To serve, line a serving bowl with the lettuce leaves and spoon the salad on top. Serve chilled.

Per Serving

Calories: 339 | fat: 24g | protein: 25g | carbs: 4g | fiber: 2g | sodium: 626mg

Wilted Kale Salad

Prep time: 10 minutes | Cook time: 5 minutes | Serves 4

2 heads kale
1 tablespoon olive oil, plus 1 teaspoon
2 cloves garlic, minced
1 cup cherry tomatoes, sliced
Sea salt and freshly ground pepper, to taste
Juice of 1 lemon

1. Rinse and dry kale. 2. Tear the kale into bite-sized pieces. 3. Heat 1 tablespoon of the olive oil in a large skillet, and add the garlic. Cook for 1 minute and then add the kale. 4. Cook just until wilted, then add the tomatoes. 5. Cook until tomatoes are softened, then remove from heat. 6. Place tomatoes and kale in a bowl, and season with sea salt and freshly ground pepper. 7. Drizzle with remaining olive oil and lemon juice, serve, and enjoy.

Per Serving

Calories: 153 | fat: 6g | protein: 10g | carbs: 23g | fiber: 9g | sodium: 88mg

Pear-Fennel Salad with Pomegranate

Prep time: 15 minutes | Cook time: 5 minutes | Serves 6

Dressing:
2 tablespoons red wine vinegar
1½ tablespoons pomegranate molasses
2 teaspoons finely chopped shallot
½ teaspoon Dijon mustard
½ teaspoon kosher salt
¼ teaspoon ground black pepper
¼ cup extra-virgin olive oil
Salad:
¼ cup walnuts, coarsely
chopped, or pine nuts
2 red pears, halved, cored, and very thinly sliced
1 bulb fennel, halved, cored, and very thinly sliced, fronds reserved
1 tablespoon fresh lemon juice
4 cups baby arugula
½ cup pomegranate seeds
⅓ cup crumbled feta cheese or shaved Parmigiano-Reggiano cheese

1. Make the Dressing: In a small bowl or jar with a lid, combine the vinegar, pomegranate molasses, shallot, mustard, salt, and pepper. Add the oil and whisk until emulsified (or cap the jar and shake vigorously). Set aside. 2. Make the Salad: In a small skillet over medium heat, toast the nuts until golden and fragrant, 4 to 5 minutes. Remove from the skillet to cool. 3. In a large bowl, combine the pears and fennel. Sprinkle with the lemon juice and toss gently. 4. Add the arugula and toss again to evenly distribute. Pour over 3 to 4 tablespoons of the dressing, just enough to moisten the arugula, and toss. Add the pomegranate seeds, cheese, and nuts and toss again. Add more dressing, if necessary, or store remainder in the refrigerator for up to 1 week. Serve the salad topped with the reserved fennel fronds.

Per Serving

Calories: 165 | fat: 10g | protein:31g | carbs: 18g | fiber: 4g | sodium: 215mg

Tricolor Tomato Summer Salad

Prep time: 10 minutes | Cook time: 0 minutes | Serves 3 to 4

¼ cup while balsamic vinegar
2 tablespoons Dijon mustard
1 tablespoon sugar
½ teaspoon freshly ground black pepper
½ teaspoon garlic salt
¼ cup extra-virgin olive oil
1½ cups chopped orange, yellow, and red tomatoes
½ cucumber, peeled and diced
1 small red onion, thinly sliced
¼ cup crumbled feta (optional)

1. In a small bowl, whisk the vinegar, mustard, sugar, pepper, and garlic salt. Next, slowly whisk in the olive oil. 2. In a large bowl, add the tomatoes, cucumber, and red onion. Add the dressing. Toss once or twice, and serve with feta crumbles (if using) on top.

Per Serving

Calories: 246 | fat: 18g | protein: 1g | carbs: 19g | fiber: 2g | sodium: 483mg

Warm Fennel, Cherry Tomato, and Spinach Salad

Prep time: 15 minutes | Cook time: 0 minutes | Serves 2

4 tablespoons chicken broth
4 cups baby spinach leaves
10 cherry tomatoes, halved
Sea salt and freshly ground
pepper, to taste
1 fennel bulb, sliced
¼ cup olive oil
Juice of 2 lemons

1. In a large sauté pan, heat the chicken broth over medium heat. Add the spinach and tomatoes and cook until spinach is wilted. Season with sea salt and freshly ground pepper to taste. 2. Remove from heat and toss fennel slices in with the spinach and tomatoes. Let the fennel warm in the pan, then transfer to a large bowl. 3. Drizzle with the olive oil and lemon juice, and serve immediately.

Per Serving

Calories: 319 | fat: 28g | protein: 5g | carbs: 18g | fiber: 6g | sodium: 123mg

Marinated Greek Salad with Oregano and Goat Cheese

Prep time: 10 minutes | Cook time: 0 minutes | Serves 4

½ cup white wine vinegar	4 to 6 long, skinny red or yellow banana peppers or other mild peppers
1 small garlic clove, minced	
1 teaspoon crumbled dried Greek oregano	
½ teaspoon salt	1 medium red onion, cut into rings
¼ teaspoon freshly ground black pepper	1 pint mixed small heirloom tomatoes, halved
2 Persian cucumbers, sliced thinly	2 ounces (57 g) crumbled goat cheese or feta

1. In a large, nonreactive (glass, ceramic, or plastic) bowl, whisk together the vinegar, garlic, oregano, salt, and pepper. Add the cucumbers, peppers, and onion and toss to mix. Cover and refrigerate for at least 1 hour. 2. Add the tomatoes to the bowl and toss to coat. Serve topped with the cheese.

Per Serving
Calories: 98 | fat: 4g | protein: 4g | carbs: 13g | fiber: 3g | sodium: 460mg

Taverna-Style Greek Salad

Prep time: 20 minutes | Cook time: 0 minutes | Serves 4

4 to 5 medium tomatoes, roughly chopped	1 teaspoon dried oregano or fresh herbs of your choice, such as parsley, cilantro, chives, or basil, divided
1 large cucumber, peeled and roughly chopped	
1 medium green bell pepper, sliced	½ cup extra-virgin olive oil, divided
1 small red onion, sliced	1 pack feta cheese
16 pitted Kalamata olives	Optional: salt, pepper, and fresh oregano, for garnish
¼ cup capers, or more olives	

1. Place the vegetables in a large serving bowl. Add the olives, capers, feta, half of the dried oregano and half of the olive oil. Mix to combine. Place the whole piece of feta cheese on top, sprinkle with the remaining dried oregano, and drizzle with the remaining olive oil. Season to taste and serve immediately, or store in the fridge for up to 1 day.

Per Serving
Calories: 320 | fat: 31g | protein: 3g | carbs: 11g | fiber: 4g | sodium: 445mg

Red Pepper, Pomegranate, and Walnut Salad

Prep time: 5 minutes | Cook time: 40 minutes | Serves 4

2 red bell peppers, halved and seeded	2 teaspoons fresh lemon juice
1 teaspoon plus 2 tablespoons olive oil	¼ teaspoon kosher salt
	⅛ teaspoon ground black pepper
4 teaspoons pomegranate molasses, divided	4 plum tomatoes, halved, seeded, and chopped

¼ cup walnut halves, chopped   parsley
¼ cup chopped fresh flat-leaf

1. Preheat the oven to 450°F (235°C). 2. Brush the bell peppers all over with 1 teaspoon of the oil and place cut side up on a large rimmed baking sheet. Drizzle 2 teaspoons of the pomegranate molasses in the cavities of the bell peppers. Roast the bell peppers until they have softened and the skins have charred, turning once during cooking, 30 to 40 minutes. Remove from the oven and cool to room temperature. Remove the skins and chop the peppers coarsely. 3. In a large bowl, whisk together the lemon juice, salt, black pepper, the remaining 2 tablespoons oil, and the remaining 2 teaspoons pomegranate molasses. Add the bell peppers, tomatoes, walnuts, and parsley and toss gently to combine. Serve at room temperature.

Per Serving
Calories: 166 | fat: 13g | protein: 2g | carbs: 11g | fiber: 3g | sodium: 153mg

Cabbage and Carrot Salad

Prep time: 10 minutes | Cook time: 0 minutes | Serves 3

½ medium head cabbage, thinly sliced, rinsed, and drained	3 tablespoons fresh lemon juice
	½ teaspoon salt
3 medium carrots, peeled and shredded	¼ teaspoon freshly ground black pepper
4 tablespoons extra virgin olive oil	1 garlic clove, minced
	8 Kalamata olives, pitted

1. Place the cabbage and carrots in a large bowl and toss. 2. In a jar or small bowl, combine the olive oil, lemon juice, salt, black pepper, and garlic. Whisk or shake to combine. 3. Pour the dressing over the salad and toss. (Note that it will reduce in volume.) 4. Scatter the olives over the salad just before serving. Store covered in the refrigerator for up to 2 days.

Per Serving
Calories: 237 | fat: 19g | protein: 3g | carbs: 16g | fiber: 6g | sodium: 570mg

Citrusy Spinach Salad

Prep time: 10 minutes | Cook time: 5 minutes | Serves 4

1 large ripe tomato	¼ cup extra-virgin olive oil
1 medium red onion	½ teaspoon salt
½ teaspoon fresh lemon zest	1 pound (454 g) baby spinach, washed, stems removed
3 tablespoons balsamic vinegar	

1. Dice the tomato into ¼-inch pieces and slice the onion into long slivers. 2. In a small bowl, whisk together the lemon zest, balsamic vinegar, olive oil, and salt. 3. Put the spinach, tomatoes, and onions in a large bowl. Pour the dressing over the salad and lightly toss to coat.

Per Serving
Calories: 172 | fat: 14g | protein: 4g | carbs: 10g | fiber: 4g | sodium: 389mg

Watermelon Burrata Salad

Prep time: 10 minutes | Cook time: 0 minutes | Serves 4

2 cups cubes or chunks watermelon
1½ cups small burrata cheese balls, cut into medium chunks
1 small red onion or 2 shallots, thinly sliced into half-moons
¼ cup olive oil
¼ cup balsamic vinegar
4 fresh basil leaves, sliced chiffonade-style (roll up leaves of basil, and slice into thin strips)
1 tablespoon lemon zest
Salt and freshly ground black pepper, to taste

1. In a large bowl, mix all the ingredients. Refrigerate until chilled before serving.

Per Serving 1 cup:
Calories: 224 | fat: 14g | protein: 14g | carbs: 12g | fiber: 1g | sodium: 560mg

Tossed Green Mediterranean Salad

Prep time: 15 minutes | Cook time: 0 minutes | Serves 4

1 medium head romaine lettuce, washed, dried, and chopped into bite-sized pieces
2 medium cucumbers, peeled and sliced
3 spring onions (white parts only), sliced
½ cup finely chopped fresh dill
⅓ cup extra virgin olive oil
2 tablespoons fresh lemon juice
¼ teaspoon fine sea salt
4 ounces (113 g) crumbled feta
7 Kalamata olives, pitted

1. Add the lettuce, cucumber, spring onions, and dill to a large bowl. Toss to combine. 2. In a small bowl, whisk together the olive oil and lemon juice. Pour the dressing over the salad, toss, then sprinkle the sea salt over the top. 3. Sprinkle the feta and olives over the top and then gently toss the salad one more time. Serve promptly. (This recipe is best served fresh.)

Per Serving
Calories: 284 | fat: 25g | protein: 7g | carbs: 10g | fiber: 5g | sodium: 496mg

Insalata Caprese

Prep time: 5 minutes | Cook time: 0 minutes | Serves 2

2 firm medium tomatoes (any variety), cut into ¼-inch slices
¼ teaspoon kosher salt
8 fresh basil leaves
7 ounces (198 g) fresh
mozzarella, cut into ¼-inch slices
¼ teaspoon dried oregano
3 teaspoons extra virgin olive oil

1. Place the sliced tomatoes on a cutting board and sprinkle them with the kosher salt. Set aside. 2. Arrange 4 basil leaves in a circular pattern on a large, round serving plate. (Tear the leaves into 2 pieces if they're large.) 3. Assemble the tomato slices and mozzarella slices on top of the basil leaves, alternating a tomato slice and then a mozzarella slice, adding a basil leaf between every 3–4 slices of tomato and mozzarella. 4.

Sprinkle the oregano over the top and then drizzle the olive oil over the entire salad. Serve promptly. (This salad is best served fresh.)

Per Serving
Calories: 361 | fat: 24g | protein: 28g | carbs: 8g | fiber: 2g | sodium: 313mg

Arugula Spinach Salad with Shaved Parmesan

Prep time: 10 minutes | Cook time: 2 minutes | Serves 3

3 tablespoons raw pine nuts
3 cups arugula
3 cups baby leaf spinach
5 dried figs, pitted and chopped
2½ ounces (71 g) shaved Parmesan cheese
For the Dressing:
4 teaspoons balsamic vinegar
1 teaspoon Dijon mustard
1 teaspoon honey
5 tablespoons extra virgin olive oil

1. In a small pan over low heat, toast the pine nuts for 2 minutes or until they begin to brown. Promptly remove them from the heat and transfer to a small bowl. 2. Make the dressing by combining the balsamic vinegar, Dijon mustard, and honey in a small bowl. Using a fork to whisk, gradually add the olive oil while continuously mixing. 3. In a large bowl, toss the arugula and baby spinach and then top with the figs, Parmesan cheese, and toasted pine nuts. Drizzle the dressing over the top and toss until the ingredients are thoroughly coated with the dressing. Serve promptly. (This salad is best served fresh.)

Per Serving
Calories: 416 | fat: 35g | protein: 10g | carbs: 18g | fiber: 3g | sodium: 478mg

Arugula and Fennel Salad with Fresh Basil

Prep time: 5 minutes | Cook time: 0 minutes | Serves 4

3 tablespoons olive oil
3 tablespoons lemon juice
1 teaspoon honey
½ teaspoon salt
1 medium bulb fennel, very thinly sliced
1 small cucumber, very thinly
sliced
2 cups arugula
¼ cup toasted pine nuts
½ cup crumbled feta cheese
¼ cup julienned fresh basil leaves

1. In a medium bowl, whisk together the olive oil, lemon juice, honey, and salt. Add the fennel and cucumber and toss to coat and let sit for 10 minutes or so. 2. Put the arugula in a large salad bowl. Add the marinated cucumber and fennel, along with the dressing, to the bowl and toss well. Serve immediately, sprinkled with pine nuts, feta cheese, and basil.

Per Serving
Calories: 237 | fat: 21g | protein: 6g | carbs: 11g | fiber: 3g | sodium: 537mg

Chapter 12 Snacks and Appetizers

Parmesan French Fries

Prep time: 10 minutes | Cook time: 25 minutes | Serves 2 to 3

2 to 3 large russet potatoes, peeled and cut into ½-inch sticks
2 teaspoons vegetable or canola oil
¾ cup grated Parmesan cheese
½ teaspoon salt
Freshly ground black pepper, to taste
1 teaspoon fresh chopped parsley

1. Bring a large saucepan of salted water to a boil on the stovetop while you peel and cut the potatoes. Blanch the potatoes in the boiling salted water for 4 minutes while you preheat the air fryer to 400°F (204°C). Strain the potatoes and rinse them with cold water. Dry them well with a clean kitchen towel. 2. Toss the dried potato sticks gently with the oil and place them in the air fryer basket. Air fry for 25 minutes, shaking the basket a few times while the fries cook to help them brown evenly. 3. Combine the Parmesan cheese, salt and pepper. With 2 minutes left on the air fryer cooking time, sprinkle the fries with the Parmesan cheese mixture. Toss the fries to coat them evenly with the cheese mixture and continue to air fry for the final 2 minutes, until the cheese has melted and just starts to brown. Sprinkle the finished fries with chopped parsley, a little more grated Parmesan cheese if you like, and serve.

Per Serving
Calories: 252 | fat: 11g | protein: 13g | carbs: 27g | fiber: 2g | sodium: 411mg

Sea Salt Potato Chips

Prep time: 30 minutes | Cook time: 27 minutes | Serves 4

Oil, for spraying
4 medium yellow potatoes
1 tablespoon oil
⅛ to ¼ teaspoon fine sea salt

1. Line the air fryer basket with parchment and spray lightly with oil. 2. Using a mandoline or a very sharp knife, cut the potatoes into very thin slices. 3. Place the slices in a bowl of cold water and let soak for about 20 minutes. 4. Drain the potatoes, transfer them to a plate lined with paper towels, and pat dry. 5. Drizzle the oil over the potatoes, sprinkle with the salt, and toss to combine. Transfer to the prepared basket. 6. Air fry at 200°F (93°C) for 20 minutes. Toss the chips, increase the heat to 400°F (204°C), and cook for another 5 to 7 minutes, until crispy.

Per Serving
Calories: 194 | fat: 4g | protein: 4g | carbs: 37g | fiber: 5g | sodium: 90mg

Cinnamon-Apple Chips

Prep time: 10 minutes | Cook time: 32 minutes | Serves 4

Oil, for spraying
2 Red Delicious or Honeycrisp apples
¼ teaspoon ground cinnamon, divided

1. Line the air fryer basket with parchment and spray lightly with oil. 2. Trim the uneven ends off the apples. Using a mandoline on the thinnest setting or a sharp knife, cut the apples into very thin slices. Discard the cores. 3. Place half of the apple slices in a single layer in the prepared basket and sprinkle with half of the cinnamon. 4. Place a metal air fryer trivet on top of the apples to keep them from flying around while they are cooking. 5. Air fry at 300°F (149°C) for 16 minutes, flipping every 5 minutes to ensure even cooking. Repeat with the remaining apple slices and cinnamon. 6. Let cool to room temperature before serving. The chips will firm up as they cool.

Per Serving
Calories: 63 | fat: 0g | protein: 0g | carbs: 15g | fiber: 3g | sodium: 1mg

Lemon-Pepper Chicken Drumsticks

Prep time: 30 minutes | Cook time: 30 minutes | Serves 2

2 teaspoons freshly ground coarse black pepper
1 teaspoon baking powder
½ teaspoon garlic powder
4 chicken drumsticks (4 ounces / 113 g each)
Kosher salt, to taste
1 lemon

1. In a small bowl, stir together the pepper, baking powder, and garlic powder. Place the drumsticks on a plate and sprinkle evenly with the baking powder mixture, turning the drumsticks so they're well coated. Let the drumsticks stand in the refrigerator for at least 1 hour or up to overnight. 2. Sprinkle the drumsticks with salt, then transfer them to the air fryer, standing them bone-end up and leaning against the wall of the air fryer basket. Air fry at 375°F (191°C) until cooked through and crisp on the outside, about 30 minutes. 3. Transfer the drumsticks to a serving platter and finely grate the zest of the lemon over them while they're hot. Cut the lemon into wedges and serve with the warm drumsticks.

Per Serving
Calories: 438 | fat: 24g | protein: 48g | carbs: 6g | fiber: 2g | sodium: 279mg

Arabic-Style Spiced Roasted Chickpeas

Prep time: 15 minutes | Cook time: 35 minutes | Serves 2

For the Seasoning Mix:
¾ teaspoon cumin
½ teaspoon coriander
½ teaspoon salt
¼ teaspoon freshly ground black pepper
¼ teaspoon paprika
¼ teaspoon cardamom
¼ teaspoon cinnamon
¼ teaspoon allspice
For the Chickpeas:
1 (15-ounce / 425-g) can chickpeas, drained and rinsed
1 tablespoon olive oil
¼ teaspoon salt

Make the Seasoning Mix: In a small bowl, combine the cumin, coriander, salt, freshly ground black pepper, paprika, cardamom, cinnamon, and allspice. Stir well to combine and set aside. Make the Chickpeas 1. Preheat the oven to 400°F (205°C) and set the rack to the middle position. Line a baking sheet with parchment paper. 2. Pat the rinsed chickpeas with paper towels or roll them in a clean kitchen towel to dry off any water. 3. Place the chickpeas in a bowl and season them with the olive oil and salt. 4. Add the chickpeas to the lined baking sheet (reserve the bowl) and roast them for about 25 to 35 minutes, turning them over once or twice while cooking. Most should be light brown. Taste one or two to make sure they are slightly crisp. 5. Place the roasted chickpeas back into the bowl and sprinkle them with the seasoning mix. Toss lightly to combine. Taste, and add additional salt if needed. Serve warm.

Per Serving
Calories: 268 | fat: 11g | protein: 11g | carbs: 35g | fiber: 10g | sodium: 301mg

Tuna Croquettes

Prep time: 40 minutes | Cook time: 25 minutes | Makes 36 croquettes

6 tablespoons extra-virgin olive oil, plus 1 to 2 cups
5 tablespoons almond flour, plus 1 cup, divided
1¼ cups heavy cream
1 (4-ounce / 113-g) can olive oil-packed yellowfin tuna
1 tablespoon chopped red
onion
2 teaspoons minced capers
½ teaspoon dried dill
¼ teaspoon freshly ground black pepper
2 large eggs
1 cup panko breadcrumbs (or a gluten-free version)

1. In a large skillet, heat 6 tablespoons olive oil over medium-low heat. Add 5 tablespoons almond flour and cook, stirring constantly, until a smooth paste forms and the flour browns slightly, 2 to 3 minutes. 2. Increase the heat to medium-high and gradually add the heavy cream, whisking constantly until completely smooth and thickened, another 4 to 5 minutes. 3. Remove from the heat and stir in the tuna, red onion, capers, dill, and pepper. 4. Transfer the mixture to an 8-inch square baking dish that is well coated with olive oil and allow to cool to room temperature. Cover and refrigerate until chilled, at least 4 hours or up to overnight. 5. To form the croquettes, set out three bowls. In one, beat together the eggs. In another, add the remaining almond flour. In the third, add the panko.

Line a baking sheet with parchment paper. 6. Using a spoon, place about a tablespoon of cold prepared dough into the flour mixture and roll to coat. Shake off excess and, using your hands, roll into an oval. 7. Dip the croquette into the beaten egg, then lightly coat in panko. Set on lined baking sheet and repeat with the remaining dough. 8. In a small saucepan, heat the remaining 1 to 2 cups of olive oil, so that the oil is about 1 inch deep, over medium-high heat. The smaller the pan, the less oil you will need, but you will need more for each batch. 9. Test if the oil is ready by throwing a pinch of panko into pot. If it sizzles, the oil is ready for frying. If it sinks, it's not quite ready. Once the oil is heated, fry the croquettes 3 or 4 at a time, depending on the size of your pan, removing with a slotted spoon when golden brown. You will need to adjust the temperature of the oil occasionally to prevent burning. If the croquettes get dark brown very quickly, lower the temperature.

Per Serving (2 croquettes)
Calories: 271 | fat: 26g | protein: 5g | carbs: 6g | fiber: 1g | sodium: 89mg

Ranch Oyster Snack Crackers

Prep time: 3 minutes | Cook time: 12 minutes | Serves 6

Oil, for spraying
¼ cup olive oil
2 teaspoons dry ranch seasoning
1 teaspoon chili powder
½ teaspoon dried dill
½ teaspoon granulated garlic
½ teaspoon salt
1 (9-ounce / 255-g) bag oyster crackers

1. Preheat the air fryer to 325°F (163°C). Line the air fryer basket with parchment and spray lightly with oil. 2. In a large bowl, mix together the olive oil, ranch seasoning, chili powder, dill, garlic, and salt. Add the crackers and toss until evenly coated. 3. Place the mixture in the prepared basket. 4. Cook for 10 to 12 minutes, shaking or stirring every 3 to 4 minutes, or until crisp and golden brown.

Per Serving
Calories: 261 | fat: 13g | protein: 4g | carbs: 32g | fiber: 1g | sodium: 621mg

Garlic-Parmesan Croutons

Prep time: 3 minutes | Cook time: 12 minutes | Serves 4

Oil, for spraying
4 cups cubed French bread
1 tablespoon grated Parmesan cheese
3 tablespoons olive oil
1 tablespoon granulated garlic
½ teaspoon unsalted salt

1. Line the air fryer basket with parchment and spray lightly with oil. 2. In a large bowl, mix together the bread, Parmesan cheese, olive oil, garlic, and salt, tossing with your hands to evenly distribute the seasonings. Transfer the coated bread cubes to the prepared basket. 3. Air fry at 350°F (177°C) for 10 to 12 minutes, stirring once after 5 minutes, or until crisp and golden brown.

Per Serving
Calories: 220 | fat: 12g | protein: 5g | carbs: 23g | fiber: 1g | sodium: 285mg

Taco-Spiced Chickpeas

Prep time: 5 minutes | Cook time: 17 minutes | Serves 3

Oil, for spraying
1 (15½-ounce / 439-g) can chickpeas, drained
1 teaspoon chili powder
½ teaspoon ground cumin
½ teaspoon salt
½ teaspoon granulated garlic
2 teaspoons lime juice

1. Line the air fryer basket with parchment and spray lightly with oil. Place the chickpeas in the prepared basket. 2. Air fry at 390°F (199°C) for 17 minutes, shaking or stirring the chickpeas and spraying lightly with oil every 5 to 7 minutes. 3. In a small bowl, mix together the chili powder, cumin, salt, and garlic. 4. When 2 to 3 minutes of cooking time remain, sprinkle half of the seasoning mix over the chickpeas. Finish cooking. 5. Transfer the chickpeas to a medium bowl and toss with the remaining seasoning mix and the lime juice. Serve immediately.
Per Serving
Calories: 208 | fat: 4g | protein: 11g | carbs: 34g | fiber: 10g | sodium: 725mg

Mexican Potato Skins

Prep time: 10 minutes | Cook time: 55 minutes | Serves 6

Olive oil
6 medium russet potatoes, scrubbed
Salt and freshly ground black pepper, to taste
1 cup fat-free refried black
beans
1 tablespoon taco seasoning
½ cup salsa
¾ cup reduced-fat shredded Cheddar cheese

1. Spray the air fryer basket lightly with olive oil. 2. Spray the potatoes lightly with oil and season with salt and pepper. Pierce each potato a few times with a fork. 3. Place the potatoes in the air fryer basket. Air fry at 400°F (204°C) until fork-tender, 30 to 40 minutes. The cooking time will depend on the size of the potatoes. You can cook the potatoes in the microwave or a standard oven, but they won't get the same lovely crispy skin they will get in the air fryer. 4. While the potatoes are cooking, in a small bowl, mix together the beans and taco seasoning. Set aside until the potatoes are cool enough to handle. 5. Cut each potato in half lengthwise. Scoop out most of the insides, leaving about ¼ inch in the skins so the potato skins hold their shape. 6. Season the insides of the potato skins with salt and black pepper. Lightly spray the insides of the potato skins with oil. You may need to cook them in batches. 7. Place them into the air fryer basket, skin-side down, and air fry until crisp and golden, 8 to 10 minutes. 8. Transfer the skins to a work surface and spoon ½ tablespoon of seasoned refried black beans into each one. Top each with 2 teaspoons salsa and 1 tablespoon shredded Cheddar cheese. 9. Place filled potato skins in the air fryer basket in a single layer. Lightly spray with oil. 10. Air fry until the cheese is melted and bubbly, 2 to 3 minutes.
Per Serving
Calories: 239 | fat: 2g | protein: 10g | carbs: 46g | fiber: 5g | sodium: 492mg

Garlic Edamame

Prep time: 5 minutes | Cook time: 10 minutes | Serves 4

Olive oil
1 (16-ounce / 454-g) bag frozen edamame in pods
½ teaspoon salt
½ teaspoon garlic salt
¼ teaspoon freshly ground black pepper
½ teaspoon red pepper flakes (optional)

1. Spray the air fryer basket lightly with olive oil. 2. In a medium bowl, add the frozen edamame and lightly spray with olive oil. Toss to coat. 3. In a small bowl, mix together the salt, garlic salt, black pepper, and red pepper flakes (if using). Add the mixture to the edamame and toss until evenly coated. 4. Place half the edamame in the air fryer basket. Do not overfill the basket. 5. Air fry at 375°F (191°C) for 5 minutes. Shake the basket and cook until the edamame is starting to brown and get crispy, 3 to 5 more minutes. 6. Repeat with the remaining edamame and serve immediately.
Per Serving
Calories: 125 | fat: 5g | protein: 12g | carbs: 10g | fiber: 5g | sodium: 443mg

Croatian Red Pepper Dip

Prep time: 10 minutes | Cook time: 30 minutes | Serves 4 to 6

4 or 5 medium red bell peppers
1 medium eggplant (about ¾ pound / 340 g)
¼ cup olive oil, divided
1 teaspoon salt, divided
½ teaspoon freshly ground black pepper, divided
4 cloves garlic, minced
1 tablespoon white vinegar

1. Preheat the broiler to high. 2. Line a large baking sheet with aluminum foil. 3. Brush the peppers and eggplant all over with 2 tablespoons of the olive oil and sprinkle with ½ teaspoon of the salt and ¼ teaspoon of the pepper. Place the peppers and the eggplant on the prepared baking sheet and broil, turning every few minutes, until the skins are charred on all sides. The peppers will take about 10 minutes and the eggplant will take about 20 minutes. 4. When the peppers are fully charred, remove them from the baking sheet, place them in a bowl, cover with plastic wrap, and let them steam while the eggplant continues to cook. When the eggplant is fully charred and soft in the center, remove it from the oven and set aside to cool. 5. When the peppers are cool enough to handle, slip the charred skins off. Discard the charred skins. Seed the peppers and place them in a food processor. 6. Add the garlic to the food processor and pulse until the vegetables are coarsely chopped. Add the rest of the olive oil, the vinegar, and remaining ½ teaspoon of salt and process to a smooth purée. 7. Transfer the vegetable mixture to a medium saucepan and bring to a simmer over medium-high heat. Lower the heat to medium-low and let simmer, stirring occasionally, for 30 minutes. Remove from the heat and cool to room temperature. Serve at room temperature.
Per Serving
Calories: 144 | fat: 11g | protein: 2g | carbs: 12g | fiber: 5g | sodium: 471mg

Vegetable Pot Stickers

Prep time: 12 minutes | Cook time: 11 to 18 minutes | Makes 12 pot stickers

1 cup shredded red cabbage
¼ cup chopped button mushrooms
¼ cup grated carrot
2 tablespoons minced onion
2 garlic cloves, minced
2 teaspoons grated fresh ginger
12 gyoza/pot sticker wrappers
2½ teaspoons olive oil, divided

1. In a baking pan, combine the red cabbage, mushrooms, carrot, onion, garlic, and ginger. Add 1 tablespoon of water. Place in the air fryer and air fry at 370ºF (188ºC) for 3 to 6 minutes, until the vegetables are crisp-tender. Drain and set aside. 2. Working one at a time, place the pot sticker wrappers on a work surface. Top each wrapper with a scant 1 tablespoon of the filling. Fold half of the wrapper over the other half to form a half circle. Dab one edge with water and press both edges together. 3. To another pan, add 1¼ teaspoons of olive oil. Put half of the pot stickers, seam-side up, in the pan. Air fry for 5 minutes, or until the bottoms are light golden brown. Add 1 tablespoon of water and return the pan to the air fryer. 4. Air fry for 4 to 6 minutes more, or until hot. Repeat with the remaining pot stickers, remaining 1¼ teaspoons of oil, and another tablespoon of water. Serve immediately.

Per Serving (1 pot stickers)
Calories: 36 | fat: 1g | protein: 1g | carbs: 6g | fiber: 0g | sodium: 49mg

Italian Crepe with Herbs and Onion

Prep time: 15 minutes | Cook time: 20 minutes per crepe | Serves 6

2 cups cold water
1 cup chickpea flour
½ teaspoon kosher salt
¼ teaspoon freshly ground black pepper
3½ tablespoons extra-virgin
olive oil, divided
½ onion, julienned
½ cup fresh herbs, chopped (thyme, sage, and rosemary are all nice on their own or as a mix)

1. In a large bowl, whisk together the water, flour, salt, and black pepper. Add 2 tablespoons of the olive oil and whisk. Let the batter sit at room temperature for at least 30 minutes. 2. Preheat the oven to 450ºF (235ºC). Place a 12-inch cast-iron pan or oven-safe skillet in the oven to warm as the oven comes to temperature. 3. Remove the hot pan from the oven carefully, add ½ tablespoon of the olive oil and one-third of the onion, stir, and place the pan back in the oven. Cook, stirring occasionally, until the onions are golden brown, 5 to 8 minutes. 4. Remove the pan from the oven and pour in one-third of the batter (about 1 cup), sprinkle with one-third of the herbs, and put it back in the oven. Bake for 10 minutes, or until firm and the edges are set. 5. Increase the oven setting to broil and cook 3 to 5 minutes, or until golden brown. Slide the crepe onto the cutting board and repeat twice more. Halve the crepes and cut into wedges. Serve warm or at room temperature.

Per Serving
Calories: 135 | fat: 9g | protein: 4g | carbs: 11g | fiber: 2g | sodium: 105mg

Spanish-Style Pan-Roasted Cod

Prep time: 15 minutes | Cook time: 25 minutes | Serves 4

4 tablespoons olive oil
8 garlic cloves, minced
½ small onion, finely chopped
½ pound (227 g) small red or new potatoes, quartered
1 (14½-ounce / 411-g) can low-sodium diced tomatoes, with their juices
16 pimiento-stuffed low-salt
Spanish olives, sliced (about ⅓ cup)
4 tablespoons finely chopped fresh parsley
4 (4-ounce / 113-g) cod fillets, about 1 inch thick
Salt and freshly ground black pepper (optional)

1. In a 10-inch skillet, heat 2 tablespoons of the olive oil and the garlic over medium heat. Cook, being careful not to let the garlic burn, until it becomes fragrant, 1 to 2 minutes. 2. Raise the temperature to medium-high heat, and add the onion, potatoes, tomatoes with their juices, olives, and 3 tablespoons of the parsley. Bring to a boil. Reduce the heat to maintain a simmer, cover, and cook for 15 to 18 minutes, until the potatoes are tender. Transfer the mixture from the skillet to a large bowl; keep warm. Wipe out the skillet and return it to the stovetop. 3. Heat the remaining 2 tablespoons olive oil in the skillet over medium-high heat. Season the cod with salt and pepper, if desired, and add it to the pan. Cook for 2 to 3 minutes, then carefully flip the fish and cook for 2 to 3 minutes more, until the fish flakes easily with a fork. 4. Divide the tomato mixture evenly among four plates and top each with a cod fillet. Sprinkle evenly with the remaining 1 tablespoon parsley and serve.

Per Serving 1 cup:
Calories: 297 | fat: 20g | protein: 9g | carbs: 20g | fiber: 4g | sodium: 557mg

Burrata Caprese Stack

Prep time: 5 minutes | Cook time: 0 minutes | Serves 4

1 large organic tomato, preferably heirloom
½ teaspoon salt
¼ teaspoon freshly ground black pepper
1 (4-ounce / 113-g) ball burrata cheese
8 fresh basil leaves, thinly sliced
2 tablespoons extra-virgin olive oil
1 tablespoon red wine or balsamic vinegar

1. Slice the tomato into 4 thick slices, removing any tough center core and sprinkle with salt and pepper. Place the tomatoes, seasoned-side up, on a plate. 2. On a separate rimmed plate, slice the burrata into 4 thick slices and place one slice on top of each tomato slice. Top each with one-quarter of the basil and pour any reserved burrata cream from the rimmed plate over top. 3. Drizzle with olive oil and vinegar and serve with a fork and knife.

Per Serving
Calories: 109 | fat: 7g | protein: 9g | carbs: 3g | fiber: 1g | sodium: 504mg

Honey-Rosemary Almonds

**Prep time: 5 minutes |Cook time: 10 minutes|
Serves: 6**

1 cup raw, whole, shelled almonds

1 tablespoon minced fresh rosemary

¼ teaspoon kosher or sea salt

1 tablespoon honey

Nonstick cooking spray

1. In a large skillet over medium heat, combine the almonds, rosemary, and salt. Stir frequently for 1 minute. 2. Drizzle in the honey and cook for another 3 to 4 minutes, stirring frequently, until the almonds are coated and just starting to darken around the edges. 3. Remove from the heat. Using a spatula, spread the almonds onto a pan coated with nonstick cooking spray. Cool for 10 minutes or so. Break up the almonds before serving.

Per Serving

Calories: 149 | fat: 12g | protein: 5g | carbs: 8g | fiber: 3g | sodium: 97mg

Salmon Niçoise Salad with Dijon-Chive Dressing

Prep time: 10 minutes | Cook time: 20 minutes | Serves 4

1 pound (454 g) baby or fingerling potatoes

½ pound (227 g) green beans

6 tablespoons olive oil

4 (4-ounce / 113-g) salmon fillets

¼ teaspoon freshly ground black pepper

2 teaspoons Dijon mustard

3 tablespoons red wine vinegar

1 tablespoon, plus 1 teaspoon finely chopped fresh chives

1 head romaine lettuce, sliced cross-wise

2 hard-boiled eggs, quartered

¼ cup Niçoise or other small black olives

1 cup cherry tomatoes, quartered

1. Put potatoes in a large saucepan and add cold water to cover. Bring the water to a boil, then reduce the heat to maintain a simmer and cook for 12 to 15 minutes, until fork-tender. Drain and set aside until cool enough to handle, then cut into cubes. Set aside. 2. Meanwhile, bring a medium saucepan of water to a boil. Add the green beans and cook for 3 minutes. Drain and rinse with cold water to stop the cooking. Set aside. 3. In a large skillet, heat 1 tablespoon of the olive oil over medium-high heat. Season the salmon with pepper. Add the salmon to the pan and cook for 4 to 5 minutes on each side. Transfer to a platter; keep warm. 4. In a small bowl, whisk together the mustard, vinegar, 1 tablespoon of chives, and remaining 5 tablespoons olive oil. 5. Divide the lettuce evenly among four plates. Add 1 salmon fillet to each plate. Divide the potatoes, green beans, eggs, olives, and tomatoes among the plates and drizzle with the dressing. 6.Sprinkle with the remaining 1 teaspoon chives and serve.

Per Serving 1 cup:

Calories: 398 | fat: 25g | protein: 15g | carbs: 30g | fiber: 8g | sodium: 173mg

Fig-Pecan Energy Bites

**Prep time: 20 minutes |Cook time: 0 minutes|
Serves: 6**

¾ cup diced dried figs (6 to 8)

½ cup chopped pecans

¼ cup rolled oats (old-fashioned or quick oats)

2 tablespoons ground flaxseed

or wheat germ (flaxseed for gluten-free)

2 tablespoons powdered or regular peanut butter

2 tablespoons honey

1. In a medium bowl, mix together the figs, pecans, oats, flaxseed, and peanut butter. Drizzle with the honey, and mix everything together. A wooden spoon works well to press the figs and nuts into the honey and powdery ingredients. (If you're using regular peanut butter instead of powdered, the dough will be stickier to handle, so freeze the dough for 5 minutes before making the bites.) 2. Divide the dough evenly into four sections in the bowl. Dampen your hands with water—but don't get them too wet or the dough will stick to them. Using your hands, roll three bites out of each of the four sections of dough, making 12 total energy bites. 3. Enjoy immediately or chill in the freezer for 5 minutes to firm up the bites before serving. The bites can be stored in a sealed container in the refrigerator for up to 1 week.

Per Serving

Calories: 196 | fat: 10g | protein: 4g | carbs: 26g | fiber: 4g | sodium: 13mg

Manchego Crackers

Prep time: 15 minutes | Cook time: 15 minutes | Makes 40 crackers

4 tablespoons butter, at room temperature

1 cup finely shredded Manchego cheese

1 cup almond flour

1 teaspoon salt, divided

¼ teaspoon freshly ground black pepper

1 large egg

1. Using an electric mixer, cream together the butter and shredded cheese until well combined and smooth. 2. In a small bowl, combine the almond flour with ½ teaspoon salt and pepper. Slowly add the almond flour mixture to the cheese, mixing constantly until the dough just comes together to form a ball. 3. Transfer to a piece of parchment or plastic wrap and roll into a cylinder log about 1½ inches thick. Wrap tightly and refrigerate for at least 1 hour. 4. Preheat the oven to 350ºF (180ºC). Line two baking sheets with parchment paper or silicone baking mats. 5. To make the egg wash, in a small bowl, whisk together the egg and remaining ½ teaspoon salt. 6. Slice the refrigerated dough into small rounds, about ¼ inch thick, and place on the lined baking sheets. 7. Brush the tops of the crackers with egg wash and bake until the crackers are golden and crispy, 12 to 15 minutes. Remove from the oven and allow to cool on a wire rack. 8. Serve warm or, once fully cooled, store in an airtight container in the refrigerator for up to 1 week.

Per Serving (2 crackers)

Calories: 73 | fat: 7g | protein: 3g | carbs: 1g | fiber: 1g | sodium: 154mg

Black Bean Corn Dip

Prep time: 10 minutes | Cook time: 10 minutes | Serves 4

½ (15-ounce / 425-g) can black beans, drained and rinsed
½ (15-ounce / 425-g) can corn, drained and rinsed
¼ cup chunky salsa
2 ounces (57 g) reduced-fat cream cheese, softened
¼ cup shredded reduced-fat Cheddar cheese
½ teaspoon ground cumin
½ teaspoon paprika
Salt and freshly ground black pepper, to taste

1. Preheat the air fryer to 325°F (163°C). 2. In a medium bowl, mix together the black beans, corn, salsa, cream cheese, Cheddar cheese, cumin, and paprika. Season with salt and pepper and stir until well combined. 3. Spoon the mixture into a baking dish. 4. Place baking dish in the air fryer basket and bake until heated through, about 10 minutes. 5. Serve hot.

Per Serving
Calories: 119 | fat: 2g | protein: 8g | carbs: 19g | fiber: 6g | sodium: 469mg

Sweet Potato Hummus

Prep time: 10 minutes | Cook time: 1 hour | Serves 8 to 10

1 pound (454 g) sweet potatoes (about 2)
1 (15-ounce / 425-g) can chickpeas, drained
4 garlic cloves, minced
2 tablespoons olive oil
2 tablespoons fresh lemon
juice
2 teaspoons ground cumin
1 teaspoon Aleppo pepper or red pepper flakes
Pita chips, pita bread, or fresh vegetables, for serving

1. Preheat the oven to 400°F (205°C). 2. Prick the sweet potatoes in a few places with a small, sharp knife and place them on a baking sheet. Roast until cooked through, about 1 hour, then set aside to cool. Peel the sweet potatoes and put the flesh in a blender or food processor. 3. Add the chickpeas, garlic, olive oil, lemon juice, cumin, and ⅓ cup water. Blend until smooth. Add the Aleppo pepper. 4. Serve with pita chips, pita bread, or as a dip for fresh vegetables.

Per Serving
Calories: 178 | fat: 5g | protein: 7g | carbs: 30g | fiber: 9g | sodium: 149mg

Goat Cheese–Mackerel Pâté

Prep time: 10 minutes | Cook time: 0 minutes | Serves 4

4 ounces (113 g) olive oil-packed wild-caught mackerel
2 ounces (57 g) goat cheese
Zest and juice of 1 lemon
2 tablespoons chopped fresh parsley
2 tablespoons chopped fresh arugula
1 tablespoon extra-virgin olive oil
2 teaspoons chopped capers
1 to 2 teaspoons fresh horseradish (optional)
Crackers, cucumber rounds, endive spears, or celery, for serving (optional)

1. In a food processor, blender, or large bowl with immersion blender, combine the mackerel, goat cheese, lemon zest and juice, parsley, arugula, olive oil, capers, and horseradish (if using). Process or blend until smooth and creamy. 2. Serve with crackers, cucumber rounds, endive spears, or celery. 3. Store covered in the refrigerator for up to 1 week.

Per Serving
Calories: 142 | fat: 10g | protein: 11g | carbs: 1g | fiber: 0g | sodium: 203mg

Charred Eggplant Dip with Feta and Mint

Prep time: 5 minutes | Cook time: 20 minutes | Makes about 1½ cups

1 medium eggplant (about 1 pound / 454 g)
2 tablespoons lemon juice
¼ cup olive oil
½ cup crumbled feta cheese
½ cup finely diced red onion
3 tablespoons chopped fresh mint leaves
1 tablespoon finely chopped flat-leaf parsley
¼ teaspoon cayenne pepper
¾ teaspoon salt

1. Preheat the broiler to high. 2. Line a baking sheet with aluminum foil. 3. Put the whole eggplant on the prepared baking sheet and poke it in several places with the tines of a fork. Cook under the broiler, turning about every 5 minutes, until the eggplant is charred on all sides and very soft in the center, about 15 to 20 minutes total. Remove from the oven and set aside until cool enough to handle. 4. When the eggplant is cool enough to handle, cut it in half lengthwise and scoop out the flesh, discarding the charred skin. 5. Add the lemon juice and olive oil and mash to a chunky purée with a fork. Add the cheese, onion, mint, parsley, cayenne, and salt. 6. Serve at room temperature.

Per Serving ½ cup:
Calories: 71 | fat: 6g | protein: 2g | carbs: 3g | fiber: 2g | sodium: 237mg

Heart-Healthful Trail Mix

Prep time: 15 minutes | Cook time: 30 minutes | Serves 10

1 cup raw almonds
1 cup walnut halves
1 cup pumpkin seeds
1 cup dried apricots, cut into thin strips
1 cup dried cherries, roughly
chopped
1 cup golden raisins
2 tablespoons extra-virgin olive oil
1 teaspoon salt

1. Preheat the oven to 300°F (150°C). Line a baking sheet with aluminum foil. 2. In a large bowl, combine the almonds, walnuts, pumpkin seeds, apricots, cherries, and raisins. Pour the olive oil over all and toss well with clean hands. Add salt and toss again to distribute. 3. Pour the nut mixture onto the baking sheet in a single layer and bake until the fruits begin to brown, about 30 minutes. Cool on the baking sheet to room temperature. Store in a large airtight container or zipper-top plastic bag.

Per Serving
Calories: 346 | fat: 20g | protein: 8g | carbs: 39g | fiber: 5g | sodium: 240mg

Taste of the Mediterranean Fat Bombs

Prep time: 15 minutes | Cook time: 0 minutes | Makes 6 fat bombs

1 cup crumbled goat cheese
4 tablespoons jarred pesto
12 pitted Kalamata olives, finely chopped
½ cup finely chopped walnuts
1 tablespoon chopped fresh rosemary

1. In a medium bowl, combine the goat cheese, pesto, and olives and mix well using a fork. Place in the refrigerator for at least 4 hours to harden. 2. Using your hands, form the mixture into 6 balls, about ¾-inch diameter. The mixture will be sticky. 3. In a small bowl, place the walnuts and rosemary and roll the goat cheese balls in the nut mixture to coat. 4. Store the fat bombs in the refrigerator for up to 1 week or in the freezer for up to 1 month.

Per Serving (1 fat bomb)

Calories: 235 | fat: 22g | protein: 10g | carbs: 2g | fiber: 1g | sodium: 365mg

Roasted Mushrooms with Garlic

Prep time: 3 minutes | Cook time: 22 to 27 minutes | Serves 4

16 garlic cloves, peeled
2 teaspoons olive oil, divided
16 button mushrooms
½ teaspoon dried marjoram
⅛ teaspoon freshly ground black pepper
1 tablespoon white wine or low-sodium vegetable broth

1. In a baking pan, mix the garlic with 1 teaspoon of olive oil. Roast in the air fryer at 350°F (177°C) for 12 minutes. 2. Add the mushrooms, marjoram, and pepper. Stir to coat. Drizzle with the remaining 1 teaspoon of olive oil and the white wine. 3. Return to the air fryer and roast for 10 to 15 minutes more, or until the mushrooms and garlic cloves are tender. Serve.

Per Serving

Calories: 57 | fat: 3g | protein: 3g | carbs: 7g | fiber: 1g | sodium: 6mg

Citrus-Marinated Olives

Prep time: 10 minutes | Cook time: 0 minutes | Makes 2 cups

2 cups mixed green olives with pits
¼ cup red wine vinegar
¼ cup extra-virgin olive oil
4 garlic cloves, finely minced
Zest and juice of 2 clementines
or 1 large orange
1 teaspoon red pepper flakes
2 bay leaves
½ teaspoon ground cumin
½ teaspoon ground allspice

1. In a large glass bowl or jar, combine the olives, vinegar, oil, garlic, orange zest and juice, red pepper flakes, bay leaves, cumin, and allspice and mix well. Cover and refrigerate for at least 4 hours or up to a week to allow the olives to marinate, tossing again before serving.

Per Serving (¼ cup)

Calories: 112 | fat: 10g | protein: 1g | carbs: 5g | fiber: 2g | sodium: 248mg

Lemony Olives and Feta Medley

Prep time: 10 minutes | Cook time: 0 minutes | Serves 8

1 (1-pound / 454-g) block of Greek feta cheese
3 cups mixed olives (Kalamata and green), drained from brine; pitted preferred
¼ cup extra-virgin olive oil
3 tablespoons lemon juice
1 teaspoon grated lemon zest
1 teaspoon dried oregano
Pita bread, for serving

1. Cut the feta cheese into ½-inch squares and put them into a large bowl. 2. Add the olives to the feta and set aside. 3. In a small bowl, whisk together the olive oil, lemon juice, lemon zest, and oregano. 4. Pour the dressing over the feta cheese and olives and gently toss together to evenly coat everything. 5. Serve with pita bread.

Per Serving

Calories: 269 | fat: 24g | protein: 9g | carbs: 6g | fiber: 2g | sodium: 891mg

Crunchy Tex-Mex Tortilla Chips

Prep time: 5 minutes | Cook time: 5 minutes | Serves 4

Olive oil
½ teaspoon salt
½ teaspoon ground cumin
½ teaspoon chili powder
½ teaspoon paprika
Pinch cayenne pepper
8 (6-inch) corn tortillas, each cut into 6 wedges

1. Spray fryer basket lightly with olive oil. 2. In a small bowl, combine the salt, cumin, chili powder, paprika, and cayenne pepper. 3. Place the tortilla wedges in the air fryer basket in a single layer. Spray the tortillas lightly with oil and sprinkle with some of the seasoning mixture. You will need to cook the tortillas in batches. 4. Air fry at 375°F (191°C) for 2 to 3 minutes. Shake the basket and cook until the chips are light brown and crispy, an additional 2 to 3 minutes. Watch the chips closely so they do not burn.

Per Serving

Calories: 118 | fat: 1g | protein: 3g | carbs: 25g | fiber: 3g | sodium: 307mg

Seared Halloumi with Pesto and Tomato

Prep time: 2 minutes | Cook time: 5 minutes | Serves 2

3 ounces (85 g) Halloumi cheese, cut crosswise into 2 thinner, rectangular pieces
2 teaspoons prepared pesto sauce, plus additional for drizzling if desired
1 medium tomato, sliced

1. Heat a nonstick skillet over medium-high heat and place the slices of Halloumi in the hot pan. After about 2 minutes, check to see if the cheese is golden on the bottom. If it is, flip the slices, top each with 1 teaspoon of pesto, and cook for another 2 minutes, or until the second side is golden. 2. Serve with slices of tomato and a drizzle of pesto, if desired, on the side.

Per Serving

Calories: 177 | fat: 14g | protein: 10g | carbs: 4g | fiber: 1g | sodium: 233mg

Quick Garlic Mushrooms

Prep time: 10 minutes | Cook time: 10 minutes | Serves 4 to 6

2 pounds (907 g) cremini mushrooms, cleaned
3 tablespoons unsalted butter
2 tablespoons garlic, minced

½ teaspoon salt
½ teaspoon freshly ground black pepper

1. Cut each mushroom in half, stem to top, and put them into a bowl. 2. Preheat a large sauté pan or skillet over medium heat. 3. Cook the butter and garlic in the pan for 2 minutes, stirring occasionally. 4. Add the mushrooms and salt to the pan and toss together with the garlic butter mixture. Cook for 7 to 8 minutes, stirring every 2 minutes. 5. Remove the mushrooms from the pan and pour into a serving dish. Top with black pepper.

Per Serving

Calories: 183 | fat: 9g | protein: 9g | carbs: 10g | fiber: 3g | sodium: 334mg

Greens Chips with Curried Yogurt Sauce

Prep time: 10 minutes | Cook time: 5 to 6 minutes | Serves 4

1 cup low-fat Greek yogurt
1 tablespoon freshly squeezed lemon juice
1 tablespoon curry powder
½ bunch curly kale, stemmed, ribs removed and discarded,

leaves cut into 2- to 3-inch pieces
½ bunch chard, stemmed, ribs removed and discarded, leaves cut into 2- to 3-inch pieces
1½ teaspoons olive oil

1. In a small bowl, stir together the yogurt, lemon juice, and curry powder. Set aside. 2. In a large bowl, toss the kale and chard with the olive oil, working the oil into the leaves with your hands. This helps break up the fibers in the leaves so the chips are tender. 3. Air fry the greens in batches at 390°F (199°C) for 5 to 6 minutes, until crisp, shaking the basket once during cooking. Serve with the yogurt sauce.

Per Serving

Calories: 98 | fat: 4g | protein: 7g | carbs: 13g | fiber: 4g | sodium: 186mg

Crunchy Orange-Thyme Chickpeas

Prep time: 5 minutes |Cook time: 20 minutes| Serves: 4

1 (15-ounce / 425-g) can chickpeas, drained and rinsed
2 teaspoons extra-virgin olive oil
¼ teaspoon dried thyme or ½

teaspoon chopped fresh thyme leaves
⅛ teaspoon kosher or sea salt
Zest of ½ orange (about ½ teaspoon)

1. Preheat the oven to 450°F (235°C). 2. Spread the chickpeas on a clean kitchen towel, and rub gently until dry. 3. Spread the chickpeas on a large, rimmed baking sheet. Drizzle with the oil, and sprinkle with the thyme and salt. Using a Microplane or citrus zester, zest about half of the orange over the chickpeas.

Mix well using your hands. 4. Bake for 10 minutes, then open the oven door and, using an oven mitt, give the baking sheet a quick shake. (Do not remove the sheet from the oven.) Bake for 10 minutes more. Taste the chickpeas (carefully!). If they are golden but you think they could be a bit crunchier, bake for 3 minutes more before serving.

Per Serving

Calories: 167 | fat: 5g | protein: 7g | carbs: 24g | fiber: 7g | sodium: 303mg

Herbed Labneh Vegetable Parfaits

Prep time: 15 minutes | Cook time: 0 minutes | Serves 2

For the Labneh:
8 ounces (227 g) plain Greek yogurt (full-fat works best)
Generous pinch salt
1 teaspoon za'atar seasoning
1 teaspoon freshly squeezed lemon juice

Pinch lemon zest
For the Parfaits:
½ cup peeled, chopped cucumber
½ cup grated carrots
½ cup cherry tomatoes, halved

Make the Labneh: 1. Line a strainer with cheesecloth and place it over a bowl. 2. Stir together the Greek yogurt and salt and place in the cheesecloth. Wrap it up and let it sit for 24 hours in the refrigerator. 3. When ready, unwrap the labneh and place it into a clean bowl. Stir in the za'atar, lemon juice, and lemon zest. Make the Parfaits 1. Divide the cucumber between two clear glasses. 2. Top each portion of cucumber with about 3 tablespoons of labneh. 3. Divide the carrots between the glasses. 4. Top with another 3 tablespoons of the labneh. 5. Top parfaits with the cherry tomatoes.

Per Serving

Calories: 143 | fat: 7g | protein: 5g | carbs: 16g | fiber: 2g | sodium: 187mg

Sweet-and-Spicy Nuts

Prep time: 5 minutes | Cook time: 20 minutes | Serves 10 to 12

Nonstick cooking spray
Zest and juice of 1 lemon
2 tablespoons honey
2 teaspoons Berbere or baharat

spice blend
1 teaspoon Aleppo pepper
1½ cups cashews
1½ cups dry-roasted peanuts

1. Preheat the oven to 375°F (190°C). Line a baking sheet with parchment paper and spray the parchment with cooking spray. 2. Spread the nuts in an even layer over the prepared baking sheet. Bake for 8 to 10 minutes, until fragrant. Remove from the oven and let cool slightly. Keep the oven on. 3. In a small bowl, stir together the lemon zest, lemon juice, honey, Berbere, and Aleppo pepper. 4. Transfer the nuts to a large bowl and pour over the honey-spice mixture. Toss to coat evenly. Return the nut mixture to the baking sheet and spread into an even layer. Bake for 8 to 10 minutes, until the nuts are caramelized. Remove from the oven and let cool completely before serving. 5. Can be stored refrigerated for up to 2 weeks.

Per Serving

Calories: 336 | fat: 27g | protein: 11g | carbs: 17g | fiber: 3g | sodium: 7mg

Roasted Rosemary Olives

Prep time: 5 minutes | Cook time: 25 minutes | Serves 4

1 cup mixed variety olives, pitted and rinsed	oil
2 tablespoons lemon juice	6 garlic cloves, peeled
1 tablespoon extra-virgin olive	4 rosemary sprigs

1. Preheat the oven to 400°F (205°C). Line the baking sheet with parchment paper or foil. 2. Combine the olives, lemon juice, olive oil, and garlic in a medium bowl and mix together. Spread in a single layer on the prepared baking sheet. Sprinkle on the rosemary. Roast for 25 minutes, tossing halfway through. 3. Remove the rosemary leaves from the stem and place in a serving bowl. Add the olives and mix before serving.

Per Serving
Calories: 100 | fat: 9g | protein: 0g | carbs: 4g | fiber: 0g | sodium: 260mg

Salmon-Stuffed Cucumbers

Prep time: 10 minutes | Cook time: 0 minutes | Serves 4

2 large cucumbers, peeled	Zest and juice of 1 lime
1 (4-ounce / 113-g) can red salmon	3 tablespoons chopped fresh cilantro
1 medium very ripe avocado, peeled, pitted, and mashed	½ teaspoon salt
1 tablespoon extra-virgin olive oil	¼ teaspoon freshly ground black pepper

1. Slice the cucumber into 1-inch-thick segments and using a spoon, scrape seeds out of center of each segment and stand up on a plate. 2. In a medium bowl, combine the salmon, avocado, olive oil, lime zest and juice, cilantro, salt, and pepper and mix until creamy. 3. Spoon the salmon mixture into the center of each cucumber segment and serve chilled.

Per Serving
Calories: 173 | fat: 13g | protein: 8g | carbs: 8g | fiber: 4g | sodium: 420mg

Warm Olives with Rosemary and Garlic

Prep time: 5 minutes | Cook time: 3 minutes | Serves 4

1 tablespoon olive oil	¼ teaspoon salt
1 clove garlic, chopped	1 cup whole cured black olives, such as Kalamata
2 sprigs fresh rosemary	

1. Heat the olive oil in a medium saucepan over medium heat. Add the garlic, rosemary, and salt. Reduce the heat to low and cook, stirring, for 1 minute. 2. Add the olives and cook, stirring occasionally, for about 2 minutes, until the olives are warm. 3. To serve, scoop the olives from the pan using a slotted spoon into a serving bowl. Pour the rosemary and garlic over the olives and serve warm.

Per Serving
Calories: 71 | fat: 7g | protein: 1g | carbs: 3g | fiber: 1g | sodium: 441mg

Marinated Olives and Mushrooms

Prep time: 10 minutes | Cook time: 0 minutes | Serves 8

1 pound (454 g) white button mushrooms	vinegar
1 pound (454 g) mixed, high-quality olives	½ tablespoon crushed fennel seeds
2 tablespoons fresh thyme leaves	Pinch chili flakes
1 tablespoon white wine	Olive oil, to cover
	Sea salt and freshly ground pepper, to taste

1. Clean and rinse mushrooms under cold water and pat dry. 2. Combine all ingredients in a glass jar or other airtight container. Cover with olive oil and season with sea salt and freshly ground pepper. Shake to distribute the ingredients. Allow to marinate for at least 1 hour. Serve at room temperature.

Per Serving
Calories: 61 | fat: 4g | protein: 2g | carbs: 5g | fiber: 2g | sodium: 420mg

Creamy Traditional Hummus

Prep time: 5 minutes | Cook time: 0 minutes | Serves 8

1 (15-ounce / 425-g) can garbanzo beans, rinsed and drained	1 teaspoon salt
2 cloves garlic, peeled	¼ cup plain Greek yogurt
¼ cup lemon juice	½ cup tahini paste
	2 tablespoons extra-virgin olive oil, divided

1. Add the garbanzo beans, garlic cloves, lemon juice, and salt to a food processor fitted with a chopping blade. Blend for 1 minute, until smooth. 2. Scrape down the sides of the processor. Add the Greek yogurt, tahini paste, and 1 tablespoon of olive oil and blend for another minute, until creamy and well combined. 3. Spoon the hummus into a serving bowl. Drizzle the remaining tablespoon of olive oil on top.

Per Serving
Calories: 189 | fat: 13g | protein: 7g | carbs: 14g | fiber: 4g | sodium: 313mg

Cherry Tomato Bruschetta

Prep time: 15 minutes | Cook time: 0 minutes | Serves 4

8 ounces (227 g) assorted cherry tomatoes, halved	oil
⅓ cup fresh herbs, chopped (such as basil, parsley, tarragon, dill)	¼ teaspoon kosher salt
	⅛ teaspoon freshly ground black pepper
1 tablespoon extra-virgin olive	¼ cup ricotta cheese
	4 slices whole-wheat bread, toasted

1. Combine the tomatoes, herbs, olive oil, salt, and black pepper in a medium bowl and mix gently. 2. Spread 1 tablespoon of ricotta cheese onto each slice of toast. Spoon one-quarter of the tomato mixture onto each bruschetta. If desired, garnish with more herbs.

Per Serving
Calories: 100 | fat: 1g | protein: 4g | carbs: 10g | fiber: 2g | sodium: 135mg

Smoky Baba Ghanoush

Prep time: 50 minutes | Cook time: 40 minutes | Serves 6

2 large eggplants, washed
¼ cup lemon juice
1 teaspoon garlic, minced
1 teaspoon salt

½ cup tahini paste
3 tablespoons extra-virgin olive oil

1. Grill the whole eggplants over a low flame using a gas stovetop or grill. Rotate the eggplant every 5 minutes to make sure that all sides are cooked evenly. Continue to do this for 40 minutes. 2. Remove the eggplants from the stove or grill and put them onto a plate or into a bowl; cover with plastic wrap. Let sit for 5 to 10 minutes. 3. Using your fingers, peel away and discard the charred skin of the eggplants. Cut off the stem. 4. Put the eggplants into a food processor fitted with a chopping blade. Add the lemon juice, garlic, salt, and tahini paste, and pulse the mixture 5 to 7 times. 5. Pour the eggplant mixture onto a serving plate. Drizzle with the olive oil. Serve chilled or at room temperature.

Per Serving
Calories: 230 | fat: 18g | protein: 5g | carbs: 16g | fiber: 7g | sodium: 416mg

Marinated Feta and Artichokes

Prep time: 10 minutes | Cook time: 0 minutes | Makes 1½ cups

4 ounces (113 g) traditional Greek feta, cut into ½-inch cubes
4 ounces (113 g) drained artichoke hearts, quartered lengthwise
⅓ cup extra-virgin olive oil

Zest and juice of 1 lemon
2 tablespoons roughly chopped fresh rosemary
2 tablespoons roughly chopped fresh parsley
½ teaspoon black peppercorns

1. In a glass bowl or large glass jar, combine the feta and artichoke hearts. Add the olive oil, lemon zest and juice, rosemary, parsley, and peppercorns and toss gently to coat, being sure not to crumble the feta. 2. Cover and refrigerate for at least 4 hours, or up to 4 days. Pull out of the refrigerator 30 minutes before serving.

Per Serving
Calories: 108 | fat: 9g | protein: 3g | carbs: 4g | fiber: 1g | sodium: 294mg

Pita Pizza with Olives, Feta, and Red Onion

Prep time: 15 minutes | Cook time: 10 minutes | Serves 4

4 (6-inch) whole-wheat pitas
1 tablespoon extra-virgin olive oil
½ cup hummus
½ bell pepper, julienned
½ red onion, julienned
¼ cup olives, pitted and

chopped
¼ cup crumbled feta cheese
¼ teaspoon red pepper flakes
¼ cup fresh herbs, chopped (mint, parsley, oregano, or a mix)

1. Preheat the broiler to low. Line a baking sheet with parchment paper or foil. 2. Place the pitas on the prepared baking sheet and brush both sides with the olive oil. Broil 1 to 2 minutes per side until starting to turn golden brown. 3. Spread 2 tablespoons hummus on each pita. Top the pitas with bell pepper, onion, olives, feta cheese, and red pepper flakes. Broil again until the cheese softens and starts to get golden brown, 4 to 6 minutes, being careful not to burn the pitas. 4. Remove from broiler and top with the herbs.

Per Serving
Calories: 185 | fat: 11g | protein: 5g | carbs: 17g | fiber: 3g | sodium: 285mg

Roasted Za'atar Chickpeas

Prep time: 5 minutes | Cook time: 1 hour | Serves 8

3 tablespoons za'atar
2 tablespoons extra-virgin olive oil
½ teaspoon kosher salt
¼ teaspoon freshly ground

black pepper
4 cups cooked chickpeas, or 2 (15-ounce / 425-g) cans, drained and rinsed

1. Preheat the oven to 400°F (205°C). Line a baking sheet with foil or parchment paper. 2. In a large bowl, combine the za'atar, olive oil, salt, and black pepper. Add the chickpeas and mix thoroughly. 3. Spread the chickpeas in a single layer on the prepared baking sheet. Bake for 45 to 60 minutes, or until golden brown and crispy. Cool and store in an airtight container at room temperature for up to 1 week.

Per Serving
Calories: 150 | fat: 6g | protein: 6g | carbs: 17g | fiber: 6g | sodium: 230mg

Apple Chips with Chocolate Tahini

Prep time: 10 minutes | Cook time: 0 minutes | Serves 2

2 tablespoons tahini
1 tablespoon maple syrup
1 tablespoon unsweetened cocoa powder
1 to 2 tablespoons warm water

(or more if needed)
2 medium apples
1 tablespoon roasted, salted sunflower seeds

1. In a small bowl, mix together the tahini, maple syrup, and cocoa powder. Add warm water, a little at a time, until thin enough to drizzle. Do not microwave it to thin it—it won't work. 2. Slice the apples crosswise into round slices, and then cut each piece in half to make a chip. 3. Lay the apple chips out on a plate and drizzle them with the chocolate tahini sauce. 4. Sprinkle sunflower seeds over the apple chips.

Per Serving
Calories: 261 | fat: 11g | protein: 5g | carbs: 43g | fiber: 8g | sodium: 21mg

Chapter 13 Staples, Sauces, Dips, and Dressings

Creamy Tomato Hummus Soup

Prep time: 10 minutes | Cook time: 10 minutes | Serves 2

1 (14½-ounce / 411-g) can crushed tomatoes with basil
1 cup roasted red pepper hummus
2 cups low-sodium chicken stock
Salt
¼ cup fresh basil leaves, thinly sliced (optional, for garnish)
Garlic croutons (optional, for garnish)

1. Combine the canned tomatoes, hummus, and chicken stock in a blender and blend until smooth. Pour the mixture into a saucepan and bring it to a boil. 2. Season with salt and fresh basil if desired. Serve with garlic croutons as a garnish, if desired.

Per Serving
Calories: 148 | fat: 6g | protein: 5g | carbs: 19g | fiber: 4g | sodium: 680mg

Vegetable Fagioli

Prep time: 30 minutes | Cook time: 60 minutes | Serves 2

1 tablespoon olive oil
2 medium carrots, diced (about ¾ cup)
2 medium celery stalks, diced (about ½ cup)
½ medium onion, diced (about ¾ cup)
1 large garlic clove, minced
3 tablespoons tomato paste
4 cups low-sodium vegetable broth
1 cup packed kale, stemmed and chopped
1 (15-ounce / 425-g) can red kidney beans, drained and rinsed
1 (15-ounce / 425-g) can cannellini beans, drained and rinsed
½ cup fresh basil, chopped
Salt
Freshly ground black pepper

1. Heat the olive oil in a stockpot over medium-high heat. Add the carrots, celery, onion, and garlic and sauté for 10 minutes, or until the vegetables start to turn golden. 2. Stir in the tomato paste and cook for about 30 seconds. 3. Add the vegetable broth and bring the soup to a boil. Cover, and reduce the heat to low. Cook the soup for 45 minutes, or until the carrots are tender. 4. Using an immersion blender, purée the soup so that it's partly smooth, but with some chunks of vegetables. If you don't have an immersion blender, scoop out about ⅓ of the soup and blend it in a blender, then add it back to the pot. 5. Add the kale, beans, and basil. Season with salt and pepper.

Per Serving
Calories: 215 | fat: 4g | protein: 11g | carbs: 36g | fiber: 11g | sodium: 486mg

Spinach and Brown Rice Soup

Prep time: 10 minutes | Cook time: 55 minutes | Serves 6

1 tablespoon olive oil
1 large onion, chopped
2 cloves garlic, minced
3 pounds (1.4 kg) spinach leaves, stems removed and
leaves chopped
8 cups chicken broth
½ cup long-grain brown rice
Sea salt and freshly ground pepper, to taste

1. Heat the olive oil in a large Dutch oven over medium heat, and add the onion and garlic. 2. Cook until the onions are soft and translucent, about 5 minutes. Add the spinach and stir. 3. Cover the pot and cook the spinach until wilted, about 3 more minutes. 4. Using a slotted spoon, remove the spinach and onions from the pot, leaving the liquid. 5. Put the spinach mixture in a food processor or blender, and process until smooth, then return to the pot. 6. Add the chicken broth and bring to a boil. 7. Add the rice, reduce heat, and simmer until rice is cooked, about 45 minutes. 8. Season to taste. 9. Serve hot.

Per Serving
Calories: 192 | fat: 6g | protein: 14g | carbs: 27g | fiber: 6g | sodium: 277mg

Mediterranean Vegetable Soup

Prep time: 20 minutes | Cook time: 6 to 8 hours | Serves 6

1 (28-ounce / 794-g) can no-salt-added diced tomatoes
2 cups low-sodium vegetable broth
1 green bell pepper, seeded and chopped
1 red or yellow bell pepper, seeded and chopped
4 ounces (113 g) mushrooms, sliced
2 zucchini, chopped
1 small red onion, chopped
3 garlic cloves, minced
1 tablespoon extra-virgin olive oil
2 teaspoons dried oregano
1 teaspoon paprika
1 teaspoon sea salt
½ teaspoon freshly ground black pepper
Juice of 1 lemon

1. In a slow cooker, combine the tomatoes, vegetable broth, green and red bell peppers, mushrooms, zucchini, onion, garlic, olive oil, oregano, paprika, salt, and black pepper. Stir to mix well. 2. Cover the cooker and cook for 6 to 8 hours on Low heat. 3. Stir in the lemon juice before serving.

Per Serving
Calories: 91 | fat: 3g | protein: 3g | carbs: 16g | fiber: 5g | sodium: 502mg

Minced Beef or Lamb Soup

Prep time: 20 minutes | Cook time: 6 to 8 hours | Serves 6

1 pound (454 g) raw ground beef or lamb
12 ounces (340 g) new red potatoes, halved, or 1 (15-ounce / 425-g) can reduced-sodium chickpeas, drained and rinsed
4 cups low-sodium beef broth
2 cups water
2 carrots, diced
2 celery stalks, diced
2 zucchini, cut into 1-inch pieces
1 large tomato, chopped
1 small onion, diced
2 garlic cloves, minced
¼ cup no-salt-added tomato paste
1 teaspoon sea salt
1 teaspoon dried oregano
1 teaspoon dried basil
½ teaspoon freshly ground black pepper
½ teaspoon dried thyme
2 bay leaves

1. In a large skillet over medium-high heat, cook the ground meat for 3 to 5 minutes, stirring and breaking it up with a spoon until it has browned and is no longer pink. Drain any grease and put the meat in a slow cooker. 2. Add the potatoes, beef broth, water, carrots, celery, zucchini, tomato, onion, garlic, tomato paste, salt, oregano, basil, pepper, thyme, and bay leaves to the ground meat. Stir to mix well. 3. Cover the cooker and cook for 6 to 8 hours on Low heat. 4. Remove and discard the bay leaves before serving.

Per Serving

Calories: 200 | fat: 6g | protein: 20g | carbs: 20g | fiber: 4g | sodium: 790mg

Lemon Chicken Soup with Orzo

Prep time: 10 minutes | Cook time: 6 to 8 hours | Serves 6

1 pound (454 g) boneless, skinless chicken thighs or 1 pound (454 g) bone-in, skinless chicken breast
4 cups low-sodium chicken broth
2 cups water
2 celery stalks, thinly sliced
1 small onion, diced
1 carrot, diced
1 garlic clove, minced
Grated zest of 1 lemon
Juice of 1 lemon
1 bay leaf
1 teaspoon sea salt
1 teaspoon dried oregano
½ teaspoon freshly ground black pepper
¾ cup dried orzo pasta
1 lemon, thinly sliced

1. In a slow cooker, combine the chicken, chicken broth, water, celery, onion, carrot, garlic, lemon zest, lemon juice, bay leaf, salt, oregano, and pepper. Stir to mix well. 2. Cover the cooker and cook for 6 to 8 hours on Low heat. 3. Remove the chicken from the slow cooker and shred it. (If you are using bone-in chicken, remove and discard the bones while shredding. The meat should be so tender that the bones just slide out.) 4. Return the chicken to the slow cooker and add the orzo and lemon slices. 5. Replace the cover on the cooker and cook for 15 to 30 minutes on Low heat, or until the orzo is tender. 6. Remove and discard the bay leaf before serving.

Per Serving

Calories: 195 | fat: 5g | protein: 15g | carbs: 22g | fiber: 3g | sodium: 561mg

Moroccan Fish Stew

Prep time: 10 minutes | Cook time: 3 to 5 hours | Serves 6

1 pound (454 g) fresh fish fillets of your choice, cut into 2-inch pieces
3 cups low-sodium vegetable broth or low-sodium chicken broth
1 (15-ounce / 425-g) can no-salt-added diced tomatoes
1 bell pepper, any color,
seeded and diced
1 small onion, diced
1 garlic clove, minced
1 teaspoon ground coriander
1 teaspoon sea salt
1 teaspoon paprika
½ teaspoon ground turmeric
½ teaspoon freshly ground black pepper
¼ cup fresh cilantro

1. In a slow cooker, combine the fish, vegetable broth, tomatoes, bell pepper, onion, garlic, coriander, salt, paprika, turmeric, and black pepper. Stir to mix well. 2. Cover the cooker and cook for 3 to 5 hours on Low heat. 3. Garnish with the fresh cilantro for serving.

Per Serving

Calories: 115 | fat: 1g | protein: 18g | carbs: 8g | fiber: 3g | sodium: 547mg

Avgolemono (Lemon Chicken Soup)

Prep time: 15 minutes | Cook time: 60 minutes | Serves 2

½ large onion
2 medium carrots
1 celery stalk
1 garlic clove
5 cups low-sodium chicken stock
¼ cup brown rice
1½ cups (about 5 ounces / 142 g) shredded rotisserie chicken
3 tablespoons freshly squeezed lemon juice
1 egg yolk
2 tablespoons chopped fresh dill
2 tablespoons chopped fresh parsley
Salt

1. Place the onion, carrots, celery, and garlic in a food processor fitted with the chopping blade and pulse it until the vegetables are minced. You can also mince them by hand. 2. Add the vegetables and chicken stock to a stockpot or Dutch oven and bring it to a boil over high heat. 3. Reduce the heat to medium-low and add the rice, shredded chicken and lemon juice. Cover, and let the soup simmer for 40 minutes, or until the rice is cooked. 4. In a small bowl, whisk the egg yolk lightly. Very slowly, while whisking with one hand, pour about ½ of a ladle of the broth into the egg yolk to warm, or temper, the yolk. Slowly add another ladle of broth and continue to whisk. Do not skip this step. 5. Remove the soup from the heat and pour the whisked egg yolk–broth mixture into the pot. Stir well to combine. 6. Add the fresh dill and parsley. Season with salt, and serve. 7. If you want to reheat any leftovers, heat it very slowly and don't let the soup come to a full boil.

Per Serving

Calories: 171 | fat: 3g | protein: 19g | carbs: 16g | fiber: 2g | sodium: 236mg

Shrimp Soup with Leeks and Fennel

Prep time: 15 minutes | Cook time: 40 minutes | Serves 6

2 tablespoons olive oil	pepper, to taste
3 stalks celery, chopped	1 tablespoon fennel seeds
1 leek, both whites and light green parts, sliced	4 cups vegetable or chicken broth
1 medium fennel bulb, chopped	1 pound (454 g) medium shrimp, peeled and deveined
1 clove garlic, minced	2 tablespoons light cream
Sea salt and freshly ground	Juice of 1 lemon

1. Heat the oil in a large Dutch oven over medium heat. 2. Add the celery, leek, and fennel, and cook for about 15 minutes, until vegetables are browned and very soft. 3. Add the garlic and season with sea salt and freshly ground pepper to taste. Add the fennel seed and stir. 4. Add the broth and bring to a boil, then reduce to a simmer and cook about 20 more minutes. 5. Add the shrimp to the soup and cook until just pink, about 3 minutes. Add the cream and lemon juice, and serve immediately.

Per Serving

Calories: 166 | fat: 7g | protein: 19g | carbs: 8g | fiber: 2g | sodium: 171mg

Roasted Eggplant Soup

Prep time: 15 minutes | Cook time: 40 minutes | Serves 6

Olive oil cooking spray	1 to 2 cups no-salt-added vegetable stock
2 pounds (907 g, 1 to 2 medium to large) eggplant, halved lengthwise	1 teaspoon pure maple syrup
2 beefsteak tomatoes, halved	1 teaspoon ground cumin
2 onions, halved	1 teaspoon ground coriander
4 garlic cloves, smashed	1 teaspoon kosher salt
4 rosemary sprigs	¼ teaspoon freshly ground black pepper
2 tablespoons extra-virgin olive oil	Lemon juice (optional)

1. Preheat the oven to 400ºF (205ºC). Line two baking sheets with parchment paper or foil. Lightly spray with olive oil cooking spray. Spread the eggplant, tomatoes, onions, and garlic on the prepared baking sheets, cut-side down. Nestle the rosemary sprigs among the vegetables. Drizzle with the olive oil and roast for 40 minutes, checking halfway through and removing the garlic before it gets brown. 2. When cool enough to touch, remove the eggplant flesh and tomato flesh from the skin and add to a high-powered blender, food processor, or Vitamix. Add the rosemary leaves, onions, garlic, 1 cup of the vegetable stock, maple syrup, cumin, coriander, salt, and black pepper. Purée until smooth. The soup should be thick and creamy. If the soup is too thick, add another cup of stock slowly, until your desired consistency is reached. Spritz with lemon juice, if desired.

Per Serving

Calories: 185 | fat: 8g | protein: 4g | carbs: 29g | fiber: 9g | sodium: 400mg

Roasted Vegetable Soup

Prep time: 20 minutes | Cook time: 30 to 35 minutes | Serves 6

2 sweet potatoes, peeled and sliced	thyme
2 parsnips, peeled and sliced	1 teaspoon salt
2 carrots, peeled and sliced	½ teaspoon freshly ground black pepper
2 tablespoons extra-virgin olive oil	4 cups vegetable or chicken broth
1 teaspoon chopped fresh rosemary	Grated Parmesan cheese for garnish (optional)
1 teaspoon chopped fresh	

1. Preheat the oven to 400ºF (205ºC). Line a baking sheet with aluminum foil. 2. In a large bowl, combine the sweet potatoes, parsnips, and carrots. Add the olive oil and toss to coat. Add the rosemary, thyme, salt, and pepper, tossing well. 3. Spread out the vegetables on the baking sheet and roast until tender and brown at the edges, 30 to 35 minutes. Remove the baking sheet from the oven and allow to cool until just warm. 4. Working in batches, transfer some of the vegetables and broth to a blender or food processor and blend until smooth. Pour each blended batch into a large saucepan. 5. When all of the vegetables have been puréed, heat the soup over low heat just until heated through. To serve, ladle into bowls and top with Parmesan cheese if desired.

Per Serving

Calories: 19 | fat: 6g | protein: 5g | carbs: 19g | fiber: 4g | sodium: 477mg

Cranberry Bean Minestrone

Prep time: 15 minutes | Cook time: 3 hours 30 minutes | Serves 6

1 quart low-sodium vegetable broth	pepper
1 (14½-ounce / 411-g) can diced tomatoes	2 (15-ounce / 425-g) cans cranberry beans, drained and rinsed
2 carrots, thinly sliced	1 small zucchini, halved lengthwise and sliced ¼' thick
2 ribs celery, thinly sliced	1½ cups whole grain ditalini or elbow pasta
1 onion, chopped	
3 cloves garlic, sliced	6 tablespoons finely grated Parmigiano-Reggiano cheese
1 tablespoon dried oregano	3 tablespoons shredded fresh basil
1 bay leaf	
½ teaspoon kosher salt	
½ teaspoon ground black	

1. In a 4- or 6-quart slow cooker, combine the broth, tomatoes, carrots, celery, onion, garlic, oregano, bay leaf, salt, and pepper. Cover and cook until the vegetables are tender, on low 6 to 8 hours or high 3 to 4 hours. 2. Remove the cover and add the beans, zucchini, and pasta. Cook on high until the pasta is tender, about 30 minutes. Remove the bay leaf and garnish each serving with the cheese and basil.

Per Serving

Calories: 321 | fat: 4g | protein: 14g | carbs: 59g | fiber: 7g | sodium: 857mg

Creamy Chickpea and Tortellini Soup

Prep time: 10 minutes | Cook time: 30 minutes | Serves 6

2 tablespoons olive oil
1 onion, diced
3 celery stalks, chopped
4 ounces (113 g) cremini (baby bella) mushrooms, quartered
6 garlic cloves, chopped
8 cups low-sodium chicken broth
2 teaspoons sea salt
1 teaspoon freshly ground black pepper
1 teaspoon Italian seasoning
¼ teaspoon paprika
10 ounces (283 g) fresh spinach or cheese tortellini
1 (15-ounce / 425-g) can chickpeas, drained and rinsed
3 to 4 ounces (85 to 113 g) baby spinach, coarsely chopped
1 cup fresh basil, coarsely chopped
½ cup heavy (whipping) cream

1. In a Dutch oven, heat the olive oil over medium heat. Add the onion and sauté for 3 minutes. Add the celery, mushrooms, and garlic and sauté until tender, about 6 minutes. Add the broth and bring to a boil. Add the salt, pepper, Italian seasoning, and paprika and stir to combine. 2. Add the tortellini and simmer for 4 to 5 minutes (or for the amount of time recommended on the package). Add the chickpeas and simmer for 2 to 3 minutes. Add the spinach, basil, and cream. Remove from the heat and stir to combine. 3. Cover the soup and let stand for 2 minutes before serving.

Per Serving
Calories: 343 | fat: 17g | protein: 12g | carbs: 39g | fiber: 5g | sodium: 614mg

Carrot Soup with Yogurt and Spices

Prep time: 10 minutes | Cook time: 20 minutes | Serves 4

2 tablespoons olive oil
1 medium onion, diced
6 medium carrots, peeled, cut into ½-inch dice
1 teaspoon salt
1 teaspoon ground coriander
1 teaspoon ground cumin
½ teaspoon ground cinnamon
¼ teaspoon ground ginger
¼ teaspoon ground turmeric
4 cups chicken broth
1 tablespoon honey
Juice of ½ lemon
1 cup plain yogurt
¼ cup chopped cilantro

1. Heat the oil in a stockpot over medium-high heat. Add the onion and cook, stirring frequently, until softened, about 5 minutes. Add the carrots, salt, coriander, cumin, cinnamon, ginger, turmeric, and broth and bring to a boil. 2. Lower the heat to low, cover, and simmer for about 15 minutes, until the carrots are tender. 3. Using an immersion blender or in batches in a countertop blender, purée the soup until smooth. Reheat if needed and stir in the honey and lemon juice. 4. Serve hot, drizzled with yogurt and garnished with cilantro.

Per Serving
Calories: 205 | fat: 11g | protein: 8g | carbs: 23g | fiber: 3g | sodium: 748mg

Cold Cucumber Soup

Prep time: 10 minutes | Cook time: 0 minutes | Serves 4

2 seedless cucumbers, peeled and cut into chunks
2 cups plain Greek yogurt
½ cup mint, finely chopped
2 garlic cloves, minced
2 cups chicken broth or
vegetable stock
3 teaspoons fresh dill
1 tablespoon tomato paste
Sea salt and freshly ground pepper, to taste

1. Purée the cucumber, yogurt, mint, and garlic in a food processor or blender. 2. Add the chicken broth, dill, tomato paste, sea salt, and pepper, and blend completely. 3. Refrigerate for at least 2 hours before serving.

Per Serving
Calories: 119 | fat: 5g | protein: 8g | carbs: 12g | fiber: 2g | sodium: 98mg

Farro Bean Soup

Prep time: 15 minutes | Cook time: 2 hours | Serves 8

2 tablespoons olive oil
1 medium onion, diced
1 celery stalk, diced
2 garlic cloves, minced
8 cups chicken broth or water
1 cup white beans, soaked overnight, rinsed, and drained
1 (14-ounce / 397-g) can diced
tomatoes, with juice
1 cup farro
½ teaspoon thyme
½ teaspoon freshly ground pepper
2 bay leaves
Sea salt and freshly ground pepper, to taste

1. Heat the olive oil in a large stockpot on medium-high heat. Sauté the onion, celery, and garlic cloves just until tender. 2. Add the broth or water, beans, tomatoes, farro, and seasonings, and bring to a simmer. 3. Cover and cook for 2 hours, or until the beans and farro are tender. Season with sea salt and freshly ground pepper to taste.

Per Serving
Calories: 253 | fat: 6g | protein: 13g | carbs: 39g | fiber: 6g | sodium: 85mg

Lentil Soup with Spinach

Prep time: 5 minutes | Cook time: 20 minutes | Serves 6

1 teaspoon olive oil
1 cup onion, chopped
1½ cups lentils
1 tablespoon curry powder
6 cups water
12 ounces (340 g) spinach

1. Heat the olive oil and sauté the onion. Add the lentils and curry powder and stir. 2. Add the water and cook until lentils are tender, about 15–20 minutes. Add the spinach and stir until wilted. 3. Serve with toasted whole-wheat bread and a green salad.

Per Serving
Calories: 48 | fat: 1g | protein: 4g | carbs: 9g | fiber: 3g | sodium: 53mg

Ribollita (Tuscan Bean, Bread, and Vegetable Stew)

Prep time: 10 minutes | Cook time: 40 minutes | Serves 6

1 tablespoon olive oil
1 onion, chopped
1 carrot, chopped
1 rib celery, chopped
2 cloves garlic, minced
1 tablespoon fresh rosemary leaves
1 tablespoon fresh thyme leaves
½ teaspoon salt
¼ teaspoon ground black pepper

1 quart low-sodium chicken broth or vegetable broth
1 (14½-ounce / 411-g) can diced tomatoes
1 (15-ounce / 425-g) can white beans, drained and rinsed
4 cups chopped kale
2 cups stale whole grain bread cubes
Parmigiano-Reggiano cheese, for garnish

1. In a large soup pot over medium heat, warm the oil. Cook the onion, carrot, and celery until softened, 5 minutes. Stir in the garlic, rosemary, thyme, salt, and pepper and cook for 1 minute. 2. Stir in the broth and tomatoes and bring to a boil. Reduce the heat to a simmer and cook for 30 minutes. 3. Add the beans and kale and cook until the kale has wilted and the beans are heated through, 5 minutes. Remove the soup from the heat and stir in the bread cubes. Serve immediately with a sprinkle of the cheese, or cool to room temperature before storing in the refrigerator.

Per Serving
Calories: 193 | fat: 4g | protein: 11g | carbs: 30g | fiber: 6g | sodium: 501mg

Greek Lemon Soup with Quinoa

Prep time: 15 minutes | Cook time: 30 minutes | Serves 6 to 8

2 tablespoons olive oil
1 large onion, chopped (about 2 cups)
4 celery stalks, diced (generous 1 cup)
5 carrots, diced (1 cup)
4 cups low-sodium vegetable broth
½ cup quinoa, well rinsed
½ cup fresh lemon juice
3 eggs
¼ teaspoon freshly ground white pepper
4 cups baby kale or spinach

1. In a 3-quart saucepan, heat the olive oil over medium heat. Add the onion, celery, and carrots and sauté until translucent, about 10 minutes. Add the broth and the quinoa. Bring the broth to a boil. Reduce the heat to maintain a simmer, cover, and cook for 15 to 20 minutes, until the quinoa is cooked through. 2. In a medium bowl, beat together the lemon juice, eggs, and white pepper. While whisking, ladle 2 cups of the hot broth into the egg mixture to temper the eggs (this prevents them from scrambling from the heat of the broth). Pour the egg mixture back into the pot and stir to combine. 3. Stir in the greens and cook just until they've wilted, then serve.

Per Serving 1 cup:
Calories: 218 | fat: 10g | protein: 8g | carbs: 25g | fiber: 5g | sodium: 367mg

Tuscan Bean Soup with Kale

Prep time: 20 minutes | Cook time: 25 minutes | Serves 4

2 tablespoons extra-virgin olive oil
1 onion, diced
1 carrot, diced
1 celery stalk, diced
1 teaspoon kosher salt
4 cups no-salt-added vegetable stock
1 (15-ounce / 425-g) can no-salt-added or low-sodium cannellini beans, drained and rinsed
1 tablespoon fresh thyme, chopped
1 tablespoon fresh sage, chopped
1 tablespoon fresh oregano, chopped
¼ teaspoon freshly ground black pepper
1 bunch kale, stemmed and chopped
¼ cup grated Parmesan cheese (optional)

1. Heat the olive oil in a large pot over medium-high heat. Add the onion, carrot, celery, and salt and sauté until translucent and slightly golden, 5 to 6 minutes. 2. Add the vegetable stock, beans, thyme, sage, oregano, and black pepper and bring to a boil. Turn down the heat to low, and simmer for 10 minutes. Stir in the kale and let it wilt, about 5 minutes. 3. Sprinkle 1 tablespoon Parmesan cheese over each bowl before serving, if desired.

Per Serving
Calories: 235 | fat: 8g | protein: 9g | carbs: 35g | fiber: 7g | sodium: 540mg

Greek Lemon-Rice Soup with Fish

Prep time: 10 minutes | Cook time: 30 minutes | Serves 8

2 tablespoons olive oil
1 medium onion, finely diced
⅔ cup Arborio rice
10 cups chicken broth
1 pound (454 g) firm white fish fillet, such as tilapia, cod, or haddock, cut into 2-inch pieces
½ cup lemon juice
2 eggs
1 teaspoon freshly ground black pepper
2 tablespoons chopped flat-leaf parsley, for garnish

1. In a stockpot, heat the olive oil over medium-high heat. Add the onion and cook, stirring frequently, until softened, about 5 minutes. Stir in the rice until the grains are well coated with oil. 2. Add the broth and bring to a boil. Reduce the heat to medium-low and simmer for about 18 minutes, until the rice is just tender. 3. Add the fish and simmer until the fish is just cooked through, about 5 minutes. 4. In a heat-safe glass measuring cup with a spout, whisk together the lemon juice, eggs, and pepper. While whisking, add a few ladles full of the hot broth to the egg mixture. Stir the egg mixture into the soup. Taste and add additional seasoning if needed. Serve immediately, garnished with the parsley.

Per Serving
Calories: 207 | fat: 7g | protein: 19g | carbs: 18g | fiber: 1g | sodium: 139mg

Greek Salad Soup

Prep time: 15 minutes | Cook time: 6 to 8 hours | Serves 6

4 tomatoes, cut into wedges
2 cucumbers, cut into 1-inch-thick rounds
2 green bell peppers, seeded and diced
1 small red onion, diced
1 cup whole Kalamata olives, pitted
4 cups low-sodium chicken broth

2 cups water
1 tablespoon extra-virgin olive oil
2 teaspoons red wine vinegar
1½ teaspoons dried oregano
1 teaspoon sea salt
½ teaspoon freshly ground black pepper
4 ounces (113 g) feta cheese, crumbled

1. In a slow cooker, combine the tomatoes, cucumbers, bell peppers, onion, olives, chicken broth, water, olive oil, vinegar, oregano, salt, and black pepper. Stir to mix well. 2. Cover the cooker and cook for 6 to 8 hours on Low heat. 3. Top each bowl with feta cheese before serving.

Per Serving
Calories: 180 | fat: 12g | protein: 6g | carbs: 13g | fiber: 3g | sodium: 976mg

Tunisian Bean Soup with Poached Eggs

Prep time: 10 minutes | Cook time: 25 minutes | Serves 4

2 tablespoons olive oil
1 small red onion, finely chopped
1 carrot, finely chopped
4 garlic cloves, minced
3 tablespoons harissa
3 cups vegetable broth

1 (15-ounce / 425-g) can chickpeas, drained
1 (5-ounce / 142-g) bag watercress or baby spinach (or red cabbage)
4 eggs

1. In a large saucepan, heat the olive oil over medium heat. Add the onion, carrot, garlic, and harissa. Cook until the vegetables are softened, 10 to 12 minutes. 2. Add the broth, chickpeas, and greens. Cook for 8 to 10 minutes, until the greens are cooked. Carefully add the eggs to the soup, one at a time. Cover; poach the eggs in the soup to your desired doneness, about 5 minutes. 3. Ladle the soup into bowls, top each with 1 egg, and serve.

Per Serving 1 cup:
Calories: 373 | fat: 20g | protein: 18g | carbs: 32g | fiber: 8g | sodium: 583mg

Red Gazpacho

Prep time: 15 minutes | Cook time: 0 minutes | Serves 4

2 pounds (907 g) tomatoes, cut into chunks
1 bell pepper, cut into chunks
1 cucumber, cut into chunks
1 small red onion, cut into chunks
1 garlic clove, smashed

2 teaspoons sherry vinegar
½ teaspoon kosher salt
¼ teaspoon freshly ground black pepper
⅓ cup extra-virgin olive oil
Lemon juice (optional)
¼ cup fresh chives, chopped,

for garnish

1. In a high-speed blender or Vitamix, add the tomatoes, bell pepper, cucumber, onion, garlic, vinegar, salt, and black pepper. Blend until smooth. With the motor running, add the olive oil and purée until smooth. Add more vinegar or a spritz of lemon juice if needed. Garnish with the chives.

Per Serving
Calories: 140 | fat: 19g | protein: 4g | carbs: 18g | fiber: 5g | sodium: 155mg

Turmeric Red Lentil Soup

Prep time: 15 minutes | Cook time: 30 minutes | Serves 6

1 tablespoon extra-virgin olive oil
1 teaspoon ground cumin
1 teaspoon ground coriander
1 teaspoon ground turmeric
1 teaspoon kosher salt
¼ teaspoon freshly ground black pepper
1 tablespoon no-salt-added tomato paste

1 onion, diced
1 carrot, diced
1 celery stalk, diced
3 garlic cloves, minced
4 cups no-salt-added vegetable stock
2 cups water
1 cup red lentils
3 tablespoons lemon juice
¼ cup fresh parsley, chopped

1. Heat the olive oil in a large stock pot over medium-high heat. Add the cumin, coriander, turmeric, salt, and black pepper and cook, stirring, for 30 seconds. Add the tomato paste and cook, stirring, for 30 seconds to 1 minute. Add the onion, carrot, and celery and sauté 5 to 6 minutes. Add the garlic and sauté 30 seconds. 2. Add the vegetable stock, water, and lentils and bring to a boil. Turn down the heat to low, and simmer, covering partially, until the lentils are tender, about 20 minutes. 3. Mix in the lemon juice and parsley.

Per Serving
Calories: 170 | fat: 3g | protein: 9g | carbs: 27g | fiber: 6g | sodium: 340mg

Chickpea Stew

Prep time: 10 minutes | Cook time: 6 to 8 hours | Serves 6

2 cups dried chickpeas, rinsed
4 cups low-sodium vegetable broth or low-sodium chicken broth
1 tablespoon extra-virgin olive oil
1 small onion, diced
1 green bell pepper, seeded and chopped

2 garlic cloves, minced
1 tablespoon drained capers
1 teaspoon ground cumin
1 teaspoon ground turmeric
½ teaspoon ground coriander
½ teaspoon sea salt
¼ teaspoon freshly ground black pepper

1. In a slow cooker, combine the chickpeas, vegetable broth, olive oil, onion, bell pepper, garlic, capers, cumin, turmeric, coriander, salt, and black pepper. Stir to mix well. 2. Cover the cooker and cook for 6 to 8 hours on Low heat.

Per Serving
Calories: 286 | fat: 6g | protein: 14g | carbs: 45g | fiber: 13g | sodium: 347mg

Avgolemono (Egg Lemon) Soup

Prep time: 10 minutes | Cook time: 15 minutes | Serves 4

1 tablespoon olive oil	1 cup cooked brown rice
1 shallot, finely chopped	1 cup shredded cooked chicken
6 cups low-sodium chicken broth	Kosher salt and ground black pepper, to taste
¼ cup fresh lemon juice	2 tablespoons chopped fresh dill
3 eggs	
3 cups baby spinach	

1. In a large saucepan over medium heat, warm the oil until shimmering. Cook the shallot, stirring, until softened, about 5 minutes. Add the broth and lemon juice and bring to a simmer. 2. In a medium bowl, whisk the eggs. Using a ladle, pour a spoonful of the broth into the eggs while whisking. Reduce the heat to low and whisk the egg mixture into the broth in the saucepan. 3. Add the spinach, rice, and chicken and cook until warmed through and the spinach is wilted, about 5 minutes. Season to taste with the salt and pepper. Serve with the dill sprinkled on top.

Per Serving

Calories: 355 | fat: 11g | protein: 33g | carbs: 31g | fiber: 3g | sodium: 304mg

Romesco Soup

Prep time: 5 minutes | Cook time: 20 minutes | Serves 6

1 tablespoon olive oil	fire-roasted tomatoes
1 onion, chopped	1 cup low-sodium chicken broth
1 teaspoon kosher salt	½ cup almond meal
6 cloves garlic, minced	1 tablespoon balsamic vinegar
½ teaspoon paprika	¼ teaspoon ground black pepper
2 (12-ounce / 340-g) jars roasted red peppers, drained and chopped	¼ cup sliced almonds, toasted
1 (28-ounce / 794-g) can diced	Chopped chives, for garnish

1. In a large pot over medium-high heat, warm the oil. Cook the onion and salt, stirring occasionally, until the onion is soft, 5 minutes. 2. Add the garlic and cook until soft, 2 minutes. Stir in the paprika and cook until fragrant, 1 minute. Add the peppers, tomatoes, and broth. Bring to a boil, reduce the heat to a simmer, cover, and cook until heated through, 15 minutes. 3. Add the almond meal and vinegar. With an immersion blender or a regular blender in batches, purée the soup until smooth. Stir in the pepper and serve topped with a sprinkle of the almonds and chives.

Per Serving

Calories: 162 | fat: 9g | protein: 5g | carbs: 17g | fiber: 4g | sodium: 701mg

Turkish Red Lentil Bride Soup

Prep time: 5 minutes | Cook time: 55 minutes | Serves 4

2 tablespoons olive oil	1 quart low-sodium chicken broth or vegetable broth
1 yellow onion, finely chopped	¼ cup chopped fresh mint
½ teaspoon hot paprika, plus more to taste	2 tablespoons fresh lemon juice
½ cup red lentils, rinsed	Kosher salt, to taste
⅓ cup bulgur wheat	
1 tablespoon tomato paste	

1. In a large saucepan over medium heat, warm the oil until shimmering. Cook the onion, stirring, until golden, about 10 minutes. 2. Stir in the paprika, lentils, and bulgur to coat in the oil. Add the tomato paste and cook, stirring, until the color darkens, about 2 minutes. 3. Add the broth and bring to a boil. Reduce the heat to a simmer and cook, stirring occasionally to avoid sticking, until the lentils and bulgur are tender and creamy, about 40 minutes. 4. Stir in the mint and lemon juice. Season to taste with the salt.

Per Serving

Calories: 206 | fat: 8g | protein: 9g | carbs: 27g | fiber: 7g | sodium: 139mg

Cauliflower & Blue Cheese Soup

Prep time: 15 minutes | Cook time: 20 minutes | Serves 5

2 tablespoons extra-virgin avocado oil	whipping cream
1 small red onion, diced	Salt and black pepper, to taste
1 medium celery stalk, sliced	1 cup crumbled goat's or sheep's blue cheese, such as Roquefort
1 medium cauliflower, cut into small florets	2 tablespoons chopped fresh chives
2 cups vegetable or chicken stock	5 tablespoons extra-virgin olive oil
¼ cup goat's cream or heavy	

1. Heat a medium saucepan greased with the avocado oil over medium heat. Sweat the onion and celery for 3 to 5 minutes, until soft and fragrant. Add the cauliflower florets and cook for 5 minutes. Add the vegetable stock and bring to a boil. Cook for about 10 minutes, or until the cauliflower is tender. Remove from the heat and let cool for a few minutes. 2. Add the cream. Use an immersion blender, or pour into a blender, to process until smooth and creamy. Season with salt and pepper to taste. Divide the soup between serving bowls and top with the crumbled blue cheese, chives, and olive oil. To store, let cool and refrigerate in a sealed container for up to 5 days.

Per Serving

Calories: 337 | fat: 30g | protein: 10g | carbs: 9g | fiber: 3g | sodium: 383mg

Spicy Carrot-Orange Soup

Prep time: 15 minutes | Cook time: 35 minutes | Serves 6

2 tablespoons olive oil
1 small onion, chopped (about 1 cup)
2 garlic cloves, chopped
4 cups no-salt-added vegetable broth or chicken broth
1 pound (454 g) carrots, coarsely chopped (2½ cups)

Zest and juice of 1 orange (about 1 tablespoon zest and ⅓ cup juice)
1 tablespoon Aleppo pepper
1 teaspoon salt
2 tablespoons Greek yogurt (optional)

1. In a large saucepan, heat the oil over medium heat. Add the onion and cook until starting to soften but not brown, 7 to 8 minutes. 2. Add the garlic and cook for 1 minute, or until fragrant. 3. Add the broth, carrots, orange zest, orange juice, and Aleppo pepper; bring to a boil. Reduce the heat to maintain a simmer and cook for 20 to 25 minutes, until the vegetables are tender. 4. Using a hand blender (or a regular blender, working in batches), blend the soup until smooth. 5. Ladle the soup into bowls, top with a little yogurt, if desired, and serve.

Per Serving 1 cup:
Calories: 125 | fat: 5g | protein: 3g | carbs: 18g | fiber: 6g | sodium: 467mg

Sweet and Crispy Roasted Pearl Onions

Prep time: 5 minutes | Cook time: 18 minutes | Serves 3

1 (14½-ounce / 411-g) package frozen pearl onions (do not thaw)
2 tablespoons extra-virgin olive oil
2 tablespoons balsamic vinegar
2 teaspoons finely chopped fresh rosemary
½ teaspoon kosher salt
¼ teaspoon black pepper

1. In a medium bowl, combine the onions, olive oil, vinegar, rosemary, salt, and pepper until well coated. 2. Transfer the onions to the air fryer basket. Set the air fryer to 400°F (204°C) for 18 minutes, or until the onions are tender and lightly charred, stirring once or twice during the cooking time.

Per Serving
Calories: 145 | fat: 9g | protein: 2g | carbs: 15g | fiber: 2g | sodium: 396mg

Parsnip Fries with Romesco Sauce

Prep time: 20 minutes | Cook time: 24 minutes | Serves 4

Romesco Sauce:
1 red bell pepper, halved and seeded
1 (1-inch) thick slice of Italian bread, torn into pieces (about 1 to 1½ cups)
1 cup almonds, toasted
Olive oil
½ Jalapeño pepper, seeded
1 tablespoon fresh parsley leaves
1 clove garlic
2 Roma tomatoes, peeled and seeded (or ⅓ cup canned crushed tomatoes)
1 tablespoon red wine vinegar
¼ teaspoon smoked paprika
½ teaspoon salt
¾ cup olive oil
3 parsnips, peeled and cut into long strips
2 teaspoons olive oil
Salt and freshly ground black pepper, to taste

1. Preheat the air fryer to 400°F (204°C). 2. Place the red pepper halves, cut side down, in the air fryer basket and air fry for 8 to 10 minutes, or until the skin turns black all over. Remove the pepper from the air fryer and let it cool. When it is cool enough to handle, peel the pepper. 3. Toss the torn bread and almonds with a little olive oil and air fry for 4 minutes, shaking the basket a couple times throughout the cooking time. When the bread and almonds are nicely toasted, remove them from the air fryer and let them cool for just a minute or two. 4. Combine the toasted bread, almonds, roasted red pepper, Jalapeño pepper, parsley, garlic, tomatoes, vinegar, smoked paprika and salt in a food processor or blender. Process until smooth. With the processor running, add the olive oil through the feed tube until the sauce comes together in a smooth paste that is barely

pourable. 5. Toss the parsnip strips with the olive oil, salt and freshly ground black pepper and air fry at 400°F (204°C) for 10 minutes, shaking the basket a couple times during the cooking process so they brown and cook evenly. Serve the parsnip fries warm with the Romesco sauce to dip into.

Per Serving
Calories: 604 | fat: 55g | protein: 7g | carbs: 55g | fiber: 8g | sodium: 319mg

Sweet-and-Sour Brussels Sprouts

Prep time: 10 minutes | Cook time: 20 minutes | Serves 2

¼ cup Thai sweet chili sauce
2 tablespoons black vinegar or balsamic vinegar
½ teaspoon hot sauce, such as Tabasco
8 ounces (227 g) Brussels sprouts, trimmed (large sprouts halved)
2 small shallots, cut into ¼-inch-thick slices
Kosher salt and freshly ground black pepper, to taste
2 teaspoons lightly packed fresh cilantro leaves

1. In a large bowl, whisk together the chili sauce, vinegar, and hot sauce. Add the Brussels sprouts and shallots, season with salt and pepper, and toss to combine. Scrape the Brussels sprouts and sauce into a cake pan. 2. Place the pan in the air fryer and roast at 375°F (191°C), stirring every 5 minutes, until the Brussels sprouts are tender and the sauce is reduced to a sticky glaze, about 20 minutes. 3. Remove the pan from the air fryer and transfer the Brussels sprouts to plates. Sprinkle with the cilantro and serve warm.

Per Serving
Calories: 106 | fat: 0g | protein: 5g | carbs: 21g | fiber: 7g | sodium: 498mg

Spinach and Sweet Pepper Poppers

Prep time: 10 minutes | Cook time: 8 minutes | Makes 16 poppers

4 ounces (113 g) cream cheese, softened
1 cup chopped fresh spinach leaves
½ teaspoon garlic powder
8 mini sweet bell peppers, tops removed, seeded, and halved lengthwise

1. In a medium bowl, mix cream cheese, spinach, and garlic powder. Place 1 tablespoon mixture into each sweet pepper half and press down to smooth. 2. Place poppers into ungreased air fryer basket. Adjust the temperature to 400°F (204°C) and air fry for 8 minutes. Poppers will be done when cheese is browned on top and peppers are tender-crisp. Serve warm.

Per Serving
Calories: 31 | fat: 2g | protein: 1g | carbs: 3g | fiber: 0g | sodium: 34mg

Five-Spice Roasted Sweet Potatoes

Prep time: 10 minutes | Cook time: 12 minutes | Serves 4

½ teaspoon ground cinnamon
¼ teaspoon ground cumin
¼ teaspoon paprika
1 teaspoon chile powder
⅛ teaspoon turmeric
½ teaspoon salt (optional)

Freshly ground black pepper, to taste
2 large sweet potatoes, peeled and cut into ¾-inch cubes (about 3 cups)
1 tablespoon olive oil

1. In a large bowl, mix together cinnamon, cumin, paprika, chile powder, turmeric, salt, and pepper to taste. 2. Add potatoes and stir well. 3. Drizzle the seasoned potatoes with the olive oil and stir until evenly coated. 4. Place seasoned potatoes in a baking pan or an ovenproof dish that fits inside your air fryer basket. 5. Cook for 6 minutes at 390ºF (199ºC), stop, and stir well. 6. Cook for an additional 6 minutes.

Per Serving
Calories: 14 | fat: 3g | protein: 1g | carbs: 14g | fiber: 2g | sodium: 327mg

Gorgonzola Sweet Potato Burgers

Prep time: 10 minutes |Cook time: 15 minutes| Serves: 4

1 large sweet potato (about 8 ounces / 227 g)
2 tablespoons extra-virgin olive oil, divided
1 cup chopped onion (about ½ medium onion)
1 cup old-fashioned rolled oats
1 large egg
1 tablespoon balsamic vinegar

1 tablespoon dried oregano
1 garlic clove
¼ teaspoon kosher or sea salt
½ cup crumbled Gorgonzola or blue cheese (about 2 ounces / 57 g)
Salad greens or 4 whole-wheat rolls, for serving (optional)

1. Using a fork, pierce the sweet potato all over and microwave on high for 4 to 5 minutes, until tender in the center. Cool slightly, then slice in half. 2. While the sweet potato is cooking, in a large skillet over medium-high heat, heat 1 tablespoon of oil. Add the onion and cook for 5 minutes, stirring occasionally. 3. Using a spoon, carefully scoop the sweet potato flesh out of the skin and put the flesh in a food processor. Add the onion, oats, egg, vinegar, oregano, garlic, and salt. Process until smooth. Add the cheese and pulse four times to barely combine. With your hands, form the mixture into four (½-cup-size) burgers. Place the burgers on a plate, and press to flatten each to about ¾-inch thick. 4. Wipe out the skillet with a paper towel, then heat the remaining 1 tablespoon of oil over medium-high heat until very hot, about 2 minutes. Add the burgers to the hot oil, then turn the heat down to medium. Cook the burgers for 5 minutes, flip with a spatula, then cook an additional 5 minutes. Enjoy as is or serve on salad greens or whole-wheat rolls.

Per Serving
Calories: 337 | fat: 16g | protein: 13g | carbs: 38g | fiber: 6g | sodium: 378mg

Garlic-Parmesan Crispy Baby Potatoes

Prep time: 10 minutes | Cook time: 15 minutes | Serves 4

Oil, for spraying
1 pound (454 g) baby potatoes
½ cup grated Parmesan cheese, divided
3 tablespoons olive oil
2 teaspoons granulated garlic
½ teaspoon onion powder

½ teaspoon salt
¼ teaspoon freshly ground black pepper
¼ teaspoon paprika
2 tablespoons chopped fresh parsley, for garnish

1. Line the air fryer basket with parchment and spray lightly with oil. 2. Rinse the potatoes, pat dry with paper towels, and place in a large bowl. 3. In a small bowl, mix together ¼ cup of Parmesan cheese, the olive oil, garlic, onion powder, salt, black pepper, and paprika. Pour the mixture over the potatoes and toss to coat. 4. Transfer the potatoes to the prepared basket and spread them out in an even layer, taking care to keep them from touching. You may need to work in batches, depending on the size of your air fryer. 5. Air fry at 400ºF (204ºC) for 15 minutes, stirring after 7 to 8 minutes, or until easily pierced with a fork. Continue to cook for another 1 to 2 minutes, if needed. 6. Sprinkle with the parsley and the remaining Parmesan cheese and serve.

Per Serving
Calories: 234 | fat: 14g | protein: 6g | carbs: 22g | fiber: 3g | sodium: 525mg

Sesame Carrots and Sugar Snap Peas

Prep time: 10 minutes | Cook time: 16 minutes | Serves 4

1 pound (454 g) carrots, peeled sliced on the bias (½-inch slices)
1 teaspoon olive oil
Salt and freshly ground black pepper, to taste
⅓ cup honey

1 tablespoon sesame oil
1 tablespoon soy sauce
½ teaspoon minced fresh ginger
4 ounces (113 g) sugar snap peas (about 1 cup)
1½ teaspoons sesame seeds

1. Preheat the air fryer to 360ºF (182ºC). 2. Toss the carrots with the olive oil, season with salt and pepper and air fry for 10 minutes, shaking the basket once or twice during the cooking process. 3. Combine the honey, sesame oil, soy sauce and minced ginger in a large bowl. Add the sugar snap peas and the air-fried carrots to the honey mixture, toss to coat and return everything to the air fryer basket. 4. Turn up the temperature to 400ºF (204ºC) and air fry for an additional 6 minutes, shaking the basket once during the cooking process. 5. Transfer the carrots and sugar snap peas to a serving bowl. Pour the sauce from the bottom of the cooker over the vegetables and sprinkle sesame seeds over top. Serve immediately.

Per Serving
Calories: 202 | fat: 6g | protein: 2g | carbs: 37g | fiber: 4g | sodium: 141mg

Garlicky Broccoli Rabe with Artichokes

Prep time: 5 minutes | Cook time: 10 minutes | Serves 4

2 pounds (907 g) fresh broccoli rabe
½ cup extra-virgin olive oil, divided
3 garlic cloves, finely minced
1 teaspoon salt
1 teaspoon red pepper flakes

1 (13¾-ounce / 390-g) can artichoke hearts, drained and quartered
1 tablespoon water
2 tablespoons red wine vinegar
Freshly ground black pepper

1. Trim away any thick lower stems and yellow leaves from the broccoli rabe and discard. Cut into individual florets with a couple inches of thin stem attached. 2. In a large skillet, heat ¼ cup olive oil over medium-high heat. Add the trimmed broccoli, garlic, salt, and red pepper flakes and sauté for 5 minutes, until the broccoli begins to soften. Add the artichoke hearts and sauté for another 2 minutes. 3. Add the water and reduce the heat to low. Cover and simmer until the broccoli stems are tender, 3 to 5 minutes. 4. In a small bowl, whisk together remaining ¼ cup olive oil and the vinegar. Drizzle over the broccoli and artichokes. Season with ground black pepper, if desired.

Per Serving

Calories: 341 | fat: 28g | protein: 11g | carbs: 18g | fiber: 12g | sodium: 750mg

Mediterranean Cauliflower Tabbouleh

Prep time: 15 minutes | Cook time: 5 minutes | Serves 6

6 tablespoons extra-virgin olive oil, divided
4 cups riced cauliflower
3 garlic cloves, finely minced
1½ teaspoons salt
½ teaspoon freshly ground black pepper
½ large cucumber, peeled, seeded, and chopped
½ cup chopped mint leaves
½ cup chopped Italian parsley
½ cup chopped pitted

Kalamata olives
2 tablespoons minced red onion
Juice of 1 lemon (about 2 tablespoons)
2 cups baby arugula or spinach leaves
2 medium avocados, peeled, pitted, and diced
1 cup quartered cherry tomatoes

1. In a large skillet, heat 2 tablespoons of olive oil over medium-high heat. Add the riced cauliflower, garlic, salt, and pepper and sauté until just tender but not mushy, 3 to 4 minutes. Remove from the heat and place in a large bowl. 2. Add the cucumber, mint, parsley, olives, red onion, lemon juice, and remaining 4 tablespoons olive oil and toss well. Place in the refrigerator, uncovered, and refrigerate for at least 30 minutes, or up to 2 hours. 3. Before serving, add the arugula, avocado, and tomatoes and toss to combine well. Season to taste with salt and pepper and serve cold or at room temperature.

Per Serving

Calories: 273 | fat: 25g | protein: 4g | carbs: 13g | fiber: 7g | sodium: 697mg

Braised Greens with Olives and Walnuts

Prep time: 5 minutes | Cook time: 20 minutes | Serves 4

8 cups fresh greens (such as kale, mustard greens, spinach, or chard)
2 to 4 garlic cloves, finely minced
½ cup roughly chopped pitted green or black olives
½ cup roughly chopped shelled

walnuts
¼ cup extra-virgin olive oil
2 tablespoons red wine vinegar
1 to 2 teaspoons freshly chopped herbs such as oregano, basil, rosemary, or thyme

1. Remove the tough stems from the greens and chop into bite-size pieces. Place in a large rimmed skillet or pot. 2. Turn the heat to high and add the minced garlic and enough water to just cover the greens. Bring to a boil, reduce the heat to low, and simmer until the greens are wilted and tender and most of the liquid has evaporated, adding more if the greens start to burn. For more tender greens such as spinach, this may only take 5 minutes, while tougher greens such as chard may need up to 20 minutes. Once cooked, remove from the heat and add the chopped olives and walnuts. 3. In a small bowl, whisk together olive oil, vinegar, and herbs. Drizzle over the cooked greens and toss to coat. Serve warm.

Per Serving

Calories: 254 | fat: 25g | protein: 4g | carbs: 6g | fiber: 3g | sodium: 137mg

Mediterranean Lentil Sloppy Joes

Prep time: 5 minutes |Cook time: 15 minutes| Serves: 4

1 tablespoon extra-virgin olive oil
1 cup chopped onion (about ½ medium onion)
1 cup chopped bell pepper, any color (about 1 medium bell pepper)
2 garlic cloves, minced (about 1 teaspoon)
1 (15-ounce / 425-g) can lentils, drained and rinsed
1 (14½-ounce / 411-g) can

low-sodium or no-salt-added diced tomatoes, undrained
1 teaspoon ground cumin
1 teaspoon dried thyme
¼ teaspoon kosher or sea salt
4 whole-wheat pita breads, split open
1½ cups chopped seedless cucumber (1 medium cucumber)
1 cup chopped romaine lettuce

1. In a medium saucepan over medium-high heat, heat the oil. Add the onion and bell pepper and cook for 4 minutes, stirring frequently. Add the garlic and cook for 1 minute, stirring frequently. Add the lentils, tomatoes (with their liquid), cumin, thyme, and salt. Turn the heat to medium and cook, stirring occasionally, for 10 minutes, or until most of the liquid has evaporated. 2. Stuff the lentil mixture inside each pita. Lay the cucumbers and lettuce on top of the lentil mixture and serve.

Per Serving

Calories: 530 | fat: 6g | protein: 31g | carbs: 93g | fiber: 17g | sodium: 292mg

Braised Fennel with radicchio, Pear, and Pecorino

Prep time: 20 minutes | Cook time: 12 minutes | Serves 4

6 tablespoons extra-virgin olive oil, divided
2 fennel bulbs (12 ounces / 340 g each), 2 tablespoons fronds chopped, stalks discarded, bulbs halved, each half cut into 1-inch-thick wedges
¾ teaspoon table salt, divided
½ teaspoon grated lemon zest plus 4 teaspoons juice

5 ounces (142 g) baby arugula
1 small head radicchio (6 ounces / 170 g), shredded
1 Bosc or Bartlett pear, quartered, cored, and sliced thin
¼ cup whole almonds, toasted and chopped
Shaved Pecorino Romano cheese

1. Using highest sauté function, heat 2 tablespoons oil in Instant Pot for 5 minutes (or until just smoking). Brown half of fennel, about 3 minutes per side; transfer to plate. Repeat with 1 tablespoon oil and remaining fennel; do not remove from pot. 2. Return first batch of fennel to pot along with ½ cup water and ½ teaspoon salt. Lock lid in place and close pressure release valve. Select high pressure cook function and cook for 2 minutes. Turn off Instant Pot and quick-release pressure. Carefully remove lid, allowing steam to escape away from you. Using slotted spoon, transfer fennel to plate; discard cooking liquid. 3. Whisk remaining 3 tablespoons oil, lemon zest and juice, and remaining ¼ teaspoon salt together in large bowl. Add arugula, radicchio, and pear and toss to coat. Transfer arugula mixture to serving dish and arrange fennel wedges on top. Sprinkle with almonds, fennel fronds, and Pecorino. Serve.

Per Serving
Calories: 290 | fat: 26g | protein: 5g | carbs: 22g | fiber: 7g | sodium: 300mg

Polenta with Mushroom Bolognese

Prep time: 5 minutes |Cook time: 25 minutes| Serves: 4

2 (8-ounce / 227-g) packages white button mushrooms
3 tablespoons extra-virgin olive oil, divided
1½ cups finely chopped onion (about ¾ medium onion)
½ cup finely chopped carrot (about 1 medium carrot)
4 garlic cloves, minced (about 2 teaspoons)
1 (18-ounce / 510-g) tube plain

polenta, cut into 8 slices
¼ cup tomato paste
1 tablespoon dried oregano, crushed between your fingers
¼ teaspoon ground nutmeg
¼ teaspoon kosher or sea salt
¼ teaspoon freshly ground black pepper
½ cup dry red wine
½ cup whole milk
½ teaspoon sugar

1. Put half the mushrooms in a food processor bowl and pulse about 15 times until finely chopped but not puréed, similar to the texture of ground meat. Repeat with the remaining mushrooms and set aside. (You can also use the food processor to chop the onion, carrot, and garlic, instead of chopping with a knife.) 2. In a large stockpot over medium-high heat, heat 2 tablespoons of oil. Add the onion and carrot and cook for 5 minutes, stirring occasionally. Add the mushrooms and

garlic and cook for 5 minutes, stirring frequently. 3. While the vegetables are cooking, add the remaining 1 tablespoon of oil to a large skillet and heat over medium-high heat. Add 4 slices of polenta to the skillet and cook for 3 to 4 minutes, until golden; flip and cook for 3 to 4 minutes more. Remove the polenta from the skillet, place it on a shallow serving dish, and cover with aluminum foil to keep warm. Repeat with the remaining 4 slices of polenta. 4. To the mushroom mixture in the stockpot, add the tomato paste, oregano, nutmeg, salt, and pepper and stir. Continue cooking for another 2 to 3 minutes, until the vegetables have softened and begun to brown. Add the wine and cook for 1 to 2 minutes, scraping up any bits from the bottom of the pan while stirring with a wooden spoon. Cook until the wine is nearly all evaporated. Lower the heat to medium. 5. Meanwhile, in a small, microwave-safe bowl, mix the milk and sugar together and microwave on high for 30 to 45 seconds, until very hot. Slowly stir the milk into the mushroom mixture and simmer for 4 more minutes, until the milk is absorbed. To serve, pour the mushroom veggie sauce over the warm polenta slices.

Per Serving
Calories: 313 | fat: 12g | protein: 7g | carbs: 41g | fiber: 4g | sodium: 467mg

Individual Asparagus and Goat Cheese Frittatas

Prep time: 15 minutes | Cook time: 15 minutes | Serves 4

1 tablespoon extra-virgin olive oil
8 ounces (227 g) asparagus, trimmed and sliced ¼ inch thick
1 red bell pepper, stemmed, seeded, and chopped
2 shallots, minced

2 ounces (57 g) goat cheese, crumbled (½ cup)
1 tablespoon minced fresh tarragon
1 teaspoon grated lemon zest
8 large eggs
½ teaspoon table salt

1. Using highest sauté function, heat oil in Instant Pot until shimmering. Add asparagus, bell pepper, and shallots; cook until softened, about 5 minutes. Turn off Instant Pot and transfer vegetables to bowl. Stir in goat cheese, tarragon, and lemon zest. 2. Arrange trivet included with Instant Pot in base of now-empty insert and add 1 cup water. Spray four 6-ounce ramekins with vegetable oil spray. Beat eggs, ¼ cup water, and salt in large bowl until thoroughly combined. Divide vegetable mixture between prepared ramekins, then pour egg mixture over top (you may have some left over). Set ramekins on trivet. Lock lid in place and close pressure release valve. Select high pressure cook function and cook for 10 minutes. 3. Turn off Instant Pot and quick-release pressure. Carefully remove lid, allowing steam to escape away from you. Using tongs, transfer ramekins to wire rack and let cool slightly. Run paring knife around inside edge of ramekins to loosen frittatas, then invert onto individual serving plates. Serve.

Per Serving
Calories: 240 | fat: 16g | protein: 17g | carbs: 6g | fiber: 2g | sodium: 500mg

Crispy Garlic Oven Potatoes

Prep time: 30 minutes | Cook time: 30 minutes | Serves 2

10 ounces (283 g) golden mini potatoes, halved
4 tablespoons extra-virgin olive oil
2 teaspoons dried, minced garlic
1 teaspoon onion salt
½ teaspoon paprika
¼ teaspoon freshly ground black pepper
¼ teaspoon red pepper flakes
¼ teaspoon dried dill

1. Preheat the oven to 400ºF (205ºC). 2. Soak the potatoes and put in a bowl of ice water for 30 minutes. Change the water if you return and the water is milky. 3. Rinse and dry the potatoes, then put them on a baking sheet. 4. Drizzle the potatoes with oil and sprinkle with the garlic, onion salt, paprika, pepper, red pepper flakes, and dill. Using tongs or your hands, toss well to coat. 5. Lower the heat to 375ºF (190ºC), add potatoes to the oven, and bake for 20 minutes. 6. At 20 minutes, check and flip potatoes. Bake for another 10 minutes, or until the potatoes are fork-tender.

Per Serving (½ cup)
Calories: 344 | fat: 28g | protein: 3g | carbs: 24g | fiber: 4g | sodium: 723mg

Parmesan and Herb Sweet Potatoes

Prep time: 10 minutes | Cook time: 18 minutes | Serves 4

2 large sweet potatoes, peeled and cubed
¼ cup olive oil
1 teaspoon dried rosemary
½ teaspoon salt
2 tablespoons shredded Parmesan

1. Preheat the air fryer to 360ºF (182ºC). 2. In a large bowl, toss the sweet potatoes with the olive oil, rosemary, and salt. 3. Pour the potatoes into the air fryer basket and roast for 10 minutes, then stir the potatoes and sprinkle the Parmesan over the top. Continue roasting for 8 minutes more. 4. Serve hot and enjoy.

Per Serving
Calories: 186 | fat: 14g | protein: 2g | carbs: 13g | fiber: 2g | sodium: 369mg

Green Beans with Potatoes and Basil

Prep time: 20 minutes | Cook time: 10 minutes | Serves 4

2 tablespoons extra-virgin olive oil, plus extra for drizzling
1 onion, chopped fine
2 tablespoons minced fresh oregano or 2 teaspoons dried
2 tablespoons tomato paste
4 garlic cloves, minced
1 (14½-ounce / 411-g) can whole peeled tomatoes,
drained with juice reserved, chopped
1 cup water
1 teaspoon table salt
¼ teaspoon pepper
1½ pounds (680 g) green beans, trimmed and cut into 2-inch lengths
1 pound (454 g) Yukon Gold potatoes, peeled and cut into

1-inch pieces
3 tablespoons chopped fresh basil or parsley
2 tablespoons toasted pine nuts
Shaved Parmesan cheese

1. Using highest sauté function, heat oil in Instant Pot until shimmering. Add onion and cook until softened, about 5 minutes. Stir in oregano, tomato paste, and garlic and cook until fragrant, about 30 seconds. Stir in tomatoes and their juice, water, salt, and pepper, then stir in green beans and potatoes. Lock lid in place and close pressure release valve. Select high pressure cook function and cook for 5 minutes. 2. Turn off Instant Pot and quick-release pressure. Carefully remove lid, allowing steam to escape away from you. Season with salt and pepper to taste. Sprinkle individual portions with basil, pine nuts, and Parmesan and drizzle with extra oil. Serve.

Per Serving
Calories: 280 | fat: 10g | protein: 7g | carbs: 42g | fiber: 8g | sodium: 880mg

Grilled Stuffed Portabello Mushrooms

Prep time: 5 minutes |Cook time: 25 minutes| Serves: 6

3 tablespoons extra-virgin olive oil, divided
1 cup diced onion (about ½ medium onion)
2 garlic cloves, minced (about 1 teaspoon)
3 cups chopped mushrooms, any variety
1 large or 2 small zucchini or summer squash, diced (about 2 cups)
1 cup chopped tomato (about 1 large tomato)
1 teaspoon dried oregano
¼ teaspoon crushed red pepper
¼ teaspoon kosher or sea salt
6 large portabello mushrooms, stems and gills removed
Nonstick cooking spray (if needed)
4 ounces (113 g) fresh mozzarella cheese, shredded
Additional dried oregano, for serving (optional)

1. In a large skillet over medium heat, heat 2 tablespoons of oil. Add the onion and cook for 4 minutes, stirring occasionally. Stir in the garlic and cook for 1 minute, stirring often. 2. Stir in the mushrooms, zucchini, tomato, oregano, crushed red pepper, and salt. Cook for 10 minutes, stirring occasionally. Remove from the heat. 3. While the veggies are cooking, heat the grill or grill pan to medium-high heat. 4. Brush the remaining tablespoon of oil over the portabello mushroom caps. Place the mushrooms bottom-side (where the stem was removed) down on the grill or pan. Cover and cook for 5 minutes. (If using a grill pan, cover with a sheet of aluminum foil sprayed with nonstick cooking spray.) 5. Flip the mushroom caps over, and spoon about ½ cup of the cooked vegetable mixture into each cap. Top each with about 2½ tablespoons of mozzarella and additional oregano, if desired. 6. Cover and grill for 4 to 5 minutes, or until the cheese melts. 7. Remove each portabello with a spatula, and let them sit for about 5 minutes to cool slightly before serving.

Per Serving
Calories: 140 | fat: 8g | protein: 10g | carbs: 11g | fiber: 3g | sodium: 254mg

Roasted Grape Tomatoes and Asparagus

Prep time: 5 minutes | Cook time: 12 minutes | Serves 6

2 cups grape tomatoes
1 bunch asparagus, trimmed
2 tablespoons olive oil

3 garlic cloves, minced
½ teaspoon kosher salt

1. Preheat the air fryer to 380ºF. 2. In a large bowl, combine all of the ingredients, tossing until the vegetables are well coated with oil. 3. Pour the vegetable mixture into the air fryer basket and spread into a single layer, then roast for 12 minutes.
Per Serving
Calories: 56 | fat: 5g | protein: 1g | carbs: 3g | fiber: 1g | sodium: 197mg

Citrus-Roasted Broccoli Florets

Prep time: 5 minutes | Cook time: 12 minutes | Serves 6

4 cups broccoli florets
(approximately 1 large head)
2 tablespoons olive oil
½ teaspoon salt

½ cup orange juice
1 tablespoon raw honey
Orange wedges, for serving
(optional)

1. Preheat the air fryer to 360ºF (182ºC). 2. In a large bowl, combine the broccoli, olive oil, salt, orange juice, and honey. Toss the broccoli in the liquid until well coated. 3. Pour the broccoli mixture into the air fryer basket and roast for 6 minutes. Stir and roast for 6 minutes more. 4. Serve alone or with orange wedges for additional citrus flavor, if desired.
Per Serving
Calories: 73 | fat: 5g | protein: 2g | carbs: 8g | fiber: 0g | sodium: 207mg

Crispy Garlic Sliced Eggplant

Prep time: 5 minutes | Cook time: 25 minutes | Serves 4

1 egg
1 tablespoon water
½ cup whole wheat bread
crumbs
1 teaspoon garlic powder
½ teaspoon dried oregano

½ teaspoon salt
½ teaspoon paprika
1 medium eggplant, sliced into
¼-inch-thick rounds
1 tablespoon olive oil

1. Preheat the air fryer to 360ºF (182ºC). 2. In a medium shallow bowl, beat together the egg and water until frothy. 3. In a separate medium shallow bowl, mix together bread crumbs, garlic powder, oregano, salt, and paprika. 4. Dip each eggplant slice into the egg mixture, then into the bread crumb mixture, coating the outside with crumbs. Place the slices in a single layer in the bottom of the air fryer basket. 5. Drizzle the tops of the eggplant slices with the olive oil, then fry for 15 minutes. Turn each slice and cook for an additional 10 minutes.
Per Serving
Calories: 137 | fat: 5g | protein: 5g | carbs: 19g | fiber: 5g | sodium: 409mg

Crispy Lemon Artichoke Hearts

Prep time: 10 minutes | Cook time: 15 minutes | Serves 2

1 (15-ounce / 425-g) can
artichoke hearts in water,
drained
1 egg
1 tablespoon water

¼ cup whole wheat bread
crumbs
¼ teaspoon salt
¼ teaspoon paprika
½ lemon

1. Preheat the air fryer to 380ºF (193ºC). 2. In a medium shallow bowl, beat together the egg and water until frothy. 3. In a separate medium shallow bowl, mix together the bread crumbs, salt, and paprika. 4. Dip each artichoke heart into the egg mixture, then into the bread crumb mixture, coating the outside with the crumbs. Place the artichokes hearts in a single layer of the air fryer basket. 5. Fry the artichoke hearts for 15 minutes. 6. Remove the artichokes from the air fryer, and squeeze fresh lemon juice over the top before serving.
Per Serving
Calories: 190 | fat: 3g | protein: 12g | carbs: 34g | fiber: 13g | sodium: 621mg

Dill-and-Garlic Beets

Prep time: 10 minutes | Cook time: 30 minutes | Serves 4

4 beets, cleaned, peeled, and
sliced
1 garlic clove, minced
2 tablespoons chopped fresh

dill
¼ teaspoon salt
¼ teaspoon black pepper
3 tablespoons olive oil

1. Preheat the air fryer to 380ºF (193ºC). 2. In a large bowl, mix together all of the ingredients so the beets are well coated with the oil. 3. Pour the beet mixture into the air fryer basket, and roast for 15 minutes before stirring, then continue roasting for 15 minutes more.
Per Serving
Calories: 136 | fat: 2g | protein: 2g | carbs: 10g | fiber: 3g | sodium: 210mg

Spiced Honey-Walnut Carrots

Prep time: 5 minutes | Cook time: 12 minutes | Serves 6

1 pound (454 g) baby carrots
2 tablespoons olive oil
¼ cup raw honey

¼ teaspoon ground cinnamon
¼ cup black walnuts, chopped

1. Preheat the air fryer to 360ºF (182ºC). 2. In a large bowl, toss the baby carrots with olive oil, honey, and cinnamon until well coated. 3. Pour into the air fryer and roast for 6 minutes. Shake the basket, sprinkle the walnuts on top, and roast for 6 minutes more. 4. Remove the carrots from the air fryer and serve.
Per Serving
Calories: 142 | fat: 8g | protein: 2g | carbs: 18g | fiber: 3g | sodium: 60mg

Rustic Cauliflower and Carrot Hash

Prep time: 10 minutes | Cook time: 10 minutes | Serves 4

3 tablespoons extra-virgin olive oil
1 large onion, chopped
1 tablespoon garlic, minced
2 cups carrots, diced

4 cups cauliflower pieces, washed
1 teaspoon salt
½ teaspoon ground cumin

1. In a large skillet over medium heat, cook the olive oil, onion, garlic, and carrots for 3 minutes. 2. Cut the cauliflower into 1-inch or bite-size pieces. Add the cauliflower, salt, and cumin to the skillet and toss to combine with the carrots and onions. 3. Cover and cook for 3 minutes. 4. Toss the vegetables and continue to cook uncovered for an additional 3 to 4 minutes. 5. Serve warm.

Per Serving
Calories: 159 | fat: 11g | protein: 3g | carbs: 15g | fiber: 5g | sodium: 657mg

Roasted Cauliflower and Tomatoes

Prep time: 5 minutes | Cook time: 25 minutes | Serves 4

4 cups cauliflower, cut into 1-inch pieces
6 tablespoons extra-virgin olive oil, divided
1 teaspoon salt, divided

4 cups cherry tomatoes
½ teaspoon freshly ground black pepper
½ cup grated Parmesan cheese

1. Preheat the oven to 425°F (220°C). 2. Add the cauliflower, 3 tablespoons of olive oil, and ½ teaspoon of salt to a large bowl and toss to evenly coat. Pour onto a baking sheet and spread the cauliflower out in an even layer. 3. In another large bowl, add the tomatoes, remaining 3 tablespoons of olive oil, and ½ teaspoon of salt, and toss to coat evenly. Pour onto a different baking sheet. 4. Put the sheet of cauliflower and the sheet of tomatoes in the oven to roast for 17 to 20 minutes until the cauliflower is lightly browned and tomatoes are plump. 5. Using a spatula, spoon the cauliflower into a serving dish, and top with tomatoes, black pepper, and Parmesan cheese. Serve warm.

Per Serving
Calories: 294 | fat: 26g | protein: 9g | carbs: 13g | fiber: 4g | sodium: 858mg

Garlicky Sautéed Zucchini with Mint

Prep time: 5 minutes | Cook time: 10 minutes | Serves 4

3 large green zucchini
3 tablespoons extra-virgin olive oil
1 large onion, chopped

3 cloves garlic, minced
1 teaspoon salt
1 teaspoon dried mint

1. Cut the zucchini into ½-inch cubes. 2. In a large skillet over medium heat, cook the olive oil, onions, and garlic for 3 minutes, stirring constantly. 3. Add the zucchini and salt to the skillet and toss to combine with the onions and garlic, cooking for 5 minutes. 4. Add the mint to the skillet, tossing to combine. Cook for another 2 minutes. Serve warm.

Per Serving
Calories: 147 | fat: 11g | protein: 4g | carbs: 12g | fiber: 3g | sodium: 607mg

Rosemary-Roasted Red Potatoes

Prep time: 5 minutes | Cook time: 20 minutes | Serves 6

1 pound (454 g) red potatoes, quartered
¼ cup olive oil
½ teaspoon kosher salt

¼ teaspoon black pepper
1 garlic clove, minced
4 rosemary sprigs

1. Preheat the air fryer to 360°F (182°C). 2. In a large bowl, toss the potatoes with the olive oil, salt, pepper, and garlic until well coated. 3. Pour the potatoes into the air fryer basket and top with the sprigs of rosemary. 4. Roast for 10 minutes, then stir or toss the potatoes and roast for 10 minutes more. 5. Remove the rosemary sprigs and serve the potatoes. Season with additional salt and pepper, if needed.

Per Serving
Calories: 134 | fat: 9g | protein: 1g | carbs: 12g | fiber: 1g | sodium: 208mg

Parmesan-Thyme Butternut Squash

Prep time: 15 minutes | Cook time: 20 minutes | Serves 4

2½ cups butternut squash, cubed into 1-inch pieces (approximately 1 medium)
2 tablespoons olive oil
¼ teaspoon salt

¼ teaspoon garlic powder
¼ teaspoon black pepper
1 tablespoon fresh thyme
¼ cup grated Parmesan

1. Preheat the air fryer to 360°F (182°C). 2. In a large bowl, combine the cubed squash with the olive oil, salt, garlic powder, pepper, and thyme until the squash is well coated. 3. Pour this mixture into the air fryer basket, and roast for 10 minutes. Stir and roast another 8 to 10 minutes more. 4. Remove the squash from the air fryer and toss with freshly grated Parmesan before serving.

Per Serving
Calories: 127 | fat: 9g | protein: 3g | carbs: 12g | fiber: 2g | sodium: 262mg

Roasted Radishes with Sea Salt

Prep time: 5 minutes | Cook time: 18 minutes | Serves 4

1 pound (454 g) radishes, ends trimmed if needed
2 tablespoons olive oil

½ teaspoon sea salt

1. Preheat the air fryer to 360°F (182°C). 2. In a large bowl, combine the radishes with olive oil and sea salt. 3. Pour the radishes into the air fryer and roast for 10 minutes. Stir or turn the radishes over and roast for 8 minutes more, then serve.
Per Serving
Calories: 80 | fat: 7g | protein: 1g | carbs: 5g | fiber: 2g | sodium: 315mg

Garlic Zucchini and Red Peppers

Prep time: 5 minutes | Cook time: 15 minutes | Serves 6

2 medium zucchini, cubed
1 red bell pepper, diced
2 garlic cloves, sliced

2 tablespoons olive oil
½ teaspoon salt

1. Preheat the air fryer to 380°F (193°C). 2. In a large bowl, mix together the zucchini, bell pepper, and garlic with the olive oil and salt. 3. Pour the mixture into the air fryer basket, and roast for 7 minutes. Shake or stir, then roast for 7 to 8 minutes more.
Per Serving
Calories: 59 | fat: 5g | protein: 1g | carbs: 4g | fiber: 1g | sodium: 200mg

Chapter 15 Vegetarian Mains

Three-Cheese Zucchini Boats

Prep time: 15 minutes | Cook time: 20 minutes | Serves 2

2 medium zucchini	cheese
1 tablespoon avocado oil	¼ teaspoon dried oregano
¼ cup low-carb, no-sugar-added pasta sauce	¼ teaspoon garlic powder
¼ cup full-fat ricotta cheese	½ teaspoon dried parsley
¼ cup shredded Mozzarella	2 tablespoons grated vegetarian Parmesan cheese

1. Cut off 1 inch from the top and bottom of each zucchini. Slice zucchini in half lengthwise and use a spoon to scoop out a bit of the inside, making room for filling. Brush with oil and spoon 2 tablespoons pasta sauce into each shell. 2. In a medium bowl, mix ricotta, Mozzarella, oregano, garlic powder, and parsley. Spoon the mixture into each zucchini shell. Place stuffed zucchini shells into the air fryer basket. 3. Adjust the temperature to 350°F (177°C) and air fry for 20 minutes. 4. To remove from the basket, use tongs or a spatula and carefully lift out. Top with Parmesan. Serve immediately.

Per Serving
Calories: 208 | fat: 14g | protein: 12g | carbs: 11g | fiber: 3g | sodium: 247mg

Crustless Spanakopita

Prep time: 15 minutes | Cook time: 45 minutes | Serves 6

12 tablespoons extra-virgin olive oil, divided	½ teaspoon freshly ground black pepper
1 small yellow onion, diced	1 cup whole-milk ricotta cheese
1 (32-ounce / 907-g) bag frozen chopped spinach, thawed, fully drained, and patted dry (about 4 cups)	4 large eggs
	¾ cup crumbled traditional feta cheese
4 garlic cloves, minced	¼ cup pine nuts
½ teaspoon salt	

1. Preheat the oven to 375°F (190°C). 2. In a large skillet, heat 4 tablespoons olive oil over medium-high heat. Add the onion and sauté until softened, 6 to 8 minutes. 3. Add the spinach, garlic, salt, and pepper and sauté another 5 minutes. Remove from the heat and allow to cool slightly. 4. In a medium bowl, whisk together the ricotta and eggs. Add to the cooled spinach and stir to combine. 5. Pour 4 tablespoons olive oil in the bottom of a 9-by-13-inch glass baking dish and swirl to coat the bottom and sides. Add the spinach-ricotta mixture and spread into an even layer. 6. Bake for 20 minutes or until the mixture begins to set. Remove from the oven and crumble the feta evenly across the top of the spinach. Add the pine nuts and drizzle with the remaining 4 tablespoons olive oil. Return to the oven and bake for an additional 15 to 20 minutes, or until the spinach is fully set and the top is starting to turn golden brown. Allow to cool slightly before cutting to serve.

Per Serving
Calories: 497 | fat: 44g | protein: 18g | carbs: 11g | fiber: 5g | sodium: 561mg

Roasted Veggie Bowl

Prep time: 10 minutes | Cook time: 15 minutes | Serves 2

1 cup broccoli florets	½ medium green bell pepper, seeded and sliced ¼ inch thick
1 cup quartered Brussels sprouts	
½ cup cauliflower florets	1 tablespoon coconut oil
¼ medium white onion, peeled and sliced ¼ inch thick	2 teaspoons chili powder
	½ teaspoon garlic powder
	½ teaspoon cumin

1. Toss all ingredients together in a large bowl until vegetables are fully coated with oil and seasoning. 2. Pour vegetables into the air fryer basket. 3. Adjust the temperature to 360°F (182°C) and roast for 15 minutes. 4. Shake two or three times during cooking. Serve warm.

Per Serving
Calories: 112 | fat: 8g | protein: 4g | carbs: 11g | fiber: 5g | sodium: 106mg

Pesto Spinach Flatbread

Prep time: 10 minutes | Cook time: 8 minutes | Serves 4

1 cup blanched finely ground almond flour	cheese
	1 cup chopped fresh spinach leaves
2 ounces (57 g) cream cheese	
2 cups shredded Mozzarella	2 tablespoons basil pesto

1. Place flour, cream cheese, and Mozzarella in a large microwave-safe bowl and microwave on high 45 seconds, then stir. 2. Fold in spinach and microwave an additional 15 seconds. Stir until a soft dough ball forms. 3. Cut two pieces of parchment paper to fit air fryer basket. Separate dough into two sections and press each out on ungreased parchment to create 6-inch rounds. 4. Spread 1 tablespoon pesto over each flatbread and place rounds on parchment into ungreased air fryer basket. Adjust the temperature to 350°F (177°C) and air fry for 8 minutes, turning crusts halfway through cooking. Flatbread will be golden when done. 5. Let cool 5 minutes before slicing and serving.

Per Serving
Calories: 387 | fat: 28g | protein: 28g | carbs: 10g | fiber: 5g | sodium: 556mg

Cheesy Cauliflower Pizza Crust

Prep time: 15 minutes | Cook time: 11 minutes | Serves 2

1 (12-ounce / 340-g) steamer bag cauliflower	2 tablespoons blanched finely ground almond flour
½ cup shredded sharp Cheddar cheese	1 teaspoon Italian blend seasoning
1 large egg	

1. Cook cauliflower according to package instructions. Remove from bag and place into cheesecloth or paper towel to remove excess water. Place cauliflower into a large bowl. 2. Add cheese, egg, almond flour, and Italian seasoning to the bowl and mix well. 3. Cut a piece of parchment to fit your air fryer basket. Press cauliflower into 6-inch round circle. Place into the air fryer basket. 4. Adjust the temperature to 360°F (182°C) and air fry for 11 minutes. 5. After 7 minutes, flip the pizza crust. 6. Add preferred toppings to pizza. Place back into air fryer basket and cook an additional 4 minutes or until fully cooked and golden. Serve immediately.

Per Serving
Calories: 251 | fat: 17g | protein: 15g | carbs: 12g | fiber: 5g | sodium: 375mg

Parmesan Artichokes

Prep time: 10 minutes | Cook time: 10 minutes | Serves 4

2 medium artichokes, trimmed and quartered, center removed	Parmesan cheese
2 tablespoons coconut oil	¼ cup blanched finely ground almond flour
1 large egg, beaten	½ teaspoon crushed red pepper flakes
½ cup grated vegetarian	

1. In a large bowl, toss artichokes in coconut oil and then dip each piece into the egg. 2. Mix the Parmesan and almond flour in a large bowl. Add artichoke pieces and toss to cover as completely as possible, sprinkle with pepper flakes. Place into the air fryer basket. 3. Adjust the temperature to 400°F (204°C) and air fry for 10 minutes. 4. Toss the basket two times during cooking. Serve warm.

Per Serving
Calories: 207 | fat: 13g | protein: 10g | carbs: 15g | fiber: 5g | sodium: 211mg

Caprese Eggplant Stacks

Prep time: 5 minutes | Cook time: 12 minutes | Serves 4

1 medium eggplant, cut into ¼-inch slices	Mozzarella, cut into ½-ounce / 14-g slices
2 large tomatoes, cut into ¼-inch slices	2 tablespoons olive oil
4 ounces (113 g) fresh	¼ cup fresh basil, sliced

1. In a baking dish, place four slices of eggplant on the bottom. Place a slice of tomato on top of each eggplant round, then Mozzarella, then eggplant. Repeat as necessary. 2. Drizzle with olive oil. Cover dish with foil and place dish into the air fryer basket. 3. Adjust the temperature to 350°F (177°C) and bake for 12 minutes. 4. When done, eggplant will be tender. Garnish with fresh basil to serve.

Per Serving
Calories: 97 | fat: 7g | protein: 2g | carbs: 8g | fiber: 4g | sodium: 11mg

Broccoli-Cheese Fritters

Prep time: 5 minutes | Cook time: 20 to 25 minutes | Serves 4

1 cup broccoli florets	1 teaspoon garlic powder
1 cup shredded Mozzarella cheese	Salt and freshly ground black pepper, to taste
¾ cup almond flour	2 eggs, lightly beaten
½ cup flaxseed meal, divided	½ cup ranch dressing
2 teaspoons baking powder	

1. Preheat the air fryer to 400°F (204°C). 2. In a food processor fitted with a metal blade, pulse the broccoli until very finely chopped. 3. Transfer the broccoli to a large bowl and add the Mozzarella, almond flour, ¼ cup of the flaxseed meal, baking powder, and garlic powder. Stir until thoroughly combined. Season to taste with salt and black pepper. Add the eggs and stir again to form a sticky dough. Shape the dough into 1¼-inch fritters. 4. Place the remaining ¼ cup flaxseed meal in a shallow bowl and roll the fritters in the meal to form an even coating. 5. Working in batches if necessary, arrange the fritters in a single layer in the basket of the air fryer and spray generously with olive oil. Pausing halfway through the cooking time to shake the basket, air fry for 20 to 25 minutes until the fritters are golden brown and crispy. Serve with the ranch dressing for dipping.

Per Serving
Calories: 388 | fat: 30g | protein: 19g | carbs: 14g | fiber: 7g | sodium: 526mg

Pesto Vegetable Skewers

Prep time: 30 minutes | Cook time: 8 minutes | Makes 8 skewers

1 medium zucchini, trimmed and cut into ½-inch slices	squares
½ medium yellow onion, peeled and cut into 1-inch squares	16 whole cremini mushrooms
	⅓ cup basil pesto
1 medium red bell pepper, seeded and cut into 1-inch	½ teaspoon salt
	¼ teaspoon ground black pepper

1. Divide zucchini slices, onion, and bell pepper into eight even portions. Place on 6-inch skewers for a total of eight kebabs. Add 2 mushrooms to each skewer and brush kebabs generously with pesto. 2. Sprinkle each kebab with salt and black pepper on all sides, then place into ungreased air fryer basket. Adjust the temperature to 375°F (191°C) and air fry for 8 minutes, turning kebabs halfway through cooking. Vegetables will be browned at the edges and tender-crisp when done. Serve warm.

Per Serving
Calories: 75 | fat: 6g | protein: 3g | carbs: 4g | fiber: 1g | sodium: 243mg

Crustless Spinach Cheese Pie

Prep time: 10 minutes | Cook time: 20 minutes | Serves 4

6 large eggs
¼ cup heavy whipping cream
1 cup frozen chopped spinach, drained

1 cup shredded sharp Cheddar cheese
¼ cup diced yellow onion

1. In a medium bowl, whisk eggs and add cream. Add remaining ingredients to bowl. 2. Pour into a round baking dish. Place into the air fryer basket. 3. Adjust the temperature to 320ºF (160ºC) and bake for 20 minutes. 4. Eggs will be firm and slightly browned when cooked. Serve immediately.

Per Serving
Calories: 263 | fat: 20g | protein: 18g | carbs: 4g | fiber: 1g | sodium: 321mg

Broccoli Crust Pizza

Prep time: 15 minutes | Cook time: 12 minutes | Serves 4

3 cups riced broccoli, steamed and drained well
1 large egg
½ cup grated vegetarian Parmesan cheese

3 tablespoons low-carb Alfredo sauce
½ cup shredded Mozzarella cheese

1. In a large bowl, mix broccoli, egg, and Parmesan. 2. Cut a piece of parchment to fit your air fryer basket. Press out the pizza mixture to fit on the parchment, working in two batches if necessary. Place into the air fryer basket. 3. Adjust the temperature to 370ºF (188ºC) and air fry for 5 minutes. 4. The crust should be firm enough to flip. If not, add 2 additional minutes. Flip crust. 5. Top with Alfredo sauce and Mozzarella. Return to the air fryer basket and cook an additional 7 minutes or until cheese is golden and bubbling. Serve warm.

Per Serving
Calories: 87 | fat: 2g | protein: 11g | carbs: 5g | fiber: 1g | sodium: 253mg

Cauliflower Rice-Stuffed Peppers

Prep time: 10 minutes | Cook time: 15 minutes | Serves 4

2 cups uncooked cauliflower rice
¾ cup drained canned petite diced tomatoes
2 tablespoons olive oil
1 cup shredded Mozzarella

cheese
¼ teaspoon salt
¼ teaspoon ground black pepper
4 medium green bell peppers, tops removed, seeded

1. In a large bowl, mix all ingredients except bell peppers. Scoop mixture evenly into peppers. 2. Place peppers into ungreased air fryer basket. Adjust the temperature to 350ºF (177ºC) and air fry for 15 minutes. Peppers will be tender and cheese will be melted when done. Serve warm.

Per Serving
Calories: 144 | fat: 7g | protein: 11g | carbs: 11g | fiber: 5g | sodium: 380mg

Vegetable Burgers

Prep time: 10 minutes | Cook time: 12 minutes | Serves 4

8 ounces (227 g) cremini mushrooms
2 large egg yolks
½ medium zucchini, trimmed and chopped
¼ cup peeled and chopped

yellow onion
1 clove garlic, peeled and finely minced
½ teaspoon salt
¼ teaspoon ground black pepper

1. Place all ingredients into a food processor and pulse twenty times until finely chopped and combined. 2. Separate mixture into four equal sections and press each into a burger shape. Place burgers into ungreased air fryer basket. Adjust the temperature to 375ºF (191ºC) and air fry for 12 minutes, turning burgers halfway through cooking. Burgers will be browned and firm when done. 3. Place burgers on a large plate and let cool 5 minutes before serving.

Per Serving
Calories: 50 | fat: 3g | protein: 3g | carbs: 4g | fiber: 1g | sodium: 299mg

Mushroom Ragù with Parmesan Polenta

Prep time: 20 minutes | Cook time: 30 minutes | Serves 2

½ ounce (14 g) dried porcini mushrooms (optional but recommended)
2 tablespoons olive oil
1 pound (454 g) baby bella (cremini) mushrooms, quartered
1 large shallot, minced (about ⅓ cup)
1 garlic clove, minced
1 tablespoon flour
2 teaspoons tomato paste

½ cup red wine
1 cup mushroom stock (or reserved liquid from soaking the porcini mushrooms, if using)
½ teaspoon dried thyme
1 fresh rosemary sprig
1½ cups water
½ teaspoon salt
⅓ cup instant polenta
2 tablespoons grated Parmesan cheese

1. If using the dried porcini mushrooms, soak them in 1 cup of hot water for about 15 minutes to soften them. When they're softened, scoop them out of the water, reserving the soaking liquid. (I strain it through a coffee filter to remove any possible grit.) Mince the porcini mushrooms. 2. Heat the olive oil in a large sauté pan over medium-high heat. Add the mushrooms, shallot, and garlic, and sauté for 10 minutes, or until the vegetables are wilted and starting to caramelize. 3. Add the flour and tomato paste, and cook for another 30 seconds. Add the red wine, mushroom stock or porcini soaking liquid, thyme, and rosemary. Bring the mixture to a boil, stirring constantly until it thickens. Reduce the heat and let it simmer for 10 minutes. 4. While the mushrooms are simmering, bring the water to a boil in a saucepan and add salt. 5. Add the instant polenta and stir quickly while it thickens. Stir in the Parmesan cheese. Taste and add additional salt if needed.

Per Serving
Calories: 451 | fat: 16g | protein: 14g | carbs: 58g | fiber: 5g | sodium: 165mg

Eggplant Parmesan

Prep time: 15 minutes | Cook time: 17 minutes | Serves 4

1 medium eggplant, ends trimmed, sliced into ½-inch rounds
¼ teaspoon salt
2 tablespoons coconut oil
½ cup grated Parmesan cheese
1 ounce (28 g) 100% cheese crisps, finely crushed
½ cup low-carb marinara sauce
½ cup shredded Mozzarella cheese

1. Sprinkle eggplant rounds with salt on both sides and wrap in a kitchen towel for 30 minutes. Press to remove excess water, then drizzle rounds with coconut oil on both sides. 2. In a medium bowl, mix Parmesan and cheese crisps. Press each eggplant slice into mixture to coat both sides. 3. Place rounds into ungreased air fryer basket. Adjust the temperature to 350°F (177°C) and air fry for 15 minutes, turning rounds halfway through cooking. They will be crispy around the edges when done. 4. Spoon marinara over rounds and sprinkle with Mozzarella. Continue cooking an additional 2 minutes at 350°F (177°C) until cheese is melted. Serve warm.

Per Serving
Calories: 208 | fat: 13g | protein: 12g | carbs: 13g | fiber: 5g | sodium: 531mg

Cauliflower Steak with Gremolata

Prep time: 15 minutes | Cook time: 25 minutes | Serves 4

2 tablespoons olive oil
1 tablespoon Italian seasoning
1 large head cauliflower, outer leaves removed and sliced lengthwise through the core into thick "steaks"
Salt and freshly ground black pepper, to taste
¼ cup Parmesan cheese
Gremolata:
1 bunch Italian parsley (about 1 cup packed)
2 cloves garlic
Zest of 1 small lemon, plus 1 to 2 teaspoons lemon juice
½ cup olive oil
Salt and pepper, to taste

1. Preheat the air fryer to 400°F (204°C). 2. In a small bowl, combine the olive oil and Italian seasoning. Brush both sides of each cauliflower "steak" generously with the oil. Season to taste with salt and black pepper. 3. Working in batches if necessary, arrange the cauliflower in a single layer in the air fryer basket. Pausing halfway through the cooking time to turn the "steaks," air fry for 15 to 20 minutes until the cauliflower is tender and the edges begin to brown. Sprinkle with the Parmesan and air fry for 5 minutes longer. 4. To make the gremolata: In a food processor fitted with a metal blade, combine the parsley, garlic, and lemon zest and juice. With the motor running, add the olive oil in a steady stream until the mixture forms a bright green sauce. Season to taste with salt and black pepper. Serve the cauliflower steaks with the gremolata spooned over the top.

Per Serving
Calories: 336 | fat: 30g | protein: 7g | carbs: 15g | fiber: 5g | sodium: 340mg

Moroccan Vegetable Tagine

Prep time: 20 minutes | Cook time: 1 hour | Serves 6

½ cup extra-virgin olive oil
2 medium yellow onions, sliced
6 celery stalks, sliced into ¼-inch crescents
6 garlic cloves, minced
1 teaspoon ground cumin
1 teaspoon ginger powder
1 teaspoon salt
½ teaspoon paprika
½ teaspoon ground cinnamon
¼ teaspoon freshly ground black pepper
2 cups vegetable stock
1 medium eggplant, cut into
1-inch cubes
2 medium zucchini, cut into ½-inch-thick semicircles
2 cups cauliflower florets
1 (13¾-ounce / 390-g) can artichoke hearts, drained and quartered
1 cup halved and pitted green olives
½ cup chopped fresh flat-leaf parsley, for garnish
½ cup chopped fresh cilantro leaves, for garnish
Greek yogurt, for garnish (optional)

1. In a large, thick soup pot or Dutch oven, heat the olive oil over medium-high heat. Add the onion and celery and sauté until softened, 6 to 8 minutes. Add the garlic, cumin, ginger, salt, paprika, cinnamon, and pepper and sauté for another 2 minutes. 2. Add the stock and bring to a boil. Reduce the heat to low and add the eggplant, zucchini, and cauliflower. Simmer on low heat, covered, until the vegetables are tender, 30 to 35 minutes. Add the artichoke hearts and olives, cover, and simmer for another 15 minutes. 3. Serve garnished with parsley, cilantro, and Greek yogurt (if using).

Per Serving
Calories: 265 | fat: 21g | protein: 5g | carbs: 19g | fiber: 9g | sodium: 858mg

Crispy Eggplant Rounds

Prep time: 15 minutes | Cook time: 10 minutes | Serves 4

1 large eggplant, ends trimmed, cut into ½-inch slices
½ teaspoon salt
2 ounces (57 g) Parmesan 100% cheese crisps, finely
ground
½ teaspoon paprika
¼ teaspoon garlic powder
1 large egg

1. Sprinkle eggplant rounds with salt. Place rounds on a kitchen towel for 30 minutes to draw out excess water. Pat rounds dry. 2. In a medium bowl, mix cheese crisps, paprika, and garlic powder. In a separate medium bowl, whisk egg. Dip each eggplant round in egg, then gently press into cheese crisps to coat both sides. 3. Place eggplant rounds into ungreased air fryer basket. Adjust the temperature to 400°F (204°C) and air fry for 10 minutes, turning rounds halfway through cooking. Eggplant will be golden and crispy when done. Serve warm.

Per Serving
Calories: 113 | fat: 5g | protein: 7g | carbs: 10g | fiber: 4g | sodium: 567mg

Spinach-Artichoke Stuffed Mushrooms

Prep time: 10 minutes | Cook time: 10 to 14 minutes | Serves 4

2 tablespoons olive oil	crumbled
4 large portobello mushrooms, stems removed and gills scraped out	½ cup chopped marinated artichoke hearts
½ teaspoon salt	1 cup frozen spinach, thawed and squeezed dry
¼ teaspoon freshly ground pepper	½ cup grated Parmesan cheese
4 ounces (113 g) goat cheese,	2 tablespoons chopped fresh parsley

1. Preheat the air fryer to 400°F (204°C). 2. Rub the olive oil over the portobello mushrooms until thoroughly coated. Sprinkle both sides with the salt and black pepper. Place top-side down on a clean work surface. 3. In a small bowl, combine the goat cheese, artichoke hearts, and spinach. Mash with the back of a fork until thoroughly combined. Divide the cheese mixture among the mushrooms and sprinkle with the Parmesan cheese. 4. Air fry for 10 to 14 minutes until the mushrooms are tender and the cheese has begun to brown. Top with the fresh parsley just before serving.

Per Serving
Calories: 284 | fat: 21g | protein: 16g | carbs: 10g | fiber: 4g | sodium: 686mg

Crispy Cabbage Steaks

Prep time: 5 minutes | Cook time: 10 minutes | Serves 4

1 small head green cabbage, cored and cut into ½-inch-thick slices	2 tablespoons olive oil
	1 clove garlic, peeled and finely minced
¼ teaspoon salt	½ teaspoon dried thyme
¼ teaspoon ground black pepper	½ teaspoon dried parsley

1. Sprinkle each side of cabbage with salt and pepper, then place into ungreased air fryer basket, working in batches if needed. 2. Drizzle each side of cabbage with olive oil, then sprinkle with remaining ingredients on both sides. Adjust the temperature to 350°F (177°C) and air fry for 10 minutes, turning "steaks" halfway through cooking. Cabbage will be browned at the edges and tender when done. Serve warm.

Per Serving
Calories: 63 | fat: 7g | protein: 0g | carbs: 1g | fiber: 0g | sodium: 155mg

Mediterranean Pan Pizza

Prep time: 5 minutes | Cook time: 8 minutes | Serves 2

1 cup shredded Mozzarella cheese	leaves
	2 tablespoons chopped black olives
¼ medium red bell pepper, seeded and chopped	2 tablespoons crumbled feta cheese
½ cup chopped fresh spinach	

1. Sprinkle Mozzarella into an ungreased round nonstick baking dish in an even layer. Add remaining ingredients on top. 2. Place dish into air fryer basket. Adjust the temperature to 350°F (177°C) and bake for 8 minutes, checking halfway through to avoid burning. Top of pizza will be golden brown and the cheese melted when done. 3. Remove dish from fryer and let cool 5 minutes before slicing and serving.

Per Serving
Calories: 108 | fat: 1g | protein: 20g | carbs: 5g | fiber: 3g | sodium: 521mg

Cheese Stuffed Zucchini

Prep time: 20 minutes | Cook time: 8 minutes | Serves 4

1 large zucchini, cut into four pieces	1 heaping tablespoon coriander, minced
2 tablespoons olive oil	2 ounces (57 g) Cheddar cheese, preferably freshly grated
1 cup Ricotta cheese, room temperature	
2 tablespoons scallions, chopped	1 teaspoon celery seeds
	½ teaspoon salt
1 heaping tablespoon fresh parsley, roughly chopped	½ teaspoon garlic pepper

1. Cook your zucchini in the air fryer basket for approximately 10 minutes at 350°F (177°C). Check for doneness and cook for 2-3 minutes longer if needed. 2. Meanwhile, make the stuffing by mixing the other items. When your zucchini is thoroughly cooked, open them up. Divide the stuffing among all zucchini pieces and bake an additional 5 minutes.

Per Serving
Calories: 242 | fat: 20g | protein: 12g | carbs: 5g | fiber: 1g | sodium: 443mg

Tangy Asparagus and Broccoli

Prep time: 25 minutes | Cook time: 22 minutes | Serves 4

½ pound (227 g) asparagus, cut into 1½-inch pieces	Salt and white pepper, to taste
	½ cup vegetable broth
½ pound (227 g) broccoli, cut into 1½-inch pieces	2 tablespoons apple cider vinegar
2 tablespoons olive oil	

1. Place the vegetables in a single layer in the lightly greased air fryer basket. Drizzle the olive oil over the vegetables. 2. Sprinkle with salt and white pepper. 3. Cook at 380°F (193°C) for 15 minutes, shaking the basket halfway through the cooking time. 4. Add ½ cup of vegetable broth to a saucepan; bring to a rapid boil and add the vinegar. Cook for 5 to 7 minutes or until the sauce has reduced by half. 5. Spoon the sauce over the warm vegetables and serve immediately. Bon appétit!

Per Serving
Calories: 93 | fat: 7g | protein: 3g | carbs: 6g | fiber: 3g | sodium: 89mg

Eggplants Stuffed with Walnuts and Feta

Prep time: 10 minutes | Cook time: 55 minutes | Serves 6

3 medium eggplants, halved lengthwise
2 teaspoons salt, divided
¼ cup olive oil, plus 2 tablespoons, divided
2 medium onions, diced
1½ pints cherry or grape tomatoes, halved
¾ cup roughly chopped walnut pieces
2¼ teaspoons ground cinnamon
1½ teaspoons dried oregano
½ teaspoon freshly ground black pepper
¼ cup whole-wheat breadcrumbs
⅔ cup (about 3 ounces / 85 g) crumbled feta cheese

1. Scoop out the flesh of the eggplants, leaving a ½-inch thick border of flesh in the skins. Dice the flesh that you removed and place it in a colander set over the sink. Sprinkle 1½ teaspoons of salt over the diced eggplant and inside the eggplant shells and let stand for 30 minutes. Rinse the shells and the pieces and pat dry with paper towels. 2. Heat ¼ cup of olive oil in a large skillet over medium heat. Add the eggplant shells, skin-side down, and cook for about 4 minutes, until browned and softened. Turn over and cook on the cut side until golden brown and soft, about 4 minutes more. Transfer to a plate lined with paper towel to drain. 3. Drain off all but about 1 to 2 tablespoons of the oil in the skillet and heat over medium-high heat. Add the onions and cook, stirring, until beginning to soften, about 3 minutes. Add the diced eggplant, tomatoes, walnuts, cinnamon, oregano, ¼ cup water, the remaining ½ teaspoon of salt, and the pepper. Cook, stirring occasionally, until the vegetables are golden brown and softened, about 8 minutes. 4. Preheat the broiler to high. 5. In a small bowl, toss together the breadcrumbs and 1 tablespoon olive oil. 6. Arrange the eggplant shells cut-side up on a large, rimmed baking sheet. Brush each shell with about ½ teaspoon of olive oil. Cook under the broiler until tender and just starting to turn golden brown, about 5 minutes. Remove the eggplants from the broiler and reduce the heat of the oven to 375ºF (190ºC). 7. Spoon the sautéed vegetable mixture into the eggplant shells, dividing equally. Sprinkle the breadcrumbs over the tops of the filled eggplants, dividing equally. Sprinkle the cheese on top, again dividing equally. Bake in the oven until the filling and shells are heated through and the topping is nicely browned and crisp, about 35 minutes.

Per Serving
Calories: 274 | fat: 15g | protein: 7g | carbs: 34g | fiber: 13g | sodium: 973mg

Provençal Ratatouille with Herbed Breadcrumbs and Goat Cheese

Prep time: 10 minutes | Cook time: 1 hour 5 minutes | Serves 4

6 tablespoons olive oil, divided
2 medium onions, diced
2 cloves garlic, minced
2 medium eggplants, halved lengthwise and cut into ¾-inch
thick half rounds
3 medium zucchini, halved lengthwise and cut into ¾-inch thick half rounds
2 red bell peppers, seeded and cut into 1½-inch pieces
1 green bell pepper, seeded and cut into 1½-inch pieces
1 (14-ounce / 397-g) can diced tomatoes, drained
1 teaspoon salt
½ teaspoon freshly ground black pepper
8 ounces (227 g) fresh
breadcrumbs
1 tablespoon chopped fresh parsley
1 tablespoon chopped fresh basil
1 tablespoon chopped fresh chives
6 ounces (170 g) soft, fresh goat cheese

1. Preheat the oven to 375ºF (190ºC). 2. Heat 5 tablespoons of the olive oil in a large skillet over medium heat. Add the onions and garlic and cook, stirring frequently, until the onions are soft and beginning to turn golden, about 8 minutes. Add the eggplant, zucchini, and bell peppers and cook, turning the vegetables occasionally, for another 10 minutes. Stir in the tomatoes, salt, and pepper and let simmer for 15 minutes. 3. While the vegetables are simmering, stir together the breadcrumbs, the remaining tablespoon of olive oil, the parsley, basil, and chives. 4. Transfer the vegetable mixture to a large baking dish, spreading it out into an even layer. Crumble the goat cheese over the top, then sprinkle the breadcrumb mixture evenly over the top. Bake in the preheated oven for about 30 minutes, until the topping is golden brown and crisp. Serve hot.

Per Serving
Calories: 644 | fat: 37g | protein: 21g | carbs: 63g | fiber: 16g | sodium: 861mg

Rustic Vegetable and Brown Rice Bowl

Prep time: 15 minutes | Cook time: 20 minutes | Serves 4

Nonstick cooking spray
2 cups broccoli florets
2 cups cauliflower florets
1 (15-ounce / 425-g) can chickpeas, drained and rinsed
1 cup carrots sliced 1 inch thick
2 to 3 tablespoons extra-virgin olive oil, divided
Salt
Freshly ground black pepper
2 to 3 tablespoons sesame seeds, for garnish
2 cups cooked brown rice
For the Dressing:
3 to 4 tablespoons tahini
2 tablespoons honey
1 lemon, juiced
1 garlic clove, minced
Salt
Freshly ground black pepper

1. Preheat the oven to 400ºF (205ºC). Spray two baking sheets with cooking spray. 2. Cover the first baking sheet with the broccoli and cauliflower and the second with the chickpeas and carrots. Toss each sheet with half of the oil and season with salt and pepper before placing in oven. 3. Cook the carrots and chickpeas for 10 minutes, leaving the carrots still just crisp, and the broccoli and cauliflower for 20 minutes, until tender. Stir each halfway through cooking. 4. To make the dressing, in a small bowl, mix the tahini, honey, lemon juice, and garlic. Season with salt and pepper and set aside. 5. Divide the rice into individual bowls, then layer with vegetables and drizzle dressing over the dish.

Per Serving
Calories: 454 | fat: 18g | protein: 12g | carbs: 62g | fiber: 11g | sodium: 61mg

Stuffed Portobellos

Prep time: 10 minutes | Cook time: 8 minutes | Serves 4

3 ounces (85 g) cream cheese, softened
½ medium zucchini, trimmed and chopped
¼ cup seeded and chopped red bell pepper
1½ cups chopped fresh spinach
leaves
4 large portobello mushrooms, stems removed
2 tablespoons coconut oil, melted
½ teaspoon salt

1. In a medium bowl, mix cream cheese, zucchini, pepper, and spinach. 2. Drizzle mushrooms with coconut oil and sprinkle with salt. Scoop ¼ zucchini mixture into each mushroom. 3. Place mushrooms into ungreased air fryer basket. Adjust the temperature to 400°F (204°C) and air fry for 8 minutes. Portobellos will be tender and tops will be browned when done. Serve warm.

Per Serving
Calories: 151 | fat: 13g | protein: 4g | carbs: 6g | fiber: 2g | sodium: 427mg

Sheet Pan Roasted Chickpeas and Vegetables with Harissa Yogurt

Prep time: 10 minutes | Cook time: 30 minutes | Serves 2

4 cups cauliflower florets (about ½ small head)
2 medium carrots, peeled, halved, and then sliced into quarters lengthwise
2 tablespoons olive oil, divided
½ teaspoon garlic powder, divided
½ teaspoon salt, divided
2 teaspoons za'atar spice mix, divided
1 (15-ounce / 425-g) can chickpeas, drained, rinsed, and patted dry
¾ cup plain Greek yogurt
1 teaspoon harissa spice paste

1. Preheat the oven to 400°F (205°C) and set the rack to the middle position. Line a sheet pan with foil or parchment paper. 2. Place the cauliflower and carrots in a large bowl. Drizzle with 1 tablespoon olive oil and sprinkle with ¼ teaspoon of garlic powder, ¼ teaspoon of salt, and 1 teaspoon of za'atar. Toss well to combine. 3. Spread the vegetables onto one half of the sheet pan in a single layer. 4. Place the chickpeas in the same bowl and season with the remaining 1 tablespoon of oil, ¼ teaspoon of garlic powder, and ¼ teaspoon of salt, and the remaining za'atar. Toss well to combine. 5. Spread the chickpeas onto the other half of the sheet pan. 6. Roast for 30 minutes, or until the vegetables are tender and the chickpeas start to turn golden. Flip the vegetables halfway through the cooking time, and give the chickpeas a stir so they cook evenly. 7. The chickpeas may need an extra few minutes if you like them crispy. If so, remove the vegetables and leave the chickpeas in until they're cooked to desired crispiness. 8. While the vegetables are roasting, combine the yogurt and harissa in a small bowl. Taste, and add additional harissa as desired.

Per Serving
Calories: 467 | fat: 23g | protein: 18g | carbs: 54g | fiber: 15g | sodium: 632mg

Quinoa with Almonds and Cranberries

Prep time: 15 minutes | Cook time: 0 minutes | Serves 4

2 cups cooked quinoa
⅓ teaspoon cranberries or currants
¼ cup sliced almonds
2 garlic cloves, minced
1¼ teaspoons salt
½ teaspoon ground cumin
½ teaspoon turmeric
¼ teaspoon ground cinnamon
¼ teaspoon freshly ground black pepper

1. In a large bowl, toss the quinoa, cranberries, almonds, garlic, salt, cumin, turmeric, cinnamon, and pepper and stir to combine. Enjoy alone or with roasted cauliflower.

Per Serving
Calories: 194 | fat: 6g | protein: 7g | carbs: 31g | fiber: 4g | sodium: 727mg

Quinoa Lentil "Meatballs" with Quick Tomato Sauce

Prep time: 25 minutes | Cook time: 45 minutes | Serves 4

For the Meatballs:
Olive oil cooking spray
2 large eggs, beaten
1 tablespoon no-salt-added tomato paste
½ teaspoon kosher salt
½ cup grated Parmesan cheese
½ onion, roughly chopped
¼ cup fresh parsley
1 garlic clove, peeled
1½ cups cooked lentils
1 cup cooked quinoa

For the Tomato Sauce:
1 tablespoon extra-virgin olive oil
1 onion, minced
½ teaspoon dried oregano
½ teaspoon kosher salt
2 garlic cloves, minced
1 (28-ounce / 794-g) can no-salt-added crushed tomatoes
½ teaspoon honey
¼ cup fresh basil, chopped

To Make the Meatballs: 1. Preheat the oven to 400°F (205°C). Lightly grease a 12-cup muffin pan with olive oil cooking spray. 2. In a large bowl, whisk together the eggs, tomato paste, and salt until fully combined. Mix in the Parmesan cheese. 3. In a food processor, add the onion, parsley, and garlic. Process until minced. Add to the egg mixture and stir together. Add the lentils to the food processor and process until puréed into a thick paste. Add to the large bowl and mix together. Add the quinoa and mix well. 4. Form balls, slightly larger than a golf ball, with ¼ cup of the quinoa mixture. Place each ball in a muffin pan cup. Note: The mixture will be somewhat soft but should hold together. 5. Bake 25 to 30 minutes, until golden brown. To Make the Tomato Sauce: 6. Heat the olive oil in a large saucepan over medium heat. Add the onion, oregano, and salt and sauté until light golden brown, about 5 minutes. Add the garlic and cook for 30 seconds. 7. Stir in the tomatoes and honey. Increase the heat to high and cook, stirring often, until simmering, then decrease the heat to medium-low and cook for 10 minutes. Remove from the heat and stir in the basil. Serve with the meatballs.

Per Serving 3 meatballs:
Calories: 360 | fat: 10g | protein: 20g | carbs: 48g | fiber: 14g | sodium: 520mg

Eggs Poached in Moroccan Tomato Sauce

Prep time: 10 minutes | Cook time: 35 minutes | Serves 4

1 tablespoon olive oil
1 medium yellow onion, diced
2 red bell peppers, seeded and diced
1¾ teaspoons sweet paprika
1 teaspoon ras al hanout
½ teaspoon cayenne pepper
1 teaspoon salt
¼ cup tomato paste
1 (28-ounce / 794-g) can diced tomatoes, drained
8 eggs
¼ cup chopped cilantro

1. Heat the olive oil in a skillet over medium-high heat. Add the onion and bell peppers and cook, stirring frequently, until softened, about 5 minutes. Stir in the paprika, ras al hanout, cayenne, salt, and tomato paste and cook, stirring occasionally, for 5 minutes. 2. Stir in the diced tomatoes, reduce the heat to medium-low, and simmer for about 15 minutes, until the tomatoes break down and the sauce thickens. 3. Make 8 wells in the sauce and drop one egg into each. Cover the pan and cook for about 10 minutes, until the whites are fully set, but the yolks are still runny. 4. Spoon the sauce and eggs into serving bowls and serve hot, garnished with cilantro.

Per Serving
Calories: 238 | fat: 13g | protein: 15g | carbs: 18g | fiber: 5g | sodium: 735mg

Creamy Chickpea Sauce with Whole-Wheat Fusilli

Prep time: 15 minutes | Cook time: 20 minutes | Serves 4

¼ cup extra-virgin olive oil
½ large shallot, chopped
5 garlic cloves, thinly sliced
1 (15-ounce / 425-g) can chickpeas, drained and rinsed, reserving ½ cup canning liquid
Pinch red pepper flakes
1 cup whole-grain fusilli pasta
¼ teaspoon salt
⅛ teaspoon freshly ground black pepper
¼ cup shaved fresh Parmesan cheese
¼ cup chopped fresh basil
2 teaspoons dried parsley
1 teaspoon dried oregano
Red pepper flakes

1. In a medium pan, heat the oil over medium heat, and sauté the shallot and garlic for 3 to 5 minutes, until the garlic is golden. Add ¾ of the chickpeas plus 2 tablespoons of liquid from the can, and bring to a simmer. 2. Remove from the heat, transfer into a standard blender, and blend until smooth. At this point, add the remaining chickpeas. Add more reserved chickpea liquid if it becomes thick. 3. Bring a large pot of salted water to a boil and cook pasta until al dente, about 8 minutes. Reserve ½ cup of the pasta water, drain the pasta, and return it to the pot. 4. Add the chickpea sauce to the hot pasta and add up to ¼ cup of the pasta water. You may need to add more pasta water to reach your desired consistency. 5. Place the pasta pot over medium heat and mix occasionally until the sauce thickens. Season with salt and pepper. 6. Serve, garnished with Parmesan, basil, parsley, oregano, and red pepper flakes.

Per Serving (1 cup pasta)
Calories: 310 | fat: 17g | protein: 10g | carbs: 33g | fiber: 7g | sodium: 243mg

Herbed Ricotta–Stuffed Mushrooms

Prep time: 10 minutes | Cook time: 30 minutes | Serves 4

6 tablespoons extra-virgin olive oil, divided
4 portobello mushroom caps, cleaned and gills removed
1 cup whole-milk ricotta cheese
⅓ cup chopped fresh herbs
(such as basil, parsley, rosemary, oregano, or thyme)
2 garlic cloves, finely minced
½ teaspoon salt
¼ teaspoon freshly ground black pepper

1. Preheat the oven to 400°F (205°C). 2. Line a baking sheet with parchment or foil and drizzle with 2 tablespoons olive oil, spreading evenly. Place the mushroom caps on the baking sheet, gill-side up. 3. In a medium bowl, mix together the ricotta, herbs, 2 tablespoons olive oil, garlic, salt, and pepper. Stuff each mushroom cap with one-quarter of the cheese mixture, pressing down if needed. Drizzle with remaining 2 tablespoons olive oil and bake until golden brown and the mushrooms are soft, 30 to 35 minutes, depending on the size of the mushrooms.

Per Serving
Calories: 308 | fat: 29g | protein: 9g | carbs: 6g | fiber: 1g | sodium: 351mg

Turkish Red Lentil and Bulgur Kofte

Prep time: 10 minutes | Cook time: 45 minutes | Serves 4

⅓ cup olive oil, plus 2 tablespoons, divided, plus more for brushing
1 cup red lentils
½ cup bulgur
1 teaspoon salt
1 medium onion, finely diced
2 tablespoons tomato paste
1 teaspoon ground cumin
¼ cup finely chopped flat-leaf parsley
3 scallions, thinly sliced
Juice of ½ lemon

1. Preheat the oven to 400°F (205°C). 2. Brush a large, rimmed baking sheet with olive oil. 3. In a medium saucepan, combine the lentils with 2 cups water and bring to a boil. Reduce the heat to low and cook, stirring occasionally, for about 15 minutes, until the lentils are tender and have soaked up most of the liquid. Remove from the heat, stir in the bulgur and salt, cover, and let sit for 15 minutes or so, until the bulgur is tender. 4. Meanwhile, heat ⅓ cup olive oil in a medium skillet over medium-high heat. Add the onion and cook, stirring frequently, until softened, about 5 minutes. Stir in the tomato paste and cook for 2 minutes more. Remove from the heat and stir in the cumin. 5. Add the cooked onion mixture to the lentil-bulgur mixture and stir to combine. Add the parsley, scallions, and lemon juice and stir to mix well. 6. Shape the mixture into walnut-sized balls and place them on the prepared baking sheet. Brush the balls with the remaining 2 tablespoons of olive oil and bake for 15 to 20 minutes, until golden brown. Serve hot.

Per Serving
Calories: 460 | fat: 25g | protein: 16g | carbs: 48g | fiber: 19g | sodium: 604mg

Beet and Carrot Fritters with Yogurt Sauce

Prep time: 15 minutes | Cook time: 15 minutes | Serves 2

For the Yogurt Sauce:
⅓ cup plain Greek yogurt
1 tablespoon freshly squeezed lemon juice
Zest of ½ lemon
¼ teaspoon garlic powder
¼ teaspoon salt
For the Fritters:
1 large carrot, peeled
1 small potato, peeled
1 medium golden or red beet, peeled

1 scallion, minced
2 tablespoons fresh minced parsley
¼ cup brown rice flour or unseasoned bread crumbs
¼ teaspoon garlic powder
¼ teaspoon salt
1 large egg, beaten
¼ cup feta cheese, crumbled
2 tablespoons olive oil (more if needed)

Make the Yogurt Sauce: 1. In a small bowl, mix together the yogurt, lemon juice and zest, garlic powder, and salt. Set aside. Make the Fritters: 2. Shred the carrot, potato, and beet in a food processor with the shredding blade. You can also use a mandoline with a julienne shredding blade or a vegetable peeler. Squeeze out any moisture from the vegetables and place them in a large bowl. 3. Add the scallion, parsley, rice flour, garlic powder, salt, and egg. Stir the mixture well to combine. Add the feta cheese and stir briefly, leaving chunks of feta cheese throughout. 4. Heat a large nonstick sauté pan over medium-high heat and add 1 tablespoon of the olive oil. 5. Make the fritters by scooping about 3 tablespoons of the vegetable mixture into your hands and flattening it into a firm disc about 3 inches in diameter. 6. Place 2 fritters at a time in the pan and let them cook for about two minutes. Check to see if the underside is golden, and then flip and repeat on the other side. Remove from the heat, add the rest of the olive oil to the pan, and repeat with the remaining vegetable mixture. 7. To serve, spoon about 1 tablespoon of the yogurt sauce on top of each fritter.

Per Serving
Calories: 295 | fat: 14g | protein: 6g | carbs: 44g | fiber: 5g | sodium: 482mg

Mozzarella and Sun-Dried Portobello Mushroom Pizza

Prep time: 10 minutes | Cook time: 10 minutes | Serves 4

4 large portobello mushroom caps
3 tablespoons extra-virgin olive oil
Salt
Freshly ground black pepper

4 sun-dried tomatoes
1 cup mozzarella cheese, divided
½ to ¾ cup low-sodium tomato sauce

1. Preheat the broiler on high. 2. On a baking sheet, drizzle the mushroom caps with the olive oil and season with salt and pepper. Broil the portobello mushrooms for 5 minutes on each side, flipping once, until tender. 3. Fill each mushroom cap with 1 sun-dried tomato, 2 tablespoons of cheese, and 2 to 3 tablespoons of sauce. Top each with 2 tablespoons of cheese.

Place the caps back under the broiler for a final 2 to 3 minutes, then quarter the mushrooms and serve.
Per Serving
Calories: 218| fat: 16g | protein: 11g | carbs: 12g | fiber: 2g | sodium: 244mg

One-Pan Mushroom Pasta with Mascarpone

Prep time: 10 minutes | Cook time: 20 minutes | Serves 2

2 tablespoons olive oil
1 large shallot, minced
8 ounces (227 g) baby bella (cremini) mushrooms, sliced
¼ cup dry sherry
1 teaspoon dried thyme
2 cups low-sodium vegetable

stock
6 ounces (170 g) dry pappardelle pasta
2 tablespoons mascarpone cheese
Salt
Freshly ground black pepper

1. Heat olive oil in a large sauté pan over medium-high heat. Add the shallot and mushrooms and sauté for 10 minutes, or until the mushrooms have given up much of their liquid. 2. Add the sherry, thyme, and vegetable stock. Bring the mixture to a boil. 3. Add the pasta, breaking it up as needed so it fits into the pan and is covered by the liquid. Return the mixture to a boil. Cover, and reduce the heat to medium-low. Let the pasta cook for 10 minutes, or until al dente. Stir it occasionally so it doesn't stick. If the sauce gets too dry, add some water or additional chicken stock. 4. When the pasta is tender, stir in the mascarpone cheese and season with salt and pepper. 5. The sauce will thicken up a bit when it's off the heat.
Per Serving
Calories: 517 | fat: 18g | protein: 16g | carbs: 69g | fiber: 3g | sodium: 141mg

Mediterranean Baked Chickpeas

Prep time: 15 minutes | Cook time: 15 minutes | Serves 4

1 tablespoon extra-virgin olive oil
½ medium onion, chopped
3 garlic cloves, chopped
2 teaspoons smoked paprika
¼ teaspoon ground cumin
4 cups halved cherry tomatoes

2 (15-ounce / 425-g) cans chickpeas, drained and rinsed
½ cup plain, unsweetened, full-fat Greek yogurt, for serving
1 cup crumbled feta, for serving

1. Preheat the oven to 425ºF (220ºC). 2. In an oven-safe sauté pan or skillet, heat the oil over medium heat and sauté the onion and garlic. Cook for about 5 minutes, until softened and fragrant. Stir in the paprika and cumin and cook for 2 minutes. Stir in the tomatoes and chickpeas. 3. Bring to a simmer for 5 to 10 minutes before placing in the oven. 4. Roast in oven for 25 to 30 minutes, until bubbling and thickened. To serve, top with Greek yogurt and feta.
Per Serving
Calories: 412 | fat: 15g | protein: 20g | carbs: 51g | fiber: 13g | sodium: 444mg

Tortellini in Red Pepper Sauce

Prep time: 15 minutes | Cook time: 10 minutes | Serves 4

1 (16-ounce / 454-g) container fresh cheese tortellini (usually green and white pasta)
1 (16-ounce / 454-g) jar roasted red peppers, drained
1 teaspoon garlic powder
¼ cup tahini
1 tablespoon red pepper oil (optional)

1. Bring a large pot of water to a boil and cook the tortellini according to package directions. 2. In a blender, combine the red peppers with the garlic powder and process until smooth. Once blended, add the tahini until the sauce is thickened. If the sauce gets too thick, add up to 1 tablespoon red pepper oil (if using). 3. Once tortellini are cooked, drain and leave pasta in colander. Add the sauce to the bottom of the empty pot and heat for 2 minutes. Then, add the tortellini back into the pot and cook for 2 more minutes. Serve and enjoy!
Per Serving
Calories: 350 | fat: 11g | protein: 12g | carbs: 46g | fiber: 4g | sodium: 192mg

Roasted Ratatouille Pasta

Prep time: 10 minutes | Cook time: 20 minutes | Serves 2

1 small eggplant (about 8 ounces / 227 g)
1 small zucchini
1 portobello mushroom
1 Roma tomato, halved
½ medium sweet red pepper, seeded
½ teaspoon salt, plus additional for the pasta water
1 teaspoon Italian herb seasoning
1 tablespoon olive oil
2 cups farfalle pasta (about 8 ounces / 227 g)
2 tablespoons minced sun-dried tomatoes in olive oil with herbs
2 tablespoons prepared pesto

1. Slice the ends off the eggplant and zucchini. Cut them lengthwise into ½-inch slices. 2. Place the eggplant, zucchini, mushroom, tomato, and red pepper in a large bowl and sprinkle with ½ teaspoon of salt. Using your hands, toss the vegetables well so that they're covered evenly with the salt. Let them rest for about 10 minutes. 3. While the vegetables are resting, preheat the oven to 400ºF (205ºC) and set the rack to the bottom position. Line a baking sheet with parchment paper. 4. When the oven is hot, drain off any liquid from the vegetables and pat them dry with a paper towel. Add the Italian herb seasoning and olive oil to the vegetables and toss well to coat both sides. 5. Lay the vegetables out in a single layer on the baking sheet. Roast them for 15 to 20 minutes, flipping them over after about 10 minutes or once they start to brown on the underside. When the vegetables are charred in spots, remove them from the oven. 6. While the vegetables are roasting, fill a large saucepan with water. Add salt and cook the pasta according to package directions. Drain the pasta, reserving ½ cup of the pasta water. 7. When cool enough to handle, cut the vegetables into large chunks (about 2 inches) and add them to the hot pasta. 8. Stir in the sun-dried tomatoes and pesto and toss everything well.
Per Serving
Calories: 612 | fat: 16g | protein: 23g | carbs: 110g | fiber: 23g | sodium: 776mg

Linguine and Brussels Sprouts

Prep time: 10 minutes | Cook time: 25 minutes | Serves 4

8 ounces (227 g) whole-wheat linguine
⅓ cup, plus 2 tablespoons extra-virgin olive oil, divided
1 medium sweet onion, diced
2 to 3 garlic cloves, smashed
8 ounces (227 g) Brussels
sprouts, chopped
½ cup chicken stock, as needed
⅓ cup dry white wine
½ cup shredded Parmesan cheese
1 lemon, cut in quarters

1. Bring a large pot of water to a boil and cook the pasta according to package directions. Drain, reserving 1 cup of the pasta water. Mix the cooked pasta with 2 tablespoons of olive oil, then set aside. 2. In a large sauté pan or skillet, heat the remaining ⅓ cup of olive oil on medium heat. Add the onion to the pan and cook for about 5 minutes, until softened. Add the smashed garlic cloves and cook for 1 minute, until fragrant. 3. Add the Brussels sprouts and cook covered for 15 minutes. Add chicken stock as needed to prevent burning. Once Brussels sprouts have wilted and are fork-tender, add white wine and cook down for about 7 minutes, until reduced. 4. Add the pasta to the skillet and add the pasta water as needed. 5. Serve with the Parmesan cheese and lemon for squeezing over the dish right before eating.
Per Serving
Calories: 502 | fat: 31g | protein: 15g | carbs: 50g | fiber: 9g | sodium: 246mg

Root Vegetable Soup with Garlic Aioli

Prep time: 10 minutes | Cook time 25 minutes | Serves 4

For the Soup:
8 cups vegetable broth
½ teaspoon salt
1 medium leek, cut into thick rounds
1 pound (454 g) carrots, peeled and diced
1 pound (454 g) potatoes, peeled and diced
1 pound (454 g) turnips, peeled
and cut into 1-inch cubes
1 red bell pepper, cut into strips
2 tablespoons fresh oregano
For the Aioli:
5 garlic cloves, minced
¼ teaspoon salt
⅔ cup olive oil
1 drop lemon juice

1. Bring the broth and salt to a boil and add the vegetables one at a time, letting the water return to a boil after each addition. Add the carrots first, then the leeks, potatoes, turnips, and finally the red bell peppers. Let the vegetables cook for about 3 minutes after adding the green beans and bringing to a boil. The process will take about 20 minutes in total. 2. Meanwhile, make the aioli. In a mortar and pestle, grind the garlic to a paste with the salt. Using a whisk and whisking constantly, add the olive oil in a thin stream. Continue whisking until the mixture thickens to the consistency of mayonnaise. Add the lemon juice. 3. Serve the vegetables in the broth, dolloped with the aioli and garnished with the fresh oregano.
Per Serving
Calories: 538 | fat: 37g | protein: 5g | carbs: 50g | fiber: 9g | sodium: 773mg

Zucchini Lasagna

Prep time: 15 minutes | Cook time: 1 hour | Serves 8

½ cup extra-virgin olive oil, divided
4 to 5 medium zucchini squash
1 teaspoon salt
8 ounces (227 g) frozen spinach, thawed and well drained (about 1 cup)
2 cups whole-milk ricotta cheese
¼ cup chopped fresh basil or 2 teaspoons dried basil

1 teaspoon garlic powder
½ teaspoon freshly ground black pepper
2 cups shredded fresh whole-milk mozzarella cheese
1¾ cups shredded Parmesan cheese
½ (24-ounce / 680-g) jar low-sugar marinara sauce (less than 5 grams sugar)

1. Preheat the oven to 425°F (220°C). 2. Line two baking sheets with parchment paper or aluminum foil and drizzle each with 2 tablespoons olive oil, spreading evenly. 3. Slice the zucchini lengthwise into ¼-inch-thick long slices and place on the prepared baking sheet in a single layer. Sprinkle with ½ teaspoon salt per sheet. Bake until softened, but not mushy, 15 to 18 minutes. Remove from the oven and allow to cool slightly before assembling the lasagna. 4. Reduce the oven temperature to 375°F (190°C). 5. While the zucchini cooks, prep the filling. In a large bowl, combine the spinach, ricotta, basil, garlic powder, and pepper. In a small bowl, mix together the mozzarella and Parmesan cheeses. In a medium bowl, combine the marinara sauce and remaining ¼ cup olive oil and stir to fully incorporate the oil into sauce. 6. To assemble the lasagna, spoon a third of the marinara sauce mixture into the bottom of a 9-by-13-inch glass baking dish and spread evenly. Place 1 layer of softened zucchini slices to fully cover the sauce, then add a third of the ricotta-spinach mixture and spread evenly on top of the zucchini. Sprinkle a third of the mozzarella-Parmesan mixture on top of the ricotta. Repeat with 2 more cycles of these layers: marinara, zucchini, ricotta-spinach, then cheese blend. 7. Bake until the cheese is bubbly and melted, 30 to 35 minutes. Turn the broiler to low and broil until the top is golden brown, about 5 minutes. Remove from the oven and allow to cool slightly before slicing.

Per Serving
Calories: 473 | fat: 36g | protein: 23g | carbs: 17g | fiber: 3g | sodium: 868mg

Freekeh, Chickpea, and Herb Salad

Prep time: 15 minutes | Cook time: 10 minutes | Serves 4 to 6

1 (15-ounce / 425-g) can chickpeas, rinsed and drained
1 cup cooked freekeh
1 cup thinly sliced celery
1 bunch scallions, both white and green parts, finely chopped
½ cup chopped fresh flat-leaf parsley
¼ cup chopped fresh mint

3 tablespoons chopped celery leaves
½ teaspoon kosher salt
⅓ cup extra-virgin olive oil
¼ cup freshly squeezed lemon juice
¼ teaspoon cumin seeds
1 teaspoon garlic powder

1. In a large bowl, combine the chickpeas, freekeh, celery, scallions, parsley, mint, celery leaves, and salt and toss lightly. 2. In a small bowl, whisk together the olive oil, lemon juice, cumin seeds, and garlic powder. Once combined, add to freekeh salad.

Per Serving
Calories: 350 | fat: 19g | protein: 9g | carbs: 38g | fiber: 9g | sodium: 329mg

Moroccan Red Lentil and Pumpkin Stew

Prep time: 10 minutes | Cook time: 30 minutes | Serves 4

2 tablespoons olive oil
1 teaspoon ground cumin
1 teaspoon ground turmeric
1 tablespoon curry powder
1 large onion, diced
1 teaspoon salt
2 tablespoons minced fresh ginger
4 cloves garlic, minced

1 pound (454 g) pumpkin, peeled, seeded, and cut into 1-inch dice
1 red bell pepper, seeded and diced
1½ cups red lentils, rinsed
6 cups vegetable broth
¼ cup chopped cilantro, for garnish

1. Heat the olive oil in a stockpot over medium heat. Add the cumin, turmeric, and curry powder and cook, stirring, for 1 minute, until fragrant. Add the onion and salt and cook, stirring frequently, until softened, about 5 minutes. Add the ginger and garlic and cook, stirring frequently, for 2 more minutes. Stir in the pumpkin and bell pepper, and then the lentils and broth and bring to a boil. 2. Reduce the heat to low and simmer, uncovered, for about 20 minutes, until the lentils are very tender. Serve hot, garnished with cilantro.

Per Serving
Calories: 405 | fat: 9g | protein: 20g | carbs: 66g | fiber: 11g | sodium: 594mg

Stuffed Pepper Stew

Prep time: 20 minutes | Cook time: 50 minutes | Serves 2

2 tablespoons olive oil
2 sweet peppers, diced (about 2 cups)
½ large onion, minced
1 garlic clove, minced
1 teaspoon oregano
1 tablespoon gluten-free vegetarian Worcestershire

sauce
1 cup low-sodium vegetable stock
1 cup low-sodium tomato juice
¼ cup brown lentils
¼ cup brown rice
Salt

1. Heat olive oil in a Dutch oven over medium-high heat. Add the sweet peppers and onion and sauté for 10 minutes, or until the peppers are wilted and the onion starts to turn golden. 2. Add the garlic, oregano, and Worcestershire sauce, and cook for another 30 seconds. Add the vegetable stock, tomato juice, lentils, and rice. 3. Bring the mixture to a boil. Cover, and reduce the heat to medium-low. Simmer for 45 minutes, or until the rice is cooked and the lentils are softened. Season with salt.

Per Serving
Calories: 379 | fat: 16g | protein: 11g | carbs: 53g | fiber: 7g | sodium: 392mg

Ricotta, Basil, and Pistachio-Stuffed Zucchini

Prep time: 15 minutes | Cook time: 25 minutes | Serves 4

2 medium zucchini, halved lengthwise
1 tablespoon extra-virgin olive oil
1 onion, diced
1 teaspoon kosher salt
2 garlic cloves, minced
¾ cup ricotta cheese
¼ cup unsalted pistachios, shelled and chopped
¼ cup fresh basil, chopped
1 large egg, beaten
¼ teaspoon freshly ground black pepper

1. Preheat the oven to 425°F (220°C). Line a baking sheet with parchment paper or foil. 2. Scoop out the seeds/pulp from the zucchini, leaving ¼-inch flesh around the edges. Transfer the pulp to a cutting board and chop the pulp. 3. Heat the olive oil in a large skillet or sauté pan over medium heat. Add the onion, pulp, and salt and sauté about 5 minutes. Add the garlic and sauté 30 seconds. 4. In a medium bowl, combine the ricotta cheese, pistachios, basil, egg, and black pepper. Add the onion mixture and mix together well. 5. Place the 4 zucchini halves on the prepared baking sheet. Fill the zucchini halves with the ricotta mixture. Bake for 20 minutes, or until golden brown.

Per Serving
Calories: 200 | fat: 12g | protein: 11g | carbs: 14g | fiber: 3g | sodium: 360mg

Asparagus and Mushroom Farrotto

Prep time: 20 minutes | Cook time: 45 minutes | Serves 2

1½ ounces (43 g) dried porcini mushrooms
1 cup hot water
3 cups low-sodium vegetable stock
2 tablespoons olive oil
½ large onion, minced (about 1 cup)
1 garlic clove
1 cup diced mushrooms (about
4 ounces / 113-g)
¾ cup farro
½ cup dry white wine
½ teaspoon dried thyme
4 ounces (113 g) asparagus, cut into ½-inch pieces (about 1 cup)
2 tablespoons grated Parmesan cheese
Salt

1. Soak the dried mushrooms in the hot water for about 15 minutes. When they're softened, drain the mushrooms, reserving the liquid. (I like to strain the liquid through a coffee filter in case there's any grit.) Mince the porcini mushrooms. 2. Add the mushroom liquid and vegetable stock to a medium saucepan and bring it to a boil. Reduce the heat to low just to keep it warm. 3. Heat the olive oil in a Dutch oven over high heat. Add the onion, garlic, and mushrooms, and sauté for 10 minutes. 4. Add the farro to the Dutch oven and sauté it for 3 minutes to toast. 5. Add the wine, thyme, and one ladleful of the hot mushroom and chicken stock. Bring it to a boil while stirring the farro. Do not cover the pot while the farro is cooking. 6. Reduce the heat to medium. When the liquid is absorbed, add another ladleful or two at a time to the pot, stirring occasionally, until the farro is cooked through. Keep an eye on the heat, to make sure it doesn't cook too quickly.

7. When the farro is al dente, add the asparagus and another ladleful of stock. Cook for another 3 to 5 minutes, or until the asparagus is softened. 8. Stir in Parmesan cheese and season with salt.
Per Serving
Calories: 341 | fat: 16g | protein: 13g | carbs: 26g | fiber: 5g | sodium: 259mg

Baked Falafel Sliders

Prep time: 10 minutes | Cook time: 30 minutes | Makes 6 sliders

Olive oil cooking spray
1 (15-ounce / 425-g) can no-salt-added or low-sodium chickpeas, drained and rinsed
1 onion, roughly chopped
2 garlic cloves, peeled
2 tablespoons fresh parsley, chopped
2 tablespoons whole-wheat flour
½ teaspoon ground coriander
½ teaspoon ground cumin
½ teaspoon baking powder
½ teaspoon kosher salt
¼ teaspoon freshly ground black pepper

1. Preheat the oven to 350°F (180°C). Line a baking sheet with parchment paper or foil and lightly spray with olive oil cooking spray. 2. In a food processor, add the chickpeas, onion, garlic, parsley, flour, coriander, cumin, baking powder, salt, and black pepper. Process until smooth, stopping to scrape down the sides of the bowl. 3. Make 6 slider patties, each with a heaping ¼ cup of mixture, and arrange on the prepared baking sheet. Bake for 30 minutes, turning over halfway through.
Per Serving 1 slider:
Calories: 90 | fat: 1g | protein: 4g | carbs:17 g | fiber: 3g | sodium: 110mg

Orzo-Stuffed Tomatoes

Prep time: 15 minutes | Cook time: 30 minutes | Serves 2

1 tablespoon olive oil
1 small zucchini, minced
½ medium onion, minced
1 garlic clove, minced
⅔ cup cooked orzo (from ¼ cup dry orzo, cooked according
to package instructions, or precooked)
½ teaspoon salt
2 teaspoons dried oregano
6 medium round tomatoes (not Roma)

1. Preheat the oven to 350°F (180°C). 2. Heat the olive oil in a large sauté pan over medium-high heat. Add the zucchini, onion, and garlic and sauté for 15 minutes, or until the vegetables turn golden. 3. Add the orzo, salt, and oregano and stir to heat through. Remove the pan from the heat and set aside. 4. Cut about ½ inch from the top of each tomato. With a paring knife, cut around the inner core of the tomato to remove about half of the flesh. Reserve for another recipe or a salad. 5. Stuff each tomato with the orzo mixture. 6. If serving hot, put the tomatoes in a baking dish, or, if they'll fit, a muffin tin. Roast the tomatoes for about 15 minutes, or until they're soft. Don't overcook them or they won't hold together. If desired, this can also be served without roasting the tomatoes.
Per Serving
Calories: 241 | fat: 8g | protein: 7g | carbs: 38g | fiber: 6g | sodium: 301mg

Balsamic Marinated Tofu with Basil and Oregano

Prep time: 10 minutes | Cook time: 30 minutes | Serves 4

¼ cup extra-virgin olive oil
¼ cup balsamic vinegar
2 tablespoons low-sodium soy sauce or gluten-free tamari
3 garlic cloves, grated
2 teaspoons pure maple syrup
Zest of 1 lemon
1 teaspoon dried basil
1 teaspoon dried oregano
½ teaspoon dried thyme
½ teaspoon dried sage
¼ teaspoon kosher salt
¼ teaspoon freshly ground black pepper
¼ teaspoon red pepper flakes (optional)
1 (16-ounce / 454-g) block extra firm tofu, drained and patted dry, cut into ½-inch or 1-inch cubes

1. In a bowl or gallon zip-top bag, mix together the olive oil, vinegar, soy sauce, garlic, maple syrup, lemon zest, basil, oregano, thyme, sage, salt, black pepper, and red pepper flakes, if desired. Add the tofu and mix gently. Put in the refrigerator and marinate for 30 minutes, or up to overnight if you desire. 2. Preheat the oven to 425ºF (220ºC). Line a baking sheet with parchment paper or foil. Arrange the marinated tofu in a single layer on the prepared baking sheet. Bake for 20 to 30 minutes, turning over halfway through, until slightly crispy on the outside and tender on the inside.

Per Serving
Calories: 225 | fat: 16g | protein: 13g | carbs: 9g | fiber: 2g | sodium: 265mg

Greek Frittata with Tomato-Olive Salad

Prep time: 10 minutes | Cook time: 25 minutes | Serves 4 to 6

Frittata:
2 tablespoons olive oil
6 scallions, thinly sliced
4 cups (about 5 ounces / 142 g) baby spinach leaves
8 eggs
¼ cup whole-wheat breadcrumbs, divided
1 cup (about 3 ounces / 85 g) crumbled feta cheese
¾ teaspoon salt
¼ teaspoon freshly ground black pepper

Tomato-Olive Salad:
2 tablespoons olive oil
1 tablespoon lemon juice
¼ teaspoon dried oregano
½ teaspoon salt
¼ teaspoon freshly ground black pepper
1 pint cherry, grape, or other small tomatoes, halved
3 pepperoncini, stemmed and chopped
½ cup coarsely chopped pitted Kalamata olives

1. Preheat the oven to 450ºF (235ºC). 2. Heat the olive oil in an oven-safe skillet set over medium-high heat. Add the scallions and spinach and cook, stirring frequently, for about 4 minutes, until the spinach wilts. 3. In a medium bowl, whisk together the eggs, 2 tablespoons breadcrumbs, cheese, ¾ cup water, salt, and pepper. Pour the egg mixture into the skillet with the spinach and onions and stir to mix. Sprinkle the remaining 2 tablespoons of breadcrumbs evenly over the top. Bake the frittata in the preheated oven for about 20 minutes, until the egg is set and the top is lightly browned. 4. While the frittata is cooking, make the salad. In a medium bowl, whisk together the olive oil, lemon juice, oregano, salt, and pepper. Add the tomatoes, pepperoncini, and olives and toss to mix well. 5.

Invert the frittata onto a serving platter and slice it into wedges. Serve warm or at room temperature with the tomato-olive salad.

Per Serving
Calories: 246 | fat: 19g | protein: 11g | carbs: 8g | fiber: 1g | sodium: 832mg

Grilled Eggplant Stacks

Prep time: 20 minutes | Cook time: 10 minutes | Serves 2

1 medium eggplant, cut crosswise into 8 slices
¼ teaspoon salt
1 teaspoon Italian herb seasoning mix
2 tablespoons olive oil
1 large tomato, cut into 4 slices
4 (1-ounce / 28-g) slices of buffalo mozzarella
Fresh basil, for garnish

1. Place the eggplant slices in a colander set in the sink or over a bowl. Sprinkle both sides with the salt. Let the eggplant sit for 15 minutes. 2. While the eggplant is resting, heat the grill to medium-high heat (about 350ºF / 180ºC). 3. Pat the eggplant dry with paper towels and place it in a mixing bowl. Sprinkle it with the Italian herb seasoning mix and olive oil. Toss well to coat. 4. Grill the eggplant for 5 minutes, or until it has grill marks and is lightly charred. Flip each eggplant slice over, and grill on the second side for another 5 minutes. 5. Flip the eggplant slices back over and top four of the slices with a slice of tomato and a slice of mozzarella. Top each stack with one of the remaining four slices of eggplant. 6. Turn the grill down to low and cover it to let the cheese melt. Check after 30 seconds and remove when the cheese is soft and mostly melted. 7. Sprinkle with fresh basil slices.

Per Serving
Calories: 354 | fat: 29g | protein: 13g | carbs: 19g | fiber: 9g | sodium: 340mg

Cauliflower Steaks with Olive Citrus Sauce

Prep time: 15 minutes | Cook time: 30 minutes | Serves 4

1 or 2 large heads cauliflower (at least 2 pounds / 907 g, enough for 4 portions)
⅓ cup extra-virgin olive oil
¼ teaspoon kosher salt
⅛ teaspoon ground black pepper
Juice of 1 orange
Zest of 1 orange
¼ cup black olives, pitted and chopped
1 tablespoon Dijon or grainy mustard
1 tablespoon red wine vinegar
½ teaspoon ground coriander

1. Preheat the oven to 400ºF (205ºC). Line a baking sheet with parchment paper or foil. 2. Cut off the stem of the cauliflower so it will sit upright. Slice it vertically into four thick slabs. Place the cauliflower on the prepared baking sheet. Drizzle with the olive oil, salt, and black pepper. Bake for about 30 minutes, turning over once, until tender and golden brown. 3. In a medium bowl, combine the orange juice, orange zest, olives, mustard, vinegar, and coriander; mix well. 4. Serve the cauliflower warm or at room temperature with the sauce.

Per Serving
Calories: 265 | fat: 21g | protein: 5g | carbs: 19g | fiber: 4g | sodium: 310mg

Roasted Portobello Mushrooms with Kale and Red Onion

Prep time: 15 minutes | Cook time: 30 minutes | Serves 4

¼ cup white wine vinegar
3 tablespoons extra-virgin olive oil, divided
½ teaspoon honey
¾ teaspoon kosher salt, divided
¼ teaspoon freshly ground black pepper
4 large (4 to 5 ounces / 113 to 142 g each) portobello
mushrooms, stems removed
1 red onion, julienned
2 garlic cloves, minced
1 (8-ounce / 227-g) bunch kale, stemmed and chopped small
¼ teaspoon red pepper flakes
¼ cup grated Parmesan or Romano cheese

1. Line a baking sheet with parchment paper or foil. In a medium bowl, whisk together the vinegar, 1½ tablespoons of the olive oil, honey, ¼ teaspoon of the salt, and the black pepper. Arrange the mushrooms on the baking sheet and pour the marinade over them. Marinate for 15 to 30 minutes. 2. Meanwhile, preheat the oven to 400°F (205°C). 3. Bake the mushrooms for 20 minutes, turning over halfway through. 4. Heat the remaining 1½ tablespoons olive oil in a large skillet or ovenproof sauté pan over medium-high heat. Add the onion and the remaining ½ teaspoon salt and sauté until golden brown, 5 to 6 minutes. Add the garlic and sauté for 30 seconds. Add the kale and red pepper flakes and sauté until the kale cooks down, about 5 minutes. 5. Remove the mushrooms from the oven and increase the temperature to broil. 6. Carefully pour the liquid from the baking sheet into the pan with the kale mixture; mix well. 7. Turn the mushrooms over so that the stem side is facing up. Spoon some of the kale mixture on top of each mushroom. Sprinkle 1 tablespoon Parmesan cheese on top of each. 8. Broil until golden brown, 3 to 4 minutes.

Per Serving
Calories: 200 | fat: 13g | protein: 8g | carbs: 16g | fiber: 4g | sodium: 365mg

Baked Mediterranean Tempeh with Tomatoes and Garlic

Prep time: 25 minutes | Cook time: 35 minutes | Serves 4

For the Tempeh:
12 ounces (340 g) tempeh
¼ cup white wine
2 tablespoons extra-virgin olive oil
2 tablespoons lemon juice
Zest of 1 lemon
¼ teaspoon kosher salt
¼ teaspoon freshly ground black pepper
For the Tomatoes and Garlic Sauce:
1 tablespoon extra-virgin olive
oil
1 onion, diced
3 garlic cloves, minced
1 (14½-ounce / 411-g) can no-salt-added crushed tomatoes
1 beefsteak tomato, diced
1 dried bay leaf
1 teaspoon white wine vinegar
1 teaspoon lemon juice
1 teaspoon dried oregano
1 teaspoon dried thyme
¾ teaspoon kosher salt
¼ cup basil, cut into ribbons

To Make the Tempeh: 1. Place the tempeh in a medium saucepan. Add enough water to cover it by 1 to 2 inches.

Bring to a boil over medium-high heat, cover, and lower heat to a simmer. Cook for 10 to 15 minutes. Remove the tempeh, pat dry, cool, and cut into 1-inch cubes. 2. In a large bowl, combine the white wine, olive oil, lemon juice, lemon zest, salt, and black pepper. Add the tempeh, cover the bowl, and put in the refrigerator for 4 hours, or up to overnight. 3. Preheat the oven to 375°F (190°C). Place the marinated tempeh and the marinade in a baking dish and cook for 15 minutes. To Make the Tomatoes and Garlic Sauce: 4. Heat the olive oil in a large skillet over medium heat. Add the onion and sauté until transparent, 3 to 5 minutes. Add the garlic and sauté for 30 seconds. Add the crushed tomatoes, beefsteak tomato, bay leaf, vinegar, lemon juice, oregano, thyme, and salt. Mix well. Simmer for 15 minutes. 5. Add the baked tempeh to the tomato mixture and gently mix together. Garnish with the basil.

Per Serving
Calories: 330 | fat: 20g | protein: 18g | carbs: 22g | fiber: 4g | sodium: 305mg

Farro with Roasted Tomatoes and Mushrooms

Prep time: 20 minutes | Cook time: 1 hour | Serves 4

For the Tomatoes:
2 pints cherry tomatoes
1 teaspoon extra-virgin olive oil
¼ teaspoon kosher salt
For the Farro:
3 to 4 cups water
½ cup farro
¼ teaspoon kosher salt
For the Mushrooms:
2 tablespoons extra-virgin olive oil
1 onion, julienned
½ teaspoon kosher salt
¼ teaspoon freshly ground black pepper
10 ounces (283 g) baby bella (crimini) mushrooms, stemmed and thinly sliced
½ cup no-salt-added vegetable stock
1 (15-ounce / 425-g) can no-salt-added or low-sodium cannellini beans, drained and rinsed
1 cup baby spinach
2 tablespoons fresh basil, cut into ribbons
¼ cup pine nuts, toasted
Aged balsamic vinegar (optional)

To Make the Tomatoes: Preheat the oven to 400°F (205°C). Line a baking sheet with parchment paper or foil. Toss the tomatoes, olive oil, and salt together on the baking sheet and roast for 30 minutes. To Make the Farro: Bring the water, farro, and salt to a boil in a medium saucepan or pot over high heat. Cover, reduce the heat to low, and simmer, and cook for 30 minutes, or until the farro is al dente. Drain and set aside. To Make the Mushrooms: 1. Heat the olive oil in a large skillet or sauté pan over medium-low heat. Add the onions, salt, and black pepper and sauté until golden brown and starting to caramelize, about 15 minutes. Add the mushrooms, increase the heat to medium, and sauté until the liquid has evaporated and the mushrooms brown, about 10 minutes. Add the vegetable stock and deglaze the pan, scraping up any brown bits, and reduce the liquid for about 5 minutes. Add the beans and warm through, about 3 minutes. 2. Remove from the heat and mix in the spinach, basil, pine nuts, roasted tomatoes, and farro. Garnish with a drizzle of balsamic vinegar, if desired.

Per Serving
Calories: 375 | fat: 15g | protein: 14g | carbs: 48g | fiber: 10g | sodium: 305mg

Baked Tofu with Sun-Dried Tomatoes and Artichokes

Prep time: 15 minutes | Cook time: 30 minutes | Serves 4

1 (16-ounce / 454-g) package extra-firm tofu, drained and patted dry, cut into 1-inch cubes
2 tablespoons extra-virgin olive oil, divided
2 tablespoons lemon juice, divided
1 tablespoon low-sodium soy sauce or gluten-free tamari
1 onion, diced
½ teaspoon kosher salt
2 garlic cloves, minced
1 (14-ounce / 397-g) can artichoke hearts, drained
8 sun-dried tomato halves packed in oil, drained and chopped
¼ teaspoon freshly ground black pepper
1 tablespoon white wine vinegar
Zest of 1 lemon
¼ cup fresh parsley, chopped

1. Preheat the oven to 400°F (205°C). Line a baking sheet with foil or parchment paper. 2. In a bowl, combine the tofu, 1 tablespoon of the olive oil, 1 tablespoon of the lemon juice, and the soy sauce. Allow to sit and marinate for 15 to 30 minutes. Arrange the tofu in a single layer on the prepared baking sheet and bake for 20 minutes, turning once, until light golden brown. 3. Heat the remaining 1 tablespoon olive oil in a large skillet or sauté pan over medium heat. Add the onion and salt; sauté until translucent, 5 to 6 minutes. Add the garlic and sauté for 30 seconds. Add the artichoke hearts, sun-dried tomatoes, and black pepper and sauté for 5 minutes. Add the white wine vinegar and the remaining 1 tablespoon lemon juice and deglaze the pan, scraping up any brown bits. Remove the pan from the heat and stir in the lemon zest and parsley. Gently mix in the baked tofu.

Per Serving

Calories: 230 | fat: 14g | protein: 14g | carbs: 13g | fiber: 5g | sodium: 500mg

Fava Bean Purée with Chicory

Prep time: 5 minutes | Cook time: 2 hours 10 minutes | Serves 4

½ pound (227 g) dried fava beans, soaked in water overnight and drained
1 pound (454 g) chicory leaves
¼ cup olive oil
1 small onion, chopped
1 clove garlic, minced
Salt

1. In a saucepan, cover the fava beans by at least an inch of water and bring to a boil over medium-high heat. Reduce the heat to low, cover, and simmer until very tender, about 2 hours. Check the pot from time to time to make sure there is enough water and add more as needed. 2. Drain off any excess water and then mash the beans with a potato masher. 3. While the beans are cooking, bring a large pot of salted water to a boil. Add the chicory and cook for about 3 minutes, until tender. Drain. 4. In a medium skillet, heat the olive oil over medium-high heat. Add the onion and a pinch of salt and cook, stirring frequently, until softened and beginning to brown, about 5 minutes. Add the garlic and cook, stirring, for another minute. Transfer half of the onion mixture, along with the oil, to the bowl with the mashed beans and stir to mix. Taste and add salt as needed. 5. Serve the purée topped with some of the remaining onions and oil, with the chicory leaves on the side.

Per Serving

Calories: 336 | fat: 14g | protein: 17g | carbs: 40g | fiber: 19g | sodium: 59mg

Kate's Warm Mediterranean Farro Bowl

Prep time: 15 minutes | Cook time: 10 minutes | Serves 4 to 6

⅓ cup extra-virgin olive oil
½ cup chopped red bell pepper
⅓ cup chopped red onions
2 garlic cloves, minced
1 cup zucchini, cut in ½-inch slices
½ cup canned chickpeas, drained and rinsed
½ cup coarsely chopped artichokes
3 cups cooked farro
Salt
Freshly ground black pepper
¼ cup sliced olives, for serving (optional)
½ cup crumbled feta cheese, for serving (optional)
2 tablespoons fresh basil, chiffonade, for serving (optional)
3 tablespoons balsamic reduction, for serving (optional)

1. In a large sauté pan or skillet, heat the oil over medium heat and sauté the pepper, onions, and garlic for about 5 minutes, until tender. 2. Add the zucchini, chickpeas, and artichokes, then stir and continue to sauté vegetables, approximately 5 more minutes, until just soft. 3. Stir in the cooked farro, tossing to combine and cooking enough to heat through. Season with salt and pepper and remove from the heat. 4. Transfer the contents of the pan into the serving vessels or bowls. 5. Top with olives, feta, and basil (if using). Drizzle with balsamic reduction (if using) to finish.

Per Serving

Calories: 367 | fat: 20g | protein: 9g | carbs: 51g | fiber: 9g | sodium: 87mg

Pistachio Mint Pesto Pasta

Prep time: 10 minutes | Cook time: 10 minutes | Serves 4

8 ounces (227 g) whole-wheat pasta
1 cup fresh mint
½ cup fresh basil
⅓ cup unsalted pistachios,
shelled
1 garlic clove, peeled
½ teaspoon kosher salt
Juice of ½ lime
⅓ cup extra-virgin olive oil

1. Cook the pasta according to the package directions. Drain, reserving ½ cup of the pasta water, and set aside. 2. In a food processor, add the mint, basil, pistachios, garlic, salt, and lime juice. Process until the pistachios are coarsely ground. Add the olive oil in a slow, steady stream and process until incorporated. 3. In a large bowl, mix the pasta with the pistachio pesto; toss well to incorporate. If a thinner, more saucy consistency is desired, add some of the reserved pasta water and toss well.

Per Serving

Calories: 420 | fat: 3g | protein: 11g | carbs: 48g | fiber: 2g | sodium: 150mg

Appendix 1: Measurement Conversion Chart

VOLUME EQUIVALENTS(DRY)

US STANDARD	METRIC (APPROXIMATE)
1/8 teaspoon	0.5 mL
1/4 teaspoon	1 mL
1/2 teaspoon	2 mL
3/4 teaspoon	4 mL
1 teaspoon	5 mL
1 tablespoon	15 mL
1/4 cup	59 mL
1/2 cup	118 mL
3/4 cup	177 mL
1 cup	235 mL
2 cups	475 mL
3 cups	700 mL
4 cups	1 L

WEIGHT EQUIVALENTS

US STANDARD	METRIC (APPROXIMATE)
1 ounce	28 g
2 ounces	57 g
5 ounces	142 g
10 ounces	284 g
15 ounces	425 g
16 ounces (1 pound)	455 g
1.5 pounds	680 g
2 pounds	907 g

VOLUME EQUIVALENTS(LIQUID)

US STANDARD	US STANDARD (OUNCES)	METRIC (APPROXIMATE)
2 tablespoons	1 fl.oz.	30 mL
1/4 cup	2 fl.oz.	60 mL
1/2 cup	4 fl.oz.	120 mL
1 cup	8 fl.oz.	240 mL
1 1/2 cup	12 fl.oz.	355 mL
2 cups or 1 pint	16 fl.oz.	475 mL
4 cups or 1 quart	32 fl.oz.	1 L
1 gallon	128 fl.oz.	4 L

TEMPERATURES EQUIVALENTS

FAHRENHEIT(F)	CELSIUS(C) (APPROXIMATE)
225 °F	107 °C
250 °F	120 °C
275 °F	135 °C
300 °F	150 °C
325 °F	160 °C
350 °F	180 °C
375 °F	190 °C
400 °F	205 °C
425 °F	220 °C
450 °F	235 °C
475 °F	245 °C
500 °F	260 °C

The Dirty Dozen and Clean Fifteen

The Environmental Working Group (EWG) is a nonprofit, nonpartisan organization dedicated to protecting human health and the environment Its mission is to empower people to live healthier lives in a healthier environment. This organization publishes an annual list of the twelve kinds of produce, in sequence, that have the highest amount of pesticide residue-the Dirty Dozen-as well as a list of the fifteen kinds ofproduce that have the least amount of pesticide residue-the Clean Fifteen.

THE DIRTY DOZEN

- The 2016 Dirty Dozen includes the following produce. These are considered among the year's most important produce to buy organic:

Strawberries	Spinach
Apples	Tomatoes
Nectarines	Bell peppers
Peaches	Cherry tomatoes
Celery	Cucumbers
Grapes	Kale/collard greens
Cherries	Hot peppers

- *The Dirty Dozen list contains two additional itemskale/collard greens and hot peppers-because they tend to contain trace levels of highly hazardous pesticides.*

THE CLEAN FIFTEEN

- The least critical to buy organically are the Clean Fifteen list. The following are on the 2016 list:

Avocados	Papayas
Corn	Kiw
Pineapples	Eggplant
Cabbage	Honeydew
Sweet peas	Grapefruit
Onions	Cantaloupe
Asparagus	Cauliflower
Mangos	

- *Some of the sweet corn sold in the United States are made from genetically engineered (GE) seedstock. Buy organic varieties of these crops to avoid GE produce.*

Appendix 4 Recipes Index

CPSIA information can be obtained
at www.ICGtesting.com
Printed in the USA
BVHW010454150822
644601BV00004BA/45